TEACHING LANGUAGE ARTS

CLASSROOM APPLICATIONS

TEACHING LANGUAGE ARTS

CLASSROOM APPLICATIONS

John N. Mangieri
Texas Christian University

Nancy K. Staley
University of South Carolina at Aiken

James A. Wilhide
South Carolina Department of Education

McGRAW-HILL BOOK COMPANY

New York   St. Louis   San Francisco   Auckland   Bogotá
Hamburg   Johannesburg   London   Madrid   Mexico   Montreal   New Delhi
Panama   Paris   São Paulo   Singapore   Sydney   Tokyo   Toronto

This book was set in Times Roman by J. M. Post Graphics, Corp.
The editors were Christina Mediate and David Dunham;
the production supervisor was Charles Hess.
The drawings were done by Burmar.
The photographs were taken by Robert W. Harper.
The cover was designed by Charles A. Carson;
the cover photograph was taken by David S. Strickler/Monkmeyer Press Photo Service.
Halliday Lithograph Corporation was printer and binder.

TEACHING LANGUAGE ARTS

Classroom Applications

1 2 3 4 5 6 7 8 9 0   HALHAL   8 9 8 7 6 5 4

ISBN 0-07-039890-9

Library of Congress Cataloging in Publication Data

Mangieri, John N.
    Teaching language arts.

    Bibliography: p.
    Includes index.
    1. Language arts (Elementary) I. Staley, Nancy K.
II. Wilhide, James A. III. Title.
LB1576.M366 1984   372.6'044   83-12068
ISBN 0-07-039890-9

To Dr. Harry W. Sartain, Dr. Charlotte S. Huck,
and the late Dr. Ruth M. Strang, who shared
their knowledge so willingly and ably with us.
May the present as well as the future generation
of students receive the quality of language arts
instruction these individuals have advocated
over the years.

CONTENTS

FOREWORD   xiii
PREFACE   xv

1   Focusing the Language Arts   **1**

WHAT ARE THE LANGUAGE ARTS?   3
BELIEFS ABOUT LANGUAGE ARTS   6
ABOUT THIS BOOK   14
SOME CAUTIONS   17
BIBLIOGRAPHY AND REFERENCES   18

2   Language Arts: Kindergarten and First Grade   **21**

OVERVIEW   21
THE CHILD   21
    Physical Characteristics   22
    Social and Emotional Characteristics   23
    Intellectual Characteristics   24
LANGUAGE ARTS IN KINDERGARTEN AND FIRST GRADE   27
LISTENING   28
    Instructional Emphases / Instructional
       Strategies / Problems / Assessment
SPEAKING   35
    Instructional Emphases / Instructional
       Strategies / Problems / Assessment
COMPOSITION   37
    Instructional Emphases / Instructional
       Strategies / Problems / Assessment
HANDWRITING   40
    Instructional Emphases / Instructional
       Strategies / Problems / Assessment
SPELLING   43
    Instructional Emphases / Instructional
       Strategies / Problems / Assessment

READING APPLICATION 47

*Instructional Emphases / Instructional
Strategies / Problems / Assessment*

BIBLIOGRAPHY AND REFERENCES 49

**3   Classroom Applications in Kindergarten
and Grade One** 53

BARBARA BROWN 53
Descriptor 53
Analysis 60
Explanation 65
LYNN SIMPSON 67
Descriptor 67
Analysis 70
Explanation 73
BIBLIOGRAPHY AND REFERENCES 80

4   Language Arts: Grades Two and Three 83

OVERVIEW 83
THE CHILD 83
Physical Characteristics 83
Social and Emotional Characteristics 84
Intellectual Characteristics 85
Summary 86
LANGUAGE ARTS IN SECOND AND THIRD GRADES 86
LISTENING 86

*Instructional Emphases / Instructional
Strategies / Problems / Assessment*

SPELLING 90

*Instructional Emphases / Instructional
Strategies / Problems / Assessment*

COMPOSITION 94

*Instructional Emphases / Instructional
Strategies / Problems / Assessment*

HANDWRITING 101

*Instructional Emphases / Instructional
Strategies / Problems / Assessment*

SPEAKING 104

*Instructional Emphases / Instructional
Strategies / Problems / Assessment*

READING APPLICATION 107

*Instructional Emphases / Instructional
Strategies / Problems / Assessment*

BIBLIOGRAPHY AND REFERENCES 112

5 **Classroom Applications in Grades Two and Three** **115**

NANCY WATSON **115**
   Descriptor **115**
   Analysis **119**
   Explanation **124**
CINDY LEE **128**
   Descriptor **128**
   Analysis **130**
   Explanation **131**
BIBLIOGRAPHY AND REFERENCES **136**

6 **Language Arts: Grades Four and Five** **139**

OVERVIEW **139**
THE CHILD **139**
   Physical Characteristics **139**
   Social and Emotional Characteristics **140**
   Intellectual Characteristics **141**
LANGUAGE ARTS IN THE INTERMEDIATE GRADES **141**
LISTENING **141**
   Instructional Emphases / Instructional
     Strategies / Problems / Assessment
SPELLING **147**
   Instructional Emphases / Instructional
     Strategies / Problems / Assessment
COMPOSITION **151**
   Instructional Emphases / Instructional
     Strategies / Problems / Assessment
HANDWRITING **163**
   Instructional Emphases / Instructional
     Strategies / Problems / Assessment
SPEAKING **166**
   Instructional Emphases / Instructional
     Strategies / Problems / Assessment
READING APPLICATION **169**
   Instructional Emphases / Instructional
     Strategies / Problems / Assessment
BIBLIOGRAPHY AND REFERENCES **174**

7 **Classroom Applications in Grades Four through Six** **179**

CAROL BEASLEY **179**
   Descriptor **179**
   Analysis **183**
   Explanation **187**

JEFFREY TATE   191
   Descriptor   191
   Analysis   194
   Explanation   197
BIBLIOGRAPHY AND REFERENCES   200

8   Language Arts in the Middle School   203

OVERVIEW   203
   Individual Needs/Societal Needs
THE CHILD   207
   Physical Characteristics   207
   Social and Emotional Characteristics   208
   Intellectual Characteristics   208
SUMMARY   208
LANGUAGE ARTS IN THE MIDDLE SCHOOL   215
LISTENING   215
   Instructional Emphases / Instructional
     Strategies / Problems / Assessment
SPELLING   218
   Instructional Emphases / Instructional
     Strategies / Problems / Assessment
COMPOSITION   223
   Instructional Emphases / Instructional
     Strategies / Problems / Assessment
HANDWRITING   227
   Instructional Emphases / Instructional
     Strategies / Problems / Assessment
SPEAKING   229
   Instructional Emphases / Instructional
     Strategies / Problems / Assessment
READING APPLICATION   233
   Instructional Emphases / Instructional
     Strategies / Problems / Assessment
CONCLUDING COMMENTS   237
BIBLIOGRAPHY AND REFERENCES   237

9   The Teacher's Role in Language Arts Instruction   241

WHAT TEACHING CHARACTERISTICS SHOULD BE AVOIDED?   241
HOW DOES A TEACHER'S VIEW ABOUT SCHOOLS AFFECT
   TEACHING STYLE?   243
WHAT DOES RESEARCH HAVE TO SAY ABOUT TEACHER
   EFFECTIVENESS?   245
WHAT ARE SOME RESEARCH IMPLICATIONS FOR THE
   LANGUAGE ARTS TEACHER?   250
CONCLUDING COMMENTS   254
BIBLIOGRAPHY AND REFERENCES   254

10   The Language Arts Program   **257**

  PROGRAM ANALYSIS   **257**
    Testing   **259**
    Perceptions   **260**
    Analysis   **261**
  PROGRAM DEVELOPMENT   **261**
    Resources   **263**
      Professional Literature / Professional Bodies /
        Schools
  IMPLEMENTATION   **265**
  FINAL COMMENTS   **266**
  APPENDIX 10-1 CRITERIA FOR PLANNING AND EVALUATION
    OF ENGLISH LANGUAGE ARTS CURRICULUM GUIDES
    (REVISED)   **267**
  APPENDIX 10-2 RATIONALE OF A LANGUAGE ARTS
    CURRICULUM   **273**
  APPENDIX 10-3 LANGUAGE ARTS COURSE OF STUDIES FOR
    THIRD GRADE   **274**
  APPENDIX 10-4 ENGLISH LANGUAGE ARTS CHECKLIST
    (ELAC)   **280**
  BIBLIOGRAPHY AND REFERENCES   **282**

  APPENDIXES   **283**
  A Literature   **285**
  B Oral Expression   **303**
  C Written Expression   **315**
  D Spelling and Handwriting   **341**
  E Professional Development   **351**
  F Dealing with Parents   **367**
  G Names and Addresses of Publishers   **377**

  INDEX   **385**

FOREWORD

Teaching Language Arts: Classroom Applications is a timely, much needed book in a critical area of the curriculum. This is a book on the language arts program at the elementary and middle school levels, by authors who are directly involved in the area they are writing about. As such, it meets the need for presenting what we know about how children learn, what is important for children to know, and ways by which children can best be taught.

The language arts dealt with in this book are listening, speaking, reading, and writing, appropriately identified as the "tools of literacy." Having survived the period in which more attention may have been directed toward language arts skills as an end in themselves, instead of as a means toward learning, teachers today are challenged to aspire to the difficult goal of developing every child to the limit of his or her ability. There can be little doubt that this goal can best be achieved by assuring that every child learns the language arts skills and develops interests which will allow him or her to learn more than was taught, to continue learning successfully beyond what was even known when she or he was in school, and to become ultimately the educated person who enjoys both the process and the results of learning.

Books in the language arts field tend to follow one of several traditional patterns. The most widely used textbooks have traditionally divided the language arts into its component parts of reading, handwriting, speaking, and listening. Some have then devoted major emphasis to the needed skills in each of these areas, while others have stressed teaching strategies intended to improve each area. Most, as would be expected, have attempted to do both, intermixing goals and strategies, sometimes in a confusing array. The complexity of this task is readily apparent, for either the length of such books has become unwieldy or the treatment has sometimes been superficial. But even more important, the problem of dealing with handwriting separately from writing (composing) and spelling has resulted in children learning spelling words for spelling class, handwriting for penmanship class, and grammar for English class, and forgetting to use these skills in social studies and science classes.

Teaching Language Arts: Classroom Applications does not succumb to this structural problem. Instead of dividing their book into sections and chapters on the basis of the belief that children's learning can be so compartmentalized, the authors have wisely taken a developmental approach, which follows the logical grade-level sequence that is the structure of our schools. After the introduction in Chapter 1, the next eight chapters are divided into 4 two-chapter units. Chapter 2 describes the kindergarten and first-grade language arts program, followed in Chapter 3 by a discussion of the language arts program in two different classrooms at these levels. This pattern is maintained throughout the elementary grades. Chapter 8, which deals with the language arts program in the middle school, is preceded by a discussion of an actual classroom at this level.

This unique approach of providing classroom models of successful language arts programs gives the reader one successful way of teaching. Instead of limiting the reader to the model provided, this approach opens the door to encourage the reader to adapt, expand, and move beyond. With a basis for judging what a good program actually contains, the reader is then free to develop his or her own program.

The practical nature of this approach, developed in a way that is easily understandable as well as challenging, is intended to promote the authors' philosophy of the interrelatedness of the language arts. If teachers are to teach this interrelatedness, then it is logical to assume that they will do so with greater understanding if this is the way in which they are taught. *Teaching Language Arts: Classroom Applications* tells how to achieve the goal of teaching children to listen, speak, read, and write as well as the ultimate goal of having children who can effectively communicate their ideas to others and receive in written and spoken form the ideas of others. To the extent that children can communicate effectively, they will become members of society who participate as thinking adults.

Walter B. Barbe

Editor-in-Chief,
Highlights for Children

Adjunct Professor,
The Ohio State University

PREFACE

The writing of any professional textbook is an arduous task. Countless hours are spent conceptualizing the book's contents, writing one's thoughts in a (we hope) coherent manner, and, most importantly, taking elaborate pains to ensure that the maximum possible meaningful content is included in the textbook.

In writing this book, we added another dimension to the preceding. We were determined to convey not only how the language arts *should* be taught to students but also to present how they *are* taught in actual classrooms. In Chapter 1, we discuss the organization of the book and the manner in which this dichotomy is integrated into our textbook.

Contrary to what some critics of education contend, we feel America's teachers are doing an excellent job in teaching the youth of our country. We know of numerous superb language arts teachers, and the teachers profiled in Chapters 3, 5, and 7 of this book are just a few of the many who could have been chosen. To the teachers described in these chapters as well as the many others who permitted us to visit their classrooms, we are grateful.

We were not "islands unto ourselves" as we wrote this book. Ideas and suggestions were discussed and received from colleagues, teachers, students, and administrators. These persons, too numerous to cite individually, gave us invaluable professional assistance. Acknowledgment is given to the authors, publishers, and organizations who permitted us to reproduce portions of prior publications; to Christine R. Swager, JoAnne M. Wilkes, Dr. Virginia B. Stanley, and Dr. Susan J. Smith, for contributions made to the textbook; to Dr. Margaret R. Corboy, for compiling the book's appendixes; to Robert W. Harper, for the photographs; to Robert K. Hess, for compiling the index; and to Joan M. Wilhide, for typing significant portions of the manuscript.

We also thank Dr. Joseph Malak of Frostburg State College, Dr. Virginia B. Stanley of Clemson University, and Dr. Anne M. Werdmann, director of the Churchill Academy in Pittsburgh, for suggesting ways in which to improve the book and for serving as reviewers for it.

Much gratitude is owed to Phillip A. Butcher, former education editor at McGraw-Hill, for encouraging the development of this endeavor and supporting it during its initial stages. We also thank Christina Mediate, education editor at McGraw-Hill, for her editorial expertise and for aiding us in dealing with the myriad issues needed to complete the writing of the book.

Finally, we thank the members of our families. They sacrificed much to permit the completion of this textbook.

John N. Mangieri

Nancy K. Staley

James A. Wilhide

TEACHING
LANGUAGE
ARTS
CLASSROOM APPLICATIONS

CHAPTER 1

FOCUSING THE LANGUAGE ARTS

Language is, and since its invention or discovery always has been, the most important tool man ever devised. Man is sometimes described as a tool-using animal; language is his basic tool. It is the tool more than any other with which he makes his living, makes his home, makes his life. As man becomes more and more a social being, as the world becomes more and more a social community, communication grows even more imperative. And language is the basis of communication. Language is also the instrument with which we think, and thinking is the rarest and most needed commodity in the world.

Charlton Laird[1]

Education is a lifelong process in which people learn to negotiate with their world. Although others play significant roles in this process, education is essentially something people must do for themselves. Language is central to the individual's process of self-discovery and self-definition. It is the means by which people explore and structure their worlds.

A distinction must be made between education and schooling. In theory, the most important purpose of the school is to provide (in Emerson's words) "not an education, but a means to an education" (22). In practice, the schools respond to the changing needs of society and the concomitant social, economic, and political considerations these changes entail. The degree to which schools respond to the aforementioned conditions is frequently the measure by which the public judges a school's effectiveness.

[1]Charlton Laird, *The Miracle of Language*. Greenwich, Conn.: Fawcett Publications, 1967.

In 1957, the Soviet Union launched Sputnik and the egos of many Americans unaccustomed to being in second place were damaged. Admiral Hyman Rickover spoke for a society which condemned John Dewey's progressive education as a "kind of gooey, precious, romantic philosophy that stressed permissiveness and life adjustment" (24). He urged that schools return to what he termed "the basics."

A result of this post-Sputnik criticism was an increased emphasis on scientific and technical education. For the first time, large sums of federal money were made available so that the teaching of these subjects could be strengthened. It was hoped, of course, that achievement gains in these areas would also occur.

The decade of the sixties was a time of great social upheaval, and the schools were charged with the task of solving, or at least ameliorating, the effects of poverty and prejudice. The Elementary and Secondary Education Act (ESEA) of 1965 provided more than a billion dollars for schools and marked the beginning of federal programs which have had a great influence on the scope and the structure of American education.

During the seventies, many schools were experimenting with diverse and innovative programs which emphasized creativity, openness, and attention to the affective domain of learning. Large sums of federal money were used to develop and support programs designed to abolish illiteracy, to solve problems associated with learning disabilities, and to help handicapped children join the mainstream of the educational system. The degree to which these ends were realized is an issue which can be debated.

In the eighties, the public schools are again being asked to respond to a changing society. There is a nationwide concern and belief that our country's public schools have failed. Parents and legislators want students and schools to score well above average on state and national assessments.

There is a belief that federal funding of programs has not worked; that instead it has created a monstrous amount of regulations and bureaucracy which interfere with, rather than aid, teachers practicing their profession. The eighties may prove to be a decade of shifting financial priorities, with financial aid to education drastically curtailed.

The swing of the pendulum is reversing; once again schools are being asked to eliminate frills and "get back to basics." John Maxwell (20), executive director of the National Council of Teachers of English (NCTE), writes:

> The critical difference in the present pendulum swing is the force being applied to curriculum change by major units of government—legislatures and state boards of education. Through legislature and regulatory language the states are increasingly specifying the curriculum, and the specifications are, at best, conservative and narrow. Future curriculum change will be made much more difficult in the face of legislative prescription of "basics." Unless something is done, the pendulum may stop swinging for a decade or two, stuck firmly at the conservative side.

Maxwell calls upon teachers to become a political force in what he foresees will be a struggle to restore openness and flexibility to the classroom. He believes teachers must be prepared to struggle at state and local levels to maintain what they know to be good educational values for children.

Teachers are in agreement with the rest of society in calling for good schools which will provide quality education for children. Although there is no consensus on the precise definition of quality education, there is agreement that it includes literacy. *How* to achieve literacy and *what kind* of literacy is needed are the questions that separate the viewpoints held by educators from those of many other members of society.

It is generally agreed that the world has become so complex that there is no longer (if there ever was) a common body of information which everyone must have. Yet all students need the tools of literacy if they are to learn to negotiate with their world. In elementary school, these tools are called the language arts; their relationship to quality education is the subject of this book.

WHAT ARE THE LANGUAGE ARTS?

Language arts is the designation used to describe the communication skills of listening, speaking, reading, and writing. Each of these facets of communication is either receptive (a message is being received by a person or persons) or expressive (a message is being sent from a person). Reading and listening are receptive; speaking and writing are expressive. For communication to take place, it is necessary to have the active participation of at least two persons—one to present a thought or idea by means of speaking or writing and the other to receive it through listening or reading.

Whether one is listening to a message sent by a speaker or reading a passage by an author, the information must be processed before it can be understood. This processing of information requires thinking. In like manner, it is important that thinking take place before a message is expressed either verbally or in written form. Moffett (21) contends that "a course of language learning is a course in thinking." Perhaps thinking should be called the fifth language art.

Many school programs continue to divide the language arts into separate skill areas. Therefore, it is understandable that many people think of reading, spelling, composition, and language as separate subject areas. Parents, legislators, and citizens' groups are demanding that schools get back to basics, especially in the language arts. For them, teaching basic skills means that teachers should isolate aspects of skills and teach and reteach them until they are mastered. The teaching of phonics is seen as the teaching of reading; drill activities devoted to punctuation, parts of speech, and grammar are seen as the teaching of writing.

It is important for teachers, the public, and parents to understand the interrelatedness of the language arts skills. Research (11) suggests that isolated teaching of skills cannot be justified; rather, "integrated approaches to language arts skills" are advocated.

In its publication entitled *What Are the Basics in English?,* the National Council of Teachers of English (10) "advocates the importance of language arts skills being used to reinforce each other. In this process of reinforcement, students explore a wide range of reading interests, get involved in a variety of related learning activities, and thereby develop a firmer grasp of all of the necessary language competencies." Figure 1-1 depicts the interrelationship of the language arts skills.

An elementary school principal, Clair Henry (12), describes what he sees when visiting the classrooms in his school. He believes teachers are overemphasizing the skills approach to language arts learning. He says:

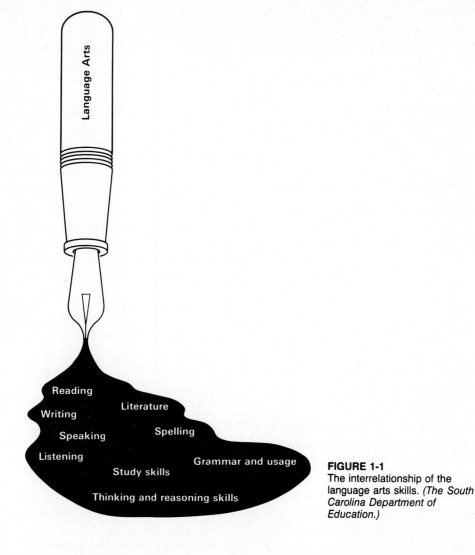

FIGURE 1-1
The interrelationship of the language arts skills. *(The South Carolina Department of Education.)*

In a first room there is phonics drill concentrating on the sounds that go with the letter 's'. In another the morning assignments include the 'b' part of the week's spelling lesson, which upon examination is found to deal with syllabication, and an exercise from the language arts book about the correct use of was and were. At one stop children are practicing vowel rules on isolated words, and in another marking accent in an assigned list of multisyllabic words. In a reading circle children are observed as they play a game to review sight words. The trip on down the hall yields a series of similar activities all related to the rote and mechanical aspects of learning. Even the bulletin boards are filled with phonics and grammar rules and reminders, with an occasional directive related to behavior or good manners.

Henry is pessimistic about the effects of these school experiences on the learning of students:

The result is a student who may do well on phonics skills tests, parts of speech in grammar, and so on, but cannot read to comprehend, cannot write a paragraph that expresses an idea, or indeed cannot generate an idea worthy of serious expression.

In the same school, another classroom reflects an integrated approach to language arts learning. As the school's principal, Henry describes it as follows:

> In this room children are using language in situations which require and permit it. Thinking is required to do the tasks at hand. Some children are writing in their daily journals. A little observation reveals that the additions deal with things that happened at home, things seen on the way to school, feelings about things, imaginings, etc. They often enjoy what they have done so much that they feel a need to share it and are able to move to another child who laughs quietly or puzzles with them over something which has been written.
>
> The teacher is working with a group around a table. They have just read a story and are considering the author's purpose in writing it and how he achieved his purpose. Someone says he doesn't think the author did achieve it. A lively counterreaction follows this reaction. There are several of the "why do you think so?" kind of question—child to child as well as teacher to child. A look at the board shows that when the group considered vocabulary for the story, phonics was used in a context setting. Children had both phonics and context for dealing with these words, which is like the real world of reading.

Henry echoes what many see as a promising move away from the skills orientation when he analyzes the teaching practices in this classroom:

> These children may not do as well on a competency test which requires mechanical response to mechanical factors. They will do all right, I believe, because they are learning to think and to "figure out" intelligent approaches to a task. They are learning much more than a competency test will require. They are learning to learn and they are learning to like to learn. They are developing study skills. They are becoming students and appreciators. These things are happening because the teacher believes that language is used in relation to something, and that language learning happens in an integrated curriculum, isolating only briefly for emphasis when such emphasis is needed, but then back into the whole it goes and learning builds on learning.

In the first example, the classrooms were led by teachers who believe that isolating aspects of skills and working on them until children master them is the best method of helping children learn the language arts. Not all principals believe as Clair Henry does; many believe the results of skills tests provide an accurate measurement of the amount of learning which has taken place. Often, parents share this belief. When their children perform well on skills tests, they are assured that the children are learning to read well and to write well, and that they are developing good communication skills.

In the last class described by Henry, the teacher has a different concept of good language arts teaching. She believes an integrated approach to learning communication skills is the best way. Her principal agrees with her; he believes that test scores are not necessarily an accurate measure of literacy. These two educators believe that language is a communication process and that the whole is greater than the sum of its parts.

It is important to realize that an individual's beliefs determine his or her behavior. All the people mentioned above—teachers, principals, and parents—have the same goal: children who possess the communication skills necessary to function well in the world. Their behavior, what they actually do in pursuit of this goal, is determined by their beliefs.

In the next section of this chapter, we will share some of our beliefs about language arts, about teachers, and about learners. We hope that this sharing will help you think about, and ultimately conceptualize, an effective approach to the teaching of language arts in the elementary classrooms.

BELIEFS ABOUT LANGUAGE ARTS

Belief One   The interrelatedness of the four aspects of the language arts—reading, writing, speaking, and listening—cannot be overemphasized.

Reading is an integral part of the language arts curriculum; the teaching of reading cannot be separated from the teaching of writing, speaking, and listening. There are many fine reading texts which attest to this fact and which are devoted to the entire reading process. This book will be concerned with reading application, which has been called "the payoff of good reading instruction" by Wayne Otto (23).

Kenneth Goodman (11) defines reading as a psycholinguistic process in which the reader (a user of language) reconstructs, as best he can, a message which has been encoded by a writer as a graphic display. According to this definition, a child could recognize letters, discriminate sounds, call out words from a word list, and use any number of phonics generalizations to decode words, but unless the child reconstructs the meaning, no reading has taken place.

Deardon (8) points out that:

> You could go through a book backwards, from bottom to top and right to left, recognizing all the words there perfectly correctly but we would hardly call this "reading" and certainly not "reading the book."

In the same vein, language is not vocabulary; nor is grammar; writing is not spelling, punctuation, or handwriting. In fact, Brown (2) believes:

> . . . there is no evidence that acquiring explicit knowledge of the structure of language in any form whatever, from sentence diagramming to the newest model of transformational grammar, has any value at all in facilitating the purposive use of language.

All of language, written and oral, deals with the getting of meaning. Language arts education is concerned with children learning to express ideas as well as understand ideas, whether they are written or spoken.

Emphasis in teaching should be placed upon the ability to use skill elements (grammar, usage, vocabulary, spelling, and so forth) in relevant language processes, and to keep those elements in perspective as being supportive of the larger processes.

Belief Two   Children learn best from interested, enthusiastic, and knowledgeable teachers.

There is general agreement among language arts educators that a good teacher has a positive effect on the learning outcomes of children. "From studies made early in this century through relatively recent studies seeking to analyze specific causes and effects, the influence of a teacher's encouragement stands out clearly" (3).

A teacher who knows individual children well enough to know their interests has a positive influence on their writing behavior. Lickteig (17) points out that "interest-awareness enables the teacher to read a child's composition and respond to the content—comment on the ideas rather than on the mechanics." It is important that the teacher be a listener and reader rather than error spotter and corrector.

If teachers are going to help children they must be competent in the language arts. Teachers need a good knowledge of language development, the reading process, and children's literature and an understanding of child development. The numerous contributions of psycholinguists and sociolinguists are important to today's teachers, and educators need to be aware of theories, concepts, and developments in these areas. If they are to promote recreational reading, teachers must value reading; they must become readers themselves.

There is reason for concern that many teachers do not possess these attributes. In an effort to determine their knowledge of children's literature and the recreational reading activities they used with children, Mangieri and Corboy (19) gave a questionnaire to 571 elementary school teachers. Ninety-one percent of the respondents were unable to name three children's books written in the past five years; 71 percent were not able to recall even one book. Eighty-nine percent of the 571 participants in the study did not know even three activities which would promote recreational reading on the part of elementary school children. These findings led the researchers to express "doubts regarding elementary educators' knowledge of recreational reading, and the extent and diversity to which it is occurring in the classroom."

Many of today's teachers have educational deficiencies which can have serious effects on the learning of young children. Roser (27) makes this point in the following anecdotes:

> Children in a fifth grade had read biographies and were preparing to share the books with classmates by donning some representative garment then sitting on a high stool in front of a classroom and conducting a press conference as the famous person. When Daniel Boone took the stool, the first few question–answer trades went smoothly. Then a waving hand was recognized and a clear voice asked, "Mr. Boone, I know you died at the Alamo. Can you tell us about that?" Daniel hesitated and then said, "Well, it was painful." There was brief laughter, but these were Texas children and they were unable to let an eyewitness account of the Alamo go untapped. So more questions followed about the Alamo and Daniel Boone faked it. "Maybe you had better tell them," I whispered to the teacher. "Tell them what?" he asked.

and

> "Kids today are so smart," beamed a fresh-faced student teacher. "Someone today—seven years old—asked me where Columbus landed."
> "What did you say?" her supervisor asked. "I said 'Florida, I think, or somewhere down there.' "

Children learn best from interested, enthusiastic, and knowledgeable teachers.

It is important for teachers to look carefully and critically at themselves. If they are going to help children gain the necessary tools with which to pursue an education, teachers must be tuned into the educational process for themselves. They must take advantage of the full range of professional development possibilities—university course work, inservice education, travel opportunities. In essence, teachers must become individuals who read for pleasure as well as for information.

Belief Three   Children need to hear good books read aloud on a regular basis.

Reading aloud to children is not only a means of interesting them in reading and writing but also a method of helping children improve their language arts competencies. Studies indicate that consistently reading to children has a positive effect on children's vocabulary and comprehension skills. One study conducted by Cohen (7) involved a special program of literature and accompanying activities which were introduced into the curriculum of disadvantaged second-grade children. Teachers were asked to read aloud every day from a selected list of trade books. Children were then asked to respond to the story in some way (through discussion, art, music, or drama). At the end of the year, the classes which had the daily story hour were significantly ahead of the control group in both vocabulary and comprehension.

Chomsky (6) studied the language development of children between six and ten years of age. She found a high correlation between their stages of language development and the amount of literature they had heard or read.

Cazden (5) recommends reading aloud as a good way of stimulating children's language growth. She found that reading aloud caused children to engage in discussion about the pictures and the stories and that it provided them with the experiences of book language and patterns of stories.

Such language arts benefits are not limited to students in the primary grades; students of all ages profit from being read to. Older children need to be introduced to good books which may be too difficult for them to read themselves but which they can understand and enjoy if someone else reads to them.

Reading provides a child with vicarious experiences and ideas. Children need many experiences to talk about, to write about, and to think about. The oral reading of children's literature serves to show again the relatedness of the language arts. Britton (1) states that when a teacher is reading to a class, at least three processes are taking place:

> First, the class is functioning as a single group . . . such communal experience becomes particularly valuable. . . . In the second place, the children who listen are gaining experience of the written forms of the English language. . . . There is an art of listening to reading that is very different from the process of listening to somebody talking. . . . If my second process was that of gaining language experience, my third is, in the simplest terms, gaining life experience.

Belief Four   Students gain competence in the areas of language arts through practice.

A good reader becomes a good reader through reading—a fact Huck (15) calls "one of the best kept secrets in education." Good readers are expected to be able to read fluently (defined in Webster's dictionary as easily, smoothly, and expressively). Hickman (13) believes that while teachers are intent on producing fluent readers, sometimes they lose sight of just what is involved in the process. The concept of fluency does not lend itself to objective research, but she makes a case that insight about the reading process can be gained through introspection coupled with observation. With this in mind, she interviewed two "extraordinarily literate" people about their reading. She concluded:

> What do fluent readers do? They read. Selectively, purposefully, critically—not just to be reading, but for a reason. For real. And how do fluent readers get to be that way? . . . Fluent readers get to be that way by reading, and by reading a great deal, from something of their own choosing.

In like manner, language is not learned passively; rather, it is learned by the speaker actively engaging in speaking. Students need many opportunities to come to grips with their thoughts in situations where they have someone with whom they wish to communicate.

Of all the language arts, listening is the one most neglected by teachers. It is incorrectly assumed that children know how to listen, although they are often faulted for not doing so. Listening is a communication process and listening skills must be developed in real communication contexts. Children become good listeners by listening to stories, by listening to each other, and by listening to their teachers.

Students need frequent opportunities for writing. While instruction and evaluation are helpful, the opportunity for actual writing practice and the expression of ideas are even more beneficial.

Yet many children do not get this necessary practice. A story is told about the father of a first-grader who collected all the school work his daughter brought home each day. At the end of the year, he had 478 sheets on which the child had practiced letter names and letter sounds, 123 sheets which had been used to practice reading sentences, 45 which the father categorized as "other," and only two pieces of original writing.

In another instance, a researcher wrote that "educational supply companies report that sales of lined composition paper are down while sales of duplicating paper used for short answers continue to rise" (6). If teachers do not provide children with opportunities for writing, children will not become proficient writers. Appropriate instruction must be provided during the practice of composition skills.

Belief Five   Classrooms must provide environments which are conducive to the growth of language arts skills.

Children need a place where they can read without being disturbed; where they can browse without disturbing others. Some teachers use such interesting objects as bathtubs, inflated inner tubes, and even carpeted cardboard cartons as "inviting" furniture in their classroom reading areas. Others construct reading lofts, so that children can go "upstairs" to read in private.

If children are to become "hooked on books," they need to be surrounded by reading materials—books, newspapers, and magazines—and be afforded adequate opportunities to use these during the school day. Huck (16) cites a study by Bisset which shows the importance of having large numbers of books available in classrooms. The researchers reported "that regardless of access to books in the home, the public library, and the school library, children in classrooms containing attractive collections read 50 percent more books than children in the same school without such collections."

A writing resource area is important in the classroom if we are to provide an appropriate environment for writing instruction and practice. Materials in this area might include picture dictionaries, motivational dictionaries (such as *The Charlie Brown Dictionary* and/or *The Super Dictionary*), regular dictionaries, lists of words in various categories, books and dictionaries of word origins, various thesauri, books of word games and puzzles, different types and sizes of writing paper and writing implements, and writing activities. Children need to have a resource area where they can seek help in their writing so they can learn to take risks in trying new words and different ways of expressing themselves.

Children and adults talk more freely in informal face-to-face contacts than they do in formal impersonal situations. Students need to practice all their communication skills with one another and they do this best in an atmosphere which not only permits talking but actively encourages it.

When children are constantly exposed to different language patterns and are encouraged to utilize these patterns in their speaking, considerable language growth can occur. Teachers should consistently encourage student dialogue, discussions, role playing, choral speaking, and self-expression as means of helping to expand the oral language skills of students.

Children are more comfortable and, therefore, more likely to try new experiences when wholesome relationships exist between the teacher and children and among the children themselves. Yet, Cazden (5) states, classrooms "are among the most crowded human environments; few adults are confined for five or more hours per day in so few square feet per person." If class sizes are large, it can be difficult for a teacher to create a classroom organization in which children are free to move about and communicate with one another. If administrators judge teaching by the noise level emanating from a classroom (the quieter the better), then it becomes difficult for teachers to create environments which facilitate children's language arts growth. It is important for teachers to have supportive principals who understand the necessity of informal environments for the learning of children.

Belief Six Blocks of time must be allocated for independent reading and writing.

This is easier to do in the primary grades than in subsequent grades in a school. Teachers in early childhood education usually work in self-contained classrooms where over half the day is often spent in language arts activities. *If* teachers value free reading, they *can* schedule time for it. A second-grade child, a student in a classroom where free reading is valued, was asked, "When do you read?" Her answer was:

Lots of times.
Sometimes with a partner.
I read my writing to the teacher.
I read books in the little library.
During SSR [sustained silent reading].
When the teacher makes books of our writing.
When my friend shows me his story.
I read the displays (25).

This child's response provides insight into her learning environment and into the attitude of her teacher toward the teaching and learning of reading.

In the middle and later grades, it may be more difficult for teachers to create a

Blocks of time must be allocated for independent reading and writing.

similar environment. Often, subjects are departmentalized and classes are scheduled at rigidly timed intervals. Language arts is taught by English teachers who often maintain that the crowded curriculum does not permit time for free reading. Yet this period of middle childhood is crucial to the development of pleasurable literacy. Teachers and administrators must commit themselves to helping children develop the practice they need to become lifetime readers.

One strategy which works well is uninterrupted sustained silent reading (USSR), which was initiated by Lyman Hunt, Jr. Hunt's goal was to get students to read voluntarily (sustain themselves) in a single book for thirty to fifty minutes. When using the USSR technique, all members of a class (including the teacher) read for an agreed length of time. Students begin by agreeing to read for ten minutes, and this quickly grows into fifteen, thirty, and then to fifty minutes of silent reading. McCracken (18, pp. 447–448), a proponent of what is commonly shortened to sustained silent reading (SSR), writes:

> Students will learn to read when reading is as important to them as speaking, and when we in schools give importance to reading. We give time to those things which we feel are important. We give time to collecting lunch money, to taking roll, to coffee breaks. . . . Students will know that teachers believe reading is important when we give time for practicing reading every school day so that every child has a time to read silently.

A similar strategy is sustained silent writing (SSW). Time is set aside for independent writing. Students are encouraged to write thought ramblings, to create poems, to keep a journal, or to write short stories. At first, the quantity of writing is emphasized and students are encouraged to write for a specified length of time. As time goes on, emphasis shifts to the quality of the writing.

Large-group, small-group, and paired writing opportunities help motivate students who find it difficult to work by themselves. Teachers can help children gain confidence in their writing abilities by moving among them and making themselves available for help and encouragement.

Belief Seven   Teachers must respect the language variations which exist among children.

People in the United States make up a linguistically diverse society. While there are just three main geographical language variations—northern, midland, and southern—there are many subvarieties within each variation. Furthermore, there is a social variation of the language which reflects such things as socioeconomic status, culture, and educational level, and which causes some variants of English to be valued more than others. For example, the dialect of Boston is held in higher esteem than the dialects of the southern Appalachians or the urban ghettos. Teachers in Massachusetts find no cause for alarm if children talk about *Cuber* (Cuba) or have great *idears* (ideas); yet many teachers feel the need to change or correct the language of children who say, "I got two cent" or "He be working now." Some linguists call such dialect modification "mischievous nonsense" (9, p. 337).

Many people, including teachers, believe there is a form of English which is "standard" (the variety used by television announcers, the college educated, and the cultured users of language). DeStefano (9, p. 336) does not agree with that viewpoint. She writes:

> . . . the United States has no true, nationally recognized, standard dialect. Someone from Columbus, Ohio will not try to sound like a New Yorker—perish the thought. Nor will a Californian try to emulate the speech of a New Englander. These regional varieties are characteristic features of American English.

Teachers who attach undue importance to language differences can have negative influences on children whose language is deemed inappropriate. It is important that teachers respect the diversity in children's language and that they prepare learning environments which facilitate growth through expansion of the existing language possessed by the children.

Students come to school fluent in the language of their homes; they have already demonstrated that they are capable of learning to communicate in their own language. Language has been learned in a nonthreatening environment; adults have not only expected them to learn but have been delighted with their progress. It is a paradox that this endeavor, which seems so effortless in the early years, becomes such a problem and causes such stress and anxiety for many children when they begin school.

School is a strange new environment for all children, but it is most foreign to the children whose language and culture differ significantly from the mainstream of middle-class American values. A classroom teacher who insists that children speak only in "complete sentences" and "correct" English can stifle the unfolding of children's language development.

To accept children's language does not imply a laissez-faire attitude on the part of teachers. Rather, it means that children will be encouraged to increase their language facility through listening, speaking, reading, and writing. Teachers can help children to learn the standard forms and the appropriate times and places for their use. Standard forms can be learned while nonstandard forms are accepted.

Successful communication is the goal of a good language arts program for all children. This goal can be attained when children learn in classrooms headed by teachers who provide children with language arts experiences based on carefully thought-out educational beliefs.

Let us now discuss how we plan to share our message with you in this book.

ABOUT THIS BOOK

In the preceding sections of this chapter, we shared with you the ingredients of the language arts as well as our beliefs about them. With this information, you now have a sense of the philosophical perspective from which we wrote this book.

The manner in which we choose to share with you our message about the language arts is unique. Our book does not devote separate chapters to listening, handwriting, spelling, reading, and composition, as most language arts textbooks have done. We deal with each of these language arts ingredients in an in-depth manner, but we do so from the *confines of a classroom* as well as from a theoretical standpoint.

Our emphasis on the classroom came as a result of our professional work with preservice education students and inservice teachers in numerous states. Supplying individuals with knowledge about the language arts was one task; getting them to implement the information properly into elementary and middle school classrooms was quite another matter. We have come into contact, over the years, with many persons who knew *what* was to be taught but were devoid of *how* specific language arts content was to be provided to students in the classroom. As we worked with future and practicing teachers, we found that our greatest success occurred when we utilized exemplary teachers whose classrooms showed how the language arts should be taught to children. Their classrooms provided our students with tangible models for teaching the language arts and helped them to see how knowledge can be implemented into practice.

Through use of this book, you will be able to "visit" vicariously the classrooms of six model teachers of the language arts. The teachers do exist, although they have been given fictitious names. They teach in urban, suburban, and rural areas in schools having both majority- and minority-group populations, thus encompassing the full range of socioeconomic levels. Also, they are not single-dimension people. Teaching is important to them but they have personal interests and commitments outside our profession, as their friends and families will attest.

While this book's focus is upon the language arts instruction provided by these teachers, it is only one of several facets of the book. Other key ingredients include the following:

1 Chapters 2 through 8 will each deal with specific grade levels of a school. Chapters 2 and 3 will concentrate on kindergarten and grade one; Chapters 4 and 5 on grades two and three; Chapters 6 and 7 on grades four and five; and Chapter 8 on grades six through eight. Thus, in the next seven chapters, you will be able to see how developmentally the language arts are taught in classrooms ranging from kindergarten through eighth grade.

2 In addition to devoting each chapter to a certain stage of school, in Chapters 2, 4, 6, and 8 we discuss *instructional emphases, instructional strategies, problems,* and *assessment measures* relative to each of the language arts at that specific stage. For example, you will be able to read about the emphases on listening for grades two and three, how it can best be taught at that level, the problems a person encounters as she or he attempts to do this, and the ways to determine whether or not listening objectives are being attained in these grades. Comparable information in the chapter will also be found regarding speaking, composition, and the other language arts as they apply to second- and third-graders. This information is meant to provide you with an understanding of each language arts aspect taught at a particular grade level.

3 A note of caution: In our discussion of language arts in Chapters 2, 4, 6, and 8 we will present some instructional emphases to be attained by children at specific stages. This section has deliberately been kept brief since the emphases are merely intended to provide you with an overview of the listening, speaking, composition, handwriting, spelling, and reading application skills to which language arts efforts are directed. The instructional emphases were determined as an outgrowth of our study of language arts curricula and materials as well as the recommendations of professional literature regarding each stage.

4 As we indicated previously, six teachers of the language arts are described in this book. These six teachers were chosen from the many excellent teachers with whom we have had contact, not only because of their competence but also because, in our estimation, they taught in classrooms similar in size, numbers of students, and conditions found most frequently in the schools throughout our country.

Two different teachers are presented in Chapters 3, 5, and 7, respectively. The teachers described in Chapter 3 teach in the grades discussed in Chapter 2. Those in Chapters 5 and 7 teach in the grades dealt with in Chapters 4, 6, and 8, respectively. The beliefs and methods of these six teachers are presented in a format we term a *descriptor*. After each descriptor, you will find our analysis of the teacher. In the analysis, we identify the aspects of the teacher we consider to be particularly noteworthy. Following each analysis, you will find an explanation of why we felt a particular practice of a teacher was noteworthy. Incidentally, each descriptor can serve as an informal test for you. While reading the descriptor, make note of the features of the teacher you consider to be positive in nature. Then compare your analysis with ours.

This look at language arts instruction in the classroom in Chapters 3, 5, and 7 gives you a fine opportunity to see how implementation of theory conveyed in Chapters 2, 4, 6, and 8 occurs. Showing you how successful teachers are providing quality instruction can aid you immeasurably as you teach the language arts to students. It is our hope that you will supplement the ideas presented with additional instructional practices and materials.

5 Chapter 8, "Language Arts in the Middle School," will focus upon the instructional emphases, instructional strategies, problems, and assessment measures occurring in grades six, seven, and eight. The constraints placed upon teaching the language arts in grades six, seven, and eight will be discussed along with some possible alternatives.

6 In Chapter 9, "The Teacher's Role in Language Arts Instruction," the emphasis will be on the teacher. We will look at complex issues involved in finding answers to questions such as, What is an effective teacher? and, Do any specific characteristics set apart effective language arts teachers from those who are not as effective? While there may be no definitive answers to each question, you will be given information which will help you to formulate a teaching philosophy which will enable you to become a teacher capable of making sound educational decisions.

7 Chapter 10, "The Language Arts Program," will describe strategies for assessing a language arts program. The chapter also presents ways in which a language arts program can be revised if facets of it are found to be deficient. Finally, the chapter offers ideas as to how language arts programmatic modifications can be implemented so that they will occur subsequently within the confines of the classroom. Included in this chapter you will find lists of the goals to be attained in the six areas designated in point 3 of this section. These areas are listening, speaking, composition, handwriting, spelling, and reading application skills. They can be found in the appendixes following Chapter 10.

If you are currently teaching in a school district, you may wish to compare your language arts program with the curricula presented in Chapter 10. If you are in the process of becoming a teacher, you may wish to visit a local school district and see how its program compares with the curricula presented in Chapter 10. In either instance, readers of this text should note that these programs' curricula represent an elaboration of the content we present in Chapters 2, 4, 6, and 8 as well as the emphases of the language arts discussed in those chapters.

8 The final ingredient of this book is its appendixes. Many hours have gone into the selection of content for this section. The material included in it was considered by language arts teachers and professors with whom we consulted to be of prime importance to novices as well as experienced teachers in making quality language arts instruction a reality in classrooms.

SOME CAUTIONS

First, in reading the descriptors and analyses contained in Chapters 3, 5, and 7, you may not consider some of the approaches used by a teacher to be new. Do not feel negative about this, since the techniques used by the teachers are sound pedagogically, they do achieve their desired goals, and, in some instances, they represent modifications of some time-honored language arts methodology.

Second, we are not suggesting that the techniques used by a teacher at a grade level are the only appropriate ones for that grade level. There are, of course, many viable vehicles for teaching the language arts to children. Our recognition of this premise is shown by the content of Chapters 3, 5, and 7. The teachers described are effective through use of the methodology presented in a descriptor, but are not carbon copies of one another. In your own instructional efforts, you are encouraged to alter the activities of a particular teacher if the needs of your students could be better met by thorough use of other techniques and materials. After all, effective teaching offers appropriate instruction in order to enable students to achieve the instructional objectives at the prescribed performance levels.

Third, although our descriptors will help you to experience the teaching of language arts in a classroom setting vicariously, we recognize that page constraints limit what we present. We have described only the conditions we felt were most important to the teaching of language arts. Omissions undoubtedly have occurred, but we still feel you will receive a thorough presentation of language arts teaching *in actual classrooms*.

Fourth, we are acutely aware that reading is one of the language arts. Given the complexity of instruction as one learns to read plus the myriad of textbooks devoted to reading, our discussion of reading will be confined to its application. We will not discuss how one learns to read and what skills are mastered in this acquisition process. Rather, we will share ways in which students can use reading for fostering the development of other language arts and/or for enjoyment.

Finally, although the format of this book differs from that of traditional textbooks, be assured that all major topics dealt with in these textbooks are described in our book. We have chosen to integrate our presentation of the language arts, to show how successful teachers provide quality instruction in actual classrooms, and to discuss with you the attributes of effective teaching of the language arts. That we do this, rather than leave you to your devices to discern how theory should be implemented in a classroom, should not be perceived as a shortcoming of our book. It can serve as a resource and reference book for your teaching as well as for discussions about preparing to teach the language arts.

BIBLIOGRAPHY AND REFERENCES

1 Britton, J. *Language and Learning*. Coral Gables, Fla.: *University of Miami Press*, 1970, pp. 150–151.
2 Brown, Roger. "Some Priorities in Language Arts Education." *Language Arts*, vol. 56, no. 5, May 1979, p. 484.
3 Burrows, A. T. *Teaching Composition*. Washington, D. C.: Department of Classroom Teachers of the National Education Association, 1966, p. 17.
4 Cazden, Courtney B. *Child Language and Education*. New York: Holt, Rinehart and Winston, 1972.
5 Cazden, Courtney B. "What We Don't Know about Teaching the Language Arts." *Phi Delta Kappan*, vol. 61, no. 9, May 1980, pp. 595–596.
6 Chomsky, Carol. "Stages in Language Development and Reading Exposure." *Harvard Educational Review*, vol. 42, February 1973, pp. 1–33.
7 Cohen, Dorothy. "Effect of Literature on Vocabulary and Reading." *Elementary English*, vol. 45, February 1968, pp. 209–213.
8 Deardon, R. F. "Curricular Implications of Developments in the Teaching of Reading." In J. Downing and A. L. Brown, (eds.), *The Second International Reading Symposium*. London: Cassell, 1967, pp. 96–97.
9 DeStefano, Johanna S., and Rentel, Victor. "Language Variation: Perspectives for Teachers." *Theory Into Practice*, vol. XIV, no. 5, December 1975, pp. 328–337.
10 Dunning, Steven, and Redd, Virginia. "What Are the Basics in English?" *SLATE Starter Sheets*, Urbana, Illinois: National Council of Teachers of English, vol. 1, no. 2, August 1976, p. 1.
11 Goodman, Kenneth S. *Analysis of Oral Reading Miscue: Applied Psycholinguistics*. New York: Holt, Rinehart and Winston, 1973, pp. 158–177.
12 Henry, Clair. "Viewpoints from an Elementary School Principal." *Language Arts*, vol. 58, no. 1, January 1981, pp. 9–11.
13 Hickman, Janet. "What Do Fluent Readers Do?" *Theory into Practice*, vol. XVI, no. 5, December 1977, pp. 372–375.
14 Howe II, Harold. *Picking up the Options*. Reston, Va.: Department of Elementary School Principals of the National Education Association, 1968, p. 151.
15 Huck, Charlotte S. *Children's Literature in the Elementary School* (3d ed.). New York: Holt, Rinehart and Winston, 1979, p. 596.
16 Huck, p. 590.
17 Lickteig, Sister M. Joan. "Research-Based Recommendations for Teachers of Writing." *Language Arts*, vol. 58, no. 1, January 1981, p. 45.
18 McCracken, Robert A. "Do We Want Real Readers?" *Journal of Reading*, March 1969, vol. 12, pp. 447–448.
19 Mangieri, John N., and Corboy, Margaret Riedell. "Recreational Reading: Do We Practice What Is Preached?" *The Reading Teacher*, vol. 34, no. 8, May 1981, pp. 923–925.
20 Maxwell, John C. "Viewpoints from a National Professional Organization." *Language Arts*, vol. 58, no. 1, January 1981, pp. 13–14.
21 Moffett, James. *A Student-Centered Language Arts Curriculum, K-13: A Handbook for Teachers*. Boston: Houghton Mifflin Company, 1973, p. 11.
22 Orth, Ralph H., and Ferguson, Alfred R. (eds.). *The Journals and Miscellaneous Notebooks of Ralph Waldo Emerson*, vol. III, 1830–1831. Cambridge, Mass.: Harvard University Press, 1977, p. 274.

23 Otto, Wayne. *Corrective and Remedial Teaching* (3d ed.). Boston: Houghton Mifflin, 1980, p. 253.

24 Postman, Neil, and Weingartener, Charles. "A Careful Guide to the School Squabble," *Psychology Today,* October 1973, p. 76.

25 Reed, Marilyn. "Reading in the Open Classroom." *Theory into Practice,* vol. XVI, no. 5, December 1977, pp. 392–400.

26 Rentel, Vistor M., and Kennedy, John J. "Effects of Pattern Drill on the Phonology, Syntax and Reading Achievement of Rural Appalachian Children." *American Educational Research Journal,* vol. 9, Winter 1972, pp. 87–100.

27 Roser, Nancy. "The Humanities in American Life: A Response," *Language Arts,* vol. 58, no. 5, May 1981, pp. 540–544.

CHAPTER **2**

LANGUAGE ARTS: KINDERGARTEN AND FIRST GRADE

OVERVIEW

The focus of this chapter will be the teaching of the language arts in kindergarten and grade one. The chapter will begin by discussing the nature of children in these grades. We will then describe the curricular emphases, instructional activities, and assessment measures associated with providing language arts instruction to children in these grades.

In this chapter, we will discuss the characteristics of children at the kindergarten and first-grade levels, followed by a discussion in six categories of language arts instruction: listening, spelling, composition, handwriting, speaking, and reading application. These topics are not to be considered in isolation in curriculum planning. They are presented in this manner as a convenience in focusing teacher attention on the pertinent issues. In many instances, these separate activities will be integrated into a total language arts program.

THE CHILD

Every classroom teacher is cognizant of the spectrum of individual differences in one classroom. Just as a classroom will have children of different heights, weights, and complexion, it will also have children in different stages of physical, emotional, and intellectual development and of readiness for learning. In the last several years, the literature on these subjects has proliferated. The brief section which follows is not intended to cover the field, even in an abridged fashion, or to dissuade the teacher from reading further in the literature. It is intended to direct teacher attention to some individual differences in children's development which impact on their language arts instruction.

Physical Characteristics

Any adult who watches children at play will be struck by their differences in physical development. Mary may swing from branches, John may climb anything upright, while Susie falls from the first rung of the ladder to the slide and stumbles over her feet as she walks down the hall. Clearly, children develop physically according to their own time clocks. All teachers of young children should consider the differences in physical abilities and their effect on the child's performance in the classroom.

Classrooms are often incorrectly thought to be homogeneous in terms of age; that is, all kindergarten children are assumed to be five years old while first-graders are presumed to be six. It is important to remember that there will be at least a one-year chronological age range within each class and that even children of the same age will reflect varied levels of development.

Children's attention spans are quite short during this period. Many young children have difficulty sitting quietly for even a fifteen-minute story. It is a good idea to have several story times of limited duration for these children rather than lose their attention by trying to force them to listen for too long a period.

Since we are concerned with language arts instruction, it is important to discuss three skills which are often included in readiness testing and which have implications for language arts learning: visual discrimination, auditory discrimination, and coordination abilities.

Visual discrimination consists of *five* skills which are important to the mastery of print:

1 Visual acuity is the accuracy of sight. Where physical examinations or school health examinations are given, there may be a notation on a child's record to the effect that his vision is adequate. This adequacy refers to acuity, and acuity is only *one* of the skills with which the teacher will be concerned.

2 Visual memory requires a child to recall from memory past visual experiences and is basic to figure names, shapes, the alphabet, and word recognition. A child who cannot remember what his name looks like is a poor candidate for instruction in the alphabet.

3 Visual tracking is the ability to follow symbols with coordinated eye movement and is essential if a child is to follow a line of print.

4 Figure–ground differentiation is the ability to select pertinent visual information from the background, an ability essential to copying, or focusing on one word or one letter in a sentence or series.

5 Consistency is the ability to recognize an object by its distinguishing features and is essential in recognizing letters of different sizes and in identifying the printing of other children as representing the same letters as his own printing, although the quality of the print may vary. This is especially important in the recognition of letters such as *a* and *g,* which have different forms in texts and teacher-printed materials (24).

Auditory discrimination includes two skills which are essential to success in phonics mastery: (1) auditory acuity, which is the accuracy of sound and the ability to differentiate between sounds, including in speech, and (2) auditory memory, which is the ability to recognize and recall past auditory experiences. Counting, reciting poetry, and sequencing alphabet all require facility in auditory memory.

The development of coordination abilities, which include eye–hand coordination, is important. In copying print from the board, a child has to attend visually to what is to be copied while controlling the movement of the hand. Young children have considerable difficulty in managing visual accuracy and motor control simultaneously. For these children, copying from the board is an exercise in frustration.

Children who have difficulty in the early stages of kindergarten and/or first grade may have developmental lags in one or several of the areas mentioned above. The teacher who wishes to provide instructional activities for the development of these physical abilities will find complete listings of activities, materials, and sources available in books such as Spache's *Good Reading for Poor Readers* (46).

Handedness is established in most children by the time they are in kindergarten, with 90 percent of the children being right-handed (3). The wise teacher will not try to force a left-handed child to change his preference. Otto and Smith note that "left-handedness is a natural and inherited trait of a small minority of children" (36, p. 306).

Social and Emotional Characteristics

A child brings his feelings to school. Children approach the classroom with expectations, anxieties (even panic), attitudes, self-concepts, interests, and values. Never before has so much been expected from them by their parents and their teachers. Yet certain school-community practices work against some children's chances for success. The legal requirement that all students must start school on the basis of chronological age causes many students to be placed in a school environment which is not conducive to their growth.

To most parents, attending school means learning to read, and a high value is placed on early reading abilities. However, some children are simply not ready to begin formal reading at this time. Their problems are exacerbated by teachers who use methods and materials which do not provide for pupils' individual differences. Reading ability is very highly valued in our society and pressures from parents, teachers, and other children often produce anxiety in children who cannot meet these unrealistic standards.

The transition from home to school can be difficult for many children. Those who speak a language other than English will be entering a new and totally different speaking environment which may produce anxiety and confusion. Children who come from other minority backgrounds may encounter situations which are oriented to the culture of the majority, and this may produce feelings of hostility and failure.

Enough research is available to document the importance of the attitudes of children toward school subjects (1, 9) and the attitudes of teachers toward children (2, 19, 31). Research on self-concept supports the hypothesis that where children expect to fail, they usually do (42). Sensitive teachers in supportive classrooms maximize student learning. Teachers must assess the emotional climate of their classrooms in terms of the feelings of the children as well as their own feelings about the teaching–learning environment. Good teachers will use methods and materials which provide for individual differences and will prepare classrooms in which children can grow socially and emotionally.

Erikson (11) describes this period of childhood as a time when the properly developing child will be learning initiative as opposed to guilt. Children who have opportunities to participate in appropriate activities develop their imaginations and their abilities to fantasize. They learn to cooperate with others and they learn to lead as well as to follow. Less fortunate children seem immobilized by guilt; they are fearful, overly dependent on adults, slower in their development of social skills, and limited in their imaginations. Teachers can facilitate children's social development by structuring learning environments rich in opportunities for children to develop their imaginations. Provision should be made for children to develop their social skills as they work and play together.

Children of this age are quite capable of working individually for short periods of time as long as they know what is expected of them. They are able to work well in small groups and in total class activities. Teachers must take advantage of these abilities as they plan their language arts programs. Classrooms must be places in which children feel at ease, in which they can talk freely with others, and in which they can develop and practice their language skills. Pinnell (41) believes that teachers should structure their efforts to "take advantage of nature's most powerful incentive for developing facility with language—the child's intention to communicate meaning to other people . . ." (p. 318).

Intellectual Characteristics

Jean Piaget describes a system for conceptualizing cognitive development which includes four stages: sensorimotor, preoperational, concrete operational, and formal operational. Children, with their differing levels of ability, knowledge, and skills, vary in the rate at which they proceed through these stages, but all children must pass through the stages in the same sequence.

Kindergarten and first-grade children are usually in the upper levels of the stage of preoperational thought, a period characterized by rapid conceptual development and the development of language. McCandles (32) describes Piaget's view of this stage: ". . . language mushrooms, symbolic play emerges, obvious modeling and imitation take place constantly (although imitation has occurred earlier) and children begin to report dreams. The child has magical notions of causation; his experiences, including his dreams, are real to him; the word is the thing, and vice versa" (p. 245).

Characteristics of preoperational children's behavior and thinking are:

1 Egocentric speech and thought. The child cannot take the role of or see the viewpoint of another.
2 Inability to attend to transformations. When a child observes a sequence of changes, he "does not focus on the process of transformation from an original state to a final state, but restricts his attention to each inbetween state when it occurs" (41, p. 73).

3 Inability to decenter. "When the child is presented with a visual stimulus, he tends to center or fix his attention on a limited perceptual aspect of the stimulus" (51, p. 75). He can only pay attention to one detail at a time; he is unable to consider two aspects of a situation at the same time.

4 Inability to reverse operations. Piaget believes reversibility "is the most clearly defined characteristic of intelligence. . . . If thought is reversible, it can follow the line of reasoning back to where it started. Preoperational thought is slow, plodding, inflexible and dominated by perceptions" (51, pp. 75–76). It is not reversible.

Piaget's analysis of cognitive stages has implications for teachers as they work with children. Biehler (4) suggests that five- and six-year-olds can profit from instruction and evaluation which is as individualized as possible. He believes that pupils should "be encouraged not just to supply answers but to explain the reasoning behind them, which provides clues to the level and nature of their thinking" (p. 119).

Over and over in his writing, Piaget (39) emphasizes the active role that the child plays in his own learning. "Knowledge is derived from action," he writes (p. 28). While relatively little is still known about how children acquire language (16) and there is disagreement among authorities regarding the source of language competence, most language theorists agree that children are active participants in their own language learning. King (29) maintains: " . . . the child is not a passive learner. He or she imitates but is not bound by imitation in learning language. The child actively constructs his or her own linguistic system" (p. 295). It is extremely important that kindergarten and first-grade teachers provide rich language environments in which students can extend and enrich their language competence.

Teachers must be certain that they are clear in their communication with children. DeStephano (8) uses the term *Language Instruction Register* (LIR) to refer to the varieties of language which are used in the teaching of reading and language arts. Included in the LIR are such words as *sound, letter, word,* and *sentence.* Teachers tend to assume that "certain concepts of language are self-evident" (10, p. 328) and that children do not need help in order to understand them. Yet research conducted by Downing (10) indicates that some primary children's concepts of these words are different from those of the teacher. Children may experience unnecessary difficulties because they do not understand the meaning of these words.

Just as young students must understand the vocabulary of language instruction, it is necessary for you to know the meaning of such terms as *perception, memory, reasoning, reflection,* and *insight* if you are to understand children's intellectual development. Perception is the process by which children detect, recognize, and interpret information from physical stimulation. Obviously this is the intellectual process accompanying the visual and auditory discriminations referred to earlier.

Important changes occur between the ages of five and seven. Younger children have difficulty focusing their attention or shifting their attention from one stimulus to another. As children mature, their selective attention improves so that not only are they able to focus on a teacher's instruction but they are also able to anticipate what might be perceived, and this anticipation allows children to respond faster, more efficiently, and more accurately. Accuracy in perception is necessary for a child to

Children need to be active in their own learning.

succeed with print, to distinguish one letter from another and one word from another. If a child has difficulty, perception can be developed through experience (18) and therefore can be improved through instruction. Gross differentiations should be required for younger children, followed by subtler differentiations as the child matures.

Memory is the ability to recognize or recall information at a later time. Recognition is the ability to identify an event or a symbol previously seen when it is again present. Recall is the ability to reconstruct an event or symbol unaided. Both recognition and recall improve with age, but recognition precedes recall. The teacher will notice the difference in children's recognition and recall abilities when teaching the alphabet. First, children will recognize letters they have seen before; later, they will remember the names; and finally, they will be able to print the letters from memory. For some children there is considerable delay before they can write letters from memory. Children develop vocabulary in the same sequence, first recognizing the word (sight vocabulary) and much later producing the word unaided (spelling). Young children have difficulty in recall because they do not have strategies for storing information (14). This may be why some young children fail to recall material which has been presented frequently.

Reasoning is the use of knowledge to make inferences and to draw conclusions. Kindergarten and first-grade children often do poorly on teacher-generated tasks or standardized tests to measure reasoning. Many children do not understand the problems because they speak a language which is different from the language of the school and they do not comprehend the vocabulary or grammar used by the teacher. Children may forget the instructions by the time the teacher has finished presenting the material. Some children have not had the opportunity for experiences which would provide them with the information they need to solve the problems. Often children will not respond because they are fearful of making a mistake. All these obstacles must be seriously considered by the teacher who is tempted to use low test scores on readiness tests as evidence of limited reasoning ability of children.

Reflection is the degree to which a child will consider the quality of his or her thinking. Children who respond rapidly, without much apparent thought, are referred to as impulsive, and those who are deliberate, as reflective. There is some research to support the hypothesis that reflective responders are fearful of making errors. Children do tend to become more reflective with age, possibly because they are increasingly concerned with making errors. Young children who respond impulsively, however, often make mistakes even though they may have the ability to perform without error. A cautious teacher must distinguish between lack of ability and lack of reflection in considering the young child's errors.

Insight is the recognition of new relationships. This power, the last to develop, continues to be refined long after elementary school. It is a lifelong process. Many kindergarten and first-grade children can entertain only one hypothesis at a time and cannot consider any other alternatives. They see things individually and do not seek to establish relationships. They see the world from their own fixed point of view. They do not "shift gears" mentally. These children will be able to focus on the differences between dogs and cats but cannot recognize any similarities between them. Such children require considerable practice in grouping and classification activities before they can recognize attributes which determine group memberships. Manipulative sorting activities are helpful in the development of insight in young children.

Many instructional materials for kindergarten and first grade are designed for the "average" child and are not designed for the proper level of all children's physical, emotional, or intellectual development. It is the task of the teacher to determine the appropriateness of the instructional materials in terms of the abilities of her or his children. A knowledge of child development can help the teacher find the right match between children's learning experiences and their levels of development.

LANGUAGE ARTS IN KINDERGARTEN AND FIRST GRADE

In this section, as well as in the following sections, we will discuss each of the language arts separately. This delineation is made for your convenience so that we can more readily describe the instructional emphases of each of the language arts, some of the instructional activities which can be used to teach them, the problems which may hinder the successful teaching of the language arts, and the ways in which the major areas of the language arts can be assessed in kindergarten and first grade.

Let us begin our discussion with the area sometimes referred to as the most neglected of the language arts—listening.

LISTENING

Listening is a receptive process in which the student derives meaning from oral presentations. Every parent and teacher will attest to its importance in communicating with young children, yet more attention is paid to the lack of listening skill than to its development. Listening comprehension can be compared with reading comprehension in that both aim to get a message from a sender to a receiver.

The child who is a reader has listening skills as well as reading ability to help him gain information. He can use text to derive meaning and he can reread for clarification. The prereader depends on his ability to listen for meaning and for instruction. Although listening is related to reading skill as a receptive process, it precedes reading and, like reading, it does not just develop with maturity. Listening, like reading, must be learned.

Just as a child varies his speech to suit his purposes and later varies his reading experiences, so, too, he needs practice in a variety of listening skills. As teachers plan classroom activities to provide this necessary practice, they must be aware that listening is, above all, a communication process. Artificial or mechanical exercises for developing listening skills detract from the true purposes of listening as a requisite for communication and as an important tool for learning.

Instructional Emphases   Listening skills should be taught in real communication contexts whenever possible. Listening games and exercises should be incorporated into the kindergarten and first-grade curriculum within this context. The teacher will provide an environment in which children can grow in the following ways: (1) Children listen so they can follow directions, understand the needs and intentions of others, and respond appropriately in a verbal environment. (2) Children listen with enjoyment to music and they enjoy participation in listening games. (3) They listen to stories and poems and grow in their appreciation of them. (4) Through listening, they begin to develop a sensitivity to language as they extend their vocabularies.

Instructional Strategies   Listen for a moment. Just stop for thirty seconds and listen. If you are reading at school, you will probably be aware of children's voices in the halls, teachers' voices from adjoining rooms, and footsteps, bells, and other sounds of activity. If you are reading at home, you may hear the hum of the refrigerator, the television, voices in your home, and traffic sounds outside it. Consider the stimuli in your environment which compete for your attention. As adults, you have learned to attend to what is important and to minimize distractions. Most kindergarten and first-grade children have not learned to do this.

The teacher must provide a classroom atmosphere in which the child can focus on tasks with a minimum of distraction. Experienced teachers have cues for attention getting. They may turn off the classroom lights, raise their hands, begin reciting a well-known nursery rhyme or doing a finger play—any one of many prearranged signals which will get the children's attention. Once the children are attending, they must be helped to identify and concentrate on the listening task. Children need not be admonished to listen; rather, they must know what is expected of them.

Children enjoy playing games such as Following Directions. This game begins with a leader giving a short command to one member of a group. After this person executes the command, she or he chooses another person to repeat that action and to complete another action also. This is repeated with a third child and a fourth and so on, each one executing the required actions and adding a new command to the sequence until a child makes an error. Then the game begins again. Games such as this provide children with practice in attending to oral directions and in holding them in their memories.

Kindergarten and first-grade students need experiences in discriminating between sounds in the environment and practice in listening for likenesses and differences in situations which maximize the differences. The teacher will need to begin with activities requiring gross discriminations and work toward finer and finer discriminations. Children need experience in perceptual tasks to make fine discriminations (18). Classroom activities might include shaker boxes into which items such as dried beans, paper clips, marbles, cotton balls, dried cereal, pins, nails, sugar cubes, sugar grains, and thumbtacks are placed. Each box is shaken separately and discussion is stimulated concerning the things which sound similar and those which sound very different. Learning-center activities can provide child-initiated practice by using similar sealed and numbered boxes.

A teacher might use a simple activity such as "What Did I Drop?" After showing the children two objects, the leader hides her hands and releases one item while the children listen for the sound of the object hitting the desk or floor. Children will listen carefully for the sounds and with practice, some children will begin to anticipate the sound of individual objects.

One teacher gave her first-graders some listening homework. Their assignment was to listen carefully at home so they would be prepared to answer the following two questions: (1) What kinds of sounds do you hear in your home when you wake in the morning? (2) Do any of these sounds have a definite, regular beat? The children came to school the next morning brimming over with reports of sounds—the ticking of clocks, the dripping of water faucets, and so on. The teacher followed up this assignment by asking the children to listen for the sounds they heard in their classroom and then to listen to hear if any of the sounds had a regular beat. During the quiet moments that followed, several children were able to hear the typewriter that was being used down the hall as well as many everyday sounds which suddenly became very interesting to them (21).

Children of this age delight in moving to music. One innovative teacher played the Introduction to the *Firebird Suite* by Igor Stravinsky. She instructed the children to listen carefully to see if they could hear different parts of the music. When the music changed from one part to another, the children were to raise their hands. After they were familiar enough with the music, she divided the children into groups and asked them to move to the music. She asked the children to think about ways that their parts of the music "told" them to move. At first, the teacher helped the children by giving them cues. Eventually, each group was able to recognize its particular part of the music (21).

Poetry offers children an opportunity to extend their vocabularies and to increase their sensitivity to language. In one first-grade class, the children enjoyed hearing their teacher read the poem "Cat" (copyright © estate of Mary Britton Miller) by Mary Britton Miller:

The black cat yawns,
Opens her jaws,
Stretches her legs,
And shows her claws.

Then she gets up
And stands on four
Long stiff legs
And yawns some more.

She shows her sharp teeth,
She stretches her lip,
Her slice of a tongue
Turns up at the tip.

Lifting herself
On her delicate toes,
She arches her back
As high as it goes.

She lets herself down
With particular care,
And pads away
With her tail in the air.

The children discussed the ritual that cats go through upon awakening. The children yawned, stretched their legs, and "showed their claws." Phrases such as "her delicate toes" and "her slice of tongue" were discussed and incorporated into their image of the cat. Finally, the children acted out the poem (21).

Kindergarten and first-grade teachers will want to read to their children frequently. Huck (26) recommends that children of five or six hear three or four stories each day "in order to provide language stimulation and enjoyment derived from hearing stories and nursery rhymes" (p. 366). Listening to stories and poems gives children opportunities to recall important details, to recognize the main idea, and to recall the sequence of events presented in the selection.

Vukelich (50, p. 890) believes that children's literature can be used more effectively to enhance listening comprehension when teachers pose carefully thought-out questions to get children to think on a deeper level than simple recall of the story demands. Vukelich's categories of questions with examples of the questioning pattern are presented below.

Type of Questions	Purpose	Example
Recall questions	Help children remember to listen for important details.	Before reading *Caps for Sale* by Esphyr Slobodkina, "See if you can remember the colors of the peddler's caps."
Vocabulary questions	Help children listen to determine word meanings from context.	"See if you can tell what the peddler's wares were in *Caps for Sale.*"
Recognition-of-main-idea questions	Help children focus on the most important point(s) in the story.	Instead of telling the children the title of the book before it is read, wait and ask them at the end of the story, "What do you think we could call this story? What was this story about?"
Sequence questions	Help children remember to listen for the order of events in the story.	Before reading *The Gingerbread Man,* "See if you can remember who ran after the Gingerbread Man first, second, third, and so on."
Predicting-outcome questions	Help children guess what might happen in the story.	"*Ask Mr. Bear,* by Marjorie Flack, is the story about a little boy who can't decide what to get his mother for her birthday. He asks a cow, who suggests milk; but she already has milk. He asks a goose, who suggests feathers for a pillow; but she already has a pillow. He asks a bear, and what do you think the bear suggested?" The key is to stop and ask the question just before the climax.

Type of Questions	*Purpose*	*Example*
Drawing-conclusion questions	Help children think about why something might have happened.	Before reading *The Three Billy Goats Gruff*, by Marcia Brown, "See if at the end of the story you can tell me why the littlest Billy Goat Gruff told the troll to wait for his bigger brother. Why did the biggest Billy Goat Gruff knock the troll to bits, body and bone?"
Interpretation-of-emotions questions	Help children label the feelings of the characters in the story.	Before reading *A Baby Sister for Frances,* by Russell Hoban, "See if you can tell me how Frances felt when her baby sister arrived."
Application-to-real-life questions	Help children apply to their own lives the ideas they have heard.	After the story is read ask, "Have you ever felt like Frances? Can you tell me how you felt and why?"

Teachers will want to prepare classroom environments which are conducive to the development of communication skills. There will be quiet times with little or no talking permitted, when children are expected to work independently on teacher-assigned tasks. At other times, children will work together in pairs or in small groups. They will talk to each other, listen to each other, and in this way expand their verbal abilities.

Children improve their listening skills by listening. In far too many classrooms, the teacher does 90 percent of the talking and only 10 percent of the listening. This ratio should be reversed. Children need to practice their communication skills and teachers need to sharpen their listening abilities. Teachers who listen learn a great deal about the needs and interests of children as they observe their interactions while they work in the learning centers or on art projects or as they respond to works of literature. An added bonus from less teacher talk is that the teacher who is a good listener becomes an excellent model for the children with whom she works.

Problems   Children who lack the physical ability to discriminate sounds will have many more difficulties developing good listening skills than those with normal hearing. While poor auditory acuity is a medical problem, it is often identified by an observant teacher or by other school personnel as a result of a school screening program. Audiometers, earphones that carry different tones and volumes, are commonly used to identify students who need to be referred to physicians.

Teachers will want to read to their students frequently.

Teachers need to be alert to other symptoms of hearing problems such as earaches, mouth breathing, incorrect pronunciation, ear rubbing, and complaints of dizziness or head noises. A child who is inattentive or has a blank expression when asked to follow directions may not be able to hear properly. Children who display any of these manifestations should be referred to a hearing specialist for diagnosis and treatment (36).

Since listening is a receptive process it is difficult for the teacher to know what the child is experiencing. Often a child who looks attentive is really withdrawn from a situation which he does not quite comprehend. If the teacher compliments him for listening, he or she is reinforcing fogginess. It is more appropriate to reinforce specific behavior with statements such as "Jim knew that the first pig built his house of straw because he was listening so well."

Another important consideration is the level of understanding of each child. As a teacher reads a story to all the children, each child's experience in that listening situation is different. Some children will have the vocabulary and experience to respond creatively or critically to the story, some children will have a more limited vocabulary and experience and respond at the literal level, and some children will lack the vocabulary and experience to respond in more than a limited fashion. Often children who do not listen do not understand. Ollila (35) cautions that "the fact that children know the name of something does not mean they have an adequate concept of it" (p. 18). For example, a child may be able to identify a fox by name, but if he does not know that a fox eats chickens he will miss some of the suspense in "Chicken Little." The teacher must be alert for evidence of limited concept development.

Much prepared material available on the market is designed to teach listening skills. The teacher must be cautious in the use of taped material for young children, especially those having the greatest difficulty in listening. These children need more than words to comprehend meaning. A reading expert relates an experience which helps to illustrate this point. He was working in India with some government officials who were proficient in their use of the English language. When he attempted to use taped materials with them he was surprised to find that they could not extract the meaning from the tapes. He speculated that although they were fluent in English, they needed more than the spoken word to get the message; they needed to see the facial expressions of the speaker, as well as the body language, pacing, and all the clues nonverbal language can provide. The speaker and listener interact in such a way that communication takes place. The speaker will adjust his vocabulary, his speed, and his emphasis as he observes the responses of the listener. This adjustment is not possible with a tape recording and therefore, just as tapes were inappropriate as materials to help the Indian government officials learn, they are also inappropriate for helping some children improve their listening skills.

Teachers often find it difficult to create classroom environments in which students get optimum amounts of practice in using their communication skills. If teachers believe their job is to control children's behavior, they find it difficult to permit the informality necessary for children to talk and listen to each other. Teachers who see themselves as dispensers of information and view children as passive receptors of this information will do most of the talking and be dismayed when so many children become poor listeners. The solution is for teachers to realize that children learn by doing; they develop listening skills by actively practicing the skills of speaking and listening.

Assessment Standardized readiness tests which include items to assess listening abilities are often used during kindergarten or at the beginning of first grade. Listening skills items are often included as one subtest in a battery of tests of prereading skills. Such a subtest attempts to assess listening abilities having to do with school language, word meanings, and auditory discrimination skills. A performance rating is computed on the basis of the scores of each specific subtest. The results of these tests should not be used to classify or label children as slow or bright, good listener or poor listener, or ready or unready. The results of these tests can provide the teacher with some useful information; careful scrutiny of individual test items can provide teachers with diagnostic information that will help them plan experiences which will promote learning.

Standardized tests are administered under conditions very different from those of actual listening and they may not be valid measures of children's listening in a normal classroom situation. For this reason, we prefer less formal methods of assessment. Teachers should use their own listening skills as well as their powers of observation to assess the listening abilities of children. Otto (36, p. 306) maintains that "the only valid way to assess a student's listening performance is to solicit a verbal response or some other overt behavior that requires them to draw on the speaker's message." Children who follow simple directions or repeat simple concrete ideas when they are asked to do so are demonstrating their listening skills. Creative teachers can find many situations in which children's listening behavior can be observed. To facilitate the observation of a pupil's listening skills, teachers can construct checklists to record examples of observed behavior.

SPEAKING

Children come to school knowing a great deal about language. They have learned to speak in the home and they have learned to speak by speaking. Studies on language acquisition agree with Bloom's conclusion that "virtually all children by five or six arrive at school able to speak their native language" (5). They are able to carry on meaningful conversations with each other and with significant adults. Children have never encountered questions such as "What does it mean to speak well?" "Whose standard of speaking should be accepted?" and yet many of them "confront linguistic demands during the early years of schooling that they can't meet and often, can't understand" (29, p. 293).

An issue which must be addressed by classroom teachers is the instruction of the child who speaks nonstandard English. The child may be unfamiliar with standard English because he lives in a home where a foreign language is spoken, where a dialect is spoken, or where a divergent form of English is used (2). The difference in instructional philosophy concerning the nonstandard English speaker is illustrated by two approaches to the writing of experience charts. Some teachers insist that the child's speech should be recorded as spoken while others demand the right to correct the syntax before recording the child's words. We believe that the child's speech should be accepted and that more formal language skills will be an outgrowth of his school language experiences. The language the child brings to school is the language of his parents, his friends, and his neighborhood. To reject a child's language is to reject her or him personally. Kenneth Goodman once thought that there would be a strong relationship between the use of dialect and beginning reading success, but his research did not support that position. He now believes that teachers must change their attitudes, if necessary, so that they can accept the language of the learner (20).

Instructional Emphases Language skills will flourish in classrooms when children feel comfortable and are assured that their contributions are welcomed. The teacher of young children must prepare such an environment. Children will dictate experience charts, they will engage in conversations with their teacher and with each other, and they will participate in in-depth discussions on topics which are generated by instructional strategies. Just as children learned to speak by speaking in their homes, they will increase their language skills within the context of the school.

Instructional Strategies   Speech is encouraged by classroom activities which allow children to contribute spontaneously to an experience chart, a discussion, a question, a game, or an activity. When children have difficulty expressing themselves, the teacher must structure activities so the child has a pattern to use in response. Kindergarten teachers play games which require children to answer in a sentence such as: "My name is _____," "I can _____," or "I like _____." Speech is imitative to a degree and children will use teacher patterns as a model.

For many children the language of the school is unfamiliar. Reading aloud to children will provide language patterns which, with repetition, begin to sound familiar. A teacher who is a storyteller or story reader may use the language of the stories for children to experience directly. Small hand puppets or stick puppets of the three little pigs, the three bears, the little red hen, and the characters related to the familiar stories may be used for informal puppet shows. As children become familiar with the stories, they learn the parts and can then use the characters' words for their parts. Sentences of familiar stories are easily learned and are of excellent quality. Such experience fosters familiarity with proper language usage.

Pilon (40) has written an excellent article entitled "Culturally Divergent Children and Creative Language Activities" in which she gives suggestions to teachers who work with children who use divergent speech patterns. Pilon recommends the use of cumulative tales, with their repetitions of standard expression as a way of helping these students develop alternate ways of expressing themselves. Children should be encouraged to join in as the teacher reads, and lines are repeated over and over. To help children hear and gain practice using past-tense -ed verbs, Pilon suggests *I Know an Old Lady* by Rose Bonne, music by Alan Mills, pictures by Abner Graboff (Scholastic Book Services, 1961). Words which have -ed endings abound in this story: "Poor old lady, she swallowed a spider, it squirmed and wiggled and turned inside her." As the children join in to say them with the teacher, they will not only be getting practice in an alternate way of speaking, but they will also be experiencing the joys and delights inherent in this literary selection.

To help children work with using *is* and *are* instead of deleting them from their speech as many black children do, Pilon suggests the book *A Hole Is to Dig* by Ruth Krauss. After the teacher reads the book to them, they are asked to repeat some of the sentences from the story, which the teacher records on the chalkboard. She writes the sentences which use *is* on one side and the ones which use *are* on the other side of the board. The teacher then develops some oral language activities using these sentences and eventually the children make up their own sentences using *is* and *are*. Throughout her article, Pilon offers a wealth of children's books which can be used as a framework for planning oral language experiences which provide practice in using such words as *was/were, has/have,* and *does/do* and the inflectional ending -s. We recommend that you read it and adapt her ideas to fit your teaching situation.

Memorizing poetry is infrequently required in the primary school, but with repetition, many children learn nursery rhymes, songs, and simple poems, and these provide sentence patterns. As children become comfortable in group recitations, they can be encouraged to contribute individually. Children who speak freely in a group provide models for other children.

Problems The teacher who accepts the child's language will correct children without rejecting them. Most teachers find that reflecting speech rather than correcting speech directly is a good method. If the child says "I got a dog," the teacher responds, "You have a dog. What is his name?" She has provided the correct verb form without rejecting the child's information. The teacher has concerns other than dialect speakers. How should she handle immature speech? Mispronunciation? Inappropriate words? Common sense would suggest that she use the same supportive style she uses in other instances.

Assessment To assess a child's ability to express his thoughts in complete, meaningful statements requires some definition of *meaningful statements*. An appropriate statement for some children would be beyond the language capabilities of others. One of us once was informed by a five-year-old first-grade child: "No, I am not working, and it is not because I do not comprehend the procedure. It is mainly because I just don't care to!" That was a meaningful statement but to use it as a standard for all first-graders would be grossly unfair. The teacher must assess progress in terms of the starting point and the final performance of a child. If children continue throughout the year to improve in their ability to communicate with the teacher and with their classmates, the program has been successful.

COMPOSITION

Writing, or composition, has been an emphasis in the language arts arena for many years, but recent competency testing and skills mastery testing have dictated more concentrated instruction and more rigorous evaluation. Although the purposes of writing, practical and creative (44), are of importance to language arts experts, the popular press has focused on what it perceives as failures in practical writing such as letter writing, directions, applications, and explanations rather than on creative expression. It is important for teachers not to overreact to such criticism and force children into a prescriptive rule-oriented world of punctuation, proper spelling, and restricted vocabulary taught during a writing period in which composition is considered an isolated phenomenon.

Instructional Emphases Children's writing flourishes in a print-filled environment where children write as they need to write, when writing is needed for a particular purpose. It is well to remember that kindergarten and first-grade children are only six or seven—they are not adults. Just as it takes time to grow into adulthood, it also takes time for communication skills to develop. It is a mistake to force children to conform to adult standards too soon.

If a child is constantly corrected when he or she speaks, the child learns to keep quiet; if the beginning writer is only permitted to write using adult models, he or she will stop writing.

Clay (7) states:

> There will always be errors in word detail if the child is motivated to express his ideas, rather than merely stay within the confines of the vocabulary with which he is familiar and the skills he can control (p. 18).

Kenneth and Yetta Goodman (20) believe that learning to read and write can be learned as easily as learning to speak and listen. They believe that the learning of both oral and written language is motivated by the child's need to communicate with others.

A first-grade teacher (33) describes her children when she writes:

> This desire to write a message—to communicate a thought in writing—is present in first graders. They do not need writing exercises to help them learn to write. Instead form and the conventions of writing emerge as the child writes whole messages with a legitimate social function (p. 180).

In short, a child learns to write by writing in real situations in order to communicate messages to other people.

Instructional Strategies   The classroom teacher who takes dictation from her students for language experiences charts, who provides rich literature in her storytelling and reading, who writes on the board concerning weather, holidays, class plans, and so on, is providing a model for her students. For many children the teacher will be the only adult model who cherishes books, writes spontaneously, and espouses creativity. Often children will write independently, and for these children a writing center with materials and references should be provided. However, all children must be instructed in composition.

A structured approach for young children is to be found in *Children's Writing: An Approach for the Primary Grades,* by Sealey, Sealey, and Millmore (43). The stages addressed in this approach are: (1) labeling and captioning, (2) writing complete statements of one-unit length, (3) writing two complete statements, (4) writing three or more complete sentences, and (5) writing thematically. Stage 1 is presented briefly here so that the teacher may get a feel for the instructional strategy. Each child is to have a booklet of about twenty unlined pages. Each day the child is expected either to draw or to paste an object of interest on the left-hand page. The teacher and child will talk about the picture. The quality of the exchange will certainly be a reflection of the teacher's sensitivity.

When the child has decided what experiences he would like written on the right-hand page, the teacher will print the word (label or caption). The child may then trace the letters with his finger or a crayon. The child will be asked to read what has been written, then to copy the word below the teacher's printing. The authors expect that the stage will be very brief, and that most children will move quickly to stage 2. Each stage is carefully described, and the book includes a rationale for writing, classroom management, materials (including instructions for making books), and writing activities. For the beginning teacher or the teacher who wishes to improve his or her composition instruction, *Children's Writing: An Approach for the Primary Grades* would be a valuable resource.

For children who do not print, who cannot recognize letters, and who cannot function in a structured writing environment readiness for composition must be developed. A child may be reluctant to make any contributions to dictation the teacher takes from the group. The teacher can still include him or her in the language process. Perhaps a friend will volunteer a sentence about the shy child and the teacher can write the friend's comment. Perhaps the teacher can ask the child a question and then include the answer in the text. Above all, the teacher can continue to structure the classroom environment so that children feel comfortable in making contributions.

Many kindergarten and first-grade teachers find that children become writers in less structured environments which are filled with opportunities for writing. In some classrooms children have mailboxes, one for each child, all ready for them even before the first day of school (30). As soon as the teacher gets the names of her new students, she sends postcards to all of them at their homes. She realizes that most of the children can't read but she also knows that getting mail is fun and she usually receives several notes from her new students on the first day of school. From that time on, the children eagerly participate in letter-writing activities.

There are many writing activities young children enjoy which are related to letter writing. Children make their own valentines, birthday cards, and Christmas cards. They enjoy being pen pals with children in other classes in the school, with university students, and even with their parents.

Young children like to write letters to favorite authors of children's books and authors are usually pleased to receive these letters. Ezra Jack Keats, the award-winning author of many books, including *Snowy Day,* is noted especially for cherishing letters from his young fans.

Children enjoy writing their own books. In some classrooms, children write rough drafts of their books, sign up for conferences with their teachers to discuss the manuscript, complete an editing process, and then carefully prepare the finished book to be donated to the classroom or school library. School librarians value these books just as they value trade books as worthwhile additions to their literature collection.

First-grade children like to keep personal journals. Each child is given a special notebook to write in each day. The teacher reads the journal but does not correct it. Sometimes she will write a note in the margin to help another adult (the parent) understand the writing. Once the journal is filled, the child takes it home to be shared with his parents.

Problems   To those who have not observed in a kindergarten or a first-grade classroom, the idea of taking dictation from twenty or thirty children might seem a formidable one. In actual practice, it is not. While all the children are encouraged to take part in the experience to be written about and to contribute to the conversation which precedes the dictation, the teacher records the ideas of only five or six of the children. To do otherwise would tax the attention spans and the interest levels of these young children. Stauffer (47) speaks to this when he writes: "Each stimulus permits the children to move about, to listen and talk to one another, to show or acquire regard for the rights of others. The whole-class accounts become a possession of each pupil, even though only five or six may have contributed literally" (p. 89).

Teachers also write experience charts for small groups within the class and for individual children. The classroom management system which enables teachers to work with small groups and individual children in other areas of the curriculum serves them here as well.

Many experienced teachers notice that young children who enjoy writing in the first few grades become less enthusiastic as they progress through the grades. Could the instruction be at fault? A third-grade teacher addressed this question and queried her students (22). The children reported that they wrote only a few sentences because, since they were going to have to copy everything over and over, the less they wrote, the less they had to copy. They were discouraged by too many red marks on their papers. They often were assigned writing activities while the teacher was busy with other instruction. Therefore, even when they knew they were making errors, there was no way to avoid them, as the teacher was not available when they needed help.

The students felt strongly about contrived purposes for writing. If children write letters to friends and relatives, they should mail them. If they write stories or poems, there needs to be opportunities to share them with their friends and opportunities to read each other's work. If they write items for newspapers or book reviews, there should be a classroom publication which would include them. A teacher would be well advised to evaluate her composition program by the standards identified by this third-grade survey.

Assessment   As in all other areas of instruction, the progress of individual children must be assessed. The child who comes to school with no exposure to books, no models for composition, no experiences with pencils and paper, no practice with the alphabet, will not be able to learn to write as easily as the child who comes to school with a rich background of experiences. The most certain way of documenting the progress of children is to keep a file of dated work for each child.

The beginning teacher may require the assistance of more experienced teachers in determining what to expect from beginning writers. When Milz (33) looks at a dated collection of writings which she compiles for each of her first-grade children she notices "patterns which different children exhibit at different times" (p. 184). These patterns are not predictable and she agrees with Marie Clay, who believes there is no fixed sequence of learning through which all children must pass in early writing. Clay (6) states: "Eventually as each convention is mastered the children acquire a common fund of concepts but the point of entry and the path of progress may be different for any two children" (p. 336).

HANDWRITING

Instructional Emphases   The discussion of handwriting in this section will be limited to manuscript writing, since most children in kindergarten and first grade use this system.

A century ago handwriting was essential to the curriculum. An examination of handwritten records from the middle and late eighteenth century would attest to the fact that carefully executed handwriting was considered a symbol of refinement and accomplishment. There is little argument that handwriting has lost its stature in the curriculum since that time. Teachers of today do not emphasize handwriting as much as they once did. Good penmanship is no longer valued as an end in itself; rather, it is seen as a tool for written expression and it is valued for its role in the communication process. The primary objective of handwriting instruction is to help children write legibly so that what they write will be understood by the reader.

Instructional emphases differ considerably from teacher to teacher and from school to school, but most teachers agree that handwriting needs some instruction. Most teachers use complete class sessions to teach children how to make the various letters and provide time for the children to practice what has been taught. The majority of school systems use one of the forty-nine commercial handwriting series as a foundation for their program. Most of those systems basically teach two forms of handwriting: manuscript for the early years and cursive writing after second or third grade.

There are those who are critical of the time it takes to teach two separate forms of handwriting. More than twenty years ago, Templin (48) argued that teaching children to make the transition from manuscript to cursive writing is not only unnecessary but a waste of childrens' time. He pointed out that in other skills areas, early learning provides a framework for later learning; only in handwriting is one form replaced by another. Other researchers agree that there is little reason to ask children to make such a drastic change (3, 12, 23).

Such criticism has led to the adoption in some school systems of an alternate writing system known as D'Nealian. This system uses letters which are oval rather than round and slanted rather than vertical. The lower-case letters are made with only one movement instead of two. At a later stage, children are taught simply to connect these letters to make the writing look very much like cursive. While this is an interesting idea which has merit, it is doubtful that this form will replace the teaching of manuscript and cursive writing in the foreseeable future.

Instructional Strategies   Handwriting is a developmental process, and as such may require quite different strategies at different levels of psychomotor maturity. Young children scribble or smear depending upon the medium. When children are performing at this level, activities must be designed to promote coordination rather than alphabet identification. Many children come to kindergarten or, where kindergartens are not compulsory, to first grade with no previous experience in using pencils or crayons. Some of these children have excellent gross motor skills, but have never had the opportunity to develop the fine motor control required for printing. These children need experiences which will enable them to develop this ability.

Years ago many first-grade classrooms had sandboxes in which children could practice lines, circles, wavy lines, and squares with a stick or a finger. Kindergarten teachers who have sandboxes in the play yard may still use them for that purpose. A large area is required for the first attempts. The chalkboard is a useful place for a child to practice. Many teachers believe that a piece of writing paper is too small a target for a child who has difficulty holding and manipulating a pencil. As the strokes are mastered (vertical and horizontal lines, circles and half-circles), the tasks should be graduated to require finer and finer motor control. Work sheets with dotted lines to follow or write-and-wipe commercial materials provide practice.

Many students come to school knowing the names of the letters and are eager to write them. If the teacher prints their names on a card and attaches it to their desks with laminating paper or clear contact paper, these children will trace and then copy their names at every opportunity. Other children will not be able to copy from the board as they have not developed the hand–eye coordination required to copy at far distances. For these children, it will be helpful to have alphabet strips attached to their desks. Board work might be written on a portable chalkboard and moved closer to the group of children who need to copy.

When children are ready to recognize and produce the alphabet, the order of presentation and the form of the letters will depend upon the practices established in the school. When writing books are used, teachers normally use the letter forms advocated by the publisher. The handwriting instruction should be coordinated with the other language arts lessons.

Earlier in this chapter, it was pointed out that about 10 percent of the population is left-handed and that this a perfectly normal attribute. When left-handed children teach themselves to write or when they do not receive careful instruction, they often develop an awkward way of holding their pencils and positioning their papers which makes handwriting an uncomfortable process for them. A sensitive teacher will see to it that the left-hander gets the individual attention and instruction he needs. Since the child cannot learn by imitating the right-handed teacher as she or he writes, the teacher must think through the operations she or he expects the child to perform and then carefully show that child the proper procedures.

In manuscript writing, the paper should be placed squarely in front of the child so he or she can make the vertical strokes without a slant. A left-handed child is likely to have a tendency to write from right to left. A teacher can help that child learn to write from left to right by putting a mark on the left side of the paper to remind him or her where to begin writing. Children should be comfortable when they write. Left-handed children should have special left-handed desks or, if they work at tables, should sit on the outside. Otto (36) points out that "Right-handed teachers need to expend some energy, both physical and psychological, if they hope to understand and to help left-handed pupils" (p. 417).

Children who are fortunate enough to work in classroom environments in which they are immersed in language arts activities will need surprisingly little formal handwriting instruction. As they work with the different aspects of the composing process, they will learn the necessity for legibility and work toward that goal.

Problems   As in all other activities considered here, the difference in the readiness levels of the children in a classroom is a major concern in handwriting instruction. Some children are practicing holding a pencil securely enough to draw circles while others are well along toward mastery. This is a real problem for some teachers. Children differ in their rates of development, so it is to be expected that children will not all demonstrate the same levels of performance.

Assessment   Basal writing programs provide standards of printing for the teacher to use as a guide. Most of these standards are commercially prepared and provide criteria which may be useful for evaluation. The degree of students' progress can best be documented by keeping a file of dated material. Samples of children's written work—their messages, poems, and stories—provide useful materials for teachers in assessing children's progress in handwriting.

SPELLING

There are few studies detailing the processes involved in spelling acquisition, especially when compared with the vast body of literature available concerning language acquisition. The work of Forester (15) is interesting in that it suggests that children go through a number of stages when they learn to spell, just as they do when they learn to speak, and that the stages for both spelling and speaking are remarkably similar (see Figure 2-1). Just as the infant begins acquiring language by babbling, so the young child initially begins writing and spelling by scribbling. Just as the small child begins with one-word sentences and progresses to two- and three-word sentences, the beginning writer–speller uses one-letter spelling (usually initial consonants) before moving on to two- and three-word sentences. Early speakers often omit certain parts of speech and use only nouns, verbs, and a few adjectives, while early spellers often omit vowels.

As children begin reading instruction and learn a number of sight words as well as some phonic generalizations, they often begin to overgeneralize known patterns or

FIGURE 2-1
Learning to spell by spelling.

STAGES OF DEVELOPMENT	
Speaking	**Writing—Spelling**
Babbling	Scribbling—pretend writing
One-word sentences	One-letter spelling
Two- and three-word sentences	Two- and three-word sentences
Self-programming of simple rules (not necessarily conforming to adult rules)	Self-programming of simple rules (not necessarily conforming to adult rules)
Overgeneralization of acquired rules	Overgeneralization of acquired rules and patterns (phonetic spelling, transfer of spelling patterns from known words)
Adoption of more precise speech	Adoption of more accurate spelling

Usual Sequence of Acquisition
Consonants (beginning, final, median)
Blends (ch, sh, bl, tr, and so on). Morphologic markers
(ed, ing, 's, and so on)
Words in frequent use (today, we, have, and so on)
Vowels

words or rules in their spelling attempts. Forester states that "as beginning speakers demonstrate the acquisition of rules by saying things like 'wented' or 'mices,' so the child learning to spell will generalize newly acquired spelling patterns to a broad range of examples before learning to discriminate more precisely" (15, p. 187).

Classroom teachers can draw several implications from Forester's work. First, just as parents were their children's models for writing and spelling development, teachers must use every opportunity to demonstrate proper writing and correct spelling. Second, if teachers are to foster spelling abilities, they must realize that early overgeneralization of spelling rules with its resultant misspellings is a result of miscues which indicate that children are progressing in their spelling acquisition.

Third, children vary in the length of time they need to progress from one stage to another. Learning to spell, just like learning to speak, is not a linear progression; rather, it is a process of gradual synthesis and integration.

Instructional Emphases   Kindergarten and first-grade teachers are concerned with the readiness components of spelling instruction. Many activities which promote auditory discrimination are provided and attention is given to the concept of rhyming words, to beginning and ending consonant sounds, and to careful pronunciation of words. As the children move into writing, the primary focus is on meaning and communication. Children learn to spell through spelling practice as they engage in meaningful writing activities.

People often are convinced that correct spelling is an important attribute of literacy as well as a means of accurate written communication. Poor spelling is seen as an indication of lack of literacy and as a reflection of the inability of the school to teach spelling. These beliefs sometimes cause spelling to become an emotional issue.

Kindergarten and first-grade teachers need to communicate their teaching philosophies to parents so that they understand that an effective spelling program focuses both on the meaning of a written message and on the spelling structures of written English (25). Spelling evolves toward more accuracy as children grow through writing experience, just as spoken language moves toward greater accuracy with practice.

There is a relationship between spelling and reading just as there is between spelling and the other language arts. Practice in one language arts area can help increase proficiency in spelling. For example, children who read widely learn to spell many words as an outgrowth of their reading. Because spelling is an encoding process and reading is a decoding process it is tempting to assume that one process is the reverse of the other, but this is not the case. Reading is concerned with getting meaning from whole words and sentences while spelling deals with abstract symbols (letters) within a word. In spelling each letter of each word requires attention.

The purpose of spelling instruction is "to equip pupils with phonetic and structural generalizations that will enable them to look at all words discriminately . . . to note agreement with or deviation from expected spelling" (30, p. 116). A pattern is introduced in reading, then applied to spelling. Basal spelling series which are well matched to the basal reading series follow this format. In addition to phonetic generalizations, spelling requires visual memory. Children need to develop the ability to recognize when a word "looks right." This, too, assumes that the child can read and visually recall the word he or she wants to spell. The child can then recognize any disparity between his or her spelling of the word and the correct spelling.

As children progress through reading instruction, they become ready for more formal spelling instruction.

Instructional Strategies   Formal spelling instruction includes the use of a spelling textbook, workbooks, and specific grade-level word lists. It is often delayed until children are in second grade and have a sufficient background of experience to profit from it. Incidental spelling is a viable approach in kindergarten and first grade before reading instruction progresses to the point where phonetic generalizations can be utilized.

The children's first encounter with spelling will be quite natural. They will learn to spell their names and perhaps a few words which are visible in the room. Teachers use conventional methods and games to introduce children to letters and their forms, names, and sounds. They write student-dictated captions under children's artwork: they write messages on the board, notes to parents. In this way they serve as models for meaningful reading and writing behavior, while children are learning that letters are not abstract or mysterious.

As children become more proficient with the alphabet they show more interest in writing and spelling. The first few attempts are usually words copied from book covers, bulletin boards, lunch boxes, and similar items. Spelling is an integral part of a child's writing. In an activity-oriented classroom it is difficult to prevent children from writing. It rarely occurs to children that they cannot write a word just because they cannot read it, and once they have written it a few times they may learn to read it. Teachers who would include spelling as part of the initial writing experience of young children must encourage creative writing, de-emphasize standard spelling, and learn to respond appropriately to nonstandard spelling (17).

The first few attempts at creative writing are usually related to drawing. A child labels his work so there is no mistaking what he drew. If teachers routinely write their dictation, there is no hesitancy on the part of the children in approaching them for help. If their teachers are busy, they may search for a word on a bulletin board or in a book, or ask another child who might know the word. As they become more confident, they try to spell the word by themselves. If their efforts are supported, they continue to experiment with writing and spelling. This is what happened with Bobby, a beginning first-grader, who drew a colorful picture of children playing in the sand and labeled it VAKSHN AT MRTL BCH (Vacation at Myrtle Beach). Bobby's teacher displayed his work in the hall and a proud Bobby continued to label and write.

Homemade dictionaries help children in their spelling development. Teachers provide lists of frequently used sight words arranged in alphabetical order. Children cut these out and paste them on sheets of paper to fashion a dictionary. As they need additional words, the teacher writes them on the board or on note cards and the children add them to their dictionaries.

When reading has progressed to where the children have sufficient sight vocabulary, the word lists may be used to teach spelling. The first take-home list should be short and simple. It might contain a few words using patterns which are in the reading; *at, bat, cat; book, look; in, pin.* The teacher might wish to avoid *done, gone,* and *cone; some, come,* and *home.* Exceptions are an important part of instruction and will not be avoided for an extended period, but the first few spelling words should be selected with care to ensure mastery for most of the children.

If the initial lists are composed of phonetically regular words, how can children learn irregular words? Such words should be included as children encounter them. A teacher might have a Spelling Stumpers (SS) list in a conspicuous place in the room. As irregular words are encountered the variation from the expected spelling should be noted and the word put on the list. It will take little encouragement to elicit contributions from the children. A child who wants to put *come* on the list because it ought to be spelled like *gum* and isn't is showing evidence of progress in spelling.

Problems   A serious problem the teacher may encounter in teaching spelling is the emotionality permeating the subject. Rote memory was not included as a strategy, yet many parents and, unfortunately, some teachers and administrators remember the good old days of spelling bees and believe that rote memory, aided by writing each word fifty to a hundred times, is the only means of helping children become good spellers. For this reason, one must be very cautious about the spelling words sent home with the children.

Teachers seem to be divided into two groups concerning their spelling philosophy. One group will not display, or send home, any written work with spelling errors. It feels obligated to bleed all over the child's work with its red pencils. The other group not only tolerates nonstandard spelling, but relishes it as evidence of a child's initiative. It not only displays the children's work but also roams the halls with handsful of children's work with other members of its group. Principals, supervisors, and parents seem to fall into the same two groups, and perfectly good arguments are advanced for each position.

A middle ground between the two positions may be in order. The teacher who wishes to encourage her children to use vocabulary beyond the few "safe" words they can spell correctly and to attempt to spell words which best reflect their feelings will remember Forester's comparison of stages of development in spelling with those in speaking. Just as the parent accepts the baby's early speech, so the teacher must accept the child's beginning spelling attempts. "Only if meaning suffers will the teacher make or ask for a correction" (15, p. 191).

As the child gains competence through practice, feedback from the teacher begins to include spelling correction. The emphasis is on the meaning of the written work, which is enhanced by correct form. Forester says it this way: "If these corrections are made in a matter-of-fact way after the child's message has been acknowledged, the pleasure of writing remains unimpaired while the spelling evolves toward more accurate standards" (15, p. 192).

Assessment   A teacher will assess a child's spelling progress in terms of his or her own philosophy. If he or she teaches from a spelling list all children are expected to master, the teacher will use formal spelling tests. If the individual differences in children require the teacher's attention he or she may consider the mastery of spelling patterns in terms of the child's reading level.

The teacher who uses incidental spelling techniques will analyze the nonstandard spelling in order to determine the child's perception of word structure. In Bobby's VAKSHN AT MRTL BCH, the teacher would note that he has an excellent beginning on the sound–symbol relationship. He had the sounds in the proper words, and the letters were in the same order as the sounds they represent. He distinguished between the SH sound in vacation and the CH sound in beach. He used the name of the letter as the sound for A, K, and B. The only vowel he used was A.

Many teachers will keep files of children's work and compare progress made over the instructional period. Such a collection during the first year in school gives the teacher useful material for assessing children's growth in the use of written language. A useful guide which helps teachers analyze samples of children's written work is Marie Clay's (7) *What Did I Write?* It assists teachers in noticing special features of children's early writing which provide clues to their thought processes as well as to their linguistic knowledge.

READING APPLICATION

Instructional Emphases   In recent years educators have become concerned with the limited recreational reading activities of students. Children who can read often do not. These children have the ability to read but lack the interest and motivation. Television viewing is preferred and children are passive rather than active participants in the communication process. Reading is not a spectator sport. Reading demands active participation. The role of the classroom teacher is to provide an atmosphere in which independent reading is a natural extension of the reading instruction. To accomplish this the teacher must help the student see himself or herself as a successful reader. The attitude of the teacher toward reading will foster or inhibit the child's interest in reading. Children will be encouraged to value reading if they observe significant others in their lives reading and valuing reading. When children come from homes in which little reading is done, the school must provide the impetus.

Instructional Strategies   Huck's interview with a kindergarten and first-grade teacher (27, p. 14) who uses children's literature as a basis for her reading program, provides a good model for teachers to use with kindergarten and first-grade children.

Teachers can help children become readers by:

1 *Providing books.* The classroom library includes many titles which appeal to children between the ages of four and eight. There are multiple copies of some of the books so children can read them together. Included in the assortment are songbooks, informational books, poetry, a dictionary, a thesaurus, supplementary texts, some wordless books, and an array of pictures.

2 *Reading aloud.* The teacher reads as many as five stories a day. Sometimes she reads to the entire group, other times she reads to four or five children and sometimes she reads to an individual child. Some stories, such as "The Three Little Pigs" and "Goldilocks and the Three Bears," are read over and over again.

3 *Reading books which stretch children's imaginations.* She reads some more difficult books such as *The Biggest Bear, Snow White,* and *Tikki, Tikki, Tembo.* When she reads these books she asks questions which lead children to make predictions about what will happen next.

4 *Using SSR.* The children and their teacher have a sustained silent reading (SSR) period which lasts for fifteen minutes at the beginning of the year and stretches to thirty minutes toward the end. The emphasis is not on silence. Sometimes children read with partners. Sometimes the teacher reads with a child; at other times she reads silently to herself.

5 *Observing.* The teacher observes children to see what they are reading. She is quoted as saying "Over and over I've discovered that once children have found 'their book,' one they read over and over again, they are on their way to becoming a reader."

6 *Using children's literature units.* The teacher usually has a theme or a unit in her classroom which emphasizes literature. Some successful units have been concerned with folktales, nursery rhymes, animals, and author–illustrators such as Pat Hutchins or Robert McCloskey.

7 *Interacting with parents.* The teacher encourages parents to read to their children and gives parents a list of "super" books to share. Parents are encouraged to visit her class and when they do, she sends several children over to the parents to read to them.

These seven strategies can provide a framework for teachers to help children become hooked on books.

You may be wondering how beginning readers cope with the decoding of words they encounter in their recreational reading. Psycholinguistic theory gives support to the idea that even beginning readers read for meaning (45). As they try to make sense from the story and reconstruct the author's message, they deal with the words and sentences in context; they do not gain comprehension by looking at each word in isolation. It is helpful if they are told the unknown word so that they can continue their efforts at getting at the meaning of the passage.

During SSR or other free reading periods, there will be times when the teacher is unavailable to explain the words to the children. When she or he is busy, the teacher may assign this responsibility to some more able readers, who will be "word helpers." Since there is normally a wide range of reading abilities within one classroom, word helpers can probably be chosen from class members. The teachers and the helpers should simply tell children what the unknown words mean without pulling them out for isolated drill. The readers will then be able to rely on the context of their reading as they strive to become more fluent readers.

There are other ways to help beginning readers with their recreational reading. When children read together with partners, they should be encouraged to help one another with unknown words. Many children enjoy reading stories while listening through earphones to the recordings of the same stories. This has been shown to be an effective strategy for improving reading vocabulary and comprehension.

Problems How can the teacher find the time to do all of this? As mentioned earlier, many primary teachers spend such a large amount of time teaching reading skills that they believe they don't have enough class time to devote to children's literature. They see reading for pleasure as something for children to do after they've finished their other work. If children are going to become readers, teachers must find the time to expose them to good literature and give them opportunities to respond to it.

Just as adults are not likely to engage in recreational reading seated at a desk and in a straight chair, so also are children not likely to pursue much recreational reading where the setting is formal and unyielding. The teacher must see to it that the classroom provides a relaxed atmosphere. When classrooms are carpeted, children may lie on the floor to read, but when they are not it is still possible to devise book corners or other comfortable reading areas.

Assessment Reading application can be assessed informally by the classroom teacher. The amount of the time the class spends in recreational reading is certainly a measure of the children's enthusiasm for reading. The teacher should be sensitive to the books which are read by individual children relative to their interests and their reading abilities.

King (28) suggests that interviews in which teachers talk with students about their reading provide useful information for reading evaluation. Statements from such interviews often tell teachers a great deal about the students "in terms of their motivations, their attitudes toward reading, and their concepts of themselves as readers" (p. 412).

BIBLIOGRAPHY AND REFERENCES

1 Alexander, J. Estill, and Filler, R. C. *Attitudes and Reading.* Newark, Del.: International Reading Association, 1976.
2 Anastasiow, N. *Oral Language: Expression of Thought.* Newark, Del.: International Reading Association, 1979.
3 Anderson, D. "Handwriting Research Movement and Quality." In T. A. Horn (ed.), *Research on Handwriting and Spelling,* Champaign, Ill.: National Council of Teachers of English.
4 Biehler, Robert F. *Psychology Applied to Teaching* (3d ed.). New York: Houghton Mifflin, 1978, p. 119.
5 Bloom, Lois. *Language Development: Form and Function in Emerging Grammars.* Cambridge, Mass.: Massachusetts Institute of Technology Press, 1970, p. 225.
6 Clay, Marie. "Exploring with a Pencil." *Theory into Practice,* vol. 16, no. 5, December 1977, p. 336.
7 Clay, Marie. *What Did I Write?* Aukland, New Zealand: Heinman Educational Books, 1975, p. 18.
8 DeStefano, Johanna, and Victor M. Rentel, "Language Variation: Perspective for Teachers." *Theory into Practice,* vol. 14, no. 5, December 1975, pp. 328–337.
9 Donaldson, M. *Children's Minds.* New York: W. W. Norton, 1978.
10 Downing, John. "Words, Words, Words." *Theory into Practice,* vol. 16, no. 5, December 1977, p. 328.
11 Erikson, E. H. *Childhood and Society* (2nd ed.). New York: Norton, 1963.

12 Farly, G. H. "Cursive Handwriting, Reading, and Spelling Achievement." *Academic Therapy,* vol. 12, Fall 1976, pp. 67–74.

13 Fern, Lief, "The Oral Model as a Strategy in Developmental Reading Instruction." *Reading Teacher,* vol. 25, 1971, p. 205.

14 Flavell, J. H. *Cognitive Development.* Englewood Cliffs, N.J.: Prentice-Hall, 1977.

15 Forester, A. D. "Learning to Spell by Spelling." *Theory into Practice,* vol. 19, no. 3, Summer 1980, pp. 186–193.

16 Garnica, Olga K. "How Children Learn to Talk." *Theory into Practice.* vol. 14, no. 5, December 1975, pp. 299–305.

17 Gentry, J. R., and Henderson, E. H. "Three Steps to Teaching Beginning Readers to Spell." In E. H. Henderson and J. W. Beers (eds.), *Developmental and Cognitive Aspects of Learning to Spell: A Reflection of Word Knowledge.* Newark, Del.: International Reading Association, 1980.

18 Gibson, E. J., and Levin, H. *The Psychology of Reading.* Cambridge, Mass.: Massachusetts Institute of Technology Press, 1975.

19 Goodman, K. S., and Buck, C. "Dialect Barriers to Reading Comprehension Revisited." *The Reading Teacher,* vol. 27, no. 1, October 1973, pp. 6–12.

20 Goodman, K. S., and Goodman, Y. "Learning to Read is Natural." Speech presented at Conference on Theory and Practice of Beginning Reading Instruction, Pittsburgh, April 13, 1976.

21 Educational Research Council of America, Greater Cleveland Humanities-for-All Program, vol. 1. Cleveland, Ohio: Educational Research Council of America, 1967.

22 Harris, J. D. "Full Speed Ahead for Written Communication." In W. T. Petty, *Issues and Problems in Elementary Language Arts: A Book of Readings.* Boston: Allyn and Bacon, 1968.

23 Harris, T. L. "Handwriting." In C. W. Harris (ed.), *Encyclopedia of Educational Research* (3rd ed.). New York: Macmillan, 1960.

24 Harrow, A. J. *A Taxonomy of the Psychomotor Domain.* New York: David McKay Company, 1972.

25 Hittleman, D. R. *Developmental Reading: A Psycholinguistic Perspective.* Chicago: Rand McNally College Publishing Company, 1978.

26 Huck, C. "Literature as the Content of Reading." *Theory into Practice,* vol. 16, no. 5, December 1977, pp. 363–371.

27 Huck, C. "Teacher Feature." *The WEB: Wonderfully Exciting Books,* vol. 4, no. 4, Summer 1980, pp. 14–17.

28 King, M. "Evaluating Reading." *Theory into Practice,* vol. 16, no. 5, December 1977, pp. 407–418.

29 King, M. L. "Language: Insights from Acquisition." *Theory into Practice,* vol. 14, no. 5, December 1975, pp. 293–297.

30 Kottmeyer, S. *Decoding and Meaning: A Modest Proposal.* New York: McGraw-Hill Book Company, 1974, p. 116.

31 Liu, S. "An Investigation of Oral Reading Miscues Made by Nonstandard Dialect Speaking Black Children." *Reading Research Quarterly,* vol. 11, no. 2, 1975–1976, pp. 193–197.

32 McCandles, Boyd R. *Adolescent's Behavior and Development.* Hinsdale, Ill.: Dryden Press, 1970.

33 Milz, V. E. "First Graders Can Write: Focus on Communication." *Theory into Practice,* vol. 19, no. 3, Summer 1980, pp. 179–185.

34 Mussen, P. M., Conger, J. J., and Kagan, J. *Child Development and Personality* (5th ed.). New York: Harper and Row, 1979.

35 Ollila, L. C. *The Kindergarten Child and Reading*. Newark, Del.: International Reading Association, 1977, p. 18.

36 Otto, W., and Smith, R. J. *Corrective and Remedial Teaching*. Boston: Houghton Mifflin, 1980, pp. 301–306.

37 Petty, W. T. *Issues and Problems in Elementary Language Arts: A Book of Readings*. Boston: Allyn and Bacon, 1968, p. 143.

38 Petty, W. T., Petty, D. C., and Becking, M. F. *Experiences in Language: Tools and Techniques for Language Arts Methods* (3rd ed.). Boston: Allyn and Bacon, 1981.

39 Piaget, Jean. *Science of Education and the Psychology of the Child*. New York: Orion, 1970, p. 28.

40 Pilon, A. Barbara. "Culturally Divergent Children and Creative Language Activities." In James L. Laffey and Roger Shuy (eds.), *Language Differences. Do They Interfere?* Newark Del.: International Reading Association, 1973.

41 Pinnell, Gay S. "Language in Primary Classrooms." *Theory into Practice,* vol. 14, no. 5, December 1975, p. 318.

42 Quandt, I. *Self-Concept and Reading*. Newark, Del.: International Reading Association, 1979.

43 Sealey, L., Sealey, N., and Millmore, M. *Children's Writing: An Approach for the Primary Grades* Newark, Del.: International Reading Association, 1979.

44 Smith, J. A. *Creative Teaching of the Language Arts in the Elementary School* (2nd ed.). Boston: Allyn and Bacon, 1973, pp. 255, 338.

45 Smith, Frank, *Understanding Reading*. New York: Holt, Rinehart and Winston, 1973.

46 Spache, G. D. *Good Reading for Poor Readers* (9th ed.). Champaign, Ill.: Garrard Publishing Company, 1974.

47 Stauffer, Russell G. *The Language-Experience Approach to the Teaching of Reading* (2nd ed.). New York: Harper and Row, 1980, p. 89.

48 Templin, E. "Research and Comment: Handwriting the Neglected R." *Elementary English,* vol. 37, 1960, pp. 386–389.

49 Veatch, Jeannette. *Reading in the Elementary School* (2d ed.). New York: John Wiley and Sons, 1978.

50 Vukelich, C. "The Developing of Listening Comprehension through Storytime." *Language Arts,* vol. 53, no. 8, November–December 1976, p. 890.

51 Wadsworth, Barry J. *Piaget's Theory of Cognitive Development*. New York: Longman, 1971.

CHAPTER **3**

CLASSROOM APPLICATIONS IN KINDERGARTEN AND GRADE ONE

In this chapter, you will find a *descriptor,* an *analysis,* and an *explanation* of the teaching practices of Barbara Brown, a kindergarten teacher, and Lynn Simpson, a first-grade teacher. As explained in Chapter 1, each descriptor is meant to serve as an informal test for the reader. When you read the descriptor, make notes of the features of the teacher's practices which you consider to be particularly good. Try to be thorough in your analysis. Then compare your analysis with our explanation of what we believe makes these practices noteworthy.

A format such as the one shown in Figure 3-1 may help you with your analysis. We hope this test and the ones in Chapters 5 and 7 will help the reader develop the ability to recognize effective teaching practices and gain an awareness of why these practices are viewed positively.

BARBARA BROWN

Descriptor

Barbara is a kindergarten teacher in a large school in a suburban school district. She returned to full-time teaching two years ago after a five-year period during which she taught half-day (only one session) in kindergarten. Her own children were small then and she enjoyed having time to spend with them. Now that they are in school, she not only teaches full time but also manages to take a graduate course each semester at a nearby extension of the state university. Her undergraduate degree is in early childhood education and her graduate work is in the same area, with the emphasis thus far on language arts courses. She is presently enrolled in a children's literature course she especially enjoys.

Barbara Brown	Effective Practices	Reasons Why
1.		
2.		
3.		
.		
.		
.		
.		
.		

Lynn Simpson	Effective Practices	Reasons Why
1.		
2.		
3.		
.		
.		
.		
.		
.		

FIGURE 3-1
This format should help you in making notes for your analysis of teaching practices.

Barbara teaches two sessions of kindergarten, each of which lasts $2\frac{1}{2}$ hours. She has a full-time aide, Marilyn, and the two adults work with twenty-five children in one session and thirty in the other. Barbara works closely with the other kindergarten teachers to plan and implement the curriculum for the children.

Children in the kindergarten classes come from a wide range of socioeconomic levels, and their families have a wide range of educational backgrounds. The children exhibit varying levels of intellectual ability. For example, some children were already reading when they came to school, while others are beginning to recognize words now, and still others will need more time to reach this level. The children also show varying levels of physical development. Billy is unable to tie his shoes, a feat Cindy mastered more than a year ago; Sherry seems to skip everywhere she goes while Gary still can't coordinate the step-hop movement necessary for him to learn to skip. There is a wide variation in student social development. Some children are very shy while some seem quite socially adept. However, the children are eager to learn and they are approaching their first school experiences in a positive way. Their backgrounds of experiences are varied, and this is reflected in the variation in their communication abilities.

Barbara's classroom is in a double portable trailer unit. It is carpeted, colorful, and attractively decorated with children's artwork displayed on the walls. There are many plants and several animals. The children enjoy caring for and observing the plants, the fish, the gerbil, and the hamster.

The classroom is set up in learning centers and children spend a large portion of the school day working in them. Barbara believes that learning centers provide a way to meet the needs of children who are functioning at various developmental levels and who have wide ranges of intellectual abilities as well as different learning styles. Barbara says, "In a way, all the centers are language arts centers; the children work together, sharing and talking—there is a lot of communication going on."

There is a writing center where children learn to work with scissors and clay and to write words and sentences and where, with Barbara's help, they write their own short stories, which they illustrate and make into books. When the stories are completed, they are put in the reading center. This area contains a wealth of reading materials. There are many trade books as well as a number of magazines, newspapers, and catalogs. Even before children become proficient readers they can use these reading materials to build on interests they bring to school with them. Some children enjoy looking through gardening magazines; others like to look at catalogs of toys and games and make wish lists for Christmas or birthdays. Many children enjoy the sports pages, the grocery advertisements, and the comics in the newspapers. They like to read the stories their classmates have written and illustrated themselves. Children often find they can read some of the trade books they have heard read to them by their parents, by Barbara or by her aide, or books they have heard in the listening center.

The listening center has many tapes of stories as well as cassettes containing recordings of music to be enjoyed and listening activities for the children to try. Barbara encourages her friends to help her add to her listening tape library by volunteering to record a favorite story for her class. A tape of Maurice Sendak's *Where the Wild Things Are* is especially cherished by her entire class—it was recorded by the superintendent of the school district!

One part of Barbara's room is devoted to a blocks center. This area is filled with blocks children use to practice skills such as part–whole relationships and visualization skills. Some of the blocks have letters on them and children use these to build words. They use larger blocks to build various shapes and objects for their dramatic play activities.

Barbara works with small groups of children in the cooking center. Here the children use their language skills as they discuss each child's contribution to the cooking task, as they help the teacher read the recipe, and as they socialize when they eat the fruits of their efforts and clean up the center so that another group can use it. Their choice of cooking experiences is often influenced by experiences generated in other areas. For example, when the children were working on learning their colors, they had "color week." On the day they devoted to *green,* Barbara read *Green Eggs and Ham* (21) by Dr. Seuss and they cooked green eggs and ham. As the children added a few drops of food coloring to the eggs they were beating, it became apparent that several of them were losing their appetites!

Barbara meets the changing interests of the children through the use of a role-playing center. Here props are changed at various intervals to transform the center into a fire station, a post office, or a grocery store. Children especially enjoy the center when it is a grocery store with its shelves of groceries, its play money, the toy cash register, and the small grocery cart. The boys and girls role play as several children place their groceries in the cart and one of the children works at the checkout counter. It is apparent to the observer that rotating among these centers provides kindergarten children with the opportunities to develop and expand concepts and to develop their language skills.

Each day begins with a group sharing time—"show and tell"—with students bringing in their drawings, personal news items, or special objects to show to their classmates. Barbara encourages all the children to talk, but she works especially hard to help the shy children overcome their fears about sharing with the group. She often asks questions which encourage interactions between the students or between the children and their teacher.

Barbara believes that children will become good listeners if other people listen to

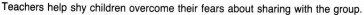

Teachers help shy children overcome their fears about sharing with the group.

them. With this in mind, she and Marilyn try to be good models for listening skills by being good listeners as the children talk.

Sharing time is more than "show and tell." It is also a planning period during which the children are involved in the organization of the session. Barbara draws from the childrens' needs and interests to plan learning activities, and the children plan with their teacher how they will carry out the morning's work.

Children know what is expected of them and they try hard to please. Barbara insists that her classroom be an orderly place with materials put back in place when children finish using them. She feels this belief is consonant with the development and maintenance of a classroom atmosphere which is conducive to effective language arts learning. Children enjoy their work and the classroom sounds like a busy workshop, but it is not chaotic. Children are working, talking, and communicating but they are using soft voices and Barbara speaks quietly when she talks to them.

There is much verbal interaction among the members of the class and between them and their teacher. The children know that Barbara cares for them and there is a mutual feeling of trust and support. She provides oral feedback to her students as they work on their activities. If a child is having difficulty, Barbara and Marilyn or another child provides assistance. The emphasis in these learning experiences is to "accentuate the positive."

Barbara's success in implementing her classroom management principles enables her to be comfortable with many activities going on at the same time. She is careful to use her time wisely and she makes good use of the efforts of her teaching aide. Marilyn helps the children understand and follow Barbara's directions. She listens to and talks with the students as she supervises some of their learning activities, and she often reads stories to the children.

One of the adults reads to the entire group of children at least once each day. In addition to this, they sometimes read to small groups and even to individual children. One day, John brought his pet white mouse to school for "show and tell." Barbara shared with him Rose Fyleman's poem "Mice" (6). He was delighted that his teacher had a poem just for him. The day Sherry came to school wiggling her loose tooth was the day Barbara read Robert McCloskey's *One Morning in Maine* (14). Barbara says, "Children enjoy stories but they become special when someone chooses one just for you."

One of the ways Barbara tries to help her children build their background of experiences is through field trips. Not long ago, she and the children visited the post office. Much preplanning took place before they went. Several parent volunteers went with them. Prior to the field trip, they formulated rules for their behavior during the trip. The children discussed desirable behavior and ultimately dictated the rules they decided upon to Barbara who wrote them on a chart. Many of the children found they could read these rules.

The field trip was a big success, with the children not only enjoying the experience but learning a great deal from it as well. Upon their return, they participated in many language arts experiences which were natural extensions of their visit. Several children were delegated to write (with Barbara's help) thank-you notes to the parents who had accompanied them. After they had written them, they discussed the process these notes would go through from the time they were written until they would be delivered to the parents' homes. This discussion was a useful evaluation technique for Barbara, who was amazed at how much the children had learned from their field trip.

As an outgrowth of this experience, the children began writing many letters. They constructed individual mailboxes out of discarded shoe boxes, and a group used red, white, and blue paint to decorate a large rectangular box to serve as a communal mailbox. Barbara capitalized on the children's interest in writing and receiving mail by helping them change the role-playing center from the grocery store to a post office. It was a simple matter to put the grocery store props in the storage area and bring out dramatic play props such as stamps (Easter seals), a homemade mail bag, packages, play money, a date stamp and ink pad, postal scales, and a cash drawer. Now when the children wrote their letters (with help from Barbara and Marilyn), the children would deposit them in the large mailbox. Several "mail carriers" would pick up the mail and take it to the post office center for sorting and canceling. As the children worked in this center, they were not only having fun but were learning as well.

Barbara believes all these language arts activities are important parts of the kindergarten curriculum and help her children meet the standards her school district lists as major language arts curricular objectives. The school district publishes a teachers' guide with specific language arts categories and specific objectives for student competency at the end of the kindergarten year. Included in this guide are suggested activities for teaching these skills. In addition to the guide, the district publishes a skills list for use in kindergarten classes. The language arts skills which are emphasized are visual, auditory, language, fine motor, and gross motor skills.

Barbara uses the district's skills list and the teachers' guide as aids when she plans her instructional program. During her planning time, she lists the skills she plans to teach the following day and she reviews the skills list for each of her students. Next, she establishes the groups of children who will work together under her direction during the next several days. These groups are not static; the grouping changes according to the skills being taught. There are normally four or five skill groups, with each group containing five or six children, but occasionally a group will have just two students. Only the children who need instruction in a specific skill are assigned to a group.

A standard readiness test is administered to each child at the beginning of the year and results are used for determining skill needs and skill groups. Strengths and weaknesses are recorded on students' progress records. This is the only formal testing which is done. Most of the assessment in Barbara's classroom is informal. She may do an activity with the children to check on a specific skill need or she may use a game to check on a skill need. She believes that teacher observation is extremely important in assessing student needs and that an effective record-keeping system is essential. Barbara marks student progress on students' skill sheets daily. She rechecks on skills periodically for maintenance of the skills. Barbara believes students need repetition of skills to broaden and to retain them.

Barbara holds a curriculum night for parents at the beginning of the school year during which she explains what they will be trying to accomplish during the year and why they will be doing what they do. She gives each parent a copy of a handbook she has developed which explains the philosophy and activities of the kindergarten program.

The district in which Barbara teaches has developed a report sheet for parents based on the kindergarten skills list. This is shared with parents at conferences during the year, and a complete report is provided at the end of the year. Parent conferences are scheduled twice a year. The first conference in the fall deals mostly with social and emotional areas, while the spring conference is devoted to going over children's progress on the skills delineated on the checklist.

Barbara communicates with parents throughout the year by telephone and through notes which contain suggested activities for them to use at home. When she was working with the children on body awareness, she sent home the following letter:

Dear Parents:

This week we've been working on a unit entitled "Body Awareness." My primary goal is to help the children acquire awareness of their bodies and to get to know themselves in relationship to their environment. Children acquire body awareness through exercises, games, and dance and through following directions.

You can reinforce our school learnings by doing some simple activities at home. I have listed a few suggestions that will help your child.

1 Trace your hands and feet and then have your child trace his. Compare the size. Count fingers and toes.

2 Have your child teach *you* "Where is Thumbkin," a song we have learned. Change the words to "Where is your elbow . . ." or "Where is your knee . . ." etc.

3 Play "Simon Says." If you don't know how to play, your child will teach you. You should be Simon first, so you can review body parts with commands such as "Simon says, 'touch your nose.' " Then ask your child to be Simon. This will be a good chance for evaluation to let you know whether your child needs more practice.

4 Make a body puzzle. Ask your child to lie on the floor on a large sheet of wrapping paper. Trace around him and then have him cut out the "paper doll." Then cut the doll in pieces to make a giant puzzle. Finally let him put himself back together!

Your help is certainly appreciated. I hope you and your child find these suggestions helpful. Enjoy!

Sincerely,

Barbara Brown

Before the end of June she sends home a letter in which she suggests summer activities which would be beneficial for the children as well as a list of good books from which they might choose some to share with their children.

In summarizing some of her feelings about teaching kindergarten, Barbara says that teachers really need to know their children, they need to know the needs of young children, and they need to know how young children learn best. The teacher also must make certain that the curriculum is responsive to the children and their needs.

Analysis

Barbara is a kindergarten teacher in a large school in a suburban school district. She returned to full-time teaching two years ago after a five-year period during which she taught half-day (only one session) in kindergarten. Her own children were small then and she enjoyed having time to spend with them. Now that they are in school, she not only teaches full time but also manages to take a graduate course each semester at a nearby extension of the state university. Her undergraduate degree is in early childhood education and her graduate work is in the same area, with the emphasis thus far on language arts courses. She is presently enrolled in a children's literature course she especially enjoys.

Barbara teaches two sessions of kindergarten, each of which lasts $2\frac{1}{2}$ hours. She has a full-time aide, Marilyn, and the two adults work with twenty-five children in one session and thirty in the other. Barbara works closely with the other kindergarten teachers to plan and implement the curriculum for the children.

Children in the kindergarten classes come from a wide range of socioeconomic levels, and their families have a wide range of educational backgrounds. The children exhibit varying levels of intellectual ability. For example, some children were already reading when they came to school, while others are beginning to recognize words now, and still others will need more time to reach this level. The children also show varying levels of physical development. Billy is unable to tie his shoes, a feat Cindy mastered more than a year ago; Sherry seems to skip everywhere she goes while Gary still can't coordinate the step-hop movement necessary for him to learn to skip. There is a wide variation in student social development. Some children are very shy while some seem quite socially adept. However, the children are eager to learn and they are approaching their first school experiences in a positive way. Their backgrounds of experiences are varied, and this is reflected in the variation in their communication abilities.

Barbara's classroom is in a double portable trailer unit. It is carpeted, colorful, and attractively decorated with children's artwork displayed on the walls. There are many plants and several animals. The children enjoy caring for and observing the plants, the fish, the gerbil, and the hamster.

The classroom is set up in learning centers[1] and children spend a large portion of the school day working in them. Barbara believes that learning centers provide a way to meet the needs of children who are functioning at various developmental levels and who have wide ranges of intellectual abilities as well as different learning styles. Barbara says, *"In a way, all the centers are language arts centers; the children work together, sharing and talking—there is a lot of communication going on."*[2]

There is a writing center where children learn to work with scissors and clay and to write words and sentences and where, with Barbara's help, they write their own short stories, which they illustrate and make into books. When the stories are completed, they are put in the reading center. This area contains a wealth of reading materials. There are many trade books as well as a number of magazines, newspapers, and catalogs. Even before children become proficient readers they can use these reading materials to build on interests they bring to school with them. Some children enjoy looking through gardening magazines while others like to look at catalogs of toys and games and make wish lists for Christmas or birthdays. Many children enjoy the sports pages, the grocery advertisements, and the comics in the newspapers. They like to read the stories their classmates have written and illustrated themselves. Children often find they can read some of the trade books they have heard read to them by their parents, by Barbara, or by her aide, or books they have heard in the listening center.

The listening center has many tapes of stories as well as cassettes containing recordings of music to be enjoyed and listening activities for the children to try. Barbara encourages her friends to help her add to her listening tape library by volunteering to record a favorite story for her class. A tape of Maurice Sendak's *Where the Wild Things Are* is especially cherished by her entire class—it was recorded by the superintendent of the school district!

One part of Barbara's room is devoted to a blocks center. This area is filled with blocks children use to practice skills such as part–whole relationships and visualization skills. Some of the blocks have letters on them and children use these to build words. They use larger blocks to build various shapes and objects for their dramatic play activities.

Barbara works with small groups of children in the cooking center. Here the children use their language skills as they discuss each child's contribution to the cooking task, as they help the teacher read the recipe, and as they socialize when they eat the fruits of their efforts and clean up the center so that another group can use it. Their choice of cooking experiences is often influenced by experiences generated in other areas. For example, when the children were working on learning their colors, they had "color week." On the day they devoted to *green,* Barbara read *Green Eggs and Ham* (21) by Dr. Seuss and they cooked green eggs and ham. As the children added a few drops of food coloring to the eggs they were beating, it became apparent that several of them were losing their appetites!

Barbara meets the changing interests of the children through the use of a role-playing center. Here props are changed at various intervals to transform the center into a fire station, a post office, or a grocery store. Children especially enjoy the center when it is a grocery store with its shelves of groceries, its play money, the toy cash register, and the small grocery cart. The boys and girls role play as several children place their groceries in the cart and one of the children works at the checkout counter. It is apparent to the observer that rotating among these centers provides kindergarten children with the opportunities to develop and expand concepts and to develop their language skills.

Each day begins with a group sharing time—"show and tell"—[3] with students bringing in their drawings, personal news items, or special objects to show to their classmates. Barbara encourages all the children to talk, but she works especially hard to help the shy children overcome their fears about sharing with the group. She often asks questions which encourage interactions between the students or between the children and their teacher.

Barbara believes that children will become good listeners if other people listen to them. With this in mind, she and Marilyn try to be good models for listening skills by being good listeners as the children talk.

Sharing time is more than "show and tell." It is also a planning period during which the children are involved in the organization of the session. Barbara draws from the childrens' needs and interests to plan learning activities, and the children plan with their teacher how they will carry out the morning's work.

Children know what is expected of them and they try hard to please. Barbara insists that her classroom be an orderly place with materials put back in place when children finish using them. She feels this belief is consonant with the development and maintenance of a classroom atmosphere which is conducive to effective language arts learning. Children enjoy their work and the classroom sounds like a busy workshop, but it is not chaotic. Children are working, talking, and communicating but they are using soft voices and Barbara speaks quietly when she talks to them.

There is much verbal interaction among the members of the class and between them and their teacher. The children know that Barbara cares for them and there is a mutual feeling of trust and support. She provides oral feedback to her students as they work on their activities. If a child is having difficulty, Barbara and Marilyn or another child provides assistance. *The emphasis in these learning experiences is to "accentuate the positive."* [4]

Barbara's success in implementing her classroom management principles enables her to be comfortable with many activities going on at the same time. She is careful to use her time wisely and she makes good use of the efforts of her teaching aide. Marilyn helps the children understand and follow Barbara's directions. She listens to and talks with the students as she supervises some of their learning activities, and she often reads stories to the children.

One of the adults reads to the entire group of children at least once each day. [5] In addition to this, they sometimes read to small groups and even to individual children. One day, John brought his pet white mouse to school for "show and tell." Barbara shared with him Rose Fyleman's poem "Mice" (6). He was delighted that his teacher had a poem just for him. The day Sherry came to school wiggling her loose tooth was the day Barbara read Robert McCloskey's *One Morning in Maine* (14). Barbara says, "Children enjoy stories but they become special when someone chooses one just for you."

One of the ways Barbara tries to help her children build their background of experiences is through field trips. Not long ago, she and the children visited the post office. Much preplanning took place before they went. Several parent volunteers went with them. Prior to the field trip, they formulated rules for their behavior during the trip. The children discussed desirable behavior and ultimately dictated the rules they decided upon to Barbara who wrote them on a chart. Many of the children found they could read these rules.

The field trip was a big success, with the children not only enjoying the experience but learning a great deal from it as well. Upon their return, they participated in many language arts experiences which were natural extensions of their visit. Several children were delegated to write (with Barbara's help) thank-you notes to the parents who had accompanied them. After they had written them, they discussed the process these notes would go through from the time they were written until they would be delivered to the parents' homes. This discussion was a useful evaluation technique for Barbara who was amazed at how much the children had learned from their field trip.

As an outgrowth of this experience, the children began writing many letters. They constructed individual mailboxes out of discarded shoe boxes, and a group used red, white, and blue paint to decorate a large rectangular box to serve as a communal mailbox. Barbara capitalized on the children's interest in writing and receiving mail by helping them change the role-playing center from the grocery store to a post office. It was a simple matter to put the grocery store props in the storage area and bring out dramatic play props such as stamps (Easter seals), a homemade mail bag, packages, play money, a date stamp and ink pad, postal scales, and a cash drawer. Now when the children wrote their letters (with help from Barbara and Marilyn), the children would deposit them in the large mailbox. Several "mail carriers" would pick up the mail and take it to the post office center for sorting and canceling. As the children worked in this center, they were not only having fun but were learning as well.

Barbara believes all these language arts activities are important parts of the kindergarten curriculum and help her children meet the standards her school district lists as major language arts curricular objectives. The school district publishes a teachers' guide with specific language arts categories and specific objectives for student competency at the end of the kindergarten year. Included in this guide are suggested activities for teaching these skills. In addition to the guide, the district publishes a skills list for use in kindergarten classes. The language arts skills which are emphasized are visual, auditory, language, fine motor, and gross motor skills.

Barbara uses the district's skills list and the teachers' guide as aids when she plans her instructional program. During her planning time, she lists the skills she plans to teach the following day and she reviews the skills list for each of her students. Next, she establishes the groups of children who will work together under her direction during the next several days. *These groups are not static; the grouping changes according to the skills being taught.*[6] There are normally four or five skill groups with each group containing five or six children, but occasionally a group will have just two students. Only the children who need instruction in a specific skill are assigned to a group.

A standard readiness test is administered to each child at the beginning of the year and results are used for determining skill needs and skill groups. Strengths and weaknesses are recorded on students' progress records. This is the only formal testing which is done. Most of the assessment in Barbara's classroom is informal. She may do something with the children to check on a specific skill need or she may use a game to check on a skill need. She believes that teacher observation is extremely important in assessing student needs *and that an effective record-keeping system is essential.*[7] Barbara marks student progress on students' skill sheets daily. She rechecks on skills periodically for maintenance of the skills. Barbara believes students need repetition of skills to broaden and to retain them.

Barbara holds a curriculum night for parents at the beginning of the school year during which she explains what they will be trying to accomplish during the year and why they will be doing what they do. She gives each parent a copy of a handbook she has developed which explains the philosophy and activities of the kindergarten program.

The district in which Barbara teaches has developed a report sheet for parents based on the kindergarten skills list. This is shared with parents at conferences during the year, and a complete report is provided at the end of the year. Parent conferences are scheduled twice a year. The first conference in the fall deals mostly with social and emotional areas, while the spring conference is devoted to going over children's progress on the skills delineated on the checklist.

Barbara communicates with parents throughout the year by telephone and through notes which contain suggested activities for them to use at home. When she was working with the children on body awareness, she sent home the following letter:

Dear Parents:

This week we've been working on a unit entitled "Body Awareness." My primary goal is to help the children acquire awareness of their bodies and to get to know themselves in relationship to their environment. Children acquire body awareness through exercises, games, and dance and through following directions.

You can reinforce our school learnings by doing some simple activities at home. I have listed a few suggestions that will help your child.

1 Trace your hands and feet and then have your child trace his. Compare the size. Count fingers and toes.

2 Have your child teach *you* "Where is Thumbkin," a song we have learned. Change the words to "Where is your elbow . . ." or "Where is your knee . . ." etc.

3 Play "Simon Says." If you don't know how to play, your child will teach you. You should be Simon first, so you can review body parts with commands such as "Simon says, 'touch your nose.' " Then ask your child to be Simon. This will be a good chance for evaluation to let you know whether your child needs more practice.

4 Make a body puzzle. Ask your child to lie on the floor on a large sheet of wrapping paper. Trace around him and then have him cut out the "paper doll." Then cut the doll in pieces to make a giant puzzle. Finally let him put himself back together!

Your help is certainly appreciated. I hope you and your child find these suggestions helpful. Enjoy!

Sincerely,

Barbara Brown

Before the end of June she sends home a letter in which she suggests summer activities which would be beneficial for the children as well as a list of good books from which they might choose some to share with their children.

In summarizing some of her feelings about teaching kindergarten, Barbara says that teachers really need to know their children, they need to know the needs of young children, and they need to know how young children learn best. The teacher also must make certain that the curriculum is responsive to the children and their needs.

Explanation

The preceding description of Barbara's kindergarten classroom identifies several positive teaching practices which are particularly noteworthy. Some of these practices may be described as follows:

1 Mellecker and Cook (15) emphasize that the use of a learning center approach helps teachers provide appropriate and relevant materials for learners.

The learning center approach can help students acquire the skills of working independently, an attribute which becomes increasingly important as the child progresses in school.

Barbara introduces new skills to small groups or to the total class and then students practice the skills for reinforcement in the learning centers. It appears that students today are taught the basic skills. In fact, there may be too much emphasis on teaching skills. Many students seem to have been introduced to too many skills without enough practice in any of them. Classroom time must be allocated for practicing skills so that students will be able to retain and apply them. We tend to spend too much time talking about the language arts skills and not enough time practicing them.

2 Barbara approaches the teaching of the language arts in an interrelated manner; she does not isolate any of the skill areas. Reading, writing, listening, and speaking are interrelated and instruction should be planned so that they are taught and practiced in an interrelated manner.

In its publication entitled "What Are the Basics in English?" (16), the National Council of Teachers of English "advocates the importance of language arts skills being used to reinforce each other. In this process of reinforcement, students explore a wide range of reading interests, get involved in a variety of related learning activities, and thereby develop a firmer grasp of all the necessary language competencies."

A strong language arts program is one in which the teacher interrelates the language arts skills throughout the entire curriculum. Social studies centers such as the grocery store or the post office often provide the content for a language development activity for individuals, small groups, or the entire class.

3 Barbara provides language development activities for her students on a daily basis. Oral language skills are necessary for the student to become proficient in all the language arts. Oral work provides readiness for written work, but it is equally important for the teacher to plan for oral work each day so that students can develop their speaking abilities.

The elementary school classroom should provide rich language experiences for the children. Langer (10) says that we have to put experience into language before knowing takes place. This could involve many aspects of the language experience approach. Numerous authors have provided a wealth of information about the importance of language experience in children's early learning. Children must be surrounded with chances to use and absorb language freely. The all-too-common drills on language skills in isolation from meaning and content should be avoided. Language is learned through experiences, not through lessons. A language development program should include a great deal of self-expression through talking, discussion, art, drama, writing, dance, and music. Activities which integrate these forms of self-expression should be used.

Teachers must provide classrooms in which a nonthreatening environment is created for language development. Teachers should encourage talk and dialogue and must provide specific opportunities for language development. The classroom plan must be developed with this goal in mind. Teachers must accept the language children bring to school and then they must help the children to further develop and refine their language skills.

4 Barbara has a positive expectancy for her students and she provides positive reinforcement regularly. Considerable research supports the fact that children seem to produce in proportion to what is expected of them. If little is expected, little will be produced. If much is expected, much will be produced, as long as the expectancy is within the child's capabilities.

This concept is extremely important. When teachers believe their students are capable of doing well, this attitude is communicated to the students, who accordingly increase in self-confidence and thus do better in their studies. Conversely, when teachers do not believe their students have much potential, the students falter. Teachers have the power to bring out the best or the worst in students.

5 Barbara reads to her students daily. It is essential for teachers to read to their students for at least fifteen minutes several times each day. Teachers should provide a variety of literature as they select books and poetry for the children.

Stewig (23) recommends that each school have a coherent, organized program for the selection of literature to be read to the students, so that what the second-grade teacher does is not in a vacuum in relation to what the fifth-grade teacher does. Children should be exposed to different kinds of literature, and this will not happen if the school does not have a structured approach to the daily reading time.

Teachers at a particular grade level often work together to develop a core literature program for students. At the kindergarten level the program would include counting books, alphabet books, concept books, wordless books, and folktales, as well as examples of some of the best of the picture books. There are several fine guides to help teachers select this core group of books wisely. The reader is directed to "Books for Ages and Stages" in Charlotte Huck's *Children's Literature for the Elementary School* (pp. 31–36) and "Guide to Story Selection According to Developmental Stage" in Bernice Cullinan's *Literature and the Child* (pp. 14–15). It is important to emphasize that a core group of books is not meant to be restrictive to the teacher. Rather, it is a list of books too good to be missed by young children. Teachers should be urged to add their own choices to the list.

6 Barbara groups her students for instruction according to their specific needs. Determining student needs through teacher observation and informal testing and then grouping children for instruction based on those needs are important skills for teachers to use. Instruction can be individualized for students by grouping them appropriately for learning experiences.

Diversity and flexibility are the keys to individualizing instruction through subgroups within a regular class. A pupil can and should belong to several groups. A student may be a part of one group working on a particular skill and belong to another group working on a very different type of skill. Groups should originate as the need arises, and each group should serve a single purpose.

7 Barbara maintains an effective and efficient record-keeping system, and she keeps parents informed of their children's progress. Teachers need a good system with which to keep track of the progress of their students. They might use a management system which lists the skills and concepts teachers plan to teach and children are expected to learn. Such a management system facilitates the process of grouping children for instruction, for practice, for reteaching, and for enrichment. The management system should be simple and quick to complete so that all the teachers' valuable instructional time is not spent on record keeping. The management system must be manageable.

Teachers use this information for communicating to parents. Parents want to know how their children are doing and they should be informed about their children's progress. Parent help and support is needed in the classroom, and good communication with parents is essential to winning that help and support. An efficient management system can be a tremendous asset to the teacher in developing an effective rapport with parents.

LYNN SIMPSON

Descriptor

Lynn is a first-grade teacher in a rural school district. Her class is composed of nineteen students, primarily from middle-class backgrounds. As in most first-grade classes, the students' standardized test results indicate differences in their intellectual abilities. However, all the children scored within the normal range, and they should be able to experience success in their first-grade work.

Within the classroom Lynn actively seeks to develop in her students favorable attitudes toward school, toward themselves, and toward the language arts. She says: "I view a classroom like a home. Everyone's comfortable. It's a safe, warm, and loving place. No one's frustrated or disgruntled and everyone's able to learn and be happy."

Lynn teaches language arts every day for a period of two hours. Language arts is taught in a "block period of time" with each skill area being integrated with other related skills. Lynn's basic organizational pattern for providing instruction is three ability groups, composed of her most able, average, and low-ability children. Within each of these groups there is a high degree of individualization. Lynn is well aware that within these groups the children are similar in their reading achievement levels but differ in their reading interests and in their specific levels of skill development. One child in the group may need additional practice on a new skill or concept while another may not. One child may be more interested in a particular story than another and will be ready for an extension from that story into a related work of children's literature. Lynn realizes that a group is not a single entity; rather, it is made up of individual children who can learn well together if provisions are made for their idiosyncrasies.

When Lynn works with one group, members of the other two groups are expected to work independently. When they are finished with assigned tasks, they are encouraged to choose from a variety of language arts enrichment activities designed to promote growth in listening, speaking, or reading. Lynn uses books such as *Reading Activities for Today's Elementary Schools,* by Burns and Roe (1), and *Encyclopedia of Activities for Teaching Grades K–3* by Malehorn (11) to provide her with ideas which she develops into independent activities to meet her students' learning needs.

Lynn spends a couple of minutes every few days with the members of each of her reading groups helping the children select easy, pleasurable books for them to read independently. Lynn says, "With television claiming so much of children's out-of-school time, we must make sure the children have time in school to read. Otherwise they never will get the reading habit."

In Lynn's school, all teachers are required to use a language arts basal series. Therefore, within her classroom, this series provides the basis of her instruction. She places special emphasis on the following objectives. She intends at the end of the first grade for each child to be able to acquire knowledge and information through listening, follow simple spoken directions, listen while others are speaking, verbally share with others what that child has read or heard, convey information orally, participate in class discussions, write thank-you letters, write creative stories, write brief statements and sentences, use proper letter formation in writing, and spell frequently used words correctly.

Lynn employs numerous activities to supplement the language arts series. Every day she presents a picture to her students, who are asked to state the action and/or mood it conveys verbally. Incomplete sentences are presented to the children, who are requested to say or write words to complete them. There is a listening center in the room and at least twice a week, the children listen to cassette tapes of stories, songs, poems, and narrative material and answer questions relative to them.

Lynn's teaching style is based upon getting a high degree of student interest and involvement. She knows a great deal about her students' hobbies, interests, and personal inclinations. She makes frequent references to each child while teaching a lesson, and whenever possible, her teaching is geared to the visual, auditory, and kinesthetic modalities. She uses visual aids, she speaks in a well-modulated voice and she gives her students ample opportunities to express themselves. Each lesson is characterized by a high degree of activity ("doing," Lynn terms it) on each child's part.

Lynn has many books in her classroom and she changes her classroom collection frequently. She reads to the children several times each day. She says "Sometimes I read a favorite story over and over. When I'm reading to them I encourage them to join in on the refrains." Her children especially enjoy Slobodkina's *Caps for Sale* (20). They delight in chiming in as she reads "first his own checked cap, then the gray caps, then the brown caps, then the blue caps, then the red caps on the very top." Another favorite is Wanda Gag's *Millions of Cats* (7). The children join in with her when they come to "Hundreds of cats, Thousands of cats, Millions and billions and trillions of cats." She has several copies of these books and children enjoy reading them again to themselves or with a partner.

Lynn shares other books which lend themselves to more in-depth discussions. She reads a story to a small group of five or six children and tries to help them discover the meaning in the story by asking carefully thought-out questions. These questions require children to supply details, to identify the main idea, and to make inferences and draw conclusions. She attempts to get her students to go beyond the selection they are reading or to which they are listening. Children are asked questions such as: "What would you have done? If you wrote this story, would it end the same way?" Sometimes she will say, "This word is unusual. Can you tell me what it means? Can you think of another word which means the same thing?" and "Does this story remind you of any other story we have read?" or "Can you think of a poem we've heard which reminds you of something which happened in the story?" She tries to give her students numerous chances to think about and respond to the story by using questions which require different levels of understanding.

Lynn explains to her students why they are doing a particular lesson, she uses praise to encourage student participation (she says, "a teacher should be a child's cheering section"), and she accepts the students' suggestions and places value on the ideas expressed by them.

Student progress is determined in a number of ways. During the school day, she observes her students as they work on certain tasks, and when a child appears to be experiencing difficulty, she asks, "Can you do this by yourself, or do you want some help?" She uses the periodic tests which accompany her commercial series to help her assess student progress. Homework is given frequently and she learns a great deal about the children's progress by how they deal with these assignments. Lynn is well aware that first-grade children work very hard during the school day and that they are tired in the evening. She structures her homework assignments around "fun" activities which are extensions of classwork. Nonetheless, these assignments provide Lynn with insight about the children's progress.

One assignment required the children to find a baby picture of themselves and write several sentences of autobiographical information around it. In order to complete this assignment children needed to interview their parents to find out where they were born, how much they weighed at birth, and other pertinent details. Some of the children needed their parents to help them write the sentences; others did not. Two other homework assignments Lynn has used are: Children were asked to bring in a report of five things in their homes which are square. They could write sentences to describe these things or draw pictures of them or, if they wished, they could just be prepared to tell about them. In like manner, they were asked to report on four things in their houses which make sounds. Assignments such as these provide parents as well as the teacher with insights into progress the children are making in language arts.

Lynn maintains an individual folder for each member of her class, and based upon observation, homework, anecdotal records, and testing, she monitors each student's strengths and deficiencies in the language arts competencies specified for first-graders. Corrective instruction is provided either with a group or with individuals when warranted.

Lynn believes that a first-grade teacher must be "a flexible person." She says:

Listening, speaking, and the other language arts are all intended to foster communication. I want to keep my students' minds open, to give them confidence in themselves, and to enable them to express their thoughts, ideas, and feelings. First-graders should not be afraid to take risks with language. Although teaching the language arts at this level is a tough task, why can't one have fun and be loving while doing it?

Analysis

Lynn is a first-grade teacher in a rural school district. Her class is composed of nineteen students, primarily from middle-class backgrounds. As in most first-grade classes, the students' standardized test results indicate differences in their intellectual abilities. However, all the children scored within the normal range, and they should be able to experience success in their first-grade work.

Within the classroom Lynn actively seeks to develop in her students favorable attitudes toward school, toward themselves, and toward the language arts.[1] She says: "I view a classroom like a home. Everyone's comfortable. It's a safe, warm, and loving place. No one's frustrated or disgruntled and everyone's able to learn and be happy."

Lynn teaches language arts every day for a period of two hours. *Language arts is taught in a "block period of time" with each skill area being integrated with other related skills.*[2] Lynn's basic organizational pattern for providing instruction is three ability groups, composed of her most able, average, and low-ability children. *Within each of these groups there is a high degree of individualization.*[3] Lynn is well aware that within these groups the children are similar in their reading achievement levels but differ in their reading interests and in their specific levels of skill development. One child in the group may need additional practice on a new skill or concept while another may not. One child may be more interested in a particular story than another and will be ready for an extension from that story into a related work of children's literature. Lynn realizes that a group is not a single entity; rather, it is made up of individual children who can learn well together if provisions are made for their idiosyncrasies.

When Lynn works with one group, members of the other two groups are expected to work independently. *When they are finished with assigned tasks, they are encouraged to choose from a variety of language arts enrichment activities designed to promote growth in listening, speaking, or reading.*[4] Lynn uses books such as *Reading Activities for Today's Elementary Schools,* by Burns and Roe (1), and *Encyclopedia of Activities for Teaching Grades K–3* by Malehorn (11) to provide her with ideas which she develops into independent activities to meet her students' learning needs.

Lynn spends a couple of minutes every few days with the members of each of her reading groups helping the children select easy, pleasurable books for them to read independently. Lynn says, "With television claiming so much of children's out-of-school time, we must make sure the children have time in school to read. Otherwise they never will get the reading habit."

In Lynn's school, all teachers are required to use a language arts basal series.[5] Therefore, within her classroom, this series provides the basis of her instruction. She places special emphasis on the following objectives. She intends at the end of the first grade for each child to be able to acquire knowledge and information through listening, follow simple spoken directions, listen while others are speaking, verbally share with others what that child has read or heard, convey information orally, participate in class discussions, write thank-you letters, write creative stories, write brief statements and sentences, use proper letter formation in writing, and spell frequently used words correctly.

Lynn employs numerous activities to supplement the language arts series. Every day she presents a picture to her students, who are asked to state the action and/or mood it conveys verbally. Incomplete sentences are presented to the children, who are requested to say or write words to complete them. There is a listening center in the room and at least twice a week, the children listen to cassette tapes of stories, songs, poems, and narrative material and answer questions relative to them.

Lynn's teaching style is based upon getting a high degree of student interest and involvement.[6] She knows a great deal about her students' hobbies, interests, and personal inclinations. She makes frequent references to each child while teaching a lesson, and whenever possible, *her teaching is geared to the visual, auditory, and kinesthetic modalities.*[7] She uses visual aids, she speaks in a well-modulated voice, and she gives her students ample opportunities to express themselves. Each lesson is characterized by a high degree of activity ("doing," Lynn terms it) on each child's part.

Lynn has many books in her classroom and she changes her classroom collection frequently. *She reads to the children several times each day.*[8] She says "Sometimes I read a favorite story over and over. When I'm reading to them I encourage them to join in on the refrains." Her children especially enjoy Slobodkina's *Caps for Sale* (20). They delight in chiming in as she reads "first his own checked cap, then the gray caps, then the brown caps, then the blue caps, then the red caps on the very top." Another favorite is Wanda Gag's *Millions of Cats* (7). The children join in with her when they come to "Hundreds of cats, Thousands of cats, Millions and billions and trillions of cats." She has several copies of these books and children enjoy reading them again to themselves or with a partner.

Lynn shares other books which lend themselves to more in-depth discussions. She reads a story to a small group of five or six children and *tries to help them discover the meaning in the story by asking carefully thought-out questions.*[9] These questions require children to supply details, to identify the main idea, and to make inferences and draw conclusions. She attempts to get her students to go beyond the selection they are reading or to which they are listening. Children are asked questions such as: "What would you have done? If you wrote this story, would it end the same way?" Sometimes, she will say, "This word is unusual. Can you tell me what it means? Can you think of another word which means the same thing?" and "Does this story remind you of any other story we have read?" or "Can you think of a poem we've heard which reminds you of something which happened in the story?" She tries to give her students numerous chances to think about and respond to the story by using questions which require different levels of understanding.

Lynn explains to her students why they are doing a particular lesson, she uses praise to encourage student participation (she says, "a teacher should be a child's

Teachers explain why they are doing a particular lesson.

cheering section"), *and she accepts the students' suggestions and places value on the ideas expressed by them.*[10]

Student progress is determined in a number of ways. During the school day, she observes her students as they work on certain tasks, and when a child appears to be experiencing difficulty, she asks, "Can you do this by yourself, or do you want some help?" She uses the periodic tests which accompany her commercial series to help her assess student progress. Homework is given frequently and she learns a great deal about the children's progress by how they deal with these assignments. Lynn is well aware that first-grade children work very hard during the school day and that they are tired in the evening. She structures her homework assignments around "fun" activities which are extensions of classwork. Nonetheless, these assignments provide Lynn with insight about the children's progress.

One assignment required the children to find a baby picture of themselves and write several sentences of autobiographical information around it. In order to complete this assignment children needed to interview their parents to find out where they were born, how much they weighed at birth, and other pertinent details. Some of the children needed their parents to help them write the sentences; others did not. Two other homework assignments Lynn has used are: Children were asked to bring in a report of five things in their homes which are square. They could write sentences to describe these things or draw pictures of them or, if they wished, they could just be prepared to tell about them. In like manner, they were asked to report on four things in their houses which make sounds. Assignments such as these provide parents as well as the teacher with insights into progress the children are making in language arts.

Lynn maintains an individual folder for each member of her class,[11] *and based upon observation, homework, anecdotal records, and testing, she monitors each student's strengths and deficiencies in the language arts competencies specified for first-graders.*[12] Corrective instruction is provided either with a group or with individuals when warranted.

Lynn believes that a first-grade teacher must be "a flexible person." She says:

> Listening, speaking, and the other language arts are all intended to foster communication. I want to keep my students' minds open, to give them confidence in themselves, and to enable them to express their thoughts, ideas, and feelings. First-graders should not be afraid to take risks with language. Although teaching the language arts at this level is a tough task, why can't one have fun and be loving while doing it?[13]

Explanation

1 Teachers should place a high priority upon the affective domain. When children enjoy coming to school, they are likely to achieve more. Frequently, the perception students have of school is shaped by the relationship they have with their teacher. Swick and Flake-Hobson (24) describe this relationship between teacher and children as it *should* exist within the confines of the classroom. They state: "Students need to be accepted for who they are, even when they make mistakes. We believe teachers should let students know that they care for them. In our own experiences with children we've found many of our 'problem students' are lonely persons who have never been valued by someone close to them."

Lynn's desire to develop a positive self-concept in each of her students is commendable. It may also be a rather infrequent occurrence if Gorman (8) is correct. Sometimes the most effective learning a student does is to develop clearly the notion that he is stupid, dirty, and undesirable.

It is unfortunate that some educators fail to recognize the importance of positive self-concept formulation. Self-concept, according to Quandt (19), "refers to all the perceptions that an individual has of himself; especially emphasized are the individual's perceptions of his value and his ability." Possessing a good self-concept is not only important for the personal development of children but it also has learning implications. In studies conducted by Brookover (3), Mangieri and Olsen (12), and others, direct relationships were found to exist between self-concept and various types of academic achievement.

Finally, we strongly endorse Lynn's desire to establish in her children a favorable attitude toward the language arts. The language arts are not merely another subject learned and forgotten in a classroom. Petty and Jensen (18) contend:

> Language is basic to humanity. We express our feelings and thoughts through language and stimulate actions and reactions through language. Language is basic for the acquisition of the understandings, attitudes, and ideals that are important to individuals, groups, and society in general.

2 The issue of which organizational pattern is the most effective means of providing language arts instruction is a subject of conjecture. Some contend that no single organizational measure is superior to any other. We agree that the period of time in which the language arts are taught will not *by itself* determine whether or not a teacher is successful.

However, efforts designed to artificially segment the language arts are, in our viewpoint, counterproductive to effective instruction. Devoting twenty minutes to listening, thirty to speaking, and so on gives the child, and possibly the teacher, the concept that each area is a discrete body of knowledge. This, of course, contradicts the very nature of the language arts. While reading, listening, composition, and the other language arts may mean the acquisition of different skills, there is nevertheless a high degree of overlap.

By allocating ample time during one portion of the school day for *all* language arts instruction as opposed to a speaking period, a listening period, and so on, it is easier to teach language arts skills which complement one another. This method will enable children to see the interrelationships among the language arts more clearly. To the teacher, it affords increased opportunities to reinforce concepts the students have previously learned. However, it also requires a more skillful teacher, one who takes the time to plan, to make associations, to relate content, and to be creative. A creative first-grade teacher will keep in mind the possibilities for language arts integration in other areas of school work.

When preplanning a unit on air transportation, for example, the teacher will not separate the language arts into the six components of reading, creative writing, speaking, listening, spelling, and handwriting. Rather, she will plan activities which will help the children expand their concepts about air transportation as they use the tools of language. Perhaps a pilot will visit the class. The teacher will work with the children prior to his or her visit on such things as interviewing techniques, discussing what sorts of questions to ask, and writing some of the questions the class decides need to be asked. During the pilot's visit the children will not only ask questions, they will also listen to the replies and interact with the speaker. After the visit, the children will write thank-you notes, and perhaps some may write an account of the visit for the school newspaper. These children will have gained practice in all six language arts areas as they expanded their social studies learning.

3 Donoghue (4) accurately describes the role language arts teachers should play and the challenges confronting them. She says:

> The teacher's most challenging responsibility is to provide a program that meets children where they are, recognizes their potential, capitalizes upon their strengths, and moves them along at a pace consonant with their ability. The teacher recognizes individual variations in ability to understand and speak standard English; abstraction; size and appropriateness of vocabulary; number and accuracy of concepts acquired; and in desire and ability to verbalize experiences.

Regardless of the form of grouping teachers employ, they will do well to remember that *individuals* comprise those groups. These individuals will be different in their ability to learn as well as in the rate at which they do learn. Also, their proficiencies and deficiencies in the language arts skill areas will vary and their interest in, and attitude toward, the language arts may be markedly different.

Given these plus myriad other uniquenesses, individualizing instruction should not be viewed as a utopian ideal. The effective teacher is well aware of these differences in children and instruction provides frequent opportunities for fostering this individualization. Teachers have many devices available for reaching this goal. Among them are learning centers, practice exercises, individual enrichment activities, and programmed materials. The effective teacher uses the form and content of material best suited to a particular student's growth in the language arts.

4 The concept of enrichment is frequently misunderstood. Although enrichment activities are typically planned—and engaged in—by the abler students in a classroom, they should not be confined to these children. Teachers should develop enrichment activities for any child in the classroom who has the time and the motivation to attempt them . . . and should *make* time for the less able students, who might not otherwise get chances to apply and enjoy newly acquired skills before going on to other skills.

What should the nature of enrichment activities be? Generally, they afford a child added opportunities for creative expression, particularly in the areas of writing, reading, and speaking. In other instances, enrichment gives a child the opportunity to acquire advanced skills beyond the language arts curriculum offered at a particular grade level. Also, enrichment can simply provide meaningful practice.

One final point should be made about enrichment. Because enrichment activities may be diverse in content or format, one should not feel that any activity can be deemed enriching. When in doubt as to whether or not an activity will be enriching to a child, you need to ask yourself two questions: Does the lesson have direct pertinence to the language arts skill(s) recently acquired by the child? Does the activity deepen and broaden the student's present level of mastery in a designated language arts area? If your answer to both questions is yes, the activity can probably serve its intended purpose(s).

5 The vast majority of our nation's elementary schools use a commercial language arts series. Most of these include reading, creative writing, speaking, listening, and reading, but many do not specifically include spelling and handwriting. Therefore, separate spelling and handwriting books are normally used. One system which is a total-language approach incorporating all the language arts components for the primary grades is published by Holt, Rinehart and Winston. School systems which use these materials do not have to purchase separate spelling and handwriting texts. Teacher who opt for a language arts block approach appreciate this particular series. All the language arts series are written by a team of authors whose expertise is well established in the field. These people have had several years of teaching experience, possess advanced degrees in language arts, and occupy prestigious positions in school districts or universities.

The language arts series produced by these authors is intended to expose and teach all the necessary skills in a logical progression from first grade through at least sixth grade, and possibly eighth grade. The series presents these skills in a detailed manner so that a teacher will know what skills children should have been taught in a series, what skills they should be learning, and what skills they should acquire by the conclusion of a school year.

Despite the elaborate details evident in the development of these series, one should not perceive them as programs of and in themselves. No matter how thorough the authors intend for the series to be, page constraints and time limitations prevent series from dealing adequately and *in a comprehensive manner* with all facets of the language arts. Thus the authors of such materials emphasize some language arts skills more than others.

The effective language arts teacher studies the curriculum and analyzes which parts of it are satisfactorily dealt with in the series. Where the series does not adequately present a skill or concept, the teacher must supplement the series. Sources of supplementary materials may be activities or lessons from another series, commercial supplementary materials, or teacher-made materials designed to teach a designated skill.

6 Capitalizing on the interests of learners is a long-established dictum of educational psychology. Pestalozzi's approach for teaching children (13) embodies the need for learner involvement in classroom activities. Lane and Beauchamp (9) describe the cognitive basis for why a teacher's voice should not be the sole one heard in a classroom. They state:

> All distinctively human behavior is social. An intelligent atmosphere involves much interchange of purposes and suggestions and free communication of them. Little effective intelligence can develop where communication is stifled, controlled, one-sided, or flowing in one direction only.

To which we add, neither can the acquisition of language arts skills.

7 The concept of learning modality has been in the educational field for quite some time. The sensory channel through which information is processed most efficiently is identified as a learning modality or strength. Basically, there are three modalities: visual, auditory, and kinesthetic. Some educators maintain that children have a preferred mode of learning. The wise teacher, they maintain, will offer instruction in a format consistent with that style of learning. For example, with an auditory learner, the teacher would use storytelling, tapes, records, cassettes, verbal discussions, and a lecture form of teaching.

Others feel that to teach primarily to a student's learning strength is not worthwhile. Spache (22) contends "that teaching to a modality is still a theoretical hypothesis. At this stage in the development of research in the area, we cannot be certain exactly what the diagnostic tests that we employ are measuring, how long the indications of the test should be followed."

Given the inconclusiveness of research on learning modalities, we do not feel that one should gear instruction primarily to a child's alleged learning strength. Not only does the premise that this is helpful lack supportive research but it also places an enormous burden on the teacher, who must then strive to devise visual, auditory, and kinesthetic activities for *each* language arts skill. Instead, we advocate a multimodal approach in which devices such as the following would be employed in a classroom: chalkboards, overhead projectors, dittos, and bulletin boards (visual activities); storytelling, cassettes, verbal discussions, and tapes (auditory activities); and writing, tracing, and manipulative materials (kinesthetic activities). Usage of multimodal techniques makes for diversity in one's teaching and avoids placing an unrealistic burden on the teacher.

8 Teachers who read aloud to children not only help them to begin to appreciate good literature and learn to like to read but also serve as models for good reading. Tiedt (25) emphasizes the importance of teachers being proficient oral readers. She urges them to practice by reading into a tape recorder. They should then evaluate their reading by asking themselves such questions as:

a Can the children hear me?
b Does the reading flow pleasantly?
c Am I reading too quickly or too slowly?
d What about expression?

After the evaluation, they should record their reading again, consciously correcting any weaknesses they have noticed. Teachers who practice in this manner find that they read much more effectively when they read to a real audience than if they had not practiced.

9 Some teachers hold the view that primary school children should be asked only simple questions. *Simple* usually means, in terms of classroom procedure, responding to factual queries. Others maintain that lower-ability children should not be asked questions of an implicit nature (that is, questions that require inferences, conclusions, predictions of outcomes, or other answers not of a direct factual nature.)

People holding either of these conceptions are incorrect. First, young children can—and should—be given opportunities to respond to *all* types of questions. Children in the primary grades enjoy questions that enable them to use their imaginative abilities. Second, the idea that only gifted or abler students should be asked "higher-level" questions is erroneous. There is ample support in professional literature for asking *all* types of questions to high-, average-, and low-ability students.

Fisher and Terry (5) describe the use of questions and questioning strategies in classrooms. They say:

> Too often teachers, in attempting to check reading comprehension or oral listening comprehension, ask primarily cognitive-memory questions. Generally speaking, the broad questions, both divergent and evaluative, provoke the greatest response from several different children. Use cognitive-memory or convergent questions to clarify facts and gain information; then use divergent and evaluative questions to extend thinking beyond that level.

10 Students, even as young as first-graders, should know *why* they are doing a particular lesson. By giving them a rationale for the task at hand, a teacher provides the learners with a state of *readiness* for the subsequent lesson. The children will know the purpose(s) of a lesson, and from what studies show, motivation and performance are likely to increase.

Lynn's use of praise is another practice we favor. In our opinion, children should receive frequent, overt, and immediate praise from a teacher. When children have done something in the language arts correctly, a teacher should use praise in the manner previously described. Almost everyone responds to praise, and students who have been praised are likely to participate more wholeheartedly in later classroom activities.

Lynn's acceptance of ideas expressed by students is another commendable practice. Just as the wise company heeds the comments of its customers, the effective teacher communicates with the children in his or her classroom. Children are the recipients of a teacher's instruction. Their questions should be answered, their responses to a lesson should be given attention, and their feelings, attitudes, and ideas should be accorded respect.

11 We cannot emphasize strongly enough our belief in the need for maintaining a language arts record of *each* child's performance during a given year. Many devices could be used to accommodate this form of classroom record keeping; we prefer using a manila folder for each child. Depending upon a teacher's needs, little or much of the child's work during the school year would be placed (after parents have reviewed it) into the folder. Minimally the folder should contain a number of dated writing samples and any significant teacher-made test administered to the child as well as the series' periodic tests in the language arts completed by the child. Any standardized language arts test or special assessment (such as of vision or hearing) is pertinent to the language arts. Other significant pieces of evaluative or diagnostic information would also be included in the child's folder.

By maintaining folders for *each* child, a teacher will not have to rely on memory when planning lessons geared to the needs of the children within a classroom. Also, maintaining a folder can help to make continuity from grade to grade possible, so that children can make optimal progress in the language arts. The folder will provide subsequent teachers with concrete information about *each* child in relation to the language arts.

John C.

Date	(+)	(−)	Criteria
____	_____		Rich vocabulary
____	_____		Uses complete sentences
____	_____		Shows imagination
____	_____		Exhibits sense of humor
____	_____		Other

FIGURE 3-2
Individual observation sheet.

12 The use of many modes for assessment purposes is a commendable practice. Teacher observation in the classroom can provide much information about the proficiencies and deficiencies of students in the language arts. By watching children in whole-class, group, and individual situations, a teacher will soon know the work habits and language arts competencies of each child in the classroom.

Teachers organize the information they gain through observation in various ways. For example, two teachers who observe children's language behavior during a discussion may use the same criteria but organize it differently. Teacher A will have a notebook with a separate sheet for each child. A page will list the child's name, the date of observation, and the criteria to be observed, and will have a line for a rating of (+) or (−) to indicate strengh or weakness. The sheet would look like the one in Figure 3-2. Teacher B might use a checklist for the same criteria in the organizational pattern used in Figure 3-3.

Homework, teacher-made tests, and tests which accompany a commercial series can provide the teacher with additional data. This information can show how well the child is progressing at daily and periodic intervals. Also, it can supplement the teacher's classroom observations of students. The additional information will support or refute

FIGURE 3-3
Observation: language behavior during discussion.

Satisfactory (S)   or Unsatisfactory (U)

Criteria   Pupils' Names

1 Rich vocabulary
2 Uses complete sentences
3 Shows imagination
4 Sense of humor
5 Other

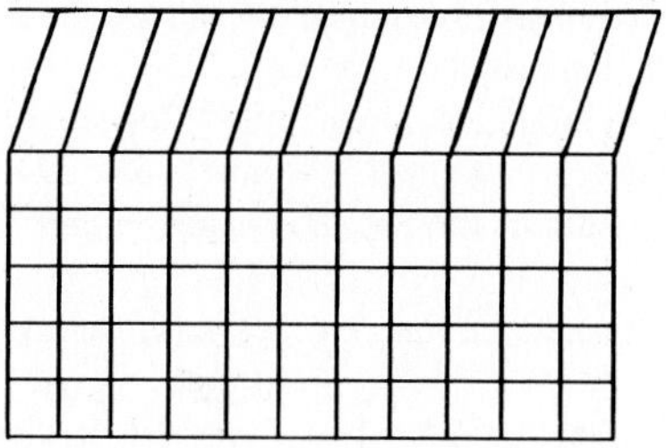

the teacher's diagnostic judgments of students formed on the basis of classroom observation(s).

13 We wholeheartedly agree with Lynn. There is an often-repeated phrase about teaching. It is: "Nobody ever said teaching was easy." Teaching is indeed hard work, but it can also be an extremely gratifying profession.

BIBLIOGRAPHY AND REFERENCES

1 Burns, Paul C., and Roe, Betty D. *Reading Activities for Today's Elementary Schools.* Chicago: Rand McNally, 1979.

2 Brookover, William B., and Erickson, Edsel. "Introduction: Symposium on Self-Concept and Its Relationship to Academic Achievement: A Longitudinal Analysis." Paper presented at the AERA meeting, Chicago, 1965.

3 Brookover, William B., Patterson, Ann, and Thomas, Sharon. "The Relationship of Self-Images to Achievement in Junior High School Subjects." Final Report of Cooperative Research Project No. 845, East Lansing, Mich. Office of Research and Publications, Michigan State University, 1962.

4 Donoghue, Mildred R. *The Child and the English Language Arts.* Dubuque, Iowa: William C. Brown Company, 1975.

5 Fisher, Carol J., and Terry, C. Ann. *Children's Language and the Language Arts.* New York: McGraw-Hill, 1977.

6 Fyleman, Rose. "Mice." In Arbuthnot, May Hill. *Time for Poetry.* Glenview, Ill.: Scott Foresman, 1951.

7 Gag, Wanda. *Millions of Cats.* New York: Coward-McCann, 1928.

8 Gorman, Alfred H. *Teachers and Learners.* Boston: Allyn and Bacon, 1974, p. 14.

9 Lane, Howard, and Beauchamp, Mary. *Understanding Human Development.* Englewood Cliffs, N.J.: Prentice-Hall, 1959, p. 82.

10 Langer, Suzanne K. *Philosophy in a New Key.* New York: Mentor Books, 1956.

11 Malehorn, Hal. *Encyclopedia of Activities for Teaching Grades K–3.* West Nyack, N.Y.: Parker Publishing Co., 1975.

12 Mangieri, John, and Olsen, Henry D. "Self-Concept-of-Achievement Ability and Reading Proficiency of Black and White Males in an Adult Education Course." *The Journal of Negro Education* vol. 46, no. 4, Fall 1977, pp. 456–461.

13 McCarthy, Melodie A., and Houston, John P. *Fundamentals of Early Childhood Education.* Cambridge, Mass.: Winthrop Publishers, 1980, p. 4.

14 McCloskey, Robert. *One Morning in Maine.* New York: Viking Press, 1953.

15 Mellecker, Janie, and Cook, Rhonda. "Why the Learning Center Approach?" *Colorado Journal of Educational Research,* vol. 19, no. 4, Summer 1980, pp. 9–10.

16 National Council of Teachers of English. "What Are the Basics in English?" *SLATE Starter Sheets,* vol. 1, no. 2, August 1976, p. 1.

17 Olsen, Henry D., and Mangieri, John. "Self-Concept-of-Academic Ability and Reading Proficiency." *Reading Horizons,* vol. 17, no. 1, Fall 1976, pp. 28–34.

18 Petty, Walter T., and Jensen, Julie M. *Developing Children's Language.* Boston: Allyn and Bacon, 1980, p. 4.

19 Quandt, Ivan. *Self-Concept and Reading.* Newark, Del.: International Reading Association, 1972.

20 Slobodkina, Esphyr. *Caps for Sale.* New York: W. R. Scott, 1947.

21 Seuss, Dr. (pseudonym of Theodor S. Geisel). *Green Eggs and Ham*. New York: Random House. 1960.

22 Spache, George D. *Investigating the Issues of Reading Disabilities*. Boston: Allyn and Bacon, 1976, p. 108.

23 Stewig, John W. *Read to Write: Using Children's Literature as a Springboard to Writing* (2d ed.). New York: Holt, Rinehart and Winston, 1980.

24 Swick, Kevin J., and Flake-Hobson, Carol. "Guidelines for Experienced Teachers." In Robert Gilstrap (ed.). *Toward Self-Discipline*. Washington, D.C.: Association for Childhood Education International, 1981, p. 35.

25 Tiedt, Iris M. *Exploring Books with Children*. Boston: Houghton Mifflin, 1979, pp. 21–22.

CHAPTER 4

LANGUAGE ARTS: GRADES TWO AND THREE

OVERVIEW

This chapter will be similar to Chapter 2 in format. The focus of this chapter will be the teaching of language arts in grades two and three. The chapter will begin by discussing the nature of children in these grades. We will then describe the curricular emphases, instructional activities, and assessment measures associated with providing language arts instruction to children in these grades.

THE CHILD

Kagan and Moss (16) have called the first four years of school a period of crystallization. They suggest that during this span, traits are formed which have been shown to be consistent with later adult behavior. Those working with children at this time must understand how seven- and eight-year-old children look, think, and feel. Why does Susan imagine the building moving back and forth when she reads the sentence, "The schoolhouse rocked with laughter"? Why does the reading group become so fidgety at ten o'clock? Why does Mark blurt out answers without thinking first? A brief look at the physical, social, emotional, and intellectual characteristics provides aid in answering such questions and solving the problems involved.

Physical Characteristics

Children of this age continue to be extremely active. Long periods of sedentary activities may cause children to release their pent-up energy through unacceptable behavior. Planning for children to move to the chalkboard to manipulate flash cards rather than merely reciting the words from their desks will provide breaks in routine and promote active involvement. As the children complete a seat-work assignment, allowing them to go to another part of the room for a different type of activity helps to provide opportunities for movement and a change of pace.

Primary-grade students continue to need rest periods. Varying activities requiring mental and physical concentration with periods of quieter and more relaxing exercises aids students in attending to learning tasks.

Some seven- and eight-year-olds may still have difficulty focusing on small objects. Alternating periods of reading with activities which do not require close visual work will furnish periods of rest. For example, after silent reading an oral discussion should be planned, rather than a written assignment.

In size and strength, boys and girls of this age are usually more similar than different (4). Although females may equal males in physical development, they will usually differ in their physical behavior. Boys tend to select activities which perpetuate the all-American boy image, where athletic success is valued. Girls, however, model behavior which matches their conception of femininity; most continue to choose less strenuous activities. It will be interesting to note the effect of our changing society on this conduct.

Social and Emotional Characteristics

During the second and third grades, closer and longer-lasting friendships occur. Many children select best friends—and worst enemies. Quarrels may develop between children or between groups, with classmates taking sides. Teachers must realize that the influence of these friendships goes beyond the playground and impacts on classroom behavior. Teachers should be aware of children who have difficulty making friends. The pairing and grouping of students for social as well as academic reasons can provide a variety of social experiences.

Seven- and eight-year-olds enjoy games and often develop complicated rule systems. These children may not comprehend the problems of extenuating circumstances; situations are viewed in literal, inflexible terms. Biehler (4) links tattling to this pattern. Keeping activities as simple as possible and anticipating potential troubling situations will eliminate many problems. Explaining games and routines carefully and being alert to signals of misunderstanding prevent most disagreements.

Seven- and eight-year-old children are more sensitive to the feelings of others. They no longer assume that everyone is exactly alike. They have become quite conscious of comparing themselves with classmates. Remembering the literal attitude of these children, we can appreciate their difficulty in accepting teasing comments, and understand their negative reaction to sarcasm.

Primary students are eager to accept responsibility and thrive on success. Housekeeping chores within the classroom may motivate, provide active involvement, or serve as a learning experience. For example, for Kay, washing the board is a reward; for Benji, it is an energy-expending break from seat work; for Carla, it is a concrete learning activity with a sponge and water.

Erikson (9) describes this period as a time for developing a sense of industry or inferiority. Children who are provided with opportunities to participate in independent and group activities will learn how things work and how objects can be manipulated. They will learn to work with others, to share, and to take turns. They will experience success and a feeling of pride in completing a task. Children who miss these opportunities or whose efforts are labeled as failures may feel inferior. This period of a search for a sense of industry can be used as a positive force by teachers who structure an active classroom environment. Designing bulletin boards, making games, and planning projects are all examples of providing a chance to gain a feeling of success through industry.

Intellectual Characteristics

Just as the key word for physical characteristics might be *active,* the key word for intellectual characteristics could be *curious.* Children's interests are varied and change rapidly. Students may seem to lack stability as they move quickly from one activity to another. A good teacher will balance this need to discover with the need to learn perseverance. Teachers can take advantage of this curiosity by creating a stimulating classroom environment. It is not sufficient, however, to fill the classroom with objects and cover the walls with posters. These articles must be made an integral part of the daily learning experience. Filling a shelf with native American artifacts is not enough. A provoking introduction will arouse children's curiosity and encourage questions. Now is the time for teaching reference skills by piquing their interest and showing them how to find the answers.

As children progress through school, differences in cognitive style become noticeable. Kagan (15) uses the terms *impulsive* and *reflective* to describe two types of responses. The impulsive thinker reacts quickly, often with the first answer that comes to mind. The reflective thinker needs time to evaluate possibilities. Kagan also refers to the *analytic,* who notes the separate details in a complex activity, and the *thematic,* who responds to the whole. The existence of these and other cognitive styles helps to explain why children of similar age and ability will respond differently to the same learning situation. Presenting material through a variety of approaches and allowing diverse methods of responses will help in matching students' styles and teachers' expectations.

According to Piaget's theory of development, the children of the second and third grades are usually in the lower level of the concrete operational stage of cognitive development. They are beginning to think in a logical fashion through the use of concrete objects. They differ from children in the preoperational stage in many important ways (11):

1 They are less ego-centered, beginning now to see the point of view of others.

2 They are able to reverse actions mentally and take them back to the first step.

3 They can conserve; they understand that the amount stays the same regardless of changes in shape.

4 They grasp the concept of multiple classification. For example, a duck can be an animal *and* a bird.

It is extremely important to note that although their thinking is logical, it is based on concrete experiences rather than abstractions.

The understanding of the cognitive levels of students should influence the classroom. For students in the concrete operational stage the necessity for providing concrete experiences becomes apparent. The environment should be equipped with manipulative objects and the routine should be structured to encourage students to explore these materials. Use of concrete objects is not *supplemental;* it is *fundamental*.

Summary

Although we can describe characteristics of second- and third-grade students, they do grow physically, emotionally, socially, and intellectually at their own pace. In addition, the stage of development is uneven; children will be at varying levels in each area.

We should also remember the interrelationships among development in these areas. For example, consider Mike who cannot compete on the playground because of physical immaturity. Because of feelings of failure, he may be hesitant to explore, to use materials, to ask questions. Thus, his intellectual growth is affected. An observant teacher notes such problems and makes adjustments for individual needs.

Finally, as discussed in Chapter 2, a child's proficiency with language is also increasing during these years. While the development of language will occur with all children in a classroom, the astute teacher recognizes that not all children will have similar facility or understanding of language. As a result, even in these early years, there will be widespread variations in the language development of students.

LANGUAGE ARTS IN SECOND AND THIRD GRADES

LISTENING

According to Smith (24), listening is the most recent addition to the language arts. In 1950, Witt's classic study found that more than half the day in elementary school was devoted to activities involving listening. It can also be observed that children spend much of their time outside the classroom in listening situations. Yet, teachers note, many students experience difficulty listening effectively. It seems evident that guidance is needed. Kellogg (18) found that direct teaching of listening habits not only increased listening ability but also increased reading achievement.

Instructional Emphases   Petty and Petty (21) suggest that some of the listening skills appropriate for the primary grades are similar to those of the preschool and first grade. Students in these grades continue to enjoy and benefit from activities involving rhyming words, rhythms, and discrimination of sounds and words. While continuing with this type of program, second- and third-grade teachers will want to extend the scope of exercises in order to increase the emphasis on comprehension and evaluative skills. In addition to these areas, appreciative skills should permeate all levels. The following goals are considered relevant for seven- and eight-year-olds.

Cognitive—Comprehension
- To recall details
- To identify main idea
- To determine sequence
- To follow directions
- To understand word meaning from context
- To draw inferences

Cognitive—Evaluation
- To distinguish reality from fantasy
- To distinguish fact from opinion
- To detect irrelevant material
- To identify simple propaganda techniques

Affective
- To derive pleasure from listening
- To compose visual images
- To value techniques such as alliteration and onomatopoeia
- To identify the mood of the selection
- To perceive humor
- To accept the importance of listening skills

It is quickly evident that these skills parallel those of reading. By helping students reach a goal through listening, we provide a foundation that will help later, when reading is required.

Instructional Strategies   Fisher and Terry (10) state that "when teaching listening, the most important factor to remember is 'integration'." Listening cannot be taught effectively as an isolated subject; listening activities should be included in all areas of the curriculum. Helping students develop skill in listening does not mean setting aside a fifteen-minute period each Friday, nor does it mean nagging the children to "Listen and pay attention." Organizing listening experiences has three aspects: taking advantage of incidental occurrences; planning activities within the context of the normal school program; and providing specific exercises in areas needing additional practice.

Every day, unplanned events arise that can be turned into teaching moments. When an unexpected storm prevents outside recess, a game that requires careful attention to directions will provide practice in listening: "Everyone in the first row, run in place. All the girls, do three jumping jacks. If you are wearing blue, hop on one foot."

Structured development of listening skills can be incorporated smoothly into any curriculum area. For example, students frequently have difficulty with word problems in math. By presenting the problems orally the teacher can guide the children to select details and detect irrelevant information. In Chapter 4 of a book by Smith (24), numerous listening activities are described. Due to the nature of these activities, they could be readily employed in any content area.

If problem areas are noted during incidental or planned experiences, lessons can be designed which focus on specific skills. For example, if some children are having

Listening activities should be included in all areas of the curriculum.

difficulty following oral directions, a specially designed tape can be placed in a listening center for those needing additional practice.

Listening may be the most neglected language art and the appreciative skills may be the most neglected listening skills. Before students can show *appreciation*, they must be made *aware* of the aspects of oral literature and music. Sharing the best of children's books and poetry and using music in a variety of ways will provide exposure, but exposure alone is insufficient; some direction and guidance are necessary.

The development of appreciative skills requires a balancing act between structure and freedom. For example, in helping students to identify the mood of a selection, teachers should provide guidance in noting the author's clues, while also encouraging individual responses. Students of primary age may experience difficulty in accepting the concept of multiple "correct" answers. Considering the rigidity and inflexibility of their thinking, it is easy to understand their confusion when the teacher encourages more than one reply per question. The lack of one-to-one correspondence or one question–one answer is baffling. Skillful teaching is required to help students to note literary patterns and to make comparisons to previous experiences in order to support their own opinions while at the same time learning to accept the view of others.

Problems   Certain conditions should be studied when planning a program of building effective listening skills. Failure to consider these aspects of teaching and learning may create situations which hinder the entire process. Teachers of children in this age range would do well to remember:

1 The short attention span of seven- and eight-year-olds requires arranging the schedule to varying listening activities with other types of classwork.

2 The avid curiosity of primary students can work as an advantage or a disadvantage. It can be a plus in gaining and maintaining attention if their interests are considered and used as starting points.

3 The experiential backgrounds of the listeners affect their comprehension. The importance of a child's background of experiences cannot be overemphasized. Reading educators refer to a child's related experiences of background knowledge as *schemata* or *schema*. Background knowledge has been found to affect reading comprehension positively. Just as teachers prepare students for reading, plans should be made for preteaching new vocabulary and concepts which appear in material to be presented orally.

4 Students of this age are unable to set purposes for their own listening. Until they have mastered this skill, teachers must provide a definite reason for listening. Aimless listening may lead to inattention and lack of comprehension. Students should also be taught that listening has a variety of purposes, depending on the listeners' needs and goals.

5 The classroom environment should be structured to keep auditory and visual distractions at a minimum. The daily routine should be maintained at appropriate noise levels, depending on the activity and the individuals involved.

6 It is the teachers who are the key to a successful listening program. The best teaching strategy is to set an example of productive listening habits. Effective teachers of listening are the teachers who *are* good listeners.

Assessment   The process of evaluation must be a continuous one. Daily observation of classroom situations provides information concerning individual and class strengths and weaknesses. To augment these observations other measures may be used to determine progress. The use of student-composed standards which list the qualities of a good listener give primary students a reminder and a guide. Students can use this model for reference and self-evaluation.

It must be stressed that hearing is not the same as listening. If, however, the teacher feels that the listening difficulty may be due to a physical problem, students should be referred for auditory screening.

Standardized tests of listening are included as subtests on many reading readiness tests and could be used to gain information about primary-age students who are experiencing problems. *The Cooperative Primary Test* (6) measures sound perception, recall, interpretation, and inference. Forms are available for grades one and two and for grades two and three. *The Durrell Listening–Reading Series* (8) is designed to compare listening and reading ability.

Commercial materials intended to teach listening skills often provide helpful pretests and posttests. They also offer activities which can be used as models for teacher-made assessments. These informal measures probably offer the most useful information of all, for they are designed to evaluate actual classroom situations. Teacher-designed listening assessments can be adapted by using any activity designed to develop listening skills.

It will be very helpful to the teacher to compose a checklist of skills to record the growth of each student. In Chapter 10, we will show the objectives, skills, and checklists of some language arts programs. This material could serve as a resource for teachers if their school district does not have an established language arts program. By maintaining a checklist of skills to be attained at a given grade level, the teacher can consolidate information from observations, informal assessments, and standardized tests in order to maintain a more efficient record-keeping system for each student. Potentially, this will help improve classroom assessment.

SPELLING

The ability to spell accurately and with ease is an asset in effective writing. Poor spellers are limited in their choice of words; they may use a word they can spell as a substitute for a more appropriate one they are unable to spell. In addition to experiencing problems in communication, the poor speller may be penalized by those who associate misspellings with carelessness and lack of effort. A well-organized spelling program should help students to master spelling skills and overcome these problems.

Instructional Emphases   Primary-grade teachers continue to provide direct instruction in spelling and also to encourage a feeling of pride in good spelling habits. Although most schools base their spelling program on a set of graded, commercial materials, it remains important for teachers to identify overall cognitive and affective objectives.

Cognitive
- To spell an increasing number of high-frequency words
- To use a method of learning to spell new words
- To utilize common phonogram patterns (*-ake, -an, -at*)

- To employ plural generalizations (*-s, -es, -ies*)
- To add some endings (*-ed, -ing*)
- To spell common homonyms (*so–sew, blew–blue*)
- To use the dictionary as a reference

Affective
- To recognize the relationship between spelling and communication
- To recognize the relationship between legible handwriting and spelling
- To use a reference or ask for help
- To take pride in good spelling habits

Systematic instruction in the use of the dictionary is important at all grade levels. The following skills are usually stressed in the second and third grades:

1 Alphabetizing words up to the third letter
2 Selecting approximate place to open the dictionary and deciding whether to turn forward or backward
3 Beginning to use key words
4 Beginning to use diacritical markings for pronunciation
5 Selecting appropriate meaning

Instructional Strategies   A balanced and effective spelling program should include experiences in six areas:

1 High-frequency words
2 Study habits
3 Word pronunciation and meaning
4 High-utility generalizations
5 Proofreading
6 Using the dictionary for spelling assistance

As teachers organize these experiences, it is necessary to consider the development of positive attitudes toward spelling. Negative attitudes may be built if students do not see the usefulness of the words or generalizations to their daily work. Other students may lack motivation to participate in spelling activities if the words are already known; the use of a pretest should solve this problem.

Knowing the five areas of concern and remembering the importance of establishing positive attitudes, teachers find that a weekly plan of instruction is an efficient organization pattern.

First day	Children are given a pretest. They check their own work and make a list or card set of those missed. Word meanings, appropriate generalizations, and pronunciation are discussed.
Second day	Experiences are provided for individual and group work relating to phonetic and structural analysis. Activities to develop visual imagery are included.

Third day   Students take a practice test on *their* words. Again, self-correction is used. Some teachers repeat the process by giving additional words to those who have mastered their original list. More work is given in studying and using the words.

Fourth day   Continued practice in using and spelling the words is provided. Games are used for enrichment. Students are encouraged to tutor each other.

Fifth day   Final test is given. Students may write each word twice: one list is for teacher correction and one for student correction. Thus, the students receive immediate feedback and the teacher is able to record progress. Misspelled words are listed for later review.

This strategy is called the "test–study" approach. Another method, referred to as "study–test," follows similar steps but omits the pretest. The "test–study" approach is preferred, as students work only on the words that are not already a part of their spelling vocabulary.

In the primary grades much attention should be devoted to teaching students how to study new words. Petty (21) points out that learning to spell a word involves alternating processes of (1) gaining an impression of the word through visual, auditory, or kinesthetic channels or a combination of these and (2) recalling the word through a visual image so that it can be written from memory. The following procedure should be used to guide students through learning to spell. Later they will be expected to follow these steps independently.

1 Look at the word and pronounce it.
2 Analyze the word by studying its parts.
3 Cover the word and try to think how it looks. If you can't remember, look again.
4 Write the word and check. If it is misspelled, start with step 1 and repeat the steps. If it is correct, write it one more time for practice.

Developing a visual image of words is important in learning to spell. Young children will need instruction which provides activities to build and strengthen this image. Some students will require additional activities for reinforcement. Students who have auditory strengths learn best when the words are pronounced frequently and spelled aloud. Others learn more efficiently if they write the word in sand or trace it. Those who learn best visually should have many opportunities to see the word in printed form. Most students will need a combination of these presentations.

Games are frequently used for extra practice. Not only do these games provide more experiences, but they also serve as motivation for learning. When using games, there are several noteworthy points to consider.

1 Spelling games should be enjoyable, but the main objective is learning to spell; therefore, games should be simple, with the main emphasis on spelling rather than on complex rules and fancy gimmicks.
2 When words are being learned, the development of the visual image is of primary importance. Games in which the letters are scrambled should be saved until after the spelling is mastered and then used for review or assessment.

Fisher and Terry (10) state the following regarding spelling games: "All games should meet two criteria: the spelling should be done in written form and *all* children should participate throughout the activity." Some of the games or activities cited by Fisher and Terry as being consistent with these criteria are crossword puzzles; classroom versions of television games; team competitions for writing various forms of words; and the commercial game, Scrabble.

Smith (24) notes a high correlation between reading ability and spelling skill. He maintains that a good reader practices his skill through independent reading, and thus has more opportunities for building visual images. That's another good reason to regard the literature program as part of the basic curriculum rather than a frill!

Although the dictionary is the essential reference book for writers, it is often regarded as the last resort. Only those who have been systematically introduced to the dictionary will ever use it to its fullest. There are dictionaries appropriate for all levels, but they often lie unopened because of lack of direct instruction in their use.

As DeHaven (7) points out, finding a word is not always a simple task. In addition to a growing knowledge of alphabetical order, the students must have some image of the spelling of the word. And if their first idea is not correct, they must continue to check out other options. Without this ability to make an educated guess first and then to try others, students will continue to cry, "I can't look it up if I can't spell it." It may be beneficial to emphasize this concept through group experiences. As an example, consider this situation.

The class is composing a group poem. It is unable to locate *sleigh* in the dictionary. One student suggests *slay* because of the word *play*. When this proves incorrect, another offers *sley* because of *hey*. Finally, one guesses *sleigh* because of *neighbor*. The teacher stresses that the *a* sound may be spelled several ways. This information is added to a class reference chart containing sounds and their many spellings.

Whatever the spelling program that is adapted and whatever organizational plan is utilized, there are other considerations to be remembered.

1 Spelling generalizations should be introduced when relevant to the words being studied. They should be taught one at a time with frequent review.

2 Instruction should stress writing the words rather than spelling them orally.

3 The program should be structured to allow flexibility in the number of words emphasized with each student.

4 Passing the test is not the goal of a spelling program. Correct spelling in actual writing activities should be stressed. This emphasizes the need for guiding students in proofreading their own first drafts.

5 Poor handwriting and spelling habits may develop if students are consistently directed to "copy each word ten times."

6 An effective spelling program employs frequent review. Attention should be called to words which are examples or exceptions to known generalizations or patterns.

Problems Following the suggested strategies and noting the listed considerations will prevent many problems; however, a few additional areas demand attention if spelling instruction is to meet the needs of all the children. Spelling instruction can be enhanced if teachers remember the following:

1 Assigning the writing of each misspelled word ten or twenty times not only fosters a negative attitude toward spelling, but also may reinforce the misspelling.

2 Using a sand tray or chalkboard to provide both kinesthetic and tactile experiences has been shown to be more effective than writing in the air, where no observable product is created.

3 For best results with more children, oral spelling should be limited or at least combined with writing.

4 Homonyms are often listed as spelling demons. Instruction should emphasize meaning and the establishment of a strong visual impression. It is considered better to teach one thoroughly before introducing the mate(s).

5 Mispronunciation of words may cause errors in spelling.

6 Overemphasis placed on phonetic generalizations may encourage overuse of these guides. Students may depend on the generalizations and fail to build visual images.

Assessment Evaluation of spelling has two purposes: measuring growth and providing information concerning strengths and weaknesses. The work of students on frequent tests and on actual written work should be analyzed for errors and *types* of errors. Anderson and Lapp (1) categorize the common patterns of mistakes as follows:

1 Omissions
2 Transpositions
3 Repetitions
4 Misperceptions
5 Inappropriate use of phonetic generalizations

Grouping misspellings of students into these categories provides information concerning group and individual needs.

Pupils should be guided in the process of self-evaluation by teaching them to (1) proofread their written expressions and to make corrections, (2) correct their own spelling tests, and (3) maintain progress charts. Helping students to assume the responsibility for finding and correcting their own spelling errors is a major objective of an effective spelling program.

COMPOSITION

The National Council of Teachers of English (19) maintains that composition is "an important medium for self-expression, for communication, and for the discovery of meaning" and that "its need (has) increased rather than decreased."

Children learn to write by writing and, therefore, the language arts curriculum must provide short, frequent, and interesting experiences in composition. Writing is a process that needs to be taught in each classroom. The process includes the steps of prewriting, planning, drafting, getting responses to the draft, revising, editing, rewriting, and publishing. Each step in the process must be taught carefully and practiced thoroughly.

Composition has received far less than its share of instructional time in most elementary school classrooms. Educators and the public share a concern about deficiencies found in children's written communication. We have become aware that composition is a national priority and that the curriculum must reflect that priority.

Instructional Emphases   In the second and third grades, the goals of the composition program might be grouped into two categories: readiness and skill development. During the readiness or prewriting period, teachers should continue to plan experiences which broaden the background of the students, expand their vocabularies, improve their observation and listening skills, and provide opportunities for oral expression. Such activities are not limited to preschool and first grade; they must be considered an integral part of the writing program at all levels. During the skill development period, teachers should plan experiences to help students master cognitive and affective objectives.

Cognitive
- To express ideas in complete sentences
- To expand kernel sentences
- To use a logical sequence of events
- To recognize irrelevant words and sentences
- To use capital letters and punctuation marks as appropriate for the primary level
- To select fitting vocabulary
- To write short paragraphs
- To write friendly letters and address the envelopes

Some of these cognitive goals need to be subdivided into more specific objectives.

I Punctuation
  A Period
    1 At the end of a declarative sentence
    2 After abbreviations
    3 After numbers in a list
    4 After an initial
  B Question Mark
    1 At the end of an interrogative sentence
  C Comma
    1 To separate day and year
    2 To separate city from state
    3 To separate objects in a series
    4 After the salutation of a friendly letter
    5 After the closing of a letter
  D Apostrophe
    1 In contractions
    2 To show possession

    E Quotation marks
        1 Before and after direct quotations
II Capitalization
        1 Names of people
        2 First word in a sentence
        3 Days of week and months of year
        4 Streets, cities, and states
        5 Names of special buildings or places
        6 The pronoun *I*
        7 First word of a salutation and the closing of a letter
        8 Titles, such as Mr., Mrs., Miss, or Ms.
        9 Abbreviations
       10 First word in each line of most poems

A caution seems warranted at this time. The preceding skills dwell upon the "how" of composition, the mechanical components of writing. Of equal, if not greater importance, are the range and quality of ideas expressed in a child's writing.

Petty (21) suggests that the primary grades are not too early to introduce the importance of neatness and attractive appearance. The following points are appropriate:

1 Margin at top, bottom, left, and right of page
2 Even spacing between letters and words
3 Indentation of first word in paragraph
4 Centered title

DeHaven (7) notes several objectives in the affective domain.

Affective
   • To demonstrate pride in written work
   • To enjoy sharing written expressions
   • To appreciate the work of others
   • To prize writing as a means of communication and self-expression

Instructional Strategies   Effective written communication occurs only after two criteria have been met. First, the writers have experienced something they want to share; and second, they have acquired the necessary skills to write so that others can read with comprehension. These competencies, however, are not developed from the use of isolated drill on individual skills. Instead, they spring from the understanding of why certain organizational patterns, such as sentences and paragraphs, and why certain mechanical skills, such as capitalization and punctuation, are important. This understanding of the relationship between writing skills and meaningful communication is introduced informally before the students are able to write independently, and it is taught formally as the students grow in writing ability.

The sentence might be called the basic unit of writing. According to DeHaven (7), "to write well-formed sentences, children must develop a sentence sense" (p. 245). Reading to, and talking with, students helps them to "develop an ear for sentences"

(p. 246). Guided dictation in which teachers ask questions requiring responses in sentences helps students learn to organize their thoughts into single ideas. Much later, they will learn ways of joining these ideas through compounding, modifying, or subordinating. Alerting students to patterns in language is another way of building an understanding of sentences and how to write them. Use a sentence such as the following:

The boy sat on the log.

Ask the students, "Where else could he sit?" and record their answers.

The boy sat on the fence.
The boy sat on the chair.

In the primary grades, experiences in writing sentences should also include direct instruction in embedding kernel sentences (7). After the students have written single sentences describing an object, show them how these can be combined to make one sentence. When the two methods are read aloud for comparison, students can hear the more rhythmic flow of the embedded sentence.

The house is white.
The house has green shutters.
The house is old.

The old, white house has green shutters.

It is important to remember that creativity can be developed in this activity, for there is more than one correct way. Students will also need to learn to join simple sentences to form a compound sentence.

Creating paragraphs is the next step in writing instruction. Rubin (23) suggests that in the upper primary grades students should be able to recognize that (1) all the sentences in a paragraph are related to one main topic and (2) these sentences are arranged in a certain sequence. Students first learn to identify a paragraph visually by observing that the first word is indented. The next steps of classifying the ideas and selecting the main topic are much more complicated.

It is wise to consider the cognitive level of the seven- and eight-year-olds. Most of them are making the transition to the concrete operational stage and will need many experiences with classification before they can comprehend the organizational pattern of paragraphs. In addition to these classification experiences, teachers need to follow a planned sequence in paragraph writing. These activities should move from structured group dictation to guided individual dictation to a combination of group and individual dictation to group discussion with individual writing to independent writing. Children in the second and third grades may be found at each of these levels.

Another paragraph development instructional measure can occur as guided group activity. In this, the chalkboard is divided into three sections. For example, in the first section, the children would dictate two or three sentences which describe an animal. In another section of the board, two or three sentences are copied which tell where the animal lives. In the third section, sentences are written which tell what the animal eats. The class then develops the material on the chalkboard into three paragraphs. Of course, variations of this activity, with different objects and actions, may be employed by the teacher in order to diversify the writing experiences of the class.

If sentences and paragraphs are going to have meaning for the reader, the writer must have the skill to select the most fitting words. Primary teachers should be vocabulary fanatics! It is often the attitude of teachers that make word study either an exciting, adventurous challenge or a dull, routine exercise. In the second and third grades, students should be introduced to categories of words, such as "happy words," "words for sounds," or "color words." Activities should be provided in learning the use of synonyms. It is also necessary to teach the importance of connotation; upper primary students will enjoy this concept.

Word banks have been used successfully in building vocabulary. Collecting their own words is not only motivating to young students; it also provides hands-on experiences; instead of watching while others work at the board, they are able to manipulate their own words, words they have chosen. A rich, lasting vocabulary does not come from simple exposure to a second- or third-grade commercial word list. Rather, it grows with varied experiences using everyday words in new ways. One of the most effective—and most pleasurable—ways of developing a wide vocabulary is to read to students, selecting the best of children's literature. It must be remembered, however, that the establishment of listening and speaking vocabularies does not automatically ensure the transfer of these words to the writing vocabulary. Students need direct instruction and encouragement to use words creatively.

Carlson (5) offers five general categories of multisensory activities for building vocabulary. These are (1) the sharing and telling of stories, (2) experiences with feelings, (3) experiences with shapes, (4) experiences with movement and sound, and (5) experiences in seeing art and color.

It has been simplistically stated that "writing is talk written down." Writing, however, lacks clues to meaning such as those given through gestures, expressions, or intonation and pitch. Punctuation and, to some extent, capitalization attempt to bridge this gap. Comments made during the dictation phase of learning to write will introduce students to basic skills such as why a period marks the end of a statement and what signals this gives the reader. After students have been introduced to several of these rules, the class could make a chart, using their own words and examples. This chart might then be used in proofreading and self-evaluation. A study of student work will show individual and group strengths and weaknesses. This information should be used in planning to emphasize certain specific skills in future lessons.

For the teacher who may need varied activities which stimulate and develop the composition abilities of children, we would like to recommend Carlson's *Writing Aids through the Grades*. This book presents 186 developmental writing activities "in which the undeveloped, immature child author can, through the use of some practical, creative ideas, be helped in improving his writing skills" (5).

Problems   Providing adequate time for writing may be one of the most persistent problems encountered in planning the composition program. Time must be scheduled for building readiness for writing, for allowing the students the chance to reflect and organize their thoughts, and for the actual writing. If time for any of these is neglected, the experiences will not be as valuable.

During the actual composition period, students should be taught that the writing process has several components. First, the ideas are recorded. Next, this rough draft is revised and improvements are made. When the content is satisfactory, editing and proofreading take place. Conferences with other students and with the teacher can help during these stages. Finally, the students copy the revised material, using their best handwriting and a pleasing format. It is not sufficient merely to ask students to read over their work; guidance must be provided. A class-designed checklist provides a reminder of appropriate standards. Reading aloud often alerts students to the need for punctuation or a change in phrasing.

The classroom environment should be structured so that it provides both the physical atmosphere and the supportive attitude that enable students to develop effective writing skills. The room should contain areas for talking and areas for writing; materials should be accessible and varied. Displaying student work is one way of showing that writing is valued.

Some students are hesitant to express themselves in writing. These students may need guidance in deciding what to write about; they may also require help in mastering the basic writing skills. They may need extra stimulation and, perhaps, extra structure. Working on joint writing projects may furnish a feeling of security. Encouraging, but not requiring, students to share their writing may help some students feel more comfortable. Of course, participation in many successful writing experiences is the most effective way to develop students who enjoy writing and who write well.

Petty (21) summarizes possible causes of writing difficulties.

- Absence of structure and direct instruction
- Inadequate vocabulary development
- Lack of mastery of writing skills
- Too little actual writing practice
- Lack of background experiences
- Overemphasis on isolated drill
- Little exposure to literature

Some children may have difficulty in writing due to their experiential backgrounds. As a result, they may feel as though they have little about which to write. Spiegel (25) offers a remedy for these children and their teachers. She states: "Children who have never traveled beyond their neighborhood, who have never been in a barn and smelled the blend of hay and animals, who have never been jostled by noisy, impersonal crowds on city sidewalks, can begin the circuitous route toward expanding the worlds in their heads by reading."

Assessment   First-graders should have been taught to proofread their work, and this practice should be continued and expanded in the primary grades. Short checklists should be available to guide the students in this process. They will encourage self-correction and self-evaluation. Mechanics conferences can be effective at this point.

Children may need guidance in deciding what to write about.

There are a number of methods available for evaluation by teachers. Individual conferences can be scheduled so that students and teachers can work together, with teachers making suggestions, asking guiding questions, and commenting on improvement. A point should be made regarding teacher conferences with students. Discussion should focus not only on the mechanical aspects (for example, spelling, grammar) of a writing assignment, but also on the content of the assignment. Teachers should also write comments on student papers which indicate good points, thus calling attention to progress.

Evaluation of students' written work has been viewed as an impossible task because of the time involved in pointing out all errors on every paper. There are several solutions to this problem. (1) Evaluate the papers during the class. By displaying selected work on a screen, teachers can emphasize pertinent points and direct discussion toward needed corrections and alternative ways of writing the same thing. This is most beneficial if it occurs before the final draft, so that students have the opportunity to make changes. (2) Collect the writing of each student in individual folders and choose only a sample for evaluation. (3) Explain to students before they write that only a specific category of errors will be noted on that particular paper.

Petty (21) doubts that traditional standardized tests are valid measures of writing ability. Although they do sample students' knowledge of certain writing skills, they do not evaluate actual performance. It seems that any attempt to measure student writing ability should be based on securing a sample of the students' writing.

HANDWRITING

Observation of most elementary classrooms shows that there is less emphasis on handwriting instruction than was found in the past. This may be due to the belief that future demands for writing by hand will decline because of increased use and availability of mechanical devices. Or less stress on handwriting skills might be caused by the proliferation of subjects making up the curriculum, leaving less time for teaching handwriting. Not only is less time devoted to instruction, but there has been a shift in perspective. No longer is handwriting regarded as an art form (Norton, 1980); it is now solely a method of communication. No longer is handwriting considered an end unto itself; it is now considered a way of sharing. Its purpose is communication. In addition, as Kean (17) points out, writing style has become increasingly individualized.

Instructional Emphases During the second grade, the objectives relate to the refinement of manuscript skills. It is usually in the beginning or middle of the third grade that students begin the transition to cursive writing. Thus, the emphasis is on maintenance of manuscript skills and introduction of cursive skills.

Cognitive—Second Grade (Manuscript)
- To use a comfortable position for writing
- To space evenly between letters and words
- To use correct letter formation of all capital and lowercase letters
- To hold writing instrument correctly

Cognitive—Third Grade (Cursive)
- To maintain all manuscript skills
- To read cursive writing
- To use correct letter formation
- To join letters correctly
- To use consistent slant
- To use cursive in some or most writing assignments

Affective—Second and Third Grades
- To recognize the need for writing legibly
- To demonstrate pride in handwriting skill growth

Petty (21) notes that cursive writing should only be introduced when students reach three goals: writing manuscript from memory and with ease, reading material written in cursive, and exhibiting an interest in learning cursive writing.

Instructional Strategies It must be remembered that the purpose for mastering handwriting skills is to ensure effective communication between the writer and the reader. To emphasize this concept, it may be helpful to guide students in discussing the problem that might occur because of illegible writing.

Bring the cot.

Does this mean bring something to sleep on? Or does it mean to bring a pet? The activities in a handwriting program should (1) provide direct instruction in specific skills and (2) reinforce these skills with practice in purposeful tasks. This practice should be a natural outcome of regular classroom activities. The importance of legibility will become evident as children are involved in writing letters, making reading games, preparing reports, and sending invitations. In planning specific lessons, DeHaven (7) notes the following areas of concern.

Forming letters
Spacing
Using appropriate and consistent size
Using lines as guides
Slanting

Most programs begin the transition from manuscript to cursive in the third grade; however, the readiness of the students, rather than commercial program guidelines or a grade level, should determine the time for change. Third grade is generally an acceptable time because most children have not mastered manuscript writing before then. When students have reached this readiness level, practice in reading cursive writing should be provided before attempts are made to write it. Fisher and Terry (10) suggest writing brief announcements or directions in both manuscript and cursive. As a group activity, the entire class could make comparisons between the two forms of writing. As the class becomes more adept in reading cursive, the manuscript copy can be gradually omitted.

Once students are comfortable in reading cursive, direct instruction in writing should be initiated. Norton (20) recommends that stress be placed on pointing out similarities and differences in the two styles. Students might list some differences which they notice in cursive writing:

1 Joining the letters in a word
2 Positioning the paper to give a slant to the writing
3 Writing the entire word before crossing or dotting letters
4 Forming letters differently

It is helpful to begin instruction with cursive letters that are similar to manuscript letters. Next, emphasis should be given to those that are unalike. Practice should be integrated into the ordinary classroom activities. Creativity is required when extra practice is needed on specific areas. If students exhibit difficulties, plan a group lesson, using the overhead projector and samples of student writing. Guide the discussion to consideration of the problem area. After showing how improvement can be made, provide an exercise which requires practice in that particular skill.

During a normal day, students are required to write a wide variety of material: a thank-you letter to a classroom guest, first drafts of a paragraph, or a spelling test, for example. A helpful teacher will remind students to consider their purpose in writing. A letter and a test require careful attention to handwriting skills; a first draft does not—and should not.

One of the major goals of an elementary handwriting program should be to help students learn to write at a reasonable speed. Speed, however, should not be emphasized during the primary years. At this point, the stress should be placed on mastering the techniques.

Exercises in tracing letters are often found in commercial material. Research, however, indicates that tracing does not improve handwriting skills and may, in fact, create poor habits. Studies by Hirsch and Niedermeyer (13) and Askov (2) show that copying is a more effective method than tracing in developing handwriting skill.

Problems   The various commercial handwriting materials may differ in the formation of certain letters. A typical second or third grade will contain students who have learned slightly modified styles because of their use of other programs. Since school districts usually adopt a handwriting series for all elementary grades, teachers should help children to learn and use the adopted model.

Most teachers are right-handed and most children are right-handed. Instruction of children who are left-handed does require that attention be paid to several considerations.

1 Many left-handed students hook their hand so that they are writing upside-down. Petty (21) suggests that providing many early experiences in writing on the board may prevent this problem. Holding the pencil further from the point allows students to see as they write, and may help them not to develop this uncomfortable position.

2 Norton (20) suggests using pencils with harder lead. Harder lead does not smear as easily.

3 The writing slant for left-handers is different. They may write more legibly and comfortably if the paper is kept straighter.

A problem may arise concerning the time for introducing cursive writing. In many areas, this transition is dictated by the handwriting materials adopted by the schools rather than the readiness of the students. Most educators agree that the beginning to the middle of third grade is best.

Sometimes handwriting problems are created through the poor practice of using handwriting excercises for disciplinary purposes. As students race to complete their punishment, they may acquire poor writing habits and negative attitudes toward handwriting.

Most classrooms allow for several different handwriting models. These may include the adopted handwriting texts, a set of letter strips which is hung on the wall, the spelling texts, the basal reader, ditto sheets the teacher may use, and the teacher as she writes on the chalkboard, on charts, or on student papers. These models should be consistent. The teacher must be sure that she does not create confusion by providing different or conflicting models.

Assessment   From the beginning of handwriting instruction, students should be shown how to evaluate their own work. Some teachers encourage students to compare their writing with commercial samples of writing by second- and third-grade students. Others prefer to display a checklist which calls attention to specific points.

It is often helpful to keep individual files of students' work so that they can see the progress that is being made. These files also provide examples of handwriting that can be shared with parents.

Teachers find checklists useful in pinpointing strengths and weaknesses. A list of points of consideration can be composed by teachers or purchased through commercial companies. A class checklist makes it easy to group students according to specific needs. As noted earlier in this chapter, examples of such checklists are presented in Chapter 10.

SPEAKING

Traditionally, schools have emphasized the reading and writing aspects of the language arts. According to Kean and Personke (17), recent research indicates that oral language is the foundation upon which the other language arts rest. This recent emphasis on speaking may seem strange, for observation of a typical primary classroom provides obvious evidence that children do talk. The language arts program, however, focuses not on aimless chatter but on developing purposeful, appropriate, and effective skills of oral communication.

Hansen-Krening (12) maintains that our society views the spoken word with suspicion. She challenges schools to accept the responsibility of teaching students not only the skills of speaking, but also the skills of evaluating. If teachers help children gain a command of oral language, "we ensure that they will *use* language rather than be *used by* language." She contends that students who have had experiences in discussing, reporting, conversing, and other methods of oral communication will appreciate the skills involved and will use appropriate standards of evaluation. They will be able to evaluate the spoken word because of their personal experiences with oral language.

Instructional Emphases   One of the reasons for our seeming deficiencies in developing competent speakers may be the lack of sequential objectives. Teachers must establish suitable goals and share these goals with the students. In the second and third grades, continued emphasis is placed on participation, courteous behavior, and the building of confidence. A list containing more specific objectives for seven- and eight-year-olds may serve as a guide for primary teachers.

Cognitive
1 To extend speaking vocabulary
2 To speak in complete sentences
3 To converse informally
4 To discuss an event in their own words and in proper sequence
5 To eliminate extraneous information

6 To avoid distracting mannerisms, such as overuse of *and,* repetitions, or long pauses

7 To speak clearly, distinctly, and at a suitable rate

8 To use correct pronunciation

9 To select appropriate speech for the classroom

Affective

1 To engage in a variety of oral activities

2 To respect both listeners and speakers

3 To gain pleasure from sharing orally

4 To engage in self-evaluation

Later, more sophisticated skills related to using nonverbal techniques, establishing audience rapport, and utilizing a variety of oral presentations will receive attention.

Instructional Strategies   Instruction in any program of oral communication skills should be focused on (1) providing experiences, (2) planning opportunities for purposeful talk, and (3) encouraging students to participate. Each of these points merits discussion. If we want students to talk, we must give them something to talk about. This simple statement could, if accepted, inaugurate sweeping changes in the classroom. More first-hand experiences would be planned, with films, tapes, manipulatives, and, of course, books to complement these direct experiences. The teacher as lecturer would cease to be the major fountain of knowledge.

A wealth of activities exists for promoting oral language skills. Speaking activities, like other language arts exercises, foster listening, reading, and writing skills. They can, and should, be included throughout the planned curriculum. Every normal school day abounds with situations that can be turned into meaningful occasions for developing oral expression. The list shown below is not exclusive to the primary grades. Some items, such as experience stories, have been introduced at the preschool and first-grade levels and need to be reviewed and extended; others, such as the interview, may be emphasized more extensively in higher grades.

Experience stories	Choral reading
"Show and tell"	Informal conversations
Puppetry	Announcements
Creative dramatics	Directions
Telephone conversations	Role playing
Oral reading	Pantomine
Storytelling	Reporting
Discussions	Interviewing

Encouraging students to take part in a variety of activities involves structuring the social, emotional, and physical environment of the room. Rubin (23) reminds teachers of the importance of creating an environment in which students feel comfortable asking questions, sharing experiences, and volunteering to participate. It is necessary to recognize the importance of teachers' attitudes toward oral contributions of the children. Teachers must be willing to accept student responses and to relinquish their traditional place at classroom center stage. In fact, in a well-managed classroom, the teacher establishes an environment in which she remains in the background—much like the director of a plan.

Teachers should maintain attitudes of respect, acceptance, and support if students are to model their behaviors with their classmates after their teachers. The seating arrangement of the classroom is related to the "speaking atmosphere." A flexible arrangement which changes with the size of the group and the type of activity is more conducive to encouraging the participation of both speakers and listeners. With young children, the use of small groups seems to be particularly effective. The constituency of such groups should be varied so that children have the opportunity to interact with many and diverse individuals.

Problems   No matter which instructional strategies are being utilized, certain points related to learning the skills or oral communication must be considered.

1 As Petty (21) points out, teachers can learn about their students by listening to their voices and watching their mannerisms as they speak. Tension, insecurity, or aggressiveness may be reflected in oral expressions. Of course, the teaching of speaking will not solve all emotional problems, but as a part of the program and the evaluation of the students, certain changes may be made in the classroom environment which help children feel more confident and comfortable. Speaking before groups causes many people to feel anxious. In order to diminish this anxiety somewhat, children should be given the opportunity to speak in small-group situations. Several such experiences will help the children to gain confidence and skill in oral expression. By teaching the prerequisite skills, creating opportunities for role playing, and arranging for observations, teachers are able to help students gain confidence in themselves.

2 Adopting certain acceptable social behaviors is necessary for classroom harmony and students' growth. Waiting turns, listening respectively, using appropriate language, and considering the volume of the voice are all a vital part of a program in oral communication. Social courtesies, such as making introductions and talking on the telephone, are also important.

3 Helping students to develop an extensive speaking vocabulary should be a major aspect of teaching oral communication skills. This means teaching the pronunciation and use of unfamiliar words as well as introducing new meanings to known words. Presenting the concept of connotation and guiding students to note relationships among words should also receive attention at this time.

4 It has been stated that the students of the second and third grades are making a transition away from egocentric thinking. They continue, however, to need direction in developing and understanding their audience. Teachers need to encourage them to speak loudly and distinctly enough to be heard and to think about what the listeners want and need to know.

Assessment   According to Tiedt and Tiedt (27), "evaluation should be the responsibility of both student and teacher, and it should always be constructive in nature." Thus plans for evaluation of speaking skills should include evaluation by teacher and student, and should contain positive plans for growth.

DeHaven (7) suggests that it may be helpful for young students to listen to a variety of speakers and make a list of the reasons they like to listen to some more than others. This exercise could be developed by the class into a set of standards for good speakers.

Taping students provides a way for them to assess themselves, using the class-designed standards. This might provide an opportunity to encourage the setting of individual goals. After evaluating themselves, each student could select one area needing improvement. Since some students have difficulty identifying their *good* points, teachers should also encourage the listing of a positive comment.

It is essential to remember the importance of immediate feedback. Short notes from the teacher could provide reinforcement of good habits. Specific comments, such as "Susan, I liked the way you looked at the class" or "Fred, you remembered to talk so everyone could hear," help students learn how to evaluate themselves and emphasize the relevant skills.

DeHaven (7) suggests that it is better to utilize informal evaluation of oral expression rather than standardized tests. Informal assessment can be conducted in natural settings and during a variety of activities. In addition to this continuous observation, teachers may want to study students' language by asking them to tell a story using a wordless book or to retell a familiar story. A checklist of speaking skills could be used to record strengths and weaknesses.

READING APPLICATION

Instructional Emphases   With the emphasis on "the basics," some teachers and administrators believe that including a literature component in the language arts curriculum is an unjustifiable addition. Reasoner (22) challenges this attitude by maintaining that a literature program is complementary, not supplementary, at all levels and for all children. At first thought, it might seem that the only objective of a literature program is to provide pleasure. While it is true that enjoyment is a goal, there are other objectives of importance for primary grade students.

Cognitive
1 To recognize and identify well-known titles, authors, and characters of children's books
2 To respond to reading through oral or written expression, art, or music
3 To recognize different types of literature
4 To comprehend material through listening or reading
5 To recognize and use new vocabulary
6 To detect language patterns and unfamiliar ways of using words
7 To develop concepts about the environment

Affective
1 To demonstrate pleasure found in listening or reading
2 To select reading as a free-choice activity
3 To share voluntarily their responses to books

Instructional Strategies   To be effective, a literature program should rely on planned rather than incidental experiences. Each of the following aspects should be considered:

Providing the time
Selecting the materials
Studying the children
Involving the students
Encouraging a response

In the already overcrowded school day, it is difficult to find time for the activities involved in a literature program. It is important to remember, however, that most of these experiences can be integrated into the already existing routine. For example, selecting and reading could become an alternative to traditional seat work while the teacher works with other groups. Sharing activities can be incorporated into periods of art, music, writing, speaking, and listening. Too often reading time is given only to those who finish their assigned work or only if all other subjects are covered for the day. "You may read if you finish your work and can't find anything else to do" or "If we finish all our lessons today, I'll read to you." What attitudes do we foster with such statements and actions? Only when time for applying reading skills becomes an accepted part of the daily lesson plan will the schools develop students who value reading as a lifelong source of pleasure and information.

In selecting the materials for a literature program, it is necessary to choose the best of children's books. The need for careful selection becomes apparent when we consider how few books can be read to children or suggested to them while they are in the second and third grades. For recommendations, refer to Huck's *Children's Literature in the Elementary School* (14) or Sutherland's *Children and Books* (26). To keep up to date with new publications, refer to the reviews found in *The Hornbook, Language Arts,* or other professional periodicals. School librarians are sometimes an untapped source of information concerning what is new and what is currently popular with children. In choosing the books, remember to include a variety of types of library genre:

Picture books
Traditional literature
Modern fantasy
Poetry
Modern fiction
Historical fiction
Biography
Informational books

In addition to applying their skills to reading the best of children's literature, students also need to have access to other materials, such as:

Magazines
Catalogs
Newspapers
Content texts
Cookbooks
Handbooks
Travelogues
Pamphlets

One overlooked source is the written work of the students. Their best work should be bound and prominently displayed for sharing.

Not only must teachers study the materials involved in a literature program, but they must also focus their attention on the children. During this transition stage, the children's thinking is becoming more flexible, they understand shifts in time and setting, and they are more accepting of the point of view of others. These changes in thinking enable them to appreciate and comprehend new types of literature. In addition to the traditional folktales, realistic fiction, and poetry enjoyed in the preschool and first grade, they will now enjoy simple biographies, historical fiction, and stories about situations outside their daily experiences. Their favorite books involve humor, fantasy, animal and nature stories, and other children. This information is helpful in choosing materials for the book center or for oral reading, but in order to recommend books to particular students, it is essential to study each child's interest. Children's interests may be discerned through use of a paper-and-pencil device such as an interest inventory and/or through a teacher's interactions with the children.

It is not enough to provide time and materials; plans must be made for bringing the students and books together. Reading aloud to the children and employing motivational activities are two approaches. A teacher of ours once remarked: "A reader is a person who was read to as a child." This thought continues to be relevant. Reading aloud should be a part of each day in the primary grades. The books should be chosen with care, practiced, introduced, read with enthusiasm, and followed up by a guided discussion or related activity.

A variety of techniques that introduce good literature to children can be organized. These activities are ways of helping books say, "Will you read me?" and encouraging children to say yes.

1 Begin a book club for sharing responses.
2 Invite special people to tell about their favorite books.
3 Design displays of books by favorite authors, books about a current topic of interest, or award-winning books.
4 Use filmstrips, films, or tapes of stories or excerpts of books.
5 Encourage parents to help the children begin a personal collection of favorites.
6 Plan special activities for National Book Week.
7 Tease the students by reading only the first paragraph of several books and making them available for reading.
8 Let students see you as you enjoy a children's book.

9 Suggest specific titles to individuals.

10 Organize contests to select "Our Book of the Month."

11 Plan regularly scheduled times for children to share their responses to their own reading.

12 Use books as a springboard to writing activities.

It has been suggested that children choose books with familiar titles or authors. If this is true, it is clear that teachers need to plan many get-acquainted experiences.

A literature program should provide opportunities for responding to books. According to Huck (14, p. 645), "to act upon the book is to know it, to make it a more memorable experience." When these responses are shared, they frequently encourage the audience to read the book. These suggestions offer ideas for responding through written or oral expression and through art or music.

1 Compose a riddle about the characters in the book.

2 Use examples of patterned language as models for original writing.

3 Make up games using words from the book.

4 Draw a map of the setting.

5 Design dioramas or shadow boxes of important sections.

6 Make puppets of the characters and dramatize a scene.

7 Construct a mobile based on important events.

8 Write rebus recipes and work with the teacher to plan cooking activities. Many books feature a food as a major part of the story.

9 Construct a homemade movie on long strips of paper.

10 Make a class quilt with the squares drawn to advertise favorite books.

11 Write letters to outstanding authors.

Problems   There are some contemporary issues in children's literature that teachers need to consider as they work with children and books. Teachers should study current information on these topics and anticipate problems in books on the level of their students. The librarian is an invaluable aid in these areas.

Examples of sexual, racial, and cultural stereotyping have been found in many children's books. Care should be taken that books for second- and third-grade students show males and females in a variety of roles and situations. All races should be portrayed in a positive manner.

Recent years have seen an increase in books for children which portray death. It is felt that literature can be a means of helping students learn about this part of life. It may be more appropriate to introduce books containing episodes about the death of animals before emphasizing those about the death of people. It is often comforting to children to learn that their classmates have similar questions and fears about the topic.

Given the rather high incidence of family separation and divorce in our society, several children's books have focused upon these topics. If handled in a judicious manner, literature experiences with these subjects and appropriate discussion of them can be beneficial to young children.

Some educators have advocated the use of books to help children understand certain personal problems. The employment of books in such a way is termed bibliotherapy. Among the topics of these books may be divorce, death, physical handicaps, moving to a new location, and family relationships. Many bibliographies of books having bibliotherapy value are currently available. We would especially recommend the fifth edition of the *Reading Ladders for Human Relations,* published by the American Council on Education.

Censorship is of concern even with books on a primary level. It has been suggested that every children's book has been controversial in some place at some time. Teachers must study both books and children before making selections for oral reading or recommendations for independent reading.

Assessment   Evaluation of progress in applying reading skills involves more than counting the number of books each student reads or giving them tests on comprehension. Periodically, teachers need to ask themselves questions about the reading habits of each of the children in the classroom. DeHaven (7) and Petty (21) suggest some of the following examples:

1 Are the students reading materials beyond what is assigned?
2 Do they select reading as a free-choice activity?
3 Do they respond to their reading through a variety of ways?
4 Are they reading a balanced diet of different types of books?
5 Do they want to share their books and responses?
6 Do they relate situations in books to those in their own life?
7 Do they select books related to content area topics?

The teacher needs to evaluate not only a student's behavior, but also his or her own attitudes and actions. The teacher should ask himself or herself the following six questions:

1 Do I enjoy reading?
2 Do my students know that I enjoy it?
3 Do I demonstrate the value I place on reading by providing a scheduled time each day for oral reading and independent, free reading?
4 Do I know children's books?
5 Do I study my children?
6 Do I plan the literature program as carefully as the "basic" areas of math and spelling?

Remember that the basis of a successful literature program lies in the ability of teachers to share their enthusiasm and appreciation of reading.

BIBLIOGRAPHY AND REFERENCES

1 Anderson, P. S., and Lapp, D. *Language Skills in Elementary Education* (3d ed.). New York: Macmillan, 1979.
2 Askov, E. N. "Handwriting: Copying versus Tracing as the Most Effective Type of Practice." *The Journal of Educational Research,* 1975, *69,* pp. 96–98.
3 Biehler, R. F. *Child Development: An Introduction.* Boston: Houghton Mifflin, 1976.
4 Biehler, R. F. *Psychology Applied to Reading* (3d ed.). Boston: Houghton Mifflin, 1978.
5 Carlson, Ruth Kearney. *Writing Aids through the Grades.* New York: Teachers College Press, Columbia University, 1970, p. viii.
6 *Cooperative Primary Test.* Princeton, N.J.: Educational Testing Service, 1967.
7 DeHaven, E. P. *Teaching and Learning the Language Arts.* Boston: Little, Brown and Company, 1979.
8 Durrell, Donald. *Durrell Listening–Reading Series.* New York: Harcourt Brace Jovanovich, 1969.
9 Erikson, E. H. *Childhood and Society* (2d ed.). New York: Norton, 1963.
10 Fisher, C. J., and Terry, C. A. *Children's Language and Language Arts.* New York: McGraw-Hill, 1977, pp. 129, 267–270.
11 Hamby, J. V. "Piaget's Theory of Cognitive Development." An unpublished paper, 1976.
12 Hanson-Krening, N. *Competency and Creativity in Language Arts: A Multiethnic Focus.* Reading, Mass.: Addison-Wesley, 1979, p. 90.
13 Hirsch, E., and Niedermeyer, F. C. "The Effect of Tracing Prompts and Discrimination Training on Kindergarten Handwriting Performance." *The Journal of Educational Research,* 1973, *67,* pp. 81–86.
14 Huck, C. S. *Children's Literature in the Elementary School* (3d ed.). New York: Holt, Rinehart and Winston, 1976.
15 Kagan, J. *Developmental Studies of Reflection and Analysis.* Cambridge, Mass.: Harvard University Press, 1964.
16 Kagan, J., and Moss, H. A. *Birth to Maturity: A Study in Psychological Development.* New York: Wiley, 1962, p. 272.
17 Kean, J. M., and Personke, C. *The Language Arts: Teaching and Learning in the Elementary School.* New York: St. Martin's Press, 1976.
18 Kellogg, Ralph E. *A Study of the Effect of a First Grade Listening Instructional Program upon Achievement in Listening and Reading.* Report No. BR-6-8469. San Diego, Calif.: San Diego County Department of Education.
19 National Council of Teachers of English Commission on Composition. "Composition: A Position Statement." *Elementary English,* 1975, *52,* pp. 194–197.
20 Norton, D. E. *The Effective Teaching of Language Arts.* Columbus, Ohio: Charles Merrill, 1980.
21 Petty, W. T., Petty D. C., and Becking, M. E. *Experiences in Language* (3d ed.). Boston: Allyn and Bacon, 1981.
22 Reasoner, C. F. *Releasing Children to Literature,* New York: Dell, 1968.
23 Rubin, D. *Teaching Elementary Language Arts* (2d ed.). New York: Holt, Rinehart and Winston, 1980.
24 Smith, J. A. *Creative Teaching of the Language Arts in the Elementary School* (2d ed.). Boston: Allyn and Bacon, 1973.
25 Spiegel, Dixie Lee. *Reading for Pleasure: Guidelines.* Newark, Del.: International Reading Association, 1981, p. 11.

26 Sutherland, Z., and Arbuthnot, M. H. *Children and Books* (5th ed.). Glenview, Ill.: Scott, Foresman, 1977.

27 Tiedt, I. M., and Tiedt, S. W. *Contemporary English in the Elementary School* (2d ed.). Englewood Cliffs, N.J.: Prentice-Hall, 1975, p. 281.

28 Wilt, M. "A Study of Teacher Awareness of Listening as a Factor in Elementary Education." *Journal of Educational Research,* 1950, *42,* pp. 626–636.

CHAPTER 5

CLASSROOM APPLICATIONS IN GRADES TWO AND THREE

The process which was used in Chapter 3 will be repeated in this chapter. We will present descriptors for two teachers—a second-grade and a third-grade teacher. Once again you will be asked to read each descriptor and then to indicate on a separate sheet of paper the practices of the two teachers which suggest the effective teaching of the language arts at these grade levels.

The second copy of the descriptor, with sentences or phrases italicized, indicates some of the effective practices we would like to call to your attention. The explanation section offers the reasons we thought the practices were exemplary. You may want to compare your analysis with ours and with others who have read this book.

NANCY WATSON

Descriptor

Nancy is an attractive teacher with a soft voice and a very warm smile. This is the third year she has taught second grade and she enjoys her work immensely. Her undergraduate degree is in early childhood education and she says she learned a great deal in college which she has been able to put into practice in her classroom.

Nancy teaches in a school district which is largely rural, and her school is located in a very small town. Most parents are employed in one of two small manufacturing plants or they commute to work. In the school district as a whole, there is a nonwhite population of 38 percent; in Nancy's school 53 percent of the students are black.

Nancy's class is one of the four second-grade groups in her school. There are twenty-three children in her class—ten girls and thirteen boys. The socioeconomic status of the parents varies considerably; about a third of the parents have college degrees while several of them have not completed high school. Twelve of the children in the class are eligible for, and receive, free lunches, an indication that their families' incomes are low enough to meet federal guidelines for participation in this program. The range of intellectual abilities within the group is wide. Although a majority of the children have test scores which place them in the average range, several children have very high abilities which may eventually qualify them for a gifted and talented program. At the other extreme, there are two children who have low achievement levels and are seen by a remedial reading teacher.

The children think of school as a pleasant place. Most of them have positive attitudes toward themselves and toward school. Nancy says: "I don't have to do much motivating—the kids come to school with smiling faces, eager to learn." She says the parents have high expectations of the children just as she does. She speaks of the cooperation she receives from the parents. "When we ask for parents to volunteer to help on a project or to go with us on a field trip, they are more than willing to help."

Nancy also is pleased with the children's positive attitude toward reading. She says: "They love to read books. In fact I can't keep enough books on my shelves. They finish one book and they're ready to get another. I have to go back to the library and get more. The librarian also has trouble keeping them from checking out more than two books at a time. They love to read!"

Nancy's classroom is a pleasant place although it certainly is neither new nor modern. The school was built in 1881 and was originally a college for women. Her classroom is the old kitchen of the college (she is proud of the fact that the original wooden cabinets are still in use as storage area). The walls are decorated with the children's artwork. Strings hanging from the ceiling have examples of the students' art, their writing, and verses of poetry they have copied attached to them.

The informal room arrangement gives children optimum freedom of movement and a feeling of space in which to work. There is a small formal instructional area for the teacher to use as she works with individuals or small groups. There are tables which can accommodate groups of four children, and there are small, movable desks which can be used by children working alone or which can be moved so students can work together. There is a book corner partitioned off with bookcases which contain a wealth of children's trade books. Nancy carpeted this herself with carpet remnants which were given to her, and she has pillows on the floor so children can be comfortable as they sit or lie on the floor to read. There is a sink in one corner of the room and next to it is the art center, where children can work on art projects. The room contains a listening–visual center which has several tape recorders with earphones, cassette tapes, a filmstrip projector, and filmstrips. It also has a writing station which has a typewriter, some handwriting books, paper, pencils, pens, a dictionary, some telephone books, and a bulletin board to display children's finished manuscripts.

Nancy's desk is in the back of the room. She says, "I'd like to get rid of it—I use it to store things. I'm a person who is all over the room. I seem to be always walking around, observing, trying to help. I try to be there when I'm needed and I try to retreat to the background when I'm not. At any rate, I never seem to find time to sit at my desk."

The informal room arrangement coupled with a facilitative teacher provides an environment in which children can learn. However, Nancy knows that without good classroom management this learning may not take place. Early in the school year, she and the children discuss and formulate rules for behavior. The children dictate these rules to Nancy who records them on charts which are posted to be read, understood, and acted upon. Learning centers are introduced slowly so children can understand what is expected of them. For example, the listening center contains tape recorders, cassettes, and blank tapes. Children are taught how to use this equipment, how to record, how to label their tapes—all the details which make it possible for groups of children to work together and separately in an orderly way. Each center is introduced in a similar manner.

Nancy believes that children learn oral communication by talking informally, but she also knows that sometimes children need a quiet environment in which to work. Therefore, from the beginning of their relationship, the children and their teacher agree on rules of behavior which will facilitate learning.

Every morning, the block of time between 8:30 and noon is devoted to language arts. The basal textbook series is a total language arts system which integrates speaking, listening, and writing with the teaching of reading. With the exception of handwriting, all skills are integrated into the reading program; there is no separate spelling book, no language book, and no separate period of the day devoted to these skills.

Initially the children were assigned to Nancy's class by the principal, who placed all the second-grade children in one of four classes based on criterion-referenced test scores from the first-grade language arts program and the results of norm-referenced reading achievements tests. The stratified cluster grouping used in this school is meant to ensure that each class has a range of achievement levels but somewhat narrower than it would be if children were randomly assigned to classes.

Of the twenty-three children in Nancy's class, twenty-one are in two formal reading groups (two of the children have reading with a special reading teacher but participate in the informal language arts learning with the entire class). Ten of the children (the Panthers) are reading in a third-grade basal reader, while eleven of them (the Tigers) are reading on grade level. Nancy follows the teachers' manuals, which she supplements with activities and ideas of her own. While she works with one group, the other group is doing language arts–related work either at their seats or at the listening, writing, or reading centers.

Nancy knows that even though children are carefully diagnosed before they are placed in reading groups, there are still ranges of achievement within each group. She makes provisions for differences in skill development through use of pretests and posttests. If children have mastered a particular skill, she does not ask them to drill on it. On the other hand, if children need more time to learn, she provides reinforcement for them. Nancy helps the children extend their reading from the basals into trade books. Children can select a book from the book corner (she changes her book collection frequently) or from the library. Children go to the library either individually or in small groups during the library "open" time each morning between 8:30 and 10:30.

Nancy believes she can best meet the varied reading needs and interests of her students through a horizontal rather than a vertical approach. She explains: "David has the ability to read anything he wants to read and he's gone through all the textbook materials through third grade. Some of the concepts in a fourth-grade book are not appropriate or not interesting to a second-grader. So instead of moving to a higher reading group, he does a lot of reading and a lot of writing on his own, and I think that is a better way for him to grow. . . ."

While membership in the two reading groups remains fairly constant, other kinds of grouping are also used. Nancy gives an example of a special-interest group:

> Several children became interested in space exploration after watching the launching of the space shuttle on television. They were filled with questions. We talked. How could they find answers to their questions? The outcome was that some children went to the library, some read newspapers, some interviewed adults, and, by the time they reported back to the class, they not only had a great deal of information, they had read, listened, talked, written— they had had good language arts experiences.

Sometimes Nancy doesn't wait for special-interest groups to form. She uses teacher-assigned groups. These work in very much the same way except the teacher assigns a topic or topics and through a brainstorming process gets the children to become enthusiastic researchers.

Nancy reads to the children at least twice a day. At the beginning of each week she plans what books and poems she will share with the children during the week. Some weeks she will focus on a particular topic, with poetry as extensions of the stories. At other times she will spotlight a particular author or poet.

A favorite poem was *The Unicorn* by Shel Silverstein. The children delighted in hearing it read until many of them had memorized it. They gathered pictures of unicorns, fashioned them out of clay, wrote a group story about a unicorn, and had a class discussion about the mythical animal.

A favorite story was *Five Chinese Brothers* by Clare Bishop. As an extension of it, the children acted it out, first with shadow puppets and ultimately with a pantomime they felt was so good they invited the parents to see it. The children not only listen to stories Nancy reads but they also read to one another. Children record stories for the listening center; these as well as professionally prepared listening tapes and tapes recorded by volunteers are valued by the children.

Nancy encourages children to develop their oral communication skills in a number of ways. She provides opportunities for two or more children to work together so they will practice expressing themselves. "Show and tell" provides an informal means for oral language development. Walking in the hall or sitting together during lunch gives the children additional practice. Nancy interacts with the children and is a good speech model for them. If a child uses an immature speech pattern or a divergent element of his or her own dialect, Nancy does not embarrass the child or tell the child he or she is wrong. She explains: "If a child says 'I seed a helicopter on the way to school,' I say 'Really, you saw a helicopter on the way to school?' and then I continue talking to the child about it."

The children have many opportunities for written expression. The writing center provides story starters for one or two children to work on individually or together. At other times, the entire class may write a group story or, after a brainstorming session, may write individual stories on the same topic. Sometimes the children make their own books. Nancy is especially proud of a book about rockets which one of the children made. After writing the story, the child designed the book in the shape of a rocket. Another writing activity which is enjoyed is a "chain story." Nancy shows the children a picture and tells them only a little about it. The children finish the story, using their own imaginations. Then they share their versions with one another. No matter what the nature of the writing activity, the students are taught to proofread their work, to edit, and to revise until the finished product is something they are proud of having written.

Nancy believes in giving the children positive feedback on their work. Her speech is punctuated with phrases such as "Much better," "You must have been practicing," and "That's coming along nicely." At least every two weeks, she sees to it that the children take home all their papers. Many of them have a "smiling face" on them. She writes notes to parents telling them interesting things the children have done; she sees no need to write about anything negative. If a child is experiencing difficulties she calls the parent or parents so they can have an informal parent–teacher conference.

Report cards are sent home with one grade given for language arts and comments from the teacher explaining the grade. Nancy evaluates the children in terms of the progress they have made as demonstrated by criterion-referenced tests (from the basal language arts program) and from her own observation.

The principal and teachers in the entire school use criterion-referenced tests, standardized tests, and observations to determine if state and school district objectives have been met. Last year, all the children in this school scored above the 50th percentile in reading achievement, a score which is quite a bit higher than many other schools with similar populations. The principal attributes this to the heavy emphasis Nancy and her colleagues put on language arts and children's literature.

Nancy is interested in improving her teaching. On one occasion, she taped a discussion between her students and herself. She thought it would be good for the children to use as a listening activity, but she found when she listened to the tape that it helped her evaluate her interactions with the children. She liked the fact that her voice was soft and pleasant; she was critical of herself for talking too much. From then on, she really tried to limit her input into the discussions.

Her principal regularly observes her teaching and gives her a written evaluation of her performance. Nancy is not threatened by this, nor is she defensive. She is aware that she and the principal are on the same instructional team and she finds constructive criticism helps her to improve her teaching. Sometimes the principal will teach her class to make possible her observation of other teachers. This not only gives her new ideas but also helps her gain insights into good teaching practices.

Analysis

Nancy is an attractive teacher with a soft voice and a very warm smile. This is the third year she has taught second grade and she enjoys her work immensely. Her undergraduate degree is in early childhood education and she says she learned a lot in college which she has been able to put into practice in her classroom.

Nancy teaches in a school district which is largely rural, and her school is located in a very small town. Most parents are employed in one of two small manufacturing plants or they commute to work. In the school district as a whole, there is a nonwhite population of 38 percent; in Nancy's school 53 percent of the students are black.

Nancy's class is one of the four second-grade groups in her school. There are twenty-three children in her class—ten girls and thirteen boys. The socioeconomic status of the parents varies considerably; about a third of the parents have college degrees while several of them have not completed high school. Twelve of the children in the class are eligible for, and receive, free lunches, an indication that their families' incomes are low enough to meet federal guidelines for participation in this program. The range of intellectual abilities within the group is wide. Although a majority of the children have test scores which place them in the average range, several children have very high abilities which may eventually qualify them for a gifted and talented program. At the other extreme, there are two children who have low achievement levels and are seen by a remedial reading teacher.

The children think of school as a pleasant place. Most of them have positive attitudes toward themselves and toward school. Nancy says: "I don't have to do much motivating—the kids come to school with smiling faces, eager to learn." She says *the parents have high expectations of the children just as she does*.[1] She speaks of the cooperation she receives from the parents. "When we ask for parents to volunteer to help on a project or to go with us on a field trip, they are more than willing to help."

Nancy also is pleased with the children's positive attitude toward reading. She says: "They love to read books. In fact *I can't keep enough books on my shelves*.[2] They finish one book and they're ready to get another. I have to go back to the library and get more. The librarian also has trouble keeping them from checking out more than two books at a time. They love to read!"

Nancy's classroom is a pleasant place although it certainly is neither new nor modern. The school was built in 1881 and was originally a college for women. Her classroom is the old kitchen of the college (she is proud of the fact that the original wooden cabinets are still in use as storage area). The walls are decorated with the children's artwork. Strings hanging from the ceiling have examples of the students' art, their writing, and verses of poetry they have copied attached to them.

The informal room arrangement gives children optimum freedom of movement and a feeling of space in which to work.[3] There is a small formal instructional area for the teacher to use as she works with individuals or small groups. There are tables which can accommodate groups of four children, and there are small, movable desks which can be used by children working alone or which can be moved so students can work together. There is a book corner partitioned off with bookcases which contain a wealth of children's trade books. Nancy carpeted this herself with carpet remnants which were given to her and she has pillows on the floor so children can be comfortable as they sit or lie on the floor to read. There is a sink in one corner of the room and next to it is the art center, where children can work on art projects. The room contains a listening–visual center which has several tape recorders with earphones, cassette tapes, a filmstrip projector, and filmstrips. It also has a writing station which has a typewriter, some handwriting books, paper, pencils, pens, a dictionary, some telephone books, and a bulletin board to display children's finished manuscripts.

Nancy's desk is in the back of the room. She says, "I'd like to get rid of it—I use it to store things. I'm a person who is all over the room. I seem to be always walking around, observing, trying to help. I try to be there when I'm needed and I try to retreat to the background when I'm not. At any rate, I never seem to find time to sit at my desk."

The informal room arrangement coupled with a facilitative teacher provides an environment in which children can learn. However, Nancy knows that *without good classroom management this learning may not take place.*[4] Early in the school year, she and the children discuss and formulate rules for behavior. The children dictate these rules to Nancy who records them on charts which are posted to be read, understood, and acted upon. Learning centers are introduced slowly so children can understand what is expected of them. For example, the listening center contains tape recorders, cassettes, and blank tapes. Children are taught how to use this equipment, how to record, how to label their tapes—all the details which make it possible for groups of children to work together and separately in an orderly way. Each center is introduced in a similar manner.

Nancy believes that children learn oral communication by talking informally, but she also knows that sometimes children need a quiet environment in which to work. Therefore, from the beginning of their relationship, the children and their teacher agree on rules of behavior which will facilitate learning.

Every morning, the block of time between 8:30 and noon is devoted to language arts. The basal textbook series is a total language arts system which integrates speaking, listening, and writing with the teaching of reading. With the exception of handwriting, all skills are integrated into the reading program; there is no separate spelling book, no language book, and no separate period of the day devoted to these skills.

Initially the children were assigned to Nancy's class by the principal, who placed all the second-grade children in one of four classes based on criterion-referenced test scores from the first-grade language arts program and the results of norm-referenced reading achievements tests. The stratified cluster grouping used in this school is meant to ensure that each class has a range of achievement levels but somewhat narrower than it would be if children were randomly assigned to classes.

Of the twenty-three children in Nancy's class, twenty-one are in two formal reading groups (two of the children have reading with a special reading teacher but participate in the informal language arts learning with the entire class). Ten of the children (the Panthers) are reading in a third-grade basal reader, while eleven of them (the Tigers) are reading on grade level. Nancy follows the teachers' manuals, which she supplements with activities and ideas of her own. While she works with one group, the other group is doing language arts–related work either at their seats or at the listening, writing, or reading centers.

Nancy knows that even though children are carefully diagnosed before they are placed in reading groups, there are still ranges of achievement within each group. She makes provisions for differences in skill development through use of pretests and posttests. If children have mastered a particular skill, she does not ask them to drill on it. On the other hand, if children need more time to learn, she provides reinforcement for them. Nancy helps the children extend their reading from the basals into trade books. Children can select a book from the book corner (she changes her book collection frequently) or from the library. *Children go to the library*[5] either individually or in small groups during the library "open" time each morning between 8:30 and 10:30.

Nancy believes she can best meet the varied reading needs and interests of her students through a horizontal rather than a vertical approach.[6] She explains: "David has the ability to read anything he wants to read and he's gone through all the textbook materials through third grade. Some of the concepts in a fourth-grade book are not appropriate or not interesting to a second-grader. So instead of moving to a higher reading group, he does a lot of reading and a lot of writing on his own, and I think that is a better way for him to grow. . . . "

While membership in the two reading groups remains fairly constant, *other kinds of grouping are also used.*[7] Nancy gives an example of a special-interest group:

> Several children became interested in space exploration after watching the launching of the space shuttle on television. They were filled with questions. We talked. How could they find answers to their questions? The outcome was that some children went to the library, some read newspapers, some interviewed adults, and, by the time they reported back to the class, they not only had a great deal of information, they had read, listened, talked, written— they had had good language arts experiences.

Sometimes Nancy doesn't wait for special-interest groups to form. She uses teacher-assigned groups. These work in very much the same way except the teacher assigns a topic or topics and through a brainstorming process gets the children to become enthusiastic researchers.

Nancy reads to the children at least twice a day. *At the beginning of each week she plans what books and poems she will share with the children during the week.*[8] Some weeks she will focus on a particular topic, with poetry as extensions of the stories. At other times she will spotlight a particular author or poet.

A favorite poem was *The Unicorn* by Shel Silverstein. The children delighted in hearing it read until many of them had memorized it. They gathered pictures of unicorns, fashioned them out of clay, wrote a group story about a unicorn, and had a class discussion about the mythical animal.

A favorite story was *Five Chinese Brothers* by Clare Bishop. *As an extension of it, the children acted it out, first with shadow puppets and ultimately with a pantomime*[9] they felt was so good they invited the parents to see it. The children not only listen to stories Nancy reads but they also read to one another. Children record stories for the listening center; these as well as professionally prepared listening tapes and tapes recorded by volunteers are valued by the children.

Nancy encourages children to develop their oral communication skills in a number of ways. She provides opportunities for two or more children to work together so they will practice expressing themselves. "Show and tell" provides an informal means for oral language development. Walking in the hall or sitting together during lunch gives the children additional practice. Nancy interacts with the children and is a good speech

Children sometimes act out stories they have read.

model for them. If a child uses an immature speech pattern or a divergent element of his or her own dialect, Nancy does not embarrass the child or tell the child he or she is wrong. She explains: "If a child says 'I seed a helicopter on the way to school,' I say 'Really, you saw a helicopter on the way to school?' and then I continue talking to the child about it."

The children have many opportunities for written expression.[10] The writing center provides story starters for one or two children to work on individually or together. At other times, the entire class may write a group story or, after a brainstorming session, may write individual stories on the same topic. Sometimes the children make their own books. Nancy is especially proud of a book about rockets one of the children made. After writing the story, the child designed the book in the shape of a rocket. Another writing activity which is enjoyed is a "chain story." Nancy shows the children a picture and tells them only a little about it. The children finish the story, using their own imaginations. Then they share their versions with one another. No matter what the nature of the writing activity, the students are taught to proofread their work, to edit, and to revise until the finished product is something they are proud of having written.

Nancy believes in giving the children positive feedback on their work. Her speech is punctuated with phrases such as "Much better," "You must have been practicing," and "That's coming along nicely." At least every two weeks, she sees to it that the children take home all their papers. Many of them have a "smiling face" on them. She writes notes to parents telling them interesting things the children have done; she sees no need to write about anything negative. If a child is experiencing difficulties she calls the parent or parents so they can have an informal parent–teacher conference.

Report cards are sent home with one grade given for language arts and comments from the teacher explaining the grade. *Nancy evaluates the children in terms of the progress they have made as demonstrated by criterion-referenced tests* (from the basal language arts program) *and from her own observation.*[11]

The principal and teachers in the entire school use criterion-referenced tests, standardized tests, and observations to determine if state and school district objectives have been met. Last year, all the children in this school scored above the 50th percentile in reading achievement, a score which is quite a bit higher than many other schools with similar populations. The principal attributes this to the heavy emphasis Nancy and her colleagues put on language arts and children's literature.

Nancy is interested in improving her teaching.[12] On one occasion, she taped a discussion between her students and herself. She thought it would be good for the children to use as a listening activity, but she found when she listened to the tape that it helped her evaluate her interactions with the children. She liked the fact that her voice was soft and pleasant; she was critical of herself for talking too much. From then on, she really tried to limit her input into the discussions.

Her principal regularly observes her teaching and gives her a written evaluation of her performance. Nancy is not threatened by this, nor is she defensive. She is aware that she and the principal are on the same instructional team and she finds constructive criticism helps her to improve her teaching. Sometimes the principal will teach her class to make possible her observation of other teachers. This not only gives her new ideas but also helps her gain insights into good teaching practices.

Explanation

1 Teachers must perceive students as people who are capable of learning and who are eager to know about life and the world in which they live. In *Pygmalion in the Classroom,* Rosenthal and Jacobson (20) introduced the idea that teachers' expectations are so powerful that they can cause a self-fulfilling prophecy to take place. Children often seem to live up to others' expectations. Teachers must base their expectations of students' behavior on accurate perceptions of children's abilities rather than on rigid stereotypes (such as that girls are better readers than boys or black children are slower than other children). Teachers who make judgments based on stereotypical thinking may treat children in a manner which causes them to dislike school (7). Ultimately, this teacher attitude may exert a negative effect on children's school performance.

2 If children are to become readers, they must have opportunities to read the best from the wealth of books published for children. There are over 40,000 children's books in print, but it is possible for a child to read widely without ever reading a significant book. Even if children read a great deal, they may read relatively few of the books appropriate to their reading interests. Huck (14) states it well:

> Assuming that a child reads one book every two weeks from the time he is 7 (when he may begin to read independently) until he is 13 or 14 (when he starts reading adult books), he will read about twenty-five books a year, or some 200 books during this period of childhood.

She suggests that a classroom library include a minimum of ten books per child. These books should be from a large variety of genre and should represent a wide range of interests and reading abilities.

Using Huck's formula, Nancy (and most teachers) would need 230 or more books at any one time. Choosing the right books for a particular child can be a formidable task. Classroom teachers find the following books and periodicals helpful in selecting appropriate books for their classes.

Huck, Charlotte S. *Children's Literature in the Elementary School.*
Zena Sutherland and May Hill Arbuthnot, *Children and Books.*
School Library Journal, published monthly during the school year, by R. R. Bowker Company, P. O. Box 67, Whitinsville, Maine 01588. $13.00 per year.
The Horn Book, published six times a year, 31 St. James Avenue, Boston, Massachusetts 02116. $12.00 per year.
Booklist, published twice a month by the American Library Association, 50 East Haron Street, Chicago, Illinois 60611. $28.00 per year.
The Bulletin of the Center of Children's Books, published monthly except August from the University of Chicago Press, 5801 Ellis Avenue, Chicago, Illinois 60637. $10.00 per year.
The WEB (Wonderfully Exciting Books) edited by Charlotte S. Huck and Janet Hickman. Published quarterly by The Ohio State University, Room 200, Ramseyer Hall, 20 West Woodruff, Columbus, Ohio 43210. $4.00 per year.

The school librarian is a good resource person who can provide assistance to teachers in book selection. Many teachers find workshops, inservice presentations, and university courses in children's literature and language arts helpful to them in their efforts to keep their knowledge current in a constantly expanding field.

3 Nancy's informal room arrangement provides a learning environment which is in agreement with the underlying philosophy of this book (Belief 5, Chapter 1). Children practice communication skills as they move around freely, talk with one another informally, and move furniture into arrangements which permit them to work together, either in pairs or in small groups.

4 Some teachers arrange their rooms informally, devise teacher-made materials, establish learning stations, develop classroom libraries, and so forth, only to find that the end result is *chaos*. Underlying all instructional plans must be the implementation of an effective classroom management structure. Children need to know what is expected of them if they are going to act responsibly in an informal classroom environment.

5 A good reading program leads to the library. Children not only learn library skills—how to use the card catalog, how to locate a book on the shelf—but they also learn to use books, magazines, and reference materials to find answers to their questions. The library should contain a wealth of reading materials and audiovisual materials. Above all, it is headed by a librarian, a trained person who provides valuable support to the language arts teacher in the attempt to bring children and books together.

6 Nancy met the needs of David, a child with above-average reading ability, by providing opportunities for him to read many books which interest him rather than asking him to move into higher-graded textbook materials written for older children in different stages of development.

Schlager (22) believes that children's stages of development, the biological aspects of their growth, determine their reading interests. She states:

> Books that reflect the child's perception of the world are the books children clamor for . . . It is useful and important to recognize that a child's perceptions change with each stage of his or her development, so that the toddler delights in aspects that will be of little interest to the seven- to twelve-year-old, and the interests of middle childhood are likewise not of interest to the young adolescent.

Just as fourth- or fifth-grade basals would be inappropriate for David, an accelerated second-grader, so would preprimers be poor choices for second-graders who are experiencing reading difficulties. Horizontal reading is a way of providing children with reading practice at a level at which they can comfortably read. Some teachers provide horizontal reading experiences for their average or below-average reading groups by choosing a book at the instructional level from an alternative basal reading series and having the children in a reading group read this second book to review and practice reading skills (4). Others use their knowledge of children's literature to bring children and books together, knowing that children will get reading practice and become better readers as they read stories which fit their interests and their developmental levels.

7 While most teachers use two or three fairly homogeneous reading groups based on reading level for instructional purposes, it is important to remember that there is no reason for children to do all their work within the framework of one group. Those who need to practice certain skills can be brought together in a special-needs group while children with similar interests can work in interest groups where they formulate common questions, find appropriate reading materials, and read and report to the class on their interests. Many times, children can work together on committees, with each group taking charge of one facet of a class project. If children hold membership in various groups, the possibility of their developing poor academic self-concepts based on their reading achievement is held to a minimum.

8 The majority of the elementary schools in the United States have no planned literature programs. This makes it even more important that individual teachers keep a record of the books they read to children, and a brief notation on the children's reaction to each book. Such a list should be shared the following year with the teacher who works with the children. This will ensure that children do not hear the same favorite over and over. Huck reports the results of a survey of an elementary school in which all but two teachers (a kindergarten and a second-grade teacher) had read *Charlotte's Web* aloud to their classes! Teachers need to plan their read-aloud programs so that there is balance in the literature program. Children need to be introduced to a variety of types of books and poems so that their appreciation for literature will be broadened.

9 Stories become more real to children as they identify with the characters and situations through creative dramatics. Pantomine is almost always a first step in the development of believable creative drama with children. Creative dramatics causes children to go back to the book and to become sensitive to the characters in the story. Since there is no written script, children are required to think on their feet and to express themselves on the basis of their own experiences (14, pp. 661–662).

10 Writing needs to be an ongoing, everyday activity in the primary grades. In some classrooms children never experience purposeful writing in which they are communicating for an authentic audience. Without a reader, writing becomes a contrived exercise with little significance.

Young children's writing is primarily expressive; that is, it reflects an experience in which they participated or an attempt to share information about themselves (9). This sort of writing is highly personal and is meant to be shared. A teacher can aid this communication process by making sure children's writing is read by a real audience. Displaying stories in the classrooms, setting aside time for sharing written work, finding ways for parents and other significant people to read children's writing are methods for effective teachers to foster writing as a communication process.

11 Evaluation is an essential component of the instructional program. Teachers need to know children's strengths and weaknesses so they can make provisions for appropriate learning experiences to take place. There are different forms of evaluation which serve different purposes. If a teacher or a principal needs to determine whether state or school district language arts objectives have been met or if progress has been made in meeting them, they will look at the results of standardized achievement tests in the specific language arts areas (reading, language arts, study skills) for all the children in a class or a school.

Children are frequently given diagnostic reading tests (usually furnished as ancillary materials with the basal textbook series) by teachers. The results of these tests help the teacher identify particular skills which children have or have not acquired. As teachers work with the children on skills they deem important to the students' educational experience, the children may be tested by using these skills as criteria for the tests. The teacher can then reteach the essential skills (not previously mastered) until the children have learned them.

Many aspects of language, particularly those related to oral language and the creative aspects of written language, do not lend themselves to paper-and-pencil tests. Teachers can gather data with informal means of evaluation which will be helpful to them in identifying the children's strengths or weaknesses.

Teachers invite children to talk to them during a carefully planned informal interview. The teacher might ask children to talk about familiar objects and listen to the way they express themselves. Story retelling is another method teachers can use to evaluate language growth. Children are read a story appropriate for their age and are asked individually to retell it. This retelling can provide data to a sensitive teacher for evaluation of comprehension and language growth.

Teachers are encouraged to keep samples of the children's writing from the beginning of the year and at intervals throughout the school year. These can provide material for assessing children's understanding of written language and for indicating the amount of progress made by children during this time period.

12 Teachers exert an important influence in the classrooms. No teacher wants to have a negative effect on students; teachers want children to learn. Yet some teaching practices are better than others. Teachers must be willing to examine their own behavior and to let others observe their teaching so they can become aware of their strengths and weaknesses and change their behaviors accordingly.

CINDY LEE

Descriptor

Cindy is a third-grade teacher in an inner-city school district. Her classroom is relatively small in size, and with thirty students in it, the classroom almost appears to be overcrowded.

The children come primarily from lower-class backgrounds and are almost equally divided in intellectual ability between high-, average-, and low-ability children. However, in terms of their attitude toward school and learning, Cindy estimates that 70 percent of her students are highly self-motivated, independent workers; 20 percent like school but need teacher direction when performing so-called independent activities; and 10 percent of the class dislikes school and the learning tasks associated with it, including the language arts.

Cindy teaches language arts every morning for eighty minutes. Like Lynn Simpson (in a previous description in Chapter 3) she uses a block period of time to teach all the language arts, with one exception. Cindy teaches handwriting separately at the end of the day.

There are four third-grade classrooms in Cindy's elementary school, with a total of 120 children. These 120 students are placed into one of ten groups on the basis of the child's previous language arts performance, teacher judgment, the diagnostic tests accompanying the language arts series used at that school, and standardized achievement results. Each teacher is then responsible for providing instruction to two or three of the groups, which are of varying size in accordance with pupil ability.

Flexibility is evident in teacher and student assignments to groups. Consideration was given to teacher preference and expertise in deciding who will teach which groups. Initial assignment of students into a particular group is precisely that: initial placement. Depending upon a child's progress, the child may move into a more able or less able group or may remain in the assigned group for the entire year.

Cindy's school requires the use of a commercial language arts series. The district, however, has developed its own language arts curriculum. This curriculum closely parallels the series; however, in some instances, differences do exist. To accommodate these differences, Cindy uses several supplementary materials. Among these are language development activities, vocabulary enrichment, comprehension builders, and creative writing aids. She also uses many recreational reading books, stories, and activities to foster an appreciation and enjoyment of reading in her pupils.

Cindy uses an individualized style of teaching. Each student in a group is given a weekly plan of instruction. This describes which activities are to be completed daily by each child. Children perform assigned tasks, they are corrected, and feedback relative to them is given to the students. If satisfactory progress is made, more difficult work is prescribed. If such progress is not made Cindy works with the child—as well as with others who have a similar difficulty—on the specific skill.

She employs several modes to convey to children and their parents the progress being made in the language arts. With the students, Cindy holds at least one conference (usually two) per week. At this session, in her words, she "tells it like it is." Cindy is honest with a student, giving praise where warranted, discussing failures, and explaining what *they* will do next.

Weekly Cindy sends home all the language arts work done by a child during that week. A parent signs this compilation on a line below the summary of the work written by Cindy. She also sends copies of "Happy Grams" to parents when their child has done superior work on a specified activity. She says "parents should share successes with their child." Finally, every six weeks (three weeks prior to issuance of report cards), Cindy sends a detailed progress report to the parents of each child. This report delineates the skills mastered by the student during a specified time period.

In addition to individualized work and conferences with students, Cindy employs many "fun" activities in her classroom. Her students devise illustrations for a story read to them by Cindy, write conclusions to an unfinished action story, perform pantomimes, write letters to famous people, do puppet shows, make murals, have choral reading, share folktales and fairy stories, dramatize poems, share books in oral discussions, and, according to Cindy, "anything else that will make the skills I teach come alive."

Cindy places much importance upon her students' ability to express themselves in speaking and writing situations. She spends a great deal of time giving the children experiences in telling stories, giving oral reports, and holding conversations. Writing activities focus on devising sentences and simple paragraphs, on composing friendly letters, and on telling about books they have read.

Listening receives a great deal of attention from Cindy. She teaches her students to be polite and attentive when someone speaks. Also, she assesses how well children listen—to each other, to stories read to them, to reports and poems, and to content material presented verbally to the students.

Finally, handwriting development is a priority in Cindy's class. She spends time with both manuscript and cursive forms of writing. Much effort goes into producing children who handle both kinds of writing legibly. Cindy says:

My attempts to wipe out messy handwriting are marked by more "losses" than "wins" at the beginning of the year. By the end of the year, just the opposite is true. Throughout the year, I praise each student every time I see even a little improvement in handwriting. All those little bits of improvement add up to a great deal by the end of the year. When I show students a handwriting sample of theirs (written at the beginning of the school year) at the end of the school year, they can't believe how poor their handwriting used to be!

Analysis

Cindy is a third-grade teacher in an inner-city school district. Her classroom is relatively small in size, and with thirty students in it, the classroom almost appears to be overcrowded.

The children come primarily from lower-class backgrounds and are almost equally divided in intellectual ability between high-, average-, and low-ability children. However, in terms of their attitude toward school and learning, Cindy estimates that 70 percent of her students are highly self-motivated, independent workers; 20 percent like school but need teacher direction when performing so-called independent activities; and 10 percent of the class dislikes school and the learning tasks associated with it, including the language arts.

Cindy teaches language arts every morning for eighty minutes. Like Lynn Simpson (in a previous description in Chapter 3) *she uses a block period of time to teach all the language arts,*[1] *with one exception.* Cindy teaches handwriting separately at the end of the day.

There are four third-grade classrooms in Cindy's elementary school, with a total of 120 children. *These 120 students are placed into one of ten groups*[2] *on the basis of the child's previous language arts performance, teacher judgment, the diagnostic tests accompanying the language arts series used at that school, and standardized achievement results.*[3] Each teacher is then responsible for providing instruction to two or three of the groups, which are of varying size in accordance with pupil ability.

Flexibility is evident in teacher and student assignments to groups. *Consideration was given to teacher preference and expertise in deciding who will teach which groups.*[4] *Initial assignment of students into a particular group is precisely that: initial placement.*[5] Depending upon a child's progress, the child may move into a more able or less able group or may remain in the assigned group for the entire year.

Cindy's school requires the use of a commercial language arts series. The district, however, has developed its own language arts curriculum. This curriculum closely parallels the series; however, in some instances, differences do exist. *To accommodate these differences, Cindy uses several supplementary materials.*[6] Among these are language development activities, vocabulary enrichment, comprehension builders, and creative writing aids. *She also uses many recreational reading books, stories, and activities to foster an appreciation and enjoyment of reading in her pupils.*[7]

Cindy uses an individualized style of teaching. Each student in a group is given a weekly plan of instruction. This describes which activities are to be completed daily by each child. Children perform assigned tasks, they are corrected, and feedback relative to them is given to the students. If satisfactory progress is made, more difficult work is prescribed. If such progress is not made, *Cindy works with the child—as well as with others who have a similar difficulty—on the specific skill.*[8]

She employs several modes to convey to children and their parents the progress being made in the language arts.[9] With the students, Cindy holds at least one conference (usually two) per week. At this session, in her words, she "tells it like it is." Cindy is honest with a student, giving praise where warranted, discussing failures, and explaining what *they* will do next.

Weekly Cindy sends home all the language arts work done by a child during that week. A parent signs this compilation on a line below the summary of the work written by Cindy. She also sends copies of "Happy Grams" to parents when their child has done superior work on a specified activity. She says "parents should share successes with their child." Finally, every six weeks (three weeks prior to issuance of report cards), Cindy sends a detailed progress report to the parents of each child.[10] This report delineates the skills mastered by the student during a specified time period.

In addition to individualized work and conferences with students, *Cindy employs many "fun" activities in her classroom.*[11] Her students devise illustrations for a story read to them by Cindy, write conclusions to an unfinished action story, perform pantomimes, write letters to famous people, do puppet shows, make murals, have choral reading, share folktales and fairy stories, dramatize poems, share books in oral discussions, and, according to Cindy, "anything else that will make the skills I teach come alive."

Cindy places much importance upon her students' ability to express themselves in speaking and writing situations. She spends a great deal of time giving the children experiences in telling stories, giving oral reports, and holding conversations. Writing activities focus on devising sentences and simple paragraphs, on composing friendly letters, and on telling about books they have read.

Listening receives a great deal of attention from Cindy. She teaches her students to be polite and attentive when someone speaks. Also, she assesses how well children listen—to each other, to stories read to them, to reports and poems, and to content material presented verbally to the students.

Finally, handwriting development is a priority in Cindy's class. She spends time with both manuscript and cursive forms of writing.[12] Much effort goes into producing children who handle both kinds of writing legibly. Cindy says,

> My attempts to wipe out messy handwriting are marked by more "losses" than "wins" at the beginning of the year. By the end of the year, just the opposite is true. Throughout the year, *I praise each student every time I see even a little improvement in handwriting.*[13] All those little bits of improvement add up to a great deal by the end of the year. When I show students a handwriting sample of theirs (written at the beginning of the school year) at the end of the school year, they can't believe how poor their handwriting used to be!

Explanation

1 We favor the concept of teaching the language arts in a block period of time for the reasons cited in the analysis of Lynn Simpson, our first-grade teacher.

2 Dividing the students into *many,* rather than one or three groups (as is prevalent in numerous classrooms), can reduce somewhat the ability range of children who will be receiving instruction. If done properly through the use of a grouping system such as this or the Joplin plan, students of *similar* ability are placed in a group to receive language arts instruction. By reducing the range of student ability differences, many teachers feel they are better able to plan instruction for the children in a group. Thus, more effective group and individual instruction can be provided to students.

A caution about this form of grouping should be offered. Although it may reduce the range of student variability relative to ability, one should not feel as though every child in a group is alike. Differences will still remain in terms of the students' interests, motivation, attitudes, and abilities.

Norton (19) offers an additional consideration. She states: "If ability is the only grouping category used in the classroom, the lower-ability child might never hear a good reader, or be motivated by the interests of other children in the class."

3 The use of information from several different sources to determine the grouping of children is a good practice. Too frequently, the score derived from a single measure determines the group—or program of instruction—to which a child will be assigned. Usually this measure is a standardized test administered during one school day. As a result, if a child scored poorly because she or he felt poorly that day, had an argument with her or his father prior to school, was reprimanded erroneously by the teacher earlier in the day and still harbored resentment, or any of a thousand and one other possible adverse occurrences, the score derived will be inaccurate. Thus the child's placement into a group will be erroneous and the child will receive instruction that is not geared to her or his ability.

When more than a single medium is employed for group placement purposes, the likelihood of one "bad" performance unduly influencing placement is diminished. With data from several sources as well as many types of assessment, those making grouping decisions will have a better opportunity to properly place children into groups commensurate with their true ability.

4 Recently at an inservice meeting, with approximately 200 elementary school teachers from several school districts using the Joplin plan in attendance, one of us asked the assembled group a series of questions. The teachers were to raise their hands to acknowledge an affirmative answer. The questions dealt with the expertise and the preference of teachers to instruct children of a certain ability. Some of the questions were: Do you prefer teaching high-ability children? medium-ability children? low-ability children? Are you best teaching high-ability students? average students? low-ability students? Do you get the opportunity to teach language arts to the type (high-, average-, low-ability) of children you are best at teaching? *Fewer* than 50 percent of the teachers responded affirmatively to the final question.

Situations such as the preceding are unfortunate. Just as care should be taken in assigning children to a group, equal consideration must be given to deciding which teacher will instruct them. The national first- and second-grade studies (24) found that the teacher was the key ingredient in determining the success of children in learning. If the teacher is such a crucial element to the teaching–learning process—a belief we also hold—why are decisions about who will teach which groups sometimes made so haphazardly?

The individual who assigns teachers to particular groups should consider the preferences of teachers as well as their expertise in working with certain children. Classroom observations, achievement performances of students taught during the prior year by the teacher, opinions held by other teachers and supervisors of the teacher, and similar factors will help to determine a teacher's expertise in working with children of a particular ability range. The assignments should not be used for punitive purposes (don't give an unpopular teacher the group with several discipline problem children as members), nor should the teacher with the most seniority get the best group and the one with the least seniority be assigned the least able children.

5 Professional literature has a plethora of quotations from language arts and reading authorities about the need for flexibility in grouping. These experts correctly maintain that depending upon children's performances, they should advance to a more able group, be placed into a less able one, or remain in the same group.

Burns and Roe (4) say: "If there has been a mistake in an original placement, if a child has a sudden spurt of growth, or if a child's growth pattern slows down, the teacher should promptly place the child in another, more appropriate group. Grouping should always be flexible. A single pattern is often misused; instead of forming a flexible schedule, rigid groups are often formed for as long as the academic year." Durkin (7) reminds us that grouping makes "it more humanly possible to achieve better instruction. Once that is accomplished, it is then up to the teacher to take advantage of new opportunities. Thus it still is the teacher who makes the greatest difference in how well and how easily children achieve. . . ."

We concur with the aforementioned statements. Grouping should facilitate instruction, not dictate it. Failure to move children properly after initial placement into a group will hinder rather than foster achievement.

Regardless of the measures used for initial placement of children into groups, the movement of individuals from one group to another is a natural occurrence. Teachers should perceive flexibility in movement among groups in a positive way and should analyze each individual's performance regularly to see if placement of that person in a designated group is resulting in the maximum achievement possible.

6 For the reasons cited in step 2 of our analysis of Lynn Simpson, the first-grade teacher, we favor supplementing the commercial series used to teach the language arts. We also endorse the use of supplements in Cindy's classroom.

7 In many classrooms, children's literature and activities which promote recreational reading are viewed as frills. People feel the aforementioned aren't really essential and should be included in a classroom "only if time permits." We hold the opposite view. As Mangieri, Bader, and Walker (18) state:

> Learning to read is a difficult process, requiring a great deal of work on the part of teacher and pupil. But learning to read is not the acquisition of a skill. Reading is an act which can afford an individual countless hours of pleasure. Reading should not be an all work–no enjoyment task. It should not be all diphthongs, workbook sheets, and the schwa sound. We support a philosophy that reading can be *fun*. Activities such as storytelling, games, and creative dramatics should be an integral part of an elementary school classroom's *modus operandi*. These activities afford children an opportunity to apply the reading skills which they have acquired. Equally important, they can foster a love of reading in children.

Recreational reading materials and activities can also serve as an ideal vehicle for an integration of the language arts. In addition to the benefits to reading to be derived from their usage, these materials and activities can provide countless instances where *meaningful* speaking, listening, and writing may occur within a classroom.

Are children's literature and recreational reading activities frills? Our answer is no.

They are *essential* ingredients in the classroom instructional program of an effective language arts teacher.

8 When a child is experiencing difficulty in acquiring a *major* skill or concept, a teacher should devote additional time to helping that student (and any others having comparable difficulty with it) to learn the skill or concept. If it is of relatively minor consequence, a teacher must weigh the time that must be spent reteaching a skill against the importance of that skill.

As children progress through the elementary school, they are confronted with progressively more difficult learning tasks. The language arts curriculum adheres to this pattern, with easier skills preceding more complex ones. Many of these skills are hierarchical and dependent so that a child must master certain skills before subsequent ones can be learned.

Therefore, Lee's reteaching of a key skill not mastered by children was time well spent. Acquisition of this skill will enhance the children's likelihood of mastering later skills for which it is a prerequisite.

9 The proper use of evaluation is a must in an elementary school classroom. Evaluation should take place on a regular basis and the data derived from it should be shared—in nontechnical language—with children and their parents. Evaluation provides the teacher with an assessment of the progress being made by the students. Children receive from it a sense of knowing their accomplishments, and it provides them with readiness for the tasks which they will be assigned. Parents will know the skills being acquired by their children. In addition, regular evaluation makes it more possible for language arts skills taught in the school to be reinforced in the children's homes. For example, the teacher could say to a child: "Here are the things *(name them)* you've learned since we last spoke. Here's what *(name a few of the skills)* we'll work to learn next week. I'm happy with how you've worked these last two weeks."

The teacher might send a letter to the parent, saying something like:

> Since I last wrote to you three weeks ago, we have been very busy. Your child has worked very hard and I'm pleased with her progress. Here is what she's learned in language arts since my last progress report to you:
>   1.
>   2.   (items would be listed here)
>   3.
>   and so on
>
> Next week, I am going to teach your child the following in the language arts:
>   1.
>   2.   (items would be listed here)
>   3.
>   and so on
>
> You can help by continuing to show an interest in what your child is learning. Please continue to sign the nightly homework assignments in language arts. Your involvement in this effort has contributed much to your child's success.

10 The previous statement addressed the issue of evaluation. The activities of Cindy in this segment relate not only to the sharing of evaluative-type information with parents but also to positive parental involvement in a child's educational program.

Saxe accurately describes what the relationship between a school and a community should be. He also offers a strategy for making this relationship occur. Saxe (21) states:

> . . . schools need to regain the trust and support once so freely, almost unquestioningly, given. This kind of trust can only be renewed if schools can become more responsive and if people are involved in important ways with matters that concern them. In this way the over-all community may support the schools again as new, mutually advantageous relationships are established. A new sharing and responsiveness can be initiated by opening up school–community relations.

Fostering the type of relationship with a community and parents advocated by Saxe is a realistic task. The modes utilized by Cindy for reporting student achievement are consistent with the aforementioned goal. Exclusive use of the report card for conveying progress in the language arts is not congruent with the goal. Lee (17) supports our viewpoint by saying: "When parents feel that the teacher is vitally concerned with the progress of their child, the channels of communication are open. The report card provides for little interaction and is a very poor device for real communication."

11 Teaching the language arts is indeed a difficult task. It need not, however, be a dull one. In conversations with effective language arts teachers—and in our observations of their classrooms—fun was a characteristic often cited by the teachers and evident in our observations of them. There was a certain vibrancy while the language arts were being taught. The children seemed genuinely delighted to be learning and using the skills associated with the language arts.

Enjoyment is *not* inconsistent with learner achievement. Teachers should strive to make the language arts a fascinating, stimulating, and loved subject in a child's day. It should *not* be, as DeStefano and Fox (6) contend, "one of the least liked subjects in the elementary school."

Enjoyment can also help to foster personal development in children. The devices employed by Cindy not only taught language arts skills but also, in some instances, served as an opportunity to engage in fanciful activities. And as Baker (3) maintains, fantasy does have a place in the elementary classroom. He states:

> To deny fantasy and the capacity to dream with purpose is to destroy the gift of mental and emotional healing with which every story is endowed. Whenever we hear or read those magic words, "Once upon a time . . . " we are projected into a world from which we return, equipped and healed, informed, wiser and more able to cope with the perplexed and perplexing world of everyday life.

12 At the beginning of this chapter, we described the language arts skills customarily taught to children in grades two and three. In our description of Cindy, the language arts skills to which she pays special attention were cited.

While the skills taught by Cindy are consistent with those specified by us earlier in the chapter, the skills per se are not of primary importance. We commend Cindy because she has specified goals or major objectives to be reached or key skills to be attained (use whichever terminology you prefer) in her classroom. We favor language arts teachers having goals for the reasons described by Allington and Strange (1). They say: "There must be goals for teaching; goals which go beyond the vague generalities and professional sounding platitudes too often associated with the various disciplines."

Enjoyment is *not* inconsistent with learner achievement.

They add: "Instructional goals should be precise enough to allow the teacher to justify each assignment in relation to them."

13 The use of praise can be a powerful vehicle when employed properly by a teacher. Children need to know through verbal or nonverbal modes of communication when their actions are positive in nature. This acknowledgment of positive actions should be made at frequent intervals to coincide with the achievement made by a student in a specified area of the language arts.

The method utilized by a teacher should be consistent with that teacher's classroom management style. Also, the child should be able to recognize it as a form of praise or positive reinforcement on the teacher's part. Gazda et al. (9) contend: "If a teacher has good relationships with students and a large repertoire of interpersonal skills, then the teacher has more potential for giving positive reinforcement. In fact, the good teacher becomes a personal reinforcer of behavior. A smile, a pat, a glance by a teacher are positive reinforcers to some students."

BIBLIOGRAPHY AND REFERENCES

1 Allington, Richard L., and Strange, Michael. "Remembering Is Not Necessarily Understanding in Content Areas." in Ernest K. Dishner, Thomas W. Bean, and John E. Readence (eds.), *Reading in the Content Areas: Improving Classroom Instruction.* Dubuque, Iowa: Kendall/Hunt Publishing Company, 1981, p. 7.

2 Auten, Anne. "ERIC/RCS: Parents as Partners in Reading." *The Reading Teacher,* vol. 34, no. 2, November 1980, pp. 228–230.

3 Baker, Donald. *Functions of Folk and Fairy Tales.* Washington, D.C.: Association for Childhood Education International, 1981, p. 3.

4 Burns, Paul C., and Roe, Betty D. *Teaching Reading in Today's Elementary Schools.* Chicago: Rand McNally College Publishing Company, 1980, p. 391.

5 Cunningham, Pat. "The Clip Sheet: Horizontal Reading," *The Reading Teacher,* vol. 34, no. 2, November 1980, pp. 222–224.

6 De Stefano, Johanna S., and Fox, Sharon E. *Language and the Language Arts.* Boston: Little, Brown and Company, 1974, p. v.

7 Durkin, Dolores. *Teaching Them to Read.* Boston: Allyn and Bacon, 1974, p. 81.

8 Dusek, Jerome B. "Do Teachers Bias Children's Learning?" *Review of Educational Research,* vol. 45, Fall 1975, pp. 661–684.

9 Gazda, George D., and others. *Human Relations Development.* Boston: Allyn and Bacon, 1977, p. 8.

10 Golden, Joanne M. "The Writer's Side: Writing for a Purpose and an Audience." *Language Arts,* vol. 57, no. 7, October 1980, pp. 756–762.

11 Goodman, Kenneth, and Goodman, Yetta. "Learning to Read Is Natural." Speech delivered at Conference on Theory and Practice of Beginning Reading Instruction, Pittsburgh, April 1976.

12 Harris, Albert J., and Sipay, Edward R. *How to Increase Reading Ability* (7th ed). New York: Longman Publishing Company, 1980.

13 Hopkins, Lee Bennett. *The Best of Book Bonanza.* New York: Holt, Rinehart and Winston, 1980.

14 Huck, Charlotte S. *Children's Literature in the Elementary School* (3d ed.). New York: Holt, Rinehart and Winston, 1979.

15 Huck, Charlotte S. "Literature as the Content of Reading." *Theory into Practice,* vol. 16, no. 5, December 1977, pp. 363–371.

16 King, Martha. "Evaluating Reading." *Theory into Practice,* vol. 16, no. 5, December 1977, pp. 407–418.

17 Lee, J. Murray. *Elementary Education Today and Tomorrow.* Boston: Allyn and Bacon, 1967, p. 224.

18 Mangieri, John N., Bader, Lois, and Walker, James E. *Teaching Elementary Reading: A Comprehensive Approach.* New York: McGraw-Hill, 1982, pp. 9–10.

19 Norton, Donna E. *The Effective Teaching of Language Arts.* Columbus, Ohio: Charles E. Merrill, 1980, p. 14.

20 Rosenthal, Robert, and Jacobson, Lenore. *Pygmalion in the Classroom.* New York: Holt, Rinehart and Winston, 1968.

21 Saxe, Richard W. *School–Community Interaction.* Berkeley, Calif.: McCuthan Publishing Corporation, 1975, p. 13.

22 Schlager, Norma. "Predicting Children's Choices in Literature: A Developmental Approach." *Children's Literature in Education,* vol. 9, no. 30, Autumn 1978.

23 Sutherland, Zena, and Arbuthnot, May Hill. *Children and Books.* New York: Scott, Foresman, 1977.

24 *The Reading Teacher.* May 1966, October 1966, May 1967, and October 1967.

CHAPTER 6

LANGUAGE ARTS:
GRADES FOUR AND FIVE

OVERVIEW

The focus of this chapter will be the teaching of the language arts in grades four and five. The chapter will begin by discussing the nature of children in these grades. We will then describe the curricular emphases, instructional activities, and assessment measures associated with providing language arts instruction to children in these grades.

THE CHILD

The study of the nature and demands of children is a feature of modern education. Its results have had substantial effects on the curriculum and teaching practices of the elementary school. The intermediate grades of the elementary school find the children in the stage of their lives when they are between great dependence on the adult world for sustenance and guidance and a point of greater maturity at which they make many of their own decisions. Since the entire scope of child development cannot adequately be addressed in this chapter, it will be necessary to focus our attention on three basic aspects of growth for the nine-, ten-, and eleven-year-old child: physical, social and emotional, and intellectual characteristics.

Physical Characteristics

Children continue to grow in size and strength from the age of nine to the age of eleven. This is usually the beginning of a period of rapid growth. The normal physical growth results in more coordination and skill in large- and small-muscle activities.

Skill at games is an important aspect in the middle years of the intermediate grades.

Children in the intermediate years exhibit significant individual differences in physical growth. It is this experience of size, skill, and sexual growth that affects the lives of the children at this stage. Adults often anticipate different behavior from these children because of their physical appearance. For example, adults tend to worry about the well-being of short and/or skinny children. Conversely, parents and teachers usually expect the tall and well-developed children of this age range to display maturity and control.

Attitudes, interests, and friendships change with physical growth and the degree of physical attractiveness. Classes of fourth- and fifth-grade students are excellent illustrations of the fact that children grow and develop at different rates. These different growth patterns present problems for the intermediate years in social relationships and self-concept. At the end of this age span, the children are moving toward the important developmental changes of puberty.

Social and Emotional Characteristics

The children in grades four and five are now a part of several important social systems—the family, the school, and the peer group. They are increasingly aware of the larger culture and the mass media. Active involvement in the process of sorting out and integrating different experiences has begun for nine-, ten-, and eleven-year-old children. Ethical concepts, peer group roles, and thought styles are not always consistent with one another as children reflect on their daily personal and schooling experiences. Family (parents and siblings) attitudes and models are an important part of this search, but there now are alternative attitudes and significant other persons to emulate. The child, who had been a taker of directions from the family, now brings changes to it in the form of new ideas and values. The family begins to experience feelings of ambiance as the child undertakes independent explorations and decisions.

By nine years of age, children have internalized many values and expectations. Some have developed a moral system with a sense of fairness and justice. Children of this age rarely tattle. Loyalty to other children is very important. The children are influenced by their emotional attitudes and understanding of the views and demands of the important people in their lives.

Games that require skill and planning (such as checkers and monopoly) as well as organized team sports (such as baseball, softball, and football) are enjoyed by the children in the intermediate grades. The activities of boys and girls are far more alike at this stage than they were many years ago as girls have become more physically active in their play. Rules of the games are very important to the children in the intermediate years as there is a move in power from adults to the peer group. Following the rules guarantees control and security for all the children in this transitional period.

The peer group is an expansion of the family-centered years. Other children become increasingly important as more time is spent in these groups. Girls usually develop one or two best friends and boys are usually seen in small groups. Frequent changes occur in both groups at this stage.

Intellectual Characteristics

Fourth- and fifth-grade students demonstrate individual differences in academic performance as well as in their thinking processes. The way children understand the world and the changes in it are affected by their personal rates of maturation. Humor, creativity, fantasy, logic, and problem solving are important aspects of children's intellectual growth.

Educators are still exploring means of presenting information and structuring classroom environments that will provide for the wide variations in the cognitive development which is likely to exist in any group of normal children. Cognitive growth is complex. The theory and investigations of Jean Piaget indicate that there are developmental trends in cognition. Piaget's theory traces many changes and describes a series of developmental stages. The stages are different from one another but they evolve in a sequence, with each stage dependent on those that have come before it.

Piaget's child is an active thinker who is trying to understand his or her world. Most children ages nine to eleven years old are into the concrete operational period, which is characterized by thought that is logical and reversible. (The distance from the door to the driveway is the same distance as from the driveway to the door. If I, a boy, have a brother, then my brother has a brother.) Children can understand the logic of classes and relationships. (It is possible for one person to be a human being, an Indian, a Pennsylvanian, a school child, and a son.) They understand and can coordinate series and subgroups when dealing with concrete objects, but at this age, they are usually still lacking in the ability to think of all possible relationships, although they understand what exists around them in reality.

At the upper end of the nine- to eleven-year-old range, some children are demonstrating some of the more complex forms of concrete logic and are entering what Piaget (53) calls the formal operational period "operations-on-operations," which involves the ability to think abstractly. It is the logical process of "If this, then this."

The way children approach tasks is defined in part by their state of development and their intellectual style. School experiences should be planned to enhance cognitive growth of all children so that they may profit from relevant experiences.

LANGUAGE ARTS IN THE INTERMEDIATE GRADES

LISTENING

What is listening? Is it hearing? As we have stated earlier, there is a definite distinction between listening and hearing. Hearing is the registration of sound stimuli using the mechanisms of the ear as receptors and the cortex as the area of registration. Listening goes beyond the physiology of hearing. It demands a conscious interaction between receiving stimuli and the organism doing the receiving. The listener must in some way respond to what he or she hears.

Listening is a receptive language process through which a large part of the school curriculum must pass on its way to learning. In 1928, Rankin (54) found that of all the time people spent daily in communication, approximately 42 percent was spent in listening and 32 percent in speaking; the remaining 25 percent were combined in reading and writing. A later investigation by Wilt (69) found that students spend an average of more than $2\frac{1}{2}$ hours of a five-hour school day listening. Because so much of students' time is spent in listening and because students differ in their listening abilities, listening should be taught as a complex mental process that demands effort and attention. A teacher cannot merely assume that the students in an intermediate grade classroom know how to listen effectively.

Instructional Emphases   Listening is the first communication skill to develop in students and it is the one upon which all others are based. It is the activity with which the majority of students feel comfortable and, in some ways, it is the most important exercise in the classroom.

We have observed that some students will come to the intermediate grades with well-developed listening skills, others will come with poor listening habits, and still others have developed inadequate habits during their short school careers. These types of listeners will have an impact on the intermediate classroom, where the emphasis is to develop a set of skills intended to make students self-directed listeners. The listening program is also directed at teaching students to listen and make distinctions among the various discourses and sounds to which they are exposed, such as humor, stories, factual information, poetry, propaganda, music, dramatizations, group discussions, informal conversations, and television and radio programs. Standards for listening are emphasized. Students are directed to analyze their own skill habits and to set definite listening goals toward which to work.

The New Hampshire Department of Education (50) has developed a listening skills assessment program. Its search of the literature located forty separate listening skills, which were then classified under five headings—"simple recall, recognizing and following spoken directions, recognizing a speaker's purpose and plan, critical listening, and higher-level listening skills." Suggestions for teaching and measuring each of these skills are included in the publication it has put out on this subject.

Instructional Strategies   The first step in planning a program to build listening skills is to ensure that all the students have the basic foundation for listening—hearing. Hearing, of course, is dependent upon whether or not one receives the sounds presented. Therefore, for classroom instructional purposes, the teacher needs only to determine that the students are receiving this input. If this gross assessment indicates that a child can physically hear sounds, a listening program can be initiated with that individual.

For instructional purposes, listening must be separated into two parts—discrimination and comprehension. During auditory discrimination practice, students listen to determine the likenesses and differences in sound, nuance, pitch, rhythm, and volume. Listening comprehension is separated into three levels—literal, interpretive, and critical. Literal comprehension is factual recall of what the speaker said. The student must repeat what was heard. Interpretation is more complex in that the student must be able to determine the meaning of what was said. Literal comprehension is required in order to interpret. The listener must be able to establish relationships among the facts he or

Listening is a process rather than a body of knowledge.

she has heard. Critical listening is the highest level of comprehension. At this level, the student must evaluate or make a judgment about what is heard.

Listening, which is a process rather than a body of knowledge, is a system of attaching meaning to the spoken word. It is considered a basic medium of learning, and listening skills must be taught. The teacher must first establish what kind of listening is expected from the students. The purposes for listening must then be determined in advance of the listening activity and communicated to the listeners. In this way, students are taught to listen effectively.

Strickland (63) has listed eight levels of listening that students may display. The list progresses from the less mature to the more mature levels and includes:

1 Little conscious listening, and then only when the interest is closely related to the student

2 Half-listening, wherein the student listens only to give her or his own ideas concerning the topic of the speaker

3 Passive listening, when the student is absorbing what the speaker is saying without any reaction

4 Listening intermittently to what the speaker says as it relates to the listener's experiential background

5 Associative listening by relating the known facts to those within the student's experiences

6 Listening in a way that the listener can react with additional comments or questions

7 Listening that involves emotional and mental participation with the speaker's theme

8 Listening for the purpose of establishing a personal interchange of ideas

An experienced teacher may be able to observe students to tell how involved they are in the listening process. The highly proficient listeners are the ones who are able to apply the type of listening that is most appropriate to the situation. The direction of the instruction is that students progress to the more mature levels of listening. The material must be presented in such a manner as to motivate the students to that goal.

Research (20) has shown that students show improvement in listening skills when: (1) the classroom environment is conducive to listening, (2) the teacher asks more open-ended questions and allows more time for responses, (3) students actively participate in the communication process with their peers in the roles of listeners and speakers, (4) a purpose is set for the listening activity which is related directly to ongoing school activities and students' interests and is presented in a variety of ways, (5) students' comments and ideas are accepted and improvements are noted and rewarded, and (6) students participate in the formulation of the class listening standards.

Students need to be instructed to listen effectively in many situations and the instruction may vary in its formality. Lessons in listening may focus on a set of skills, on activities that require listening for specific purposes, and on other subject areas that call for listening. In the intermediate grades as in the primary grades, the possibilities for listening activities are many. The following list is illustrative:

Listening to oral reports and readings and in listening and speaking situations with fellow students

Listening to directions, stories, and lectures by the teachers

Listening to music, drama, newscasts, and instruction by radio, tape, cassette recordings, records, and television

Listening to live music, dramatic presentations, group and panel discussions, and demonstrations

Some specific suggestions for activities to improve listening skills in various curriculum areas are provided by Lundsteen (42).

Techniques and Their Uses in the Listening Center

I Instruction that is used annually

  A Individual instruction

    1 For high-ability students

    2 For low-ability students

B Reteaching a skill
    1 For those who have been absent
    2 For those who need to relearn
C Testing
    1 Practice for tests (pretest)
    2 The test itself
II Building listening skills
    A On a one-to-one basis
    B On a group basis
    C Step-by-step instructions
    D A series of instructions
III Enjoying cultural experiences
    A Music
    B Literature or stories
IV Creative thinking
    A Open-ended or unfinished stories
    B Problem solving
        1 Math
        2 Science
        3 Social studies
    C Discovery method
        1 Math
        2 Science
V Children's recordings
    A Plays, choral reading, oral interpretation of stories
    B Measuring reading growth (oral)

Some Ideas for Using a Listening Center in the Areas We Are Currently Teaching
I Art and music
    A Interpreting music through art
    B Listening to a story and drawing
        1 A character in the story
        2 A favorite part of the story
    C Listening to a story; just before it ends, stop and ask the children to make their own ending.
II Language arts
    A Creative writing
        1 Tell a short problem story about friends.
           Have the children develop their own solutions.
        2 Record a story but leave it unfinished.
           Have the children create their own ending.
    B English
        1 How to use a dictionary
        2 How to make a book report

    C Foreign-language resources. Some school systems have complete tapes on conversational Spanish and French, as well as songs and dances of these cultures.

    D Listening to stories for enjoyment

    E Radio plays

    F Spelling

        1 Individualized spelling program

        2 Weekly tests for regular spelling programs

III Math

    A Mr. Arithmetic number fact drill

        1 Addition

        2 Subtraction

        3 Multiplication

        4 Division

        5 Percentages

    B Guided seat work

    C Math games

    D Story problems

    E Discovery method using Cuisenaire Rods

IV Reading

    A Diagnostic tests

    B Science Research Associates *Listening Skill Builders*

    C Enrichment activity to follow a reading-group story

    D Introduction of new words in reading

    E Guided seat work

    F Phonics lessons (commercial records are available)

    G Listening to a story to master sequence and retention skills

    H Recording improvement in expression in oral reading. Children enjoy hearing their own voices. A measure of growth in this area for the pupil, parent, and teacher can be made by comparing reading samples from the beginning of the year with those from the end of the year.

    I Reading games

V Science

    A Individual science experiments

    B How to record data

    C Listening to read-aloud excerpts from science books and learning to draw conclusions

VI Social studies

    A How to make reports

    B Practicing reporting

    C Reading selections from books

    D Interviewing a resource person who is unable to visit the class and recording the interview

Problems   Little, if any, emphasis is placed upon teaching listening skills in most teacher-training courses. The teacher-training institutions and classroom practices appear to suggest that listening ability may be taken for granted. Students come to school capable of listening, and it is often assumed that they are listening when in fact they are just passively sitting with folded hands, good posture, and attentive eyes!

Studies (39) have shown that schools do very little to improve the listening ability of students. Yet students spend much of their time in school listening in order to learn. Listening has a high degree of respect among educators, but little effort or time is devoted to it as a separate skill area. Many listening suggestions may be listed in the classroom, but very few ideas are given on how *to teach* students to become better listeners. An examination of the language arts textbooks commonly used in elementary classrooms reveals only a few pages concerning listening skills. Listening is the language arts medium students use most frequently, but it is seldom stressed. If listening is taught too incidentally, the listening results that are desired for students may not be attained.

Assessment   The teacher and the student need to know if effective listening habits are developing through the planned listening activities of the classroom.

Evidence, required to measure growth, may be found in well-designed lessons, standards, checklists, and teacher-made and standardized tests. Organized listening lessons will provide feedback to the teacher and the student as to whether the listening required was effective for the purposes defined. Students may design and set up their own standards for listening and assess their listening behaviors against their standards as an individual class member and as a class. Statements of standards may be converted into checklists which can be used to provide a written record of progress toward the stated listening goals and habits.

Sequential Tests of Educational Progress (STEP) and *Durrell Listening–Reading Series,* both published by Educational Testing Service, are standardized tests designed to measure students' listening abilities in the intermediate grades. The *Listening Skills Assessment* from the New Hampshire Department of Education (50) measures the listening skills listed earlier in this chapter. Teacher-made tests can be designed to measure growth in specific listening areas, such as distinguishing fact from opinion, getting the main idea and supporting details, and recognizing propaganda. These may be modeled after a standardized format.

SPELLING

Unlike listening—a neglected aspect of the language arts—spelling is the focal point of a great deal of attention from both educators and the public. A student may not spell very well or students may not spell some words well, but everyone acknowledges that the schools should do something about it. Improvement in spelling instruction continues to capture the interest of researchers and teachers as both seek better methods and procedures.

Instructional Emphases Spelling instruction at the intermediate grades continues from the skills and words acquired in the primary grades and builds upon these.

Today's concern for better student writing and communication skills—words used correctly and spelled accurately—demands that spelling instruction be designed to be important and effective. The intermediate grades spelling program emphasizes the acquisition of a spelling vocabulary, its maintenance, and the transfer of those words into a "bank" of familiar writing vocabulary.

"Learning to spell is a matter of acquiring knowledge rather than habits . . ." say Henderson and Beers (29). Their publication provides valuable insights into the teaching of spelling, for the primary as well as for the intermediate teacher. In the same book, Zutell (72) states that "it seems reasonable to conclude that learning to spell is not simply a matter of enough drill work and/or rote memorization. The development of spelling proficiency seems to involve both cognitive and linguistic processes and, as such, it requires the active, exploring participation of the learner." He continues by saying,

> Furthermore, classroom practices like extensive phonics drills and the typical weekly spelling list–test cycle hardly encourage essential active participation and concept formation. It would seem more profitable to construct learning environments in which children have the opportunity to formulate, test, and evaluate their own hypotheses about the orthography. Such environments might logically include activities which encourage and stimulate natural language use through extensive speaking, reading, and writing as means of communication and expression.
>
> Children also need opportunities to compare and contrast words on a variety of levels (sound, structure, syntax, semantics) so that they might systematically discover and utilize both intraword and interword patterns of organization. Activities that foster such comparisons need not be especially complicated or time consuming. Henderson (14) briefly suggests a word sorting procedure in which the child sorts or piles word-bank words under examples of useful classifications. It may be helpful for children to see the relationship between the spelling of past tense (typically-*ed*) and its various but systematic pronunciations. Children may be asked to classify their -*ed* words as more like *raked, cheated,* or *played.* (Of course there will be some exceptions, and other examples may be thought of as the child proceeds with the activity.)
>
> Dale (8) and O'Rourke (17) describe the technique of "word webbing" as another activity through which older children may discover word patterns and relationships. In a root web, for instance, words like *sympathy, pathetic,* and *pathology* are linked through their common root *path-,* from *pathos* (suffer). By constructing such webs and checking their accuracy, students can simultaneously extend both their spelling and vocabulary growth through the discovery of underlying, systematic patterns of meaning and spelling.
>
> In effect, children need the opportunity and encouragement to *discover* for themselves the structures governing English spelling, just as they *invent* (in Piaget's terms) the structures which enable them to assimilate reality, and tacitly *construct* the transformational rules which govern the structure of spoken and written language.

These studies are supported by Hodges (31), who reported that "the ability to spell is a highly complex and active intellectual accomplishment, and not, as it has historically been viewed, a low-order memory task."

Instructional Strategies   The spelling program in a majority of elementary class-rooms is largely determined by the textbook used. The textbooks provide a prescribed word list and a method of teaching and learning. In addition, some classes may draw other word lists for spelling from students' writings or other areas of the curriculum. Utilization of the textbook gives teachers confidence that the common words of English are learned progressively.

Spelling research over the last sixty years has set forth significant elements that should be reflected in published spelling programs. These research-supported proce-dures (14) are as follows:

1 Spelling words should initially be presented in a list form and later be studied in sentence or paragraph form.

2 Words used most frequently by students should be the first words to be mastered.

3 Spelling games are devices to stimulate students' interests.

4 The single most important factor in learning to spell words is the student correcting his or her own spelling test under the teacher's supervision.

5 It is not necessary for students to learn the meaning of the majority of their spelling words.

6 The whole-word method of learning words is a better technique than learning words by syllables.

7 To teach spelling by phonic rules is questionable due to the nature of the English language.

8 The study of spelling should be between an hour and seventy-five minutes per week.

9 The test–study method is better than the study–test method with most students. Spelling can be taught effectively if the instruction is based on information that research and practice have provided.

A typical weekly lesson plan from a commercial spelling program requires ap-proximately a fifteen-minute period and incorporates the following features:

First day. The teacher gives the pretest of the words in the lesson. The student checks his or her own test and records his or her individual word study list.

Second day. The teacher directs study of the function and structural and phonemic patterns in the words. Each student studies his or her individual spelling list.

Third day. The teacher gives dictation in sentences containing words from this lesson and previous lessons to provide maintenance and practice of spelling words.

Fourth day. The student continues activities and practices in the lesson and studies misspelled words from third day.

Fifth day. The teacher administers and corrects the final test. The students record words, if any, that are still causing difficulty.

A word study procedure is recommended for each student, since spelling is learned by a series of steps involving impression and recall. For example, the following method of study includes visual, auditory, and kinesthetic impressions and recall—seeing in the mind and writing from memory.

When you study a word:

1 Look at the word and say it correctly.
2 Close your eyes and recall the image of the word as you say the word.
3 Look at the word again.
4 Cover the word and write it as you think about how it looks.
5 Check your spelling. Correct errors. If you have no errors continue on to the next word.

Spelling enrichment activities and games are used to stimulate student interest, to provide for individual needs, and to ensure variety in the program. They often require reading, comparing, contrasting, retrieving, selecting, and writing the list words to attain spelling growth and maintenance.

Hodges (31) points out that "children learn to spell not from a study of isolated words but from a rich interaction with written language through daily reading and writing." He further contends that word games are a valuable part of the teaching of spelling and that their value is not merely in the enjoyment they offer, "but in their potential to promote inquiry and experimentation." His book, *Learning to Spell*, explains forty-one word games children, teachers, and parents can play to enhance the spelling program.

The learning styles of children should be reflected by the type of spelling programs in which they are involved. Visual learners would probably rely on the configuration of words, auditory learners would probably benefit from a phonics approach, and kinesthetic learners may need to write the words to see if they feel right (4).

Problems There appears to be a serious gap between the current research in spelling and the practices of the classroom. Improvement in spelling instruction has been slow. Many research-supported techniques and procedures have not been used effectively. There is evidence that some practices and activities implemented in some spelling programs have no logic or basis in research. Some examples of these are looking for "hard spots" in a word to improve spelling ability, studying spelling words before a pretest, writing words in the air as a valuable means of helping a student practice the spelling of a word, and learning words by syllables rather than by the whole-word presentation.

Assessment Tests and checklists may be used to measure a student's ability to spell words in the basic word list and in functional writing. The general spelling program should include at least two weekly tests, a review test at the end of a unit or some other interval, and a semester or term test. Each of these should include only the words the student should have learned during the given time period. Checklists or progress charts for the student and teacher may record the student's development during a lesson and throughout the year as words are used in day-to-day writing. Standardized achievement tests, administered at the end of the year, can give an estimate or indication of a student's spelling ability through the spelling section. The tests from the spelling section are useful only as guides, due to the limited number of words in the instruments.

COMPOSITION

As a powerful means of understanding the function and value of language, writing is the most difficult language skill to acquire. Still, it has the potential for developing all the components of the language arts program. Writing is one of the most complex processes in which man engages.

Words are the "stuff" of writing. Writers work with words. They are the tools that must be selected and ordered in composing a sentence, a paragraph, a poem, or a composition. Jacobs (34) has expressed what he calls the range of words. "Words certainly do have their ways. They grow out of human experiences. They may be regarded as labels. They are used for walls or fences. They are intended to be vehicles for the conveyance of ideas—sometimes facts, sometimes opinions, sometimes sales talks, sometimes directions and sometimes feelings."

One of the most important things students will learn in school is how to communicate. It is a skill that is essential to success no matter what career is chosen. Tech-

One of the most important things that students will learn in school is how to communicate.

nology has changed many of the means of communicating, but the written word is still important. Words are a means of preserving thoughts, feelings, and opinions and have the power to influence others. Writing is one of the best means for students to discover and display what they have learned. The everyday classroom presents many opportunities for students to write. Students become writers by writing, if they receive good instruction in improving their writing.

Instructional Emphases   The sequential study of composition continues at this level, with the same concepts, skills, and attitudes that were begun in the primary grades, and builds upon that foundation. Emphases are placed upon the increased awareness of the need for composition as one of the means for communication. The content of the composition program draws upon the current needs and experiences of students and includes prewriting, purpose, audience, organization, composition types (such as narration, description, exposition, and persuasion), revision, and the related skills of handwriting, spelling, capitalization, punctuation, grammatical usage, and sentence structure. The student will be assisted to: (1) continue to explore and use personal experiences and experiences of others as the basis of composition; (2) select topics to write about that are appropriate to the audience and the purpose of the communication; (3) organize writing assignments with attention to concise and fig-urative language, sentence variety, point of view and language mechanics; and (4) write compositions that have a beginning, a middle, and an end through prewriting, writing, and revision.

The following observations, drawn from a review of professional literature, are listed by Haley-James (25):

1 Children learn to write by writing.

2 Even young children whose knowledge of letter formations and spelling patterns is limited can and should write.

3 Regular and meaningful writing benefits learning to read.

4 Writing frequently on self-selected topics is important to developing skill in writing.

5 When children feel a need or a desire to write for some purpose or audience, they write more effectively.

6 Children should write from their experiences, and expectations for their writing should be in line with their stage of experiential and mental development.

7 Oral language processing of the ideas and content being expressed should precede writing and occur during writing.

8 Real and varied audiences for their work are important to the development of children as writers and to their incentive to write.

9 Writing purpose and a developing concept of audience lead children to a logical need for revising selected pieces of their writing.

10 Formal study of grammar should be delayed until grade eight or nine: until then revising writing in view of the audience for the writing should be the basis of grammar-related language study.

11 Teacher and peer conferences with the writer are appropriate means of helping children process their writing orally and progress from first drafts, in which primary concern is with getting meaning out on paper, to improved drafts.

12 Holistic and primary trait scoring are useful means of assessing both the progress of groups of children and the effectiveness of writing programs.

Instructional Strategies   *Stages of Composition*   Researchers like James Britton, Charles Cooper, Paul Diedrich, Donald Graves, Richard Lloyd-Jones, and James Moffet have provided insights into the writing process and writing evaluation. Their findings appear to indicate that the composition process is a multistaged process. Teachers who are aware of the requirements at the various stages of writing are able to assist and instruct students to become better writers.

One teaching method based on a skill approach recognizes the importance of three stages of composition—prewriting, writing, and postwriting or revision.

Prewriting is a period for exploration and discovery before the composition is begun. Prewriting includes planning and provision for involving students' participation and discussion of the writing assignment. During brainstorming and discussion activities, ideas and vocabulary can be developed for use in the composition. The students talk to clarify and to gather and sort information on the audience, purpose, and content of the composition and to develop main points.

The audience, from a friend to the community at large, would determine what kind of information and appropriate language is to be used in the writing. The purpose of the composition considers why the writing is being done and what effect it should have on its audience. Content is determined by the kind and amount of information the composition will transmit. The interrelationship among audience, purpose, and content will shape the general outline of the composition. The prewriting talk will help students to examine their own thoughts as well as those of other students and to discuss special features and problems. This interaction is important in the learning process of writing.

Writing is centered on all the activities—outlining, the false starts and rough drafts, the additions and deletions, and so on—that will culminate in the communication of an idea that has a logical beginning, a middle, and an end. The only concern here should be for content, the getting of ideas down on paper.

The teacher may confer with individuals or groups of students about the work in progress. Students may confer in pairs or in small groups of four or five. They can learn a great deal from each other as they ask and respond to such questions as "What do you like about my composition?" "What do you want to know about my story?" and "What should I do to improve my compositon?" Many ideas will be exchanged which can help students to improve their content. Students may accept and reject various ideas which are received because they must maintain "ownership" of the composition in order to want to continue to improve it. The writer needs to be sure that the intended meaning has been conveyed and that the audience will understand the message clearly. The concept of using conferences as a strategy for helping students to improve their writing is supported by Graves (23) and other researchers.

Postwriting or revision begins when the first draft of the composition is completed. This final stage includes revising, reorganizing, and resequencing, to ascertain that the audience, purpose, and content of the composition have been met. Editing and proofreading for correctness complete the final steps. Revising and editing need to be taught and practiced as separate entities. The revision should be for improving the content of the composition. The students should not be concerned with grammar and usage at this stage but, rather, with being certain that the composition states what is really intended.

Editing is the time when students examine the mechanics of their writing. They check for spelling, capitalization, punctuation, errors in grammar, and so on. It is important to recognize that the skills of editing must be taught carefully and practiced regularly. When the students complete these stages, the compositions should be the best that they are capable of doing at that time. Thus a final draft is the result of much preliminary work.

After the *postwriting* stage is completed, the piece of writing should be delivered to the intended audience. This is usually referred to as the *publication* stage and may range from displaying student writings in the classroom or throughout the school, to publication in a school or districtwide newspaper, to mailing the piece to an intended audience, to being bound and placed in the classroom or school library, to being sent to a commercial publisher, or to being made available to potential readers in other ways. The teacher and students may devise many creative ways to publish their writing. Suggestions for binding children's books may be found in the Appendixes.

Holdzkom et al. (32, pp. 56–58) suggest the following activities teachers might use during the stages of composition.

Classroom Activities Using the Process Approach

Prewriting. Most classrooms offer countless opportunities for prewriting experiences. The important thing is to recognize these opportunities and to verbalize them. Drawing, for example, can be an important prewriting activity for very young children. As they grow older, children move to writing before they draw.

All of the content areas, for example, should be taken advantage of. Before children are taken on science or social studies field trips, the teacher can let them know that they will have an opportunity to write about the experience, either during the trip or after they return— during the return trip on the bus, they can talk to the person they are sitting with about their ideas for the writing task. Talk is an important prewriting activity and can be encouraged in many ways. It can include teacher/student, student/student, and group interactions.

Reading is also an important prewriting activity. Children can use books, newspapers, magazines, and even other children's writing to generate ideas for their own writing.

Oral language activities such as reading aloud to children, playing records, storytelling, and talking in small groups can be used as stimuli for writing.

Prewriting should be, at least in part, a private experience. Children need time to explore their own thoughts and feelings, to organize and jot down ideas, and to develop a strategy for how they will approach the writing.

Drafting. Writing of the first draft can be done as a group activity but will more often be an individual experience. The teacher should be available to the students for short conferences during this stage and the following stages. For young children, this can mean moving from child to child and making short comments—asking questions and showing interest. As children grow older, the teacher might also be writing a first draft, so conferences might be scheduled, or children might have a peer who serves as a sounding board and, later, as a student editor. During the drafting stage, the focus should be on the content of the message, not the conventions of writing.

Revising. During the revision stage, children have an opportunity to go back over their writing and make whatever changes they feel are necessary. This might mean changes in syntax, sentence structure, organization, and, in some cases, starting over completely. For the teacher, this may also be the most difficult stage to teach. Young children and older students alike resist the notion that their first draft is not final.

Calkins, as quoted in Gentry (5), suggests that beginning writers are reluctant to revise because they view writing as a one-step process. She has attempted to describe the early stages of revision for third graders and to offer suggestions for how teachers can help children move on to the next stage:

Revision Stage	*Suggestions for Next Step*
1 Children don't independently reread or consider either their words or their mechanics. Writing is final, and for these children, it is extremely hard to put anything on paper at all.	These children can revise in other media. They should also be encouraged to reread what they write. Questions like "What is your favorite part?" help them begin to look back.
2 Some children reread and correct their papers. They only make small editing changes, and they erase rather than cross-out. They see each draft as a final copy.	If the teacher listens carefully to what this child writes and asks honest, real questions, the writer can learn that the reader needs more information. Content revision begins as "adding on." Usually children first add on to the end of their piece, and later they add on to middle sections through inserts.
3 Some children independently recopy their pieces. This is a step ahead of the child who merely corrects the original paper. Once there are two drafts, handwriting and spelling can be relegated to a later stage in the process, and the child can worry about content and language only. Also, as the child recopies, he or she often changes the original.	The next step is to learn to make the first draft into a working manuscript. Write all over it. Star it. Change it. Use it.

Editing. During the editing stage, students take a final look at their writing—correct misspellings, check their grammar, perhaps still change a word or phrase here and there. They might also do this for other students.

The degree to which the edited, final draft will be correct depends upon the developmental maturity of the student. Very young children will proudly hand their teacher a paper filled with invented spellings and mechanical errors. Many of these "mistakes" represent learning in progress and should not be of concern to the teacher. For older students, this might still be the case, but errors might also be indications of a need for guidance for the teacher.

In teaching writing, it is especially important for the teacher to be with the students and move among them as they write. Active participation on the teacher's part is perceived by the students as commitment to support their writing efforts. As an added dimension to this commitment, teachers may share samples of their writing with the students. This would demonstrate that the teachers do write and their writings may serve as models.

The Role of Grammar Instruction   In many intermediate-grade classrooms, the bulk of language arts instruction is devoted to the teaching of grammar and usage. Often, however, this teaching of grammar and usage is not related to teaching composition. It is often spent in memorizing rules, in labeling parts of speech, and in completing isolated drills on ditto sheets or in workbooks. It is important for teachers and administrators to know what the research presents in this area.

Holdzkom et al. (32, pp. 61–68) review the research and make some specific suggestions:

> Research does not support the notion that an ability to perform grammatical analysis leads to improvement of students' oral or written communication. Indeed, some researchers feel that children younger than 13 cannot work with abstraction so instruction in the abstractness of grammar may be counter-productive. However, when grammar instruction springs from and links back to children's own writing, children will see the connection and use the new structures in their work. Grammar instruction as an end in itself is unlikely to translate into better compositions.

Very few questions, however, are as emotionally charged as the one posed here. Much of the recent research on writing pays very slight attention to the teaching of grammar in the composing process. Indeed, in a recent review of research on writing, several experts are cited who recommend that grammar instruction not be attempted before grade 7. This recommendation is made because many children have difficulty with the abstract nature of grammar, or because such study will retard the development of the child's own language.

Other educators feel, however, that grammar instruction is necessary to help children learn to write well, to be able to use language correctly, or to be able to express themselves clearly. Parents often reinforce this idea. Traditionally in American education, the grammar school has been seen as the institution created by a nation of immigrants to homogenize the culture through language.

Before we can look at the role of grammar instruction in improving students' compositions, we need to define clearly what is meant by the term "grammar." From there, we can proceed to discuss effective instruction and ways to integrate that instruction naturally in the student's writing.

Most teachers mean a subject matter when they say "grammar." "Grammar" is taught by English teachers and consists of a set of rules which can be learned and which, when used, will allow the speaker or writer to duplicate the language used by the social class whose dialect is the standard of the language. In this definition, differences among dialect groups are usually viewed as deficiencies which should be remediated. Thus, the view of "grammar" taken is a *prescriptive* one.

In this view, "grammar" becomes a value-laden term. By speaking "grammatically," the speaker is using the language conventions used by the socially prestigious class. Deviation from standard indicates an imperfect use of language, a less than complete understanding of how the language really works. Because dialect, usage, and other conventions of language are all cultural phenomena, the listener (or reader) very often can have stereotyped reactions to the speaker (or writer).

It is this prescriptive view of grammar that dominates most "grammar" instruction. Children are taught to make subjects and verbs "agree" in number, to begin sentences with capital letters and end them with periods, question marks or exclamation points, to insure that "every sentence is a complete thought." Often, this instruction takes the form of memorizing grammar rules. Unfortunately, the knowledge of a rule does not necessarily lead to the employment of the rule (Petroskey, 1977).

If by grammar however, we mean the rules underlying our use of language, then every child comes to school with a working knowledge of grammar. While students may not be able to talk about how language works, they can use language. The teacher does not teach grammar, then, in the same way that he or she teaches reading. Rather, by allowing children to use language—to speak and to write—the teacher can foster the development of language skills. By organizing instruction so that a child's growing ability to write is encouraged, several things will happen:

1. Children will develop fluency in the "physical" or "mechanical" aspects of writing. Writing difficulty may stem from two different problems: what to say and how to transfer the thought from the mind to the page. If this second area of difficulty can be reduced, then the writer's attention will be focused primarily on the first area. In order to reduce the difficulty of the physical act of writing, the muscles of the hand and eyes must be developed to the point that writing is not the literally painful task that it is for nonwriters. Frequent opportunities to flex these muscles will reduce the physical difficulty.

It is the same for the "mechanical" aspects of language. Frequent opportunities for writing will develop the child's ability to use words, spelling, and punctuation in an almost automatic way. Frequent steps to check spelling, to erase, to revise on the mechanical level will not be required.

2. Frequent opportunities to write will also underscore, for the child, the differences between what can be said and what can be written (Britton). Not only will there be a desire to extend the repertoire of written forms at the child's command, there will be a need for more grammatical features which will arise from the child's desire to communicate. Thus, the "teachable moment" will be created.

3. Children will learn from each other. While it is possible to describe the stages of language development in children as a statistical group, it is clear that children develop language fluency and control different grammatical structures at times and rates which vary from individual to individual. Such individual differences are especially evident in classrooms in which children from various socioeconomic backgrounds come together (Loban, 1976). Thus, by encouraging children to talk and listen to one another and to work in writing/editing groups, teachers will invite the flow of grammatical information from child to child as writing pieces develop. Children, then, will teach one another (Slavin).

4. By presenting "grammar" in the context of the child's own writing, application of conventions will be made clear and practical. As early as 1908, George Carpenter and his colleagues questioned the ability of children younger than 13 years to understand the *abstract* nature of syntax. It is, of course, precisely this abstractness which is emphasized when we teach "grammar," meaning a system of rules of how language operates. If, however, syntax were taught in relation to the child's own writing and speaking then the abstract nature would disappear and the child would be able to apply the syntactic feature for which a need is exhibited. Moreover, by delaying the attention to "grammar" until the editing stage of the writing process, the child has already wrestled with one of the major difficulties (what to say) and can now turn attention to the second difficulty (how to say it).

5. By helping students develop a sense of audience and of appropriateness of communication, the teacher can help children understand that the effectiveness of language use depends upon factors outside the child. Depending upon the nature of the communication, whether oral or written, children may need to use variations of standard English. As the child's sense of purpose of communication develops, the need for selecting from among several linguistic items will be perceived. The language used when writing to a friend is different from the language used when writing to the principal of the school. Similarly, language used to convince a general audience of the rightness of a given proposition is different from the language used to write a ghost story. By setting writing tasks which are different in purpose and audience, the teacher can establish different language demand situations, thus creating a need to increase the number of language features available.

This is not to suggest that "grammar" instruction should occur only in an accidental or undirected way with each child deciding when, or even if he or she needs to learn particular items of the language system. However, teachers do need to make a distinction between teaching "grammar" and teaching mechanics of use, and teaching writing.

By mechanics, we mean a series of conventions which help writers express extra-linguistic features of language. Mechanics includes use of punctuation, handwriting, beginning sentences with capital letters, spelling conventionally. This system of symbols can conveniently be taught within the context of the children's writing, and in the revising phase.

Invented spellings and grammar "errors" may also be viewed as important indications of the problem-solving process used by the child and can provide important data about the child's progress in learning to read and to develop writing fluency. What is commonly seen as a problem (the child's inability to include pronouns, for example) might better be seen as an opportunity for instruction. If the child's writing exhibits no need for pronouns, it is unlikely that a worksheet on pronoun reference will have much impact. If, however, the child is using pronouns in an awkward way, he or she may be very accepting of a teacher's demonstration of how pronouns can make the sentence more fluent. Similarly, showing a child how commas can help readers to understand the child's sentence will lead to more effective use of commas than will work on worksheets.

Many teachers found that teaching students to combine sentences leads to more fluent use of language. By practicing the embedding of one sentence or idea within another sentence, students can learn to create sentences which are more interesting and can learn to use a variety of syntactic patterns.

The underlying notion of sentence combining is that fluent writers use longer, more complex sentences than do less fluent writers. Through a series of guided exercises, students are shown how several short sentences may be combined into longer ones. For example, a poor writer may write these sentences:

William Hearst owned a newspaper.
He wanted to increase sales.
He wrote about atrocities in Cuba.

A more competent writer might combine the first two sentences:

Newspaper-owner William Hearst wanted to increase sales. He wrote about atrocities in Cuba.

A still more competent writer might get all three ideas into one sentence:

Wishing to increase sales, newspaper-owner William Hearst wrote about atrocities in Cuba.

To increase fluency and add variety to students' writing, sentence combining can be very effective. Often, conjunctions or relative pronouns can be added in the exercises to guide the combinations:

The car was stolen.
It was red. (that)
The car that was stolen was red.

Other signals might include underlying parts of one sentence to be embedded in the main sentence or using the word SOMETHING in capitals:

Joanna ate the fish.
The fish was *broiled*.
Joanna ate the broiled fish.

and

We thought SOMETHING.
We would pass the test. (that)
We thought that we would pass the test.

Sentence combining exercises have been shown to improve the fluency of students' writing, if fluency is determined by length. Hunt analyzed writing samples of 72 writers (drawn equally from Grades 4, 8, and 12 and a group of writers published in *Harper's* and *Atlantic*). He found that, indeed, older writers write longer sentences. But he found that the major difference between student writers and adult writers was that adults tended to increase clause length, not total number of clauses used. Whereas younger writers string clauses together, either with coordinating or subordinating conjunctions, adult writers used more nonclause elements to pack meaning into clauses (6).

Mellon urges caution, however, when using sentence combining activities. As early as 1969, Mellon conducted experiments which showed that merely giving students practice in sentence combining could actually have an adverse effect on student writing unless sentence combining practice was linked to helping students look at sentence effectiveness (8). Again, such an activity sets the stage for students' writing to occur. It cannot replace students' writing and thinking about their writing. Practice on controlled exercises is only a first step. It will be the students' ability to use the *results* of these exercises in their own writing which will determine whether the grammar instruction has contributed to students' growth as writers.

Sentence combining is a good example of grammar instruction which will extend the student's repertoire of writing skills and which will lead to better composition writing. Other exercises in grammatical analysis can be undertaken based on real writing produced by the students.

The teacher's role, then, in teaching grammar is quite different from being the guardian of correct usage and the arbiter of elegant standards. As a helper or coach, the teacher responds to the communication of the child, suggesting ways to strengthen the child's writing, or offering information about how language can be used to state the child's thought more precisely. As Constance Weaver points out, the teacher's knowledge of grammar in a formal sense is far more important than the student's. As a coach or editor, the teacher who understands the grammatical relationships conveyed by words and sentences will see many ways to strengthen students' writing. These variations can be taught to students both directly— as in sentence combining—and indirectly, through editorial conferences.

As a role model, the teacher has two kinds of responsibility. One is the modelling of effective language structures. If children hear and see practiced the kinds of language which they are expected to use, they will be more apt to do so.

The second responsibility is for the teacher to be accepting of the child's language. This acceptance is important for all children, but is especially so for children for whom standard English is not a first dialect or language or who may be developmentally or physically disabled. By working with the language used by the child, the teacher will not prescribe language change, but will facilitate language growth and communication skills development. By avoiding judgments about the "correctness" of language use, the teacher will provide a friendly environment in which children can explore and "try-on" differing language styles, and can decide which language structures are appropriate, given the communicative purpose and the audience. Finally, by refusing to divorce grammar instruction from the reality of language use, the teacher will be able to help children develop an enthusiasm for the systemic nature of language and an eagerness to use that system to enhance their own writing.

Summary

How can grammar instruction help make students better writers? If the instruction is integrally related to students' own writing, and if the instruction is geared toward application, grammar can make a difference. Sentence combining activities have been shown to relate to improvements in children's writing. But, even these exercises must be presented so that the reasons for the effectiveness of the combined sentence are clear to the young writer.

The new view of grammar articulated by Francis Christensen suggests some new directions for teaching students to vary the texture and direction of their writing to increase interest.

What is clear is that the "memorize the rules" approach to grammar teaching does not—and probably cannot—lead to improvement in writing. Indeed, this approach may prove damaging to the writer's attitudes toward writing and in any case will take time away from the real task: writing, writing, and more writing.

Classroom Climate for Composition   Motivation to write will not be high unless students' writing is valued and rewarded. Teachers must create a classroom atmosphere of acceptance and appreciation of writing. This means seeing errors not always as deficiencies, but as signs of growth. Praise and encouragement will foster positive attitudes, and when students begin to understand they can succeed, they will feed on that success and continue to grow.

Effective writing is a process that develops through years of practice and instruction. No student is going to be a master at the beginning. Despite most teachers' efforts, students in the intermediate grades do not *all* possess adequate writing skills. Writing, in some instances, has been a small part of their language arts program. However, students who do write learn, through their practice, all areas of the curriculum. They learn to read, to spell, to use correct grammar and punctuation, and to use legible handwriting. They also learn to integrate the knowledge they are gaining in other subject areas—science, health, social studies, math—through the writing process. A rich environment of children's and adolescent literature and of oral language development can contribute significantly to the composition program.

Opportunities for Writing   Making writing a daily part of the classroom curriculum is essential if students are to develop any reasonable degree of facility. The day-to-day activities of the modern classroom provide unlimited opportunities for students' personal and practical writing. Children need to be encouraged to express themselves through writing. The following are examples of situations that lead to writing:

Personal letters, pen pal letters, and notes of invitation and thanks
Business letters or requests for information for class activities
Notices, advertisements, announcements, and directions
Outlines, class notes, club minutes, science and social studies summaries and records, and research reports
News articles, plays, stories, poems, jokes, songs, and games
Descriptive, sequence, factual, opinion, and summary paragraphs
Diaries, journals, and logs
The Dial-an-Author program suggested by Bantam Books

Since these writings are a part of the other *real* experiences, students learn that writing can serve life situations and can be utilized for different purposes.

Problems   There is little writing in today's schools, according to Donald Graves (23). Daily writing is not part of the students' school life and, at best, there is only the once-a-week composition. There is evidence that adults, including teachers, write even less than students do. Writing is a basic of education and has been neglected in school and in society.

The back-to-basics movement has had a dramatic impact on composition. Suddenly writing, once the domain of junior and senior high school English teachers, has become a concern of elementary teachers. The elementary school has for many years placed a high premium on teaching students to read and on requiring them to listen. Little time or instruction has been given to the area of writing. Elementary students have spent the majority of the time in their language arts program in basal reading instruction, with numerous supplementary practice sheets and workbooks. Writing has been a very small part of their program—usually a fifteen- to twenty-minute period a week. This small time period has been devoted to language skills such as grammar and punctuation taught in a drill format from a textbook, a practice that is partly responsible for poor writing in the elementary school.

Writing has often been used for discipline purposes in the school. The assigned punishment composition, "How I Plan to Change My Attitude, Study Habits, and so on" has not contributed to the view that writing is a craft and a very personal valued means of communication.

Beginning writing is difficult not only for students but also for their teachers. Teachers have expressed a negative attitude toward writing. They do not want to teach writing because so few of them have been trained to do so. Many do not enjoy the act of writing and do not write unless required to do so. They often feel that they are poor writers and that the demands of teaching so many subject areas do not leave them time to teach compositon or to improve their own writing skills.

Writing is a lonely, painfully hard, but rewarding task. It is an important dimension of the language arts program and requires deliberate planning and teaching. Without a facilitative teacher to provide time and instruction in writing, it is no wonder that students complain that they have nothing to say or nothing of value about which to write. The teacher must be able to help students release ideas and express what they know, and must have experiences in teaching composition that employ the conventions of edited English. Writing must become a valued daily necessity for students and teachers.

Assessment   Evaluation of composition is an integral part of the language arts program which promotes, measures, and encourages growth in writing. Evaluation should be viewed as a cooperative task of the teacher and the student. The following procedures may be used to evaluate compositions throughout the school year:

1 Student writing folders may be kept to aid the teacher, the student, and the parents in comparing and assessing progress in writing performance from the beginning, middle, and end of the year. Writing is a long-term process and should not be evaluated on a single piece of writing. Grades in a grade book cannot show progress or lack of progress, but five or six writing samples can.

2 Dictated paragraphs may be used as an informal evaluation of students' writing abilities. Skills in correct punctuation, capitalization, spelling, and paragraph form are assessed.

3 Original paragraphs may be used to determine the degree of proficiency in organization, vocabulary, and mechanics.

4 Student–teacher conferences to evaluate a composition for specific objectives during the writing process may prove an effective means for the teacher and the student to receive feedback and diagnose problems. Corrections made under teacher guidance provide aid in analysis and evaluation in locating errors.

5 General or holistic evaluation methods may be used to get a total impression of a written work. General comments and impressions can be recorded.

6 Students may work in pairs or as a group to edit individual or class compositions against a class or standard guidelines. Editing groups provide means of expanding ideas, responding to the writings of others, increasing critical reading skills, and developing realistic writing standards.

7 Students may evaluate their own written work against a standard. Original (first-draft) and edited compositions may be used as evidence of skills in self-evaluation.

Evaluation of student compositions should take place after the revising and editing stages and after the student has completed the final draft. Prior to this time in the writing process, teachers should be helping students to improve their writing for content and for mechanics. Too often, evaluation comes after the first draft instead of after the final draft. In such cases, the first draft is the final draft. Teachers need to teach students to write as many drafts as may be necessary in order to make the composition the best that the student is capable of writing. After the evaluation, it might be beneficial for the student to do a revision, incorporating the suggestions for improvement.

As teachers plan for the evaluation of student compositions, they must be certain that they have established goals and objectives for the composition program, that they have an instructional program which meets the goals and objectives, and that the evaluation component is designed to show whether or not the instruction has been effective and whether or not the goals and objectives have been met.

It is evident that the best way to evaluate students' abilities as writers is through the use of writing samples rather than through the use of multiple choice or fill-in-the-blank-type tests. It is unfortunate that most assessments of writing are done through multiple choice or fill-in-the-blank-type testing. It is refreshing to see that several statewide writing assessments (for example, in New York, South Carolina, Texas) are utilizing writing samples.

All student compositions do not need to be evaluated. There are many ways, including peer evaluation, for assessing the compositions which are selected for teacher evaluation. It is important for teachers to point out student strengths as well as to diagnose deficiencies as they evaluate student compositions. Underlining "beautiful thoughts," noting growth in vocabulary, and praising individual improvements can be excellent motivators for student writers.

Three common methods for evaluating student compositions are holistic scoring, analytic scoring, and primary-trait scoring. An explanation of these scoring procedures follows.

1 *Holistic Scoring*. Briefly, holistic scoring involves reviewing a paper for an overall or "whole" impression. Individual characteristics such as grammar, usage, syntax, spelling, and creativity undoubtedly affect a rater's response, but none of these factors is addressed directly. Generally, a four-point scale is used in ranking papers; model papers are used as guides in assigning scores.

2 *Analytical Scoring*. Analytical scoring is quite different in that it involves isolating the characteristics of "good" writing—for instance, organization, syntax, mechanics, style—and scoring them one by one. Again, a four-point scale may be used. However, in addition to model papers, readers receive a scoring guide which defines each characteristic in explicit terms and offers specific criteria for assigning scores at each level. This scoring approach allows one to report not just how students performed overall, but how they performed with respect to syntax, word choice, or some other trait.

3 *Primary-Trait Scoring*. Primary-trait scoring presumes that all writing is done in terms of an audience, and that successful writing is that which has the desired effect upon that audience: For example, a set of directions for assembling a bike provides clear, orderly information; a campaign speech arouses support. The most important— or *primary*—traits in a piece of writing are those which cause it to have its desired effect. These traits are isolated and scored independently. Whereas analytical scoring focuses on traits important to *any* piece of writing in *any* context, primary traits differ from case to case, depending on audience and situation. The primary traits for the bike assembly instructions, for instance, might be organization and clarity; for the campaign speech, word choice and syntax. Primary-trait scoring does not provide a broad profile of student performance; nevertheless it's an excellent means of scoring specific writing skills. As with analytical scoring, raters follow a written guide; they may also use model papers in assigning scores (10).

Teachers could also use modifications of these scoring procedures as they work with writing samples for intermediate-grade students. The evaluation processes may lead to adjustments in the pace and in the plan for instruction for individuals or for student groups.

HANDWRITING

Handwriting is a physical skill that students may be helped to develop. As a tool, it is a means of self-expression and a function important to the part of the school's curriculum in which written expression and communication are needed and required. Yet it has been assigned low priority by many educators, and this neglect is clearly evident in the handwriting of many students and teachers. The current emphasis on the return to basics has caused a revival of interest in the teaching of handwriting. Legibility is part of the criteria for the evaluation of many direct-assessment writing tests.

Instructional Emphases   The handwriting program in grades four and five is continued from earlier grades and builds upon the skills taught and mastered during those years. The skill of cursive handwriting is generally developed during the last half of second grade or the beginning of third grade. This should be a districtwide practice and all teachers should follow the same time frame. Cursive writing is joined script—usually termed real writing by the elementary students. Cursive writing requires increased small-muscle control and is taught so that students will gain more speed in writing. Learning to write in cursive script does not mean that students will substitute cursive writing for their use of manuscript writing or abandon the latter.

Manuscript writing instruction and practice should continue throughout the intermediate grades so that students may retain and improve the level of skill achieved in the earlier grades. Printing takes on added importance as students are required to write more and for more purposes. Signs, labels, records, charts, posters, and applications are examples of items that may require the more easily read and highly legible manuscript style. Thus, increased legibility and speed in manuscript and cursive writing become the focus of handwriting instruction in the intermediate grades.

Instructional Strategies   An analysis of handwriting skill reveals that students must be able to: (1) discriminate and identify shapes by sight and touch and (2) form the shapes by muscular movement. Since vision and muscles must be coordinated, handwriting is a sensorimotor activity and should be approached on a multisensory level. Students hear and say the letter strokes at the same time they write or see them. Thus, there is auditory and visual stimulation accompanied by physical movement.

Training in large- and small-muscle movements supports handwriting instruction. Games and crafts are to be considered a viable support of a multisensory approach to handwriting. Directionality, left–right eye movement, and visual perception training will be carried over into other language arts areas.

Cursive writing is the fourth stage in the mechanics of handwriting. The other stages are readiness skills, manuscript writing, and transition from manuscript to cursive. Each of these stages requires specific and sequential skills to be taught through direct and systematic instruction.

Instruction in grades four and five will increasingly center on the use of writing to communicate. Creative writing, poetry, reports, letters, announcements, and so on are logical extensions of the handwriting instruction when basic letter formations are mastered. Real writing situations foster an understanding of the importance of legible handwriting to communicate.

Students working at developing and maintaining manuscript and cursive writing need individual assistance and group instruction. Group instruction would emphasize the elements of legibility—letter formation, spacing, slant, alignment, size, proportion, and line quality. Handwriting must be legible and students should understand these elements and acquire skill in them. Correct posture and paper and pencil position are also stressed in group instruction. Fatigue may result from poor posture, and correct paper and pencil position promotes ease of hand and arm movement. After a time, group instruction, except for specific common problems, is not needed. The instruction then becomes highly individualized as students practice to improve their own skills.

Some attention to speed is necessary in the intermediate grades after letter formations are learned. The teacher may assist students in transferring good penmanship to writing in the content areas by timed exercises. Legibility and speed are emphasized. The following from Zaner-Bloser (1) is offered as a guide in determining speed attainments in cursive writing by grade level.

Grade	Letters per Line	Letters per Minute
4	20–22	50
5	22–25	60
6	25–28	67

The type of writing—tests, personal correspondence, or school assignments—requires students to make appropriate adjustments in speed.

Good handwriting requires practice. For the student in the intermediate grades, the grade expectancy is one of improved performance. Handwriting is an all-day-long skill. To be taught effectively, instruction must permeate the total curriculum and not be crammed into a ten- to fifteen-minute period usually dominated by commercial textbooks and materials.

Does illegible handwriting interfere with spelling? There is some evidence that it does. In her dissertation research, Strickling (64) found that the oral spelling scores of a group of fifth-graders were higher than their written scores. The conclusion that Strickling drew was that handwriting errors were the source of the discrepancy between oral and written scores, because words missed on the written test were spelled correctly on the oral test. The difference between oral and written spelling errors was approximately 20 percent.

Milone, Wilhide, and Wasylyk (44) conducted a similar study with sixth-grade students in South Carolina. Their study suggests that there is a strong relationship between spelling ability and handwriting. Their data supported the conclusion that poor handwriting is related to poor written spelling ability.

Hodges (31, p. 13) states that "In ordinary circumstances, whenever one writes one also spells. Handwriting has a special importance in spelling because misformed and illegible letters cause words to appear to be misspelled, to be misunderstood, or not to be understood at all." He continues that ". . . since spelling and writing are simultaneous and inseparable activities, spelling and handwriting instruction can be carried on together."

These reports indicate that there is a relationship between handwriting and spelling and that students with poor handwriting are at something of a disadvantage when it comes to written spelling ability. Their handwriting seems to interfere with their spelling in the testing situation, and it is not an illogical leap to assume that the same interference is working in all written assignments.

Problems   Many elementary teachers are not trained in the techniques of teaching handwriting. Therefore, they either teach it incidentally or not at all after the letter formation models are presented. This presents a problem as it is the handwriting teacher's responsibility to understand the developmental nature of handwriting skills and provide effective teaching skills and procedures for a quality program. The teacher requirements are knowing (1) how to write and (2) how to teach handwriting. In manuscript and cursive, the teacher's handwriting will serve as a model for the students in the class.

The model provided by the teacher and other referents (such as alphabet strips, ditto sheets, and charts) must be consistent. The need to write neatly on lined paper as well as on unlined surfaces such as the chalkboard, chart, or overhead projector are apparent. Skills in diagnosing and prescribing instruction for persistent problems in handwriting, such as confusion in visual discrimination, poor muscle control, reversals, left-handedness, and poor evaluation, are needed in the implementation of a handwriting program. It is the teacher who brings direction to the program.

Assessment   Handwriting evaluation may bring about more successful application of the fundamentals and provide insight into the facets of legibility. The evaluation process can be effective if self-evaluation, peer evaluation, and teacher evaluation are employed. The purpose of these evaluations is to locate strengths and weaknesses in the elements of legibility so that appropriate instruction and practice may be determined. Published handwriting scales may be used by students and their peers as a basis for making judgments about the legibility of handwriting samples. The teacher might want to examine the Ayers Handwriting Scale (University of Iowa), the Zaner-Bloser Evaluation Scales, and others. Checklists which include the elements of legible handwriting may be used to evaluate handwriting as well as to provide a record of progress in handwriting skills. Individual handwriting logs are useful for periodic evaluations and may provide writing samples that can be ranked from weak to improved.

Practice in handwriting should grow from diagnosis. Westbrooks (68) cleverly labeled common mistakes in handwriting as handwriting diseases: "Giantwritytis, Tinywritytis, Frillyosis (unnecessary decorations), Slumps (words written above or below the line), 'T'sless (uncrossed *t*'s), Unmeasles (undotted *i*'s), Broken letter (gaps in letters such as *a*, *o*, and *s*), Looptheria, Squeezles (squeezed too close together), Disjointed, and Sloppox (sloppy writing)." Verbalization by students of their weaknesses and their efforts to improve would enhance the evaluation process.

Schools have never been successful in making the handwriting of all students exactly the same; nor is it a particularly desired goal. Schools appear to accept individuality in handwriting if legibility and reasonable speed are maintained.

SPEAKING

Speaking (oral language) has been slighted in many elementary schools. The assumption has been made and accepted by many that when students come to school they do not require instruction in speech as they do in other language art skills. As a result, maturity alone has been responsible for the development of students' speaking abilities. Educators now question this neglect of speech and face the fact that the language arts develop together and that the work in oral communication is basic to all the rest. Oral language skills and instruction should be purposeful, ongoing, and responsive to the needs of elementary students.

Instructional Emphases   To develop speaking abilities in the intermediate grades, the instructional program should be a continuation of the developmental foundation begun in the primary grades. The same kinds of speaking skills and activities are used throughout the grades. They are practiced again, but in the intermediate grades a greater degree of refinement is expected. The content of the speech instruction is the skill performance necessary to deliver or communicate the message (ideas of a story told, a poem read or recited, a report presented) to a listener or listeners. Practiced in more varied and structured situations, speech skills in the intermediate grades will emphasize the factors that promote effective speech for individual and group performances.

Instructional Strategies   Skills in oral language result from practice. The intermediate-grade students should be given opportunities to participate in many different types of oral language activities, such as meetings, conversations, discussions, debates, interviews, reports, explanations, choral reading, problem solving, and creative interpretations. Direct attention at this level should be given to the following factors which contribute to effective speech: control and vocal mechanism, use of nonverbal expression, and adaptation to an audience (52).

Voice Control   By the time students reach the intermediate grades, they have a wide range of speaking skills available to them. The skills they have may be correct, or they may be hampered with habits that need correcting. Voice quality, tone, pitch, and tempo are indicators of a student's emotional state. Under normal circumstances, a student adjusts the volume of her or his voice to fit the needs of the particular speaking environment. Within the school situation, environments might include the classroom, playground, gym class, music class, library, lunchroom, and bus.

Choral reading is an excellent means of facilitating instruction to produce speech that is suitable in tempo and volume for the purpose, the content, and the audience. It provides the means whereby the student can understand the importance of rate, pitch, rhythm, stress, and pause. Experimentation with the different lines may help illustrate how these factors contribute to fluent speech. The selection of choral reading material available is vast. Poems can be found with the arrangements already worked out in many anthologies of verse. Choral speaking can aid in developing good speech as well as in providing self-confidence to shy students and enrichment to the language arts classroom.

Recorded speeches and choral readings may help students discover and assess their own strengths and weaknesses in voice control. This evaluation, in a classroom environment in which students feel free, comfortable, and secure in participating in speaking situations, is focused on self-improvement.

In teaching production of speech and sound and voice control, the teacher may discover students with speech defects which interfere with their ability to communicate. These defects should be brought to the attention of the speech specialist or a person trained in speech correction. The speech specialist can help the teacher in working more effectively with these speech inadequacies.

The teacher's voice, diction, and means of expression are tremendously important. The teacher is the model and example of clear and pleasant speech that is integrated with all activities.

Nonverbal Expressions   Speaking often includes more than just words. Nonverbal elements also carry real meaning. Sometimes the meaning reinforces what the words say. Sometimes the two are contradictory.

Studies by Mehrabian and Ferris (43) show that of any given message, only 35 percent is verbal. The remaining 65 percent is communicated through the various nonverbal channels of the hand, eye, head, and arm movement and by body attitude or position. Students need to become aware of these gestures and their uses.

The teaching task is to help students study and expand their understanding of the nature of body language. Creative dramatics, music, literature, and pantomime are means by which students may be stimulated to study and perform nonverbal elements of speech. These activities provide a variety of roles and contribute to real-life situations. The study of other systems of gestures, such as those of referees, policemen, movie and television directors, music directors or conductors, and the deaf will demonstrate the effective use of body control and movement in communicating. These studies should aid the students' delivery in speaking situations.

Audience   The purpose of speaking is to communicate and only if the message is received by the intended person(s) has communication taken place. As in composition, students must be helped to develop sensitivity to their audience. Their attention must be directed to the ideas to be transmitted and to the person(s) for whom the message is directed. The range of audiences includes classmates, teachers, peers, employers, family, and the community.

With teacher and class assistance, students can plan and clarify thinking and presentations. A variety of methods may be used to express their topics and ideas in creative ways. These may take the form of props, models, audiovisual materials, puppets, charts, and/or maps.

In delivering the speech or presentation, students must learn to establish eye contact and rapport with the audience. Watching the audience for reactions will provide the speaker with information regarding the acceptance of the speaker's message. The speaker can learn to interpret audience feelings and modify his discussion and delivery in terms of these indicators. This is a difficult process and requires many experiences in presenting information. Experiences as a speaker and as part of an audience will enhance the procedure for all students.

Problems   In many instances, teachers dominate the classrooms and do most of the talking, with the result that students have few opportunities to use talk creatively. Talk is a learning activity to be guided by the teacher. Although in many classrooms time is devoted to "show and tell," current events, or sharing time, students often make little progress toward becoming effective speakers in these situations. This is partly due to the fact that these sharing situations have become rituals rather than valid learning opportunities. Getting students into and out of structured talk environments is a very challenging task for the teacher. In most situations, the teacher is facing this problem without an oral language curriculum or structured guidelines (36).

Correctness in English and changing speech patterns poses a dilemma for the teacher. The standard for good English, as far as the elementary school is concerned, is the informal standard level. Many students will come to school speaking a dialect divergent from the standard English of the region in which they live, and their needs must be met.

Assessment Standardized tests to evaluate students' oral language are not available. To measure growth, teachers may depend on class speech standards and checklists. The evaluation of speech tends to be somewhat subjective. Therefore, evaluation ideally should be a shared responsibility between student and teacher to assess individual abilities, needs, and achievements. Ideas for developing checklists of speaking skills are provided in Burns' (7) *Diagnostic Teaching of the Language Arts*. Evaluation should be made at regular intervals and comparisons should be made of growth during the period. Tape recordings may also be useful in providing a record of students' growth.

READING APPLICATION

Reading has long been considered the most important area of the school curriculum. The concern of American people to teach their children to read began early in the colonial days and continues today. This interest and concern with reading are also reflected in the huge amount of literature available and in the research that has been done in this field. More has been written about reading than about any other single subject area. Yet the inquiries into the who, what, when, where, and how of reading and reading instruction continue.

Instructional Emphases Students learn at different rates and are not all ready for any particular learning at any given grade level. As reading is a developmental process, the student will progress through the reading program at an individual rate. Once the students reach the intermediate grades of the elementary school, they are expected to do more reading in the various subject-matter areas. This produces a transitional period for reading instruction that must overlap between learning to read and reading to learn. The program will contain reinforcement and extension of the basic reading skills begun in the primary grades and begin a new emphasis on reading as a tool for gaining information and pleasure.

Instructional Strategies *Reading—A Tool for Learning* In the intermediate grades, the number of subjects that students are required to study increases. All these areas require reading ability. Therefore, much more of the student's day is spent in reading, and the content of much of the reading becomes the content of the individual school subjects. Students who have little or no difficulty with basal readers at a particular grade level may encounter obstacles in reading content subject textbooks written for that same grade level. Study skills are, then, an integral part of teaching all subject areas and not just part of the language arts program. Study skills are taught as a guide to independent reading and study.

Study Procedures   One popular study strategy is a method suggested by Robinson (55). That procedure, SQ3R, has five steps: survey, question, read, recite, and review. The first step is to survey the material to be read to determine what it concerns and how much time may be needed to read it. This includes skimming the table of contents, introductory and summary paragraphs, and headings and briefly studying illustrations or graphics. The second step requires the readers to develop questions from headings, subheadings, and/or topic sentences. This step establishes a purpose and focus of attention for improved comprehension. Next is the reading of the material to answer the questions formed in the second step. The fourth step is for the student to recite the answers to the questions. This step provides a summary and evaluation of step 3. The final step is to review in order to aid in retaining the material.

Outlining is another study skill which intermediate students may use to organize and record information, locating the first main idea, the details, the next main idea, the details, the next main idea, the details, and so on until all the material has been covered. Outline format is a simple form of using roman numerals for the main topics, capital letters for the main ideas, and arabic numbers for the details. Outlining helps students to improve comprehension skills by locating main ideas and supporting details which may lead to logical conclusions, cause-and-effect relationships, or the prediction of outcomes. Outlining can be introduced and practiced with stories and poems and then expanded into the various content areas.

Teachers should teach a standard outline form and then give the students many opportunities to practice, using this form. An example follows.

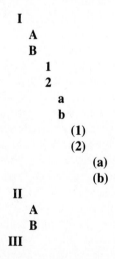

Fogelberg's (16) outline exercises, which are shown in Figure 6-1, may be used as one example of a student activity for practicing the skills of outlining. Teachers could put each word on a 3 × 5 index card and students could then lay the cards out in outline form. The information could then be transferred to an outline form.

Scrambled	Unscrambled
No. 1 Short	**I** Distances
Long	**A** Long
Distances	**B** Medium
Medium	**C** Short
No. 2 Chevrolet	**I** Cars
Cars	**A** Buick
Ford	**B** Chevrolet
Buick	**C** Ford
No. 3 Chainsaw	**I** Tools
Tools	**A** Hand Tools
Screwdriver	**1** Hammer
Power tools	**2** Screwdriver
Hammer	**3** Pliers
Pliers	**B** Power Tools
Electric drill	**1** Electric drill
Hand tools	**2** Chainsaw
No. 4 Feet	**I** Measurement
Metric	**A** Metric
Meters	**1** Kilometers
Yards	**2** Meters
English	**3** Centimeters
Centimeters	**B** English
Miles	**1** Miles
Kilometers	**2** Yards
Measurement	**3** Feet

FIGURE 6-1
Outline exercises.

Note taking is introduced at this level, but is refined in the secondary schools. It is employed when students are in a lecture or are using content books, encyclopedias, or other reference books. This study skill demands selective thinking or thoughtful reading. Intermediate students must be guided to select key words and learn to summarize ideas in their own words. A listening guide suggested by Castallo (8) may be used as a preliminary step to note taking. The students are given an incomplete outline to study before a lecture. The students fill in the outline during the lecture as the teacher does the same on an overhead projector and provides a model or standard.

Reading—A Source of Recreation   A reading program cannot be successful unless the students enrolled in it develop such an interest in reading that they seek out reading as a leisure-time activity and a method for gaining information of interest to them. To encourage such reading, the instructional program must provide reading material related to students' needs and interests and provide time during a busy school day to develop the habit.

Teachers can establish a reading nook for purposeful and meaningful reading situations. Materials are chosen with great regard to relevance and interest and set up in a section of the classroom designed for recreational reading. The students may establish the rules for using the nook and may participate in supplying and looking for additional reading materials. Interest inventories and interest charts may be used to determine what interests students have and what recreational activities they enjoy. The interest inventory in Figure 6-2 is an example of what teachers might use to assess student interest.

Teachers may employ such resources as *Adventuring with Books* from the National Council of Teachers of English, *Popular Reading* from the American Association of School Librarians, or *Best Books for Children* from R. R. Bowker Company as a means of knowing what books to suggest for specific students.

Time to read during a hectic school day may come with the practice of sustained silent reading. For a specific number of minutes a day, everyone reads—the teacher and the whole class; nothing else is allowed. The choice of reading material is left to the individual student. There is no test on the material and no reporting of what was read. It is important for the teacher to read during this time period. Students need a model to emulate, since many students find no examples of readers in their homes.

FIGURE 6-2
Interest inventory. What You Read

1. Do you read a newspaper regularly? _____
2. Number according to your likes the first four parts of the paper that are your favorites.

News:	Crossword puzzle
local	Astrology/horoscope
national	Inspirational articles
Sports	Entertainment items:
Editorial	movies
Fashion	television
Society	art
Want ads	theater
Comics	restaurant
Cartoons	Medical columns
	"Dear Abby"-type columns

3. Do you read magazines regularly? _____ If so, name your favorite two. _____
4. Do you enjoy reading comic books? _____
5. List three of your favorite books.
   _____ _____ _____
6. Name anything else you read. _____
7. Number in order of preference your first five favorite types of reading material.

Short story	Science fiction	Detective
Novel	Mysteries	Spy
Biography	Adventure	Fairy tales
Poetry	"How to do it"	Ghost
Newspaper:	materials	Western
news	Religious	Animal
sports	Motor magazines	Hobby
Essays	Love stories	Humor
Plays	History	
Comics	Family	

From Smith, Susan (ed.). *Teaching Reading in South Carolina Secondary Schools*. Columbia, S.C.: South Carolina Department of Education, 1978, p. 84.

Sustained reading has increased reading interest for many students, contributed to practice of reading skills, and given importance to individualized reading in the curriculum.

Another way to bring various forms of literature alive is the use of oral reading. The oral reading may be done by the teacher or by a student. The material read should be new and close to the interest of the students. After considerable practice on the part of the teacher and the student, the selection should be presented to the class. Oral reading can provide satisfaction to the reader and the listeners as contact is maintained with the world of written words. Intermediate-grade teachers should read to their students for at least fifteen minutes daily. A good balance of prose and poetry should be selected, and teachers should read materials they enjoy. Stewig (61) offers specific suggestions for using literature as a base for teaching various language skills to children.

Additional activities for the recreational reading time might include book talks (given by students, teachers, librarians, and parents), storytelling (this is a way to involve numerous community resources), creative dramatics, puppetry, and readers' theater. Each of these activities can provide enrichment and meaningful involvement of students as they apply the skills of reading. Some suggestions may be found in the Appendixes.

Problems Many students are quite serious about high achievement in school by the time they reach the intermediate grades. They are receptive to analyzing their strengths and weaknesses in reading and its applications in the other subject areas. They learn that they acquire additional skills which are needed for reading the various materials in the content subjects and for applying the reading skills of reference and study that will enable them to learn from the textbooks on their own. For these students, motivation is self-generated. For other students, who have not done as well in reading or in school and see little payoff in education, motivation is a real problem.

The failure of students to read outside of school has been blamed on many things, such as television, movies, radio, and comic books. Today's children spend far more time watching television than they do reading for pleasure. The results of Winn's (70) survey of more than 500 fourth- and fifth-grade children indicated that the children were unanimous in their preferences for watching television over reading books of any kind. Moody (47) cites a report from the National Association of Librarians that circulation in children's libraries has decreased by 15 percent during the last ten years. She states that "television—not print—is the children's literature of our times" (p. 65).

A successful reading program must develop students who can read and who *do* read for pleasure. The fact is that if reading is not pleasurable, students will avoid it and do other things with their spare time. However, if students love to read, they will find time for it in their lives. Teachers should give priority to working to develop positive attitudes toward reading and to encouraging students to read regularly for pleasure and enjoyment. Teachers could also use the suggestions in the International Reading Association pamphlet entitled *You Can Use Television to Stimulate Your Child's Reading Habits.*

Assessment   Standardized achievement tests contain subtests that measure study and reference skills. However, such tests usually contain too few items pertaining to a single skill to provide reliable information about individual students. These tests may not, in some cases, even sample the skills that the school has chosen for its curriculum. Criterion-referenced tests based on the school's study and reference skills objectives may be useful in determining students' mastery level. Checklists and teacher observations are possibly the best methods for assessing students' study skills as these skills are utilized in carrying out daily class assignments.

Because evaluation instruments are not available to assess the recreational reading program, it must be evaluated through the use of informal techniques. These may include attitude and interest inventories, logs, observations, checklists, and interviews. Many suggestions for various inventories are offered by Strang (62). All these techniques depend on subjective judgments by the teacher and the students. Teachers can devise and implement various activities for motivating and rewarding recreational reading. Rewards and incentives may be intrinsic and extrinsic; the creative teacher has unlimited resources in this area.

BIBLIOGRAPHY AND REFERENCES

1 Barbe, Walter B. *Evaluating Handwriting: Cursive.* Columbus, Ohio: Zaner-Bloser, 1979.
2 Barbe, Walter B., and Lucas, Virginia H. "Instruction in Handwriting: A New Look." *Childhood Education,* vol. 50, no. 4, February 1974, pp. 207–209.
3 Barbe, Walter B., Lucas, Virginia H., Hackney, Clinton S., and McAllister, Constance. *Creative Growth with Handwriting* (2d ed.). Columbus, Ohio: Zaner-Bloser, 1979.
4 Barbe, Walter B., Swassing, Raymond H., and Milone, Michael N., Jr. *Swassing–Barbe Checklist of Observable Modality Strength Characteristics.* Columbus, Ohio: Zaner-Bloser, 1980.
5 Billig, Edith, "Children's Literature as a Springboard to Content Areas." *The Reading Teacher,* vol. 30, May 1977, pp. 855–859.
6 Bingham, Alma, and Dusenbery, Bea. "Just Talking Isn't Enough." *Language Arts,* vol. 56, March 1979, pp. 275–278.
7 Burns, Paul C. *Diagnostic Teaching of the Language Arts.* Itasca, Ill.: F. E. Peacock, 1974, pp. 62–78.
8 Castallo, Richard. "Listening Guide—A First Step Toward Notetaking and Listening Skills." *Journal of Reading,* vol. 19, January 1976, pp. 289–290.
9 Chenfeld, Mimi B. *Teaching Language Arts Creatively.* New York: Harcourt Brace Jovanovich, 1978.
10 Clearinghouse for Applied Performance Testing. *CAPT Newsletter,* vol. 5, January 1980, pp. 4–5.
11 Cohen, Leonard S., Craun, Marlus J., and Johnson, Susan K. "Spelling Difficulty—A Survey of the Research." *Review of Educational Research,* vol. 41, no. 4, 1971, pp. 281–301.
12 Cooper, Charles R., and Odell, Lee. *Evaluating Writing: Describing Measuring, Judging.* Urbana, Ill.: National Council of Teachers of English, 1977.
13 Ediger, Marlow. "The Pupil, the Teacher, and Handwriting." *Reading Improvement,* vol. 11, Spring 1974, pp. 62–64.

14 Fitzsimmons, Robert J., and Loomer, Bradley M. *Spelling: Learning and Instruction—Research and Practice*. Iowa City: University of Iowa, 1978.

15 Fletcher, David B. "ERIC/RCS Report: Oral Language and the Language Arts Teacher." *Language Arts,* vol. 58, February 1981, pp. 219–223.

16 Fogelberg, Donald D. "Outline Exercises." A handout presented during a talk at the National Council of Teachers of English spring convention, Minneapolis, Minn. April 1982.

17 Furner, Beatrice A. "An Analysis of the Effectiveness of a Program of Instruction Emphasizing the Perceptual–Motor Nature of Learning Handwriting." *Elementary English,* vol. 47, January 1970, pp. 61–69.

18 Gesell, Arnold, and Ilg, Frances L. *The Child from Five to Ten*. New York: Harper and Brothers, 1946.

19 Gold, Yvonne. "Improvement of Teaching Listening Skills." *Reading Improvement,* vol. 10, Winter 1973, pp. 14–16.

20 Gold, Yvonne. "Teaching Listening? Why Not?" *Elementary English,* vol. 52, March 1975, pp. 421–422.

21 Golden, Joanne M. "The Writer's Side: Writing for a Purpose and an Audience." *Language Arts,* vol. 57, October 1980, pp. 756–762.

22 Graves, Donald H. "Research Update of Spelling Texts and Structural Analysis Methods." *Language Arts,* vol. 54, January 1977, pp. 86–90.

23 Graves, Donald H. *Balance the Basics: Let Them Write*. New York: Ford Foundation Papers on Research about Learning, 1978.

24 Graves, Donald H. "We Won't Let Them Write." *Language Arts,* vol. 55, May 1978, pp. 635–640.

25 Haley-James, Shirley (ed.). *Perspectives on Writing in Grades 1–8*. Urbana, Ill.: National Council of Teachers of English, 1981.

26 Hanna, P. R. "The Teaching of Spelling." *National Elementary Principal,* vol. 45, November 1965, pp. 19–28.

27 Harris, Albert J., and Sipay, Edward R. *How to Increase Reading Ability*. New York: David McKay, 1975.

28 Harris, Albert J., and Sipay, Edward R. *How to Teach Reading*. New York: Longman, 1979.

29 Henderson, Edmund H., and Beers, James W. (eds.). *Developmental and Cognitive Aspects of Learning to Spell: A Reflection of Word Knowledge*. Newark, Del.: International Reading Association, 1980, p. 112.

30 Hillerich, Robert L. "Developing Written Expression: How to Raise—Not Raze—Writers." *Language Arts,* vol. 56, October 1979, pp. 769–776.

31 Hodges, Richard E. *Learning to Spell*. Urbana, Ill.: ERIC Clearinghouse on Reading and Communication Skills and National Council of Teachers of English, 1981.

32 Holdzkom, David, Reed, Linda J., Porter, E. Jane, and Rubin, Donald L. *Research within Reach: Oral and Written Communication*. St. Louis: CEMREL, Inc., 1981

33 Horn, Ernest. "Spelling." *Encyclopedia of Research* (3d ed.). New York: Macmillan, 1960.

34 Jacobs, Leland B. "Teaching Children More about Words and Their Ways." *Elementary English,* vol. 41, January 1964, pp. 30–34.

35 Johnson, Terry D., Langford, Kenneth G., and Quorn, Kerry C. "Characteristics of an Effective Spelling Program." *Language Arts,* vol. 58, May 1981, pp. 581–588.

36 Klein, Marvin L. *Talk in the Language Arts Classroom*. Urbana, Ill.: National Council of Teachers of English and ERIC Clearinghouse on Reading and Communication Skills, 1977.

37 Klein, Marvin L. "Designing a Talk Environment for the Classroom." *Language Arts,* vol. 56, September 1979, pp. 647–656.

38 Landry, D. L. "The Neglect of Listening." *Elementary English,* vol. 46, 1969, pp. 599–605.

39 Lewis, Maurice S. "Teaching Children to Listen." *Education,* vol. 80, April 1960, pp. 455–459.

40 Lindheim, Elaine, Lettieri, Carol, and Ruggles, John. *Teaching the Skills of Composition.* Los Angeles, Calif.: Instructional Objectives Exchange, 1980.

41 Lucas, Virgina H. *Persistent Problems in Penmanship.* Columbus, Ohio: Zaner-Bloser, Inc.

42 Lundsteen, Sarah W. *Listening: Its Impact on Reading and Other Language Arts.* Urbana, Ill.: National Council of Teachers of English and ERIC Clearinghouse on the Teaching of English, 1971.

43 Mehrabian, Albert, and Ferris, Susan R. "Inference of Attitude from Non-Verbal Communication in Two Channels." *Journal of Consulting Psychology,* vol. 31, June 1967, pp. 248–252.

44 Milone, Michael N., Jr., Wilhide, James A., and Wasylyk, Thomas M. *Spelling and Handwriting: Is There a Relationship?* A paper presented at the National Council of Teachers of English spring convention, Minneapolis, Minn., April 1982.

45 Minuchin, Patricia P. *The Middle Years of Childhood.* Monterey, Calif.: Brooks/Cole, 1977.

46 Moffett, James, and Wagner, Betty Jane. *Student-Centered Language Arts and Reading, K–13.* Boston: Houghton Mifflin, 1976.

47 Moody, Kate. *Growing Up on Television.* New York: Times Books, 1980.

48 Mussen, Paul Henry, Conger, John Janeway, and Kagan, Jerome. *Child Development and Personality.* New York: Harper & Row, 1979.

49 Myers, Miles. "Five Approaches to the Teaching of Writing." *Learning,* vol. 6, April 1978, pp. 38–41.

50 New Hampshire Department of Education. *Listening Skills Assessment: Manual and Script.* Concord, N.H.: 1981.

51 Noyce, Ruth M. "Another Slant on Mastery Writing Instruction." *Language Arts,* vol. 56, March 1979, pp. 251–255.

52 Petty, Walter T., Petty, Dorothy C., and Becking, Marjorie F. *Experiences in Language.* Boston: Allyn and Bacon, 1976.

53 Pulaski, Mary Ann Spencer. *Understanding Piaget.* New York: Harper & Row, 1971.

54 Rankin, Paul T. "The Importance of Listening Ability." *English Journal,* vol. 17, 1928, pp. 623–630.

55 Robinson, Francis P. *Effective Study.* New York: Harper & Row, 1961.

56 Smith, Nila B., and Robinson, H. Alan. *Reading Instruction for Today's Children.* Englewood Cliffs, N.J.: Prentice-Hall, 1980.

57 Smith, Susan (ed.). *Teaching Reading in South Carolina Secondary Schools.* Columbia, S.C.: South Carolina Department of Education, 1978.

58 "Standards for Basic Skills Writing Programs." *Language Arts,* vol. 56, October 1979, pp. 836–838.

59 *Standards for Effective Oral Communication Programs.* Prepared by American Speech–Language–Hearing Association and Speech–Communication Association.

60 Stewig, John Warren. "Nonverbal Communication: 'I *See* What You Say.' " *Language Arts,* vol. 56, February 1979, pp. 150–155.

61 Stewig, John Warren. *Read to Write.* New York: Holt, Rinehart and Winston, 1980.

62 Strang, Ruth. *Diagnostic Teaching of Reading.* New York: McGraw-Hill, 1964.

63 Strickland, Ruth G. *The Language Arts in the Elementary School* (3d ed.). Lexington, Mass.: D. C. Heath and Company, 1969.

64 Strickling, C. "The Effect of Handwriting and Related Skills upon the Spelling Score of Above Average and Below Average Readers in the Fifth Grade." Doctoral dissertation, University of Maryland, College Park, 1973.

65 Tutolo, Daniel. "Cognitive Approach to Teaching Listening." *Language Arts,* vol. 54, March 1977, pp. 262–265.

66 Wagner, Betty Jane. "Using Drama to Create an Environment for Language Development." *Language Arts,* vol. 56, March 1979, pp. 268–273.

67 Way, J. G. "Teaching Listening Skills." *The Reading Teacher,* vol. 26, February 1973, pp. 472–476.

68 Westbrooks, Linda K. "Prescription for Ailing Penmanship." *–Teacher,* vol. 94, September 1976, pp. 100ff.

69 Wilt, Miriam. "A Study of Teacher Awareness of Listening as a Factor in Elementary Education." *Journal of Educational Research,* vol. 43, April 1950, pp. 626–636.

70 Winn, Marie. *The Plug-In Drug: Television, Children and the Family.* New York: The Viking Press, 1977.

71 Wiseman, Donna, and Watson, Dorothy. "The Good News about Becoming a Writer." *Language Arts,* vol. 57, October 1980, pp. 750–755.

72 Zutell, Jerry. "Children's Spelling Strategies and Their Cognitive Development." In Edmund H. Henderson and James W. Beers (eds.), *Developmental and Cognitive Aspects of Learning To Spell: A Reflection of Word Knowledge.* Newark, Del.: International Reading Association, 1980, pp. 52–73.

CHAPTER 7

CLASSROOM APPLICATIONS IN GRADES FOUR THROUGH SIX

This chapter will repeat the format used in Chapters 3 and 5. In this chapter, descriptors for Carol Beasley, a fourth-grade teacher, and Jeffrey Tate, a sixth-grade teacher, will be presented. Following each of these descriptors, a second copy of the descriptor is presented with sentences or phrases italicized to indicate some of the teacher's effective practices which we felt were meritorious. In the explanation section, we discuss why we considered the practices to be noteworthy.

Once again, we encourage you to view these descriptors as tests which will provide you with opportunities to see how your responses compare with ours and others.

CAROL BEASLEY

Descriptor

Carol teaches fourth grade in a rural school district. Her classroom is on the second floor of an old building which was once a junior high school. The walls are freshly painted and the floor is carpeted. The room is large with windows across the back providing a light, sunny atmosphere which is heightened by the many examples of children's work displayed around the room. A large bulletin board on one side of the room is partially completed. Children work together on committees to plan and prepare the projects which are displayed on it.

Twenty-five children are in this class—twelve girls and thirteen boys. They have been assigned by the school principal, who places all the children in classes based on their previous year's reading test scores. Carol's class is composed of three distinct reading achievement groups. One group is made up of children who read well above grade level, one group reads on grade level, and the children in the third group read about $1\frac{1}{2}$ years below grade level. There is a strong correlation between the intellectual abilities of these children and their reading levels. Almost a third of them demonstrate very high intellectual abilities, a third of the children are in the average range, and the remaining students perform at a lower than average level of ability.

The socioeconomic status of the children's parents varies widely. Although most of the parents have finished high school and have completed some college work (including parents with earned doctorates), there are also some who have not finished high school.

School is a very important part of these children's lives and they really seem to enjoy it. Carol says, "Fourth-grade children come to school knowing a great deal about the learning process." During their preceding school years, they have learned many skills and formed many new behaviors. She sees her task as that of helping them build on what they already know by getting them to channel their natural curiosity and vitality in ways that ensure a continuity in their learning experiences.

At the beginning of each year, Carol works with the children to create a classroom environment in which students are not afraid to make mistakes. She believes children must learn that many problems are too complex to have only one right answer. She also emphasizes that it is worthwhile to explore options and that it is important to make tentative decisions rather than only final decisions. Carol believes language arts activities should provide many opportunities for children to think and to grapple with ideas, and the classroom environment must be conducive to such thinking.

The children have positive attitudes toward learning and healthy self-concepts. They are comfortable in speaking during class discussions, they share their creative writing with each other, and they accept constructive criticism from one another as well as from the teacher.

Carol says many of the children think the skills pages, which emphasize dictionary or other skills, in their language arts workbooks are "a drag," but they will do them if she assigns them to be completed. She notices more and more that the children use the dictionary when they write stories, although some still ask her how to spell a word. Carol is pleased with the way these children use reference books for their committee work; she believes this is the real test of their study skills knowledge.

In Carol's school district, a basal textbook series is used by each child, as are separate English books, spelling books, and handwriting books. Children are issued these various textbooks according to their reading levels. Therefore, in Carol's class with its three-group composition, the members of each group have reading, English, and spelling books in accordance with their reading level. The children are provided with these books and the principal insists that they be used. Carol uses them to supplement what she views as a total language arts program. She sees herself as the instructional leader and the textbooks as tools to be used to help children learn.

Each morning begins with a meeting between Carol and her students. During this time, the entire day is planned and delineated on a daily plan sheet. The students choose activities from a list of assigned and free-choice items. They have designated work times, special area classes (art, music, physical education), literature and reading times, and sharing and clean-up periods. The planning includes provision for projects, skills, and whole-class activities.

The teacher's input into the planning period includes teacher-assigned activities (often from the textbook), ideas for free-choice items (these are also generated by the students), and teacher-designated work times. Carol believes learning doesn't just happen; rather, it is planned.

Two blocks of time are set aside for work periods each day. The only apparent difference in them is the amount of talking and interaction which is encouraged. Since the teacher is working with reading groups during the early morning work time, the children (not receiving direct instruction from the teacher) work on activities they can participate in quietly during this period. Even though one is quieter than the other, both work periods are busy, active community times in which talking and moving about are natural and appropriate. The students are involved in previously planned and spontaneous activities. They are developing socialization skills along with their language skills; their creative efforts are generating needs for spelling, handwriting, reading, and writing.

During the $1\frac{1}{2}$ hour block of time following the planning period, Carol works with the children in reading groups, using their basal textbooks. The emphasis of the series intermediate program is on reading skill maintenance and usage and on study skills development. Dictionary, glossary, and library skills are introduced and reinforced, and practice is provided for using these and other resources for locating and organizing information. One group of children is working in a basal text which is below the fourth-grade level in difficulty. These children are working on basic decoding skills while reinforcing those which were introduced at lower levels.

The student books at all three levels contain legends and folktales, fantasy, some biography, and some poetry. The textbook authors try to select good examples from the wealth of children's literature, although some of the stories are written especially for the grade-level text. Carol uses the stories as examples of an author's work or as examples of a genre and encourages the children to move from the basal into the other works of children's literature.

Literature is an important ingredient of the language arts program. She reads aloud to the children every day. Sometimes she reads a story because a child asks her to do so. For the past several years, her children have asked her to read some of Judy Blume's books. Carol says, "I read only a bit, enough to interest the children who haven't read any of Blume's books. I don't read the whole book. I stop. I know that the children will finish the book on their own."

Carol chooses to read books to the entire class which her children might ordinarily not read. She feels this will stretch them a little. Such a book is E. L. Konigsburg's *From the Mixed Up Files of Mrs. Basil E. Frankweiler*. This rather sophisticated, humorous survival story is about a child who feels unappreciated at home (she had to empty the dishwasher and set the table while her brothers did nothing). She runs away to the Metropolitan Museum of Art, taking her younger brother with her because he has some money.

The children particularly enjoyed this book and Carol capitalized on their enthusiasm by giving special attention to the book through extension activities, such as writing poetry and reading information books. In this case, the school librarian located a book about sculpture, a book about mummies, and another book, *Pantheon Story of Art for*

Young People by Ariane Batterberry, which several of the children really liked. Carol found some poems about hiding places which she shared with the children.

Carol and the class had a brainstorming discussion period to see what activities or extensions could come from their interest in this book. It was decided that some children would make a map of the art museum, some would make a diorama, while still others planned an imaginary trip to the Metropolitan Museum of Art. Several of the children did a soap sculpture while two wrote a diary of "a week spent in an art museum." These activities caused children to reread the book or parts of it for themselves. Carol believes that these activities enriched the children's experiences and helped make the reading of the book a memorable experience for them.

Children at this age prefer an uninterrupted time for independent reading. With this in mind, Carol makes certain there are quiet periods (no talking permitted) when the children and their teacher read silently. The books are chosen by each student from classroom bookshelves or from the school library for independent, individual reading. At other times, group reading occurs. Two or three children will decide to read the same title and discuss the book together.

The children keep a book log in which they record the books they have read. These logs are filed in the back of their journals. All students keep a journal of important events, projects, and other experiences. They write in them at least once a week and these become chronological records of significant happenings during the school year.

A writing time is scheduled each day as a whole-class, quiet, private activity in which the children write on self-chosen or teacher-suggested topics. Carol may show a picture to stimulate writing, suggest a general topic to the class, or put a title on the board which the class can use if it wishes. At other times, the writing assignment is more focused. Children are encouraged to work on a topic which interests them— perhaps something from their social studies work or a book they've recently read. They research the topic, organize the information, and do a written report.

Some of the children's best writing has occurred as an outgrowth of the literature program. Sometimes the children write point-of-view stories in which they retell a story from the point of view of a different character. Some children enjoy writing stories which continue where the book ended. These fourth-graders loved Michael Bond's series of books about *A Bear Named Paddington*. Several students wrote stories about what might have happended if Paddington had lived in their neighborhood. Mechanical skills such as spelling, punctuation, and handwriting are developed and reinforced as children write, edit, and revise their creative stories.

Carol has a good rapport with the parents of her students. At the beginning of each school year, she telephones each child's parents, introduces herself, and assures them of her interest in the child's progress and of her readiness to be available for parent–teacher conferences. Many of the parents work, so telephone conferences are arranged for them. Once a week the children take home examples of their written work and frequently they share a book or a special poem with their parents. Carol writes notes to parents commenting on particularly good actions by their children. She provides recommended lists of books appropriate for fourth-graders which help parents select good books for birthday or Christmas presents.

Carol meets with her students on a regular basis to confer with them regarding their progress in their school studies. On the report cards she is required to use, each of the separate elements of the language arts (such as handwriting or spelling) is graded, and the grade level on which the child is working is recorded. A child who is reading in a second-grade basal reader could get an A in reading, but the level (second grade) is indicated on the report card.

Carol believes education is a continuous process and that children grow and develop in language arts at their own rate. She believes grades are an attempt to evaluate students' work. However, she feels that the conference which emphasizes student progress and attempts to ameliorate difficulties adds meaning to the evaluation process and is far better than the report card alone.

Analysis

Carol teaches fourth grade in a rural school district. Her classroom is on the second floor of an old building which was once a junior high school. The walls are freshly painted and the floor is carpeted. The room is large with windows across the back providing a light, sunny atmosphere which is heightened by the many examples of children's work displayed around the room. A large bulletin board on one side of the room is partially completed. Children work together on committees to plan and prepare the projects which are displayed on it.

Twenty-five children are in this class—twelve girls and thirteen boys. They have been assigned by the school principal, who places all the children in classes based on their previous year's reading test scores. *Carol's class is composed of three distinct reading achievement groups.*[1] One group is made up of children who read well above grade level, one group reads on grade level, and the children in the third group read about $1\frac{1}{2}$ years below grade level. There is a strong correlation between the intellectual abilities of these children and their reading levels. Almost a third of them demonstrate very high intellectual abilities, a third of the children are in the average range, and the remaining students perform at a lower than average level of ability.

The socioeconomic status of the children's parents varies widely. Although most of the parents have finished high school and have completed some college work (including parents with earned doctorates), there are also some who have not finished high school.

School is a very important part of these children's lives and they really seem to enjoy it. Carol says, "Fourth-grade children come to school knowing a great deal about the learning process." During their preceding school years, they have learned many skills and formed many new behaviors. *She sees her task as that of helping them build on what they already know*[2] by getting them to channel their natural curiosity and vitality in ways that ensure a continuity in their learning experience.

At the beginning of each year, *Carol works with the children to create a classroom environment in which students are not afraid to risk making mistakes.*[3] She believes children must learn that many problems are too complex to have only one right answer. She also emphasizes that it is worthwhile to explore options and that it is important

It is important for children to have positive attitudes toward learning.

to make tentative decisions rather than only final decisions. Carol believes language arts activities should provide opportunities for children to think and to grapple with ideas, and the classroom environment must be conducive to such thinking.

The children have positive attitudes toward learning and healthy self-concepts.[4] They are comfortable in speaking during class discussions, they share their creative writing with each other, and they accept constructive criticism from one another as well as from the teacher.

Carol says many of the children think the skill pages, which emphasize dictionary or other skills, in their language arts workbooks are "a drag," but they will do them if she assigns them to be completed. She notices more and more that the children use the dictionary when they write stories, although some still ask her how to spell a word. Carol is pleased with the way these children use reference books for their committee work; she believes this is the real test of their study skills knowledge.

In Carol's school district, a basal textbook series is used by each child, as are separate English books, spelling books, and handwriting books. Children are issued these various textbooks according to their reading levels. Therefore, in Carol's class with its three-group composition, the members of each group have reading, English, and spelling books in accordance with their reading level. *The children are provided with these books and the principal insists that they be used.*[5] Carol uses them to supplement what she views as a total language arts program. She sees herself as the instructional leader and the textbooks as tools to be used to help children learn.

Each morning begins with a meeting between Carol and her students.[6] During this time, the entire day is planned and is delineated on a daily plan sheet. The students choose activities from a list of assigned and free-choice items. They have designated work times, special area classes (art, music, physical education), literature and reading times, and sharing and clean-up periods. The planning includes provision for projects, skills, and whole-class activities.

The teacher's input into the planning period includes teacher-assigned activities (often from the textbook), ideas for free-choice items (these are also generated by the students), and teacher-designated work times. Carol believes learning doesn't just happen; rather, it is planned.

Two blocks of time are set aside for work periods each day. The only apparent difference in them is the amount of talking and interaction which is encouraged. Since the teacher is working with reading groups during the early morning work time, the children (not receiving direct instruction from the teacher) work on activities they can participate in quietly during this period. Even though one is quieter than the other, both work periods are busy, active community times in which talking and moving about are natural and appropriate. The students are involved in previously planned and spontaneous activities. *They are developing socialization skills along with their language skills;*[7] their creative efforts are generating needs for spelling, handwriting, reading, and writing.

During the 1½ hour block of time following the planning period, Carol works with the children in reading groups, using their basal textbooks. The emphasis of the series intermediate program is on reading skill maintenance and usage and on study skills development. Dictionary, glossary, and library skills are introduced and reinforced, and practice is provided for using these and other resources for locating and organizing information. One group of children is working in a basal text which is below the fourth-grade level in difficulty. These children are working on basic decoding skills while reinforcing those which were introduced at lower levels.

The student books at all three levels contain legends and folktales, fantasy, some biography, and some poetry. The textbook authors try to select good examples from the wealth of children's literature, although some of the stories are written especially for the grade-level text. Carol uses the stories as examples of an author's work or as examples of a genre and encourages the children to move from the basal into the other works of children's literature.

Literature is an important ingredient of the language arts program. *She reads aloud to the children every day.*[8] Sometimes she reads a story because a child asks her to do so. For the past several years, her children have asked her to read some of Judy Blume's books. Carol says, "I read only a bit, enough to interest the children who haven't read any of Blume's books. I don't read the whole book. I stop. I know that the children will finish the book on their own."

Carol chooses to read books to the entire class which her children might ordinarily not read. She feels this will stretch them a little. Such a book is E. L. Konigsburg's *From the Mixed Up Files of Mrs. Basil E. Frankweiler*. This rather sophisticated, humorous survival story is about a child who feels unappreciated at home (she had to empty the dishwasher and set the table while her brothers did nothing). She runs away to the Metropolitan Museum of Art, taking her younger brother with her because he has some money.

The children particularly enjoyed this book and Carol capitalized on their enthusiasm by giving special attention to the book through extension activities, such as writing poetry and reading information books. In this case, the school librarian located a book about sculpture, a book about mummies, and another book, *Pantheon Story of Art for Young People* by Ariane Batterberry, which several of the children really liked. Carol found some poems about hiding places which she shared with the children.

Carol and the class had a brainstorming discussion period to see what activities or extensions could come from their interest in this book.[9] It was decided that some children would make a map of the art museum, some would make a diorama, while still others planned an imaginary trip to the Metropolitan Museum of Art. Several of the children did a soap sculpture while two wrote a diary of "a week spent in an art museum." These activities caused children to reread the book or parts of it for themselves. Carol believes that these activities enriched the children's experiences and helped make the reading of the book a memorable experience for them.

Children at this age prefer an uninterrupted time for independent reading. With this in mind, Carol makes certain there are quiet periods (no talking permitted) when the children and their teacher read silently. The books are chosen by each student from classroom bookshelves or from the school library for independent, individual reading. At other times, group reading occurs. Two or three children will decide to read the same title and discuss the book together.

The children keep a book log in which they record the books they have read. These logs are filed in the back of their journals. All students keep a journal of important events, projects, and other experiences. They write in them at least once a week and these become chronological records of significant happenings during the school year.

A writing time is scheduled each day as a whole-class, quiet, private activity in which the children write on self-chosen or teacher-suggested topics. Carol may show a picture to stimulate writing, suggest a general topic to the class, or put a title on the board which the class can use if it wishes. At other times, the writing assignment is more focused. Children are encouraged to work on a topic which interests them—

perhaps something from their social studies work or a book they've recently read. They research the topic, organize the information, and do a written report.

Some of the children's best writing has occurred as an outgrowth of the literature program. Sometimes the children write point-of-view stories in which they retell a story from the point of view of a different character. Some children enjoy writing stories which continue where the book ended. These fourth-graders loved Michael Bond's series of books about *A Bear Named Paddington*. Several students wrote stories about what might have happened if Paddington had lived in their neighborhood. *Mechanical skills such as spelling, punctuation, and handwriting are developed and reinforced as children write,*[10] edit, and revise their creative stories.

Carol has a good rapport with the parents of her students.[11] At the beginning of each school year, she telephones each child's parents, introduces herself, and assures them of her interest in the child's progress and of her readiness to be available for parent–teacher conferences. Many of the parents work, so telephone conferences are arranged for them. Once a week the children take home examples of their written work and frequently they share a book or a special poem with their parents. Carol writes notes to parents commenting on particularly good action by their children. She provides recommended lists of books appropriate for fourth-graders which help parents select good books for birthday or Chirstmas presents.

Carol meets with her students on a regular basis to confer with them regarding their progress in their school studies. On the report cards she is required to use, each of the separate elements of the language arts (such as handwriting or spelling) is graded, and the grade level on which the child is working is recorded. A child who is reading in a second-grade basal reader could get an A in reading, but the level (second grade) is indicated on the report card.

Carol believes education is a continuous process and that children grow and develop in language arts at their own rate. She believes grades are an attempt to evaluate students' work. However, she feels that the conference which emphasizes student progress and attempts to ameliorate difficulties adds meaning to the evaluation process and is far better than the report card alone.

Explanation

1 Even though children are tested carefully before being placed in reading groups, there are still differences among individual students in the groups. No two children are precisely the same regardless of how similar their test results are. Children vary in their interests and in their abilities. A wise teacher understands that children can learn in group situations only when the differences among them are known and taken into consideration (10). Instructional decisions are based on individual needs which can be met within the context of a group. At times, a teacher needs to work with an individual child; sometimes learning can best take place within a small group, and at other times the teacher should work with the class as a whole.

2 Bloom summarized a number of studies which indicate that learning during the early elementary school grades has a strong influence on the child's educational development. He cites evidence that approximately 50 percent of general achievement at the end of high school had been reached by the beginning of fourth grade. The research shows that the first three grades in school are significant to the development of children's attitudes toward school and their subsequent academic achievement (2).

Fourth-grade children know a great deal about the learning process. As Piaget's research has shown, children bring many systems and networks of understandings to their interactions with their environment. The production of invented spellings and the use of a nonstandard dialect are examples of child-constructed systems which help them understand and organize aspects of their world.

Sister Rosemary Winkeljohann (27) believes that at times the school attempts to guide children into systems of understanding which conflict with what the children understand. She believes it is important that teachers know that children possess their own systems of understanding and that teachers value them even if they do not conform to the school's standards. If a child is not learning that which is being taught, it does not mean that child is slow or lazy or unattentive. It may be that the child's self-constructed understanding systems conflict with the understanding systems of the school.

Winkeljohann believes the systems-in-conflict concept has implications for the teacher's role in children's learning. She states the child must learn:

> that his or her systems of understanding are not always adequate. Broader, deeper and more mature understanding develops when we are confronted by experiences which cannot be accounted for by what we already know and believe to be true (p. 662).

3 An environment which is conducive to language arts learning must permit children to risk making mistakes. A child who is constantly corrected when speaking learns to keep quiet. Children learn to write by writing, to speak by speaking, and so forth, and teachers must accept the language the children possess and help them build on it. Pilon (21, p. 136) explains:

> . . . a child must hear the words and languages . . . patterns we would like him to use as alternatives for parts of his language . . . he must be reinforced for using this convergent language. . . . He must not be punished for saying what is ordinary normal and "correct" for him to say.

She believes children's stories and poems can be used to help children become attuned to some standard expressions which may be troublesome for them.

The development of the competencies necessary to be proficient in reading, writing, speaking, and listening is a process which takes time. Teachers who repeatedly point out mistakes often impede progress because children learn to focus on form rather than on meaning. As a result, they do not develop confidence in their ability to communicate. Teachers should look at children's mistakes from an analytical rather than a corrective perspective. Clay (6) writes "The significant question at any stage of progress is not 'How much does he know?' but rather 'What operations does he carry out and what kinds of operations has he neglected to use?' " A careful consideration of Clay's questions will help teachers to determine the educational experiences each child needs to improve his or her competencies in the language arts.

4 Consistently, research has shown that a persistent and significant relationship exists between one's self-concept and academic achievement (23). Additional studies (4, 17, 19) have established that positive self-concepts of children are significantly related to reading achievement. This research clearly shows that classroom teachers must structure learning environments in ways which strengthen self-esteem and meet children's social and emotional needs as well as their academic ones. In a book by Quandt (24), many suggestions for developing positive self-concepts in children are offered.

5 The use of a basal series is common to more than 90 percent of the classrooms in the nation. Many teachers are required by their school districts to use them, while other teachers prefer them because of the structure which basals give to a developmental reading program. Many of the basal reading programs are total language arts systems which make use of the interrelatedness of reading, writing, speaking, and listening.

It is important for teachers to realize that they, rather than the textbooks, are the instructional leaders in children's language arts programs. Lessons must be adapted to the needs and interests of the children. Questions which are suggested in the teachers' guides may need to be expanded, extended, or even skipped. The authors of most basal textbooks series encourage teachers to use them to suit the needs of individual children. Yet many teachers are hesitant to do this; they believe that "authorities" have written the teachers' guides and that these experts know more about their children than the teachers themselves. Teachers need to realize that they are the highest authorities in the classroom—not the materials. When teachers formulate this attitude, they can begin to concentrate on using materials intelligently.

6 While Carol believes that the teacher must play a key role in preparing the learning environment and determining relevant education experiences, she also knows that participation in teacher–student planning periods necessitates language arts practice. As children discuss their activities from a list of assigned items and record their plans, they are reading, writing, speaking, and listening. Furthermore, children who are taking part in the planning of their educational experiences are making strides toward becoming responsible for their own behavior. This is, of course, a worthwhile learning outcome.

7 In this book, Wadsworth (26) explains that children in the concrete operational stage are becoming less egocentric; they are becoming aware that others can arrive at different conclusions. Because of this new awareness, children seek validation of their thoughts. Wadsworth writes:

> Piaget states that social interaction is one of the variables that facilitates cognitive development. His writing suggests that social interactions are any behaviors that involve a real interchange between two or more persons. Thus, when language becomes functionally communicative, it is a form of social interaction (p. 9).

As children become less egocentric they become able to listen to others and to respond thoughtfully. Petty and Jensen (20) believe that "socialized speech," the ability to talk to and respond to the talk of others, is a requisite for instruction in many school subjects.

In her book, *The Unreluctant Years,* Smith (25) suggests that bringing books and children together is an important endeavor:

> The impact of even one good book on a child's mind is surely an end in itself, a valid experience which helps him to form standards of judgment and taste at the time when his mind is most sensitive to impressions of every kind.

Hillman (14) suggests that reading aloud to children benefits them in a number of ways. Their receptive vocabularies are increased by hearing words used in context, their listening skills are developed, and they are introduced to alternate ways of expressing themselves.

After analyzing the classic studies of Chomsky, Cohen and Durkin, and others, McCormick (18, p. 143) states: "Research now provides evidence of the direct relationship between reading aloud to children and reading performance, language development, and the development of reading interests."

Some fourth-grade teachers feel guilty when they take time away from "teaching" to do something as enjoyable as reading aloud to children. They erroneously feel that reading to a class should be done only in the primary grades. These teachers need to become aware of research which indicates that this activity is of great value to children of all ages. Thus, reading aloud to children is not only fun; it is also conducive to achievement.

9 Intermediate-grade children need to read widely so that they can become fluent readers, and they need to have books read to them which will develop their imaginations further and help them become appreciative readers. D. W. Harding (12) would agree with Carol's choice of *From the Mixed Up Files of Mrs. Basil E. Frankweiler* instead of an "easier" book. He writes:

> Since the purpose of presentation by the teacher is to promote the student's understanding of and engagement with the literary work, such direct presentation should normally be reserved for selections difficult for students; works which are accessible to the individual reader should be read by students on their own (p. 384).

Hickman (13) believes that an environment which facilitates children's interaction with literature must include a wealth of children's books, read-aloud periods, and discussions of literature as well as:

> Opportunities . . . for children to work with literature through various other activities—art, writing, drama and the like—with allowance for the necessary time, space and material . . . (p. 529).

10 Children in Carol's class have many opportunities for written expression and she has found that the mechanical skills of composition are developed as the children write. Calkins (5) aptly says: "The urge to tell leads children to struggle with punctuation and language mechanics." Calkins observed third-grade children in two classrooms over a period of one year. In one of the classrooms, punctuation was used in context, while in the other, it was taught in isolation. Her research findings are consistent with the behaviors of Carol's students. She wrote:

> The third grade "writers" who had not had formal instruction in punctuation could define/explain an average of 8.66 kinds of punctuation. The children who had studied punctuation through classwork, drills and tests, but had rarely written, were only able to define/explain 3.85 kinds of punctuation.

It is important to note that both teachers believe children need punctuation skills. They differ in their beliefs about the best method of teaching them. Carol's teaching is in agreement with the teacher in the study who believes children learn mechanical skills better in the context of their own writing than through isolated practice.

11 Parent–teacher cooperation has a positive influence on children's learning. Research has shown time and time again that parents are the primary models for their children's behavior. If teachers encourage parents to become actively involved and concerned with educational matters, the effect on the children will be positive.

Not all parents are free to volunteer to help at school or with a field trip; many of them work. Still, teachers can provide parents with practical suggestions to help them to be good models for their children. Teachers can suggest such resources as *How Can I Help My Child Build Positive Attitudes toward Reading* (28), in which parents are encouraged to make use of television, newspaper stories, and shopping expeditions as teaching aids for their children.

Parents can be advised to take their children to the public library and to read to them daily. Nancy Larrick's (16) *A Parent's Guide to Children's Reading* is an excellent resource for parents. It lists recommended fiction, nonfiction, magazines, and audiovisual materials for children of all ages and explains ways to prepare good home reading environments for children. In Appendix F of this book, we have presented numerous additional devices which can promote positive parental involvement in the education of their children.

JEFFREY TATE

Descriptor

Jeffrey is a member of a four-teacher team in the sixth grade. Each teacher teaches reading and one of the four major content areas. Jeffrey teaches one class of reading and four classes of language arts. He has 120 students in the four language arts classes, which are heterogeneously grouped. Each class meets for fifty minutes daily.

The school, which is located in a suburban area, houses students in grades six, seven, eight, and nine. There are ten units of sixth-graders in the school. The socioeconomic status of families ranges from low to high average, with the majority in the average to high average bracket. Students have a good attitude toward school and they generally have positive self-concepts. This is undoubtedly enhanced by their stable home conditions. The sixth-graders are eager to please their teachers when they arrive at the school, although the students are often afraid and inhibited as they enter a new school. They are very guarded, and many are afraid to express themselves verbally at the beginning of the year.

The team of teachers plans together daily. Language arts skills are stressed in social studies and science and the teachers reinforce the skills in all content areas. All teachers try to use nonobjective tests in which they ask students to write their answers in complete sentences and paragraphs. Teachers provide feedback to their students on their language usage.

The school's practice of scheduling reading as a separate class from the other language arts necessitates some isolation of language arts skills. The basal reading program is a total language arts series; however, since reading is during a separate period, it focuses mainly on comprehension and vocabulary. The language arts class focuses on language growth and usage, spelling, handwriting, listening, speaking, and composition. The scope and sequence are different for the two classes.

The real pressure under which Jeffrey works is in trying to teach all the language arts skills effectively in a daily period of fifty minutes. He uses the prescribed state-adopted texts and tries to interrelate the various skills. The school district has developed a K–12 language arts curriculum guide which specifies the instructional program. Teachers in the district are to use the texts and teacher-developed resources as tools for teaching the identified skills and concepts. Jeffrey does not have enough class time to utilize many other commercial materials. He uses very few duplicated materials because he wants students to learn to write and to have adequate practice in writing.

Jeffrey uses a teacher-developed resource for teaching the parts of speech and their functional role in language usage. He calls the procedure the "Parts of Speech Family." Family members include pa verb, mother noun, big sister pronoun (she takes her mother's place when mother is not there), big brother preposition, adjective and adverb twins (adverb is the cheerleader and is always jumping around), Andy conjunction (the little brother who likes to put things together all the time), and interjection (Snoopy the dog, who barks and interrupts). Each character is made of cardboard and is hung on the wall in the classroom. Jeffrey explains that "Each character has a place in the family. When students associate these things, they remember them. They associate the parts of speech with their role and the duties they have." This procedure works quite effectively with Jeffrey's students.

Jeffrey also has his students engage in journal writing on a weekly basis. Students are encouraged to express themselves freely and Jeffrey writes comments to the students in response to their journal entries. Jeffrey notes that the students are able to see progress in their journal writing as the year progresses and that they are proud of their journals at the end of the year. The practice of journal writing becomes a habit which many of Jeffrey's students continue through later years.

Jeffrey includes a number of teacher-made and commercially produced games to enrich the instructional program. Numerous language arts skills lend themselves to this form of enrichment and practice.

School-wide grouping is practiced for reading and mathematics classes, but students are placed heterogeneously for their other classes. Jeffrey feels that this heterogeneous grouping works well in language arts because students of differing ability levels learn a great deal from each other and stimulate each other. He does utilize subgrouping within his classes for various aspects of the program. For example, Jeffrey varies the number and type of spelling words assigned according to the instructional and developmental level of the students.

He assesses the readiness level of his students for instruction in specific skills by observing student performance on classroom activities. For example, Jeffrey places an emphasis on composition and he determines which students need specific instruction in various aspects of grammar and usage, spelling, and handwriting by using the student's actual writing as a diagnostic source. He feels strongly that students learn to write by writing and that teachers learn the strengths and weaknesses of students by examining their writing carefully. Otherwise, it is like trying to learn to swim by reading a book. Therefore, he teaches grammar and usage, spelling, and handwriting in the context of composition.

Included in the composition instruction is practice in writing complete sentences, writing a good paragraph, writing a three-paragraph report, making and following an outline, writing creatively, preparing a rough draft, editing and proofreading, writing the final draft, and responding to a specific writing prompt. Students follow the writing process and develop their skills as prescribed in the state's basic skills writing program. Writing is an important part of the curriculum and is used to tie together the various components of the language arts program.

In developing listening skills, Jeffrey stresses following oral and written directions. He works to develop good listening habits as he reads to his students regularly.

Jeffrey considers the area of speaking as "one of my things." He uses many activities which encourage oral expression, including some public speaking. All students have the opportunity to participate in some speech contests during the year, and a number of students enter oratorical contests in which they write, memorize, and deliver a speech. This aspect of the curriculum also integrates many language arts skills.

Student progress is reported formally through a six-week report card, the school's standard procedure. In addition, Jeffrey sends student work home for parents to examine and he conducts many student and parent conferences. A checklist which shows student progress on skills listed in the curriculum guide is kept for each student and used to assess progress during conferences. He also sends interim reports to parents of students who are having problems during the grading period. Usually when parent conferences are held, all four unit teachers meet with the parents so a complete picture of the child can be presented. The parent can share information with, and ask questions of, all teachers. This method of conferencing seems to work well and is appreciated by the parents.

Jeffrey maintains a file folder for each student in which he keeps samples of the student's writing so that the student, the teacher, and the parents can see progress over a period of time. One can note growth in the student's ability to use language, to express herself or himself clearly and concisely, to use legible handwriting, and to spell accurately. Students are often surprised to see the amount of improvement they have made over a period of time.

Jeffrey stresses that teachers must make the language arts fun if they want to be successful. He says that aspects of the language arts can be dry and the teacher must work to make these as enjoyable and meaningful as possible. "You need to get to know your students well and help them to know that you care about them. The first thing you have to do is get the kids on your side. I find it is important to let the students know that I know my subject well but that I am still learning too. I encourage them to find mistakes that I make and I try to allow for a relaxed atmosphere."

Jeffrey praises his students when it is deserved and he gives them special attention. He writes "Happy Grams" to his students on special occasions. He finds that the students respond very positively to the comments he writes in their journals. Students warm up to the teacher fast and they seem to feel freer to express themselves in class.

Jeffrey provides special help for students at any time it seems to be needed. He has prepared some special packets of material for use in class and at home to provide practice in various skill areas. Jeffrey also helps students during recess and after school as needed. Additional special help is available through learning disability classes, reading resource classes, and Title I classes.

The classroom bulletin boards are used for creative and involvement activities. They may focus on writing poetry or developing an ongoing short story. Bulletin boards are used to promote learning and student creativity rather than for displaying trite sayings and/or teacher-made exhibits.

The enthusiasm Jeffrey has for teaching, the fun he has while teaching, the competence he exhibits in his teaching field, and his concern for the development of his students make Jeffrey's classroom a stimulating one for his sixth-graders.

Analysis

Jeffrey is a member of a four-teacher team in the sixth grade. Each teacher teaches reading and one of the four major content areas. Jeffrey teaches one class of reading and four classes of language arts. He has 120 students in the four language arts classes which are heterogeneously grouped. Each class meets for fifty minutes daily.

The school, which is located in a suburban area, houses students in grades six, seven, eight, and nine. There are ten units of sixth-graders in the school. The socio-economic status of families ranges from low to high average, with the majority in the average to high average bracket. Students have a good attitude toward school and they generally have positive self-concepts. This is undoubtedly enhanced by their stable home conditions. The sixth-graders are eager to please their teachers when they arrive at the school, although the students are often afraid and inhibited as they enter a new school. They are very guarded, and many are afraid to express themselves verbally at the beginning of the year.

The team of teachers plans together daily.[1] *Language arts skills are stressed in social studies and science and the teachers reinforce the skills in all content areas.*[2] All teachers try to use nonobjective tests in which they ask students to write their answers in complete sentences and paragraphs. Teachers provide feedback to their students on their language usage.

The school's practice of scheduling reading as a separate class from the other language arts necessitates some isolation of language arts skills. The basal reading program is a total language arts series; however, since reading is during a separate period, it focuses on language growth and usage, spelling, handwriting, listening, speaking, and composition. The scope and sequence are different for the two classes.

The real pressure under which Jeffrey works is in trying to teach all the language arts skills effectively in a daily period of fifty minutes. *He uses the prescribed state-adopted texts and tries to interrelate the various skills.*[3] The school district has developed a K–12 language arts curriculum guide which specifies the instructional program. *Teachers in the district are to use the texts and teacher-developed resources as tools for teaching the identified skills and concepts.*[4] Jeffrey does not have enough class time to utilize many other commercial materials. *He uses very few duplicated materials because he wants students to learn to write and to have adequate practice in writing.*[5]

Jeffrey uses a teacher-developed resource for teaching the parts of speech and their functional role in language usage.[6] He calls this procedure the "Parts of Speech Family." Family members include pa verb, mother noun, big sister pronoun (she takes her mother's place when mother is not there), big brother preposition, adjective and adverb twins (adverb is the cheerleader and is always jumping around), Andy conjunction (the little brother who likes to put things together all the time), and interjection

(Snoopy the dog, who barks and interrupts). Each character is made of cardboard and is hung on the wall in the classroom. Jeffrey explains that "Each character has a place in the family. When students associate these things, they remember them. They associate the parts of speech with their role and the duties they have." This procedure works quite effectively with Jeffrey's students.

Jeffrey also has his students engage in journal writing on a weekly basis.[7] Students are encouraged to express themselves freely and Jeffrey writes comments to the students in response to their journal entries. Jeffrey notes that the students are able to see progress in their journal writing as the year progresses and that they are proud of their journals at the end of the year. The practice of journal writing becomes a habit which many of Jeffrey's students continue through later years.

Jeffrey includes a number of teacher-made and commercially produced games to enrich the instructional program.[8] Numerous language arts skills lend themselves to this form of enrichment and practice.

School-wide grouping is practiced for reading and mathematics classes, but students are placed heterogeneously for their other classes. *Jeffrey feels that this heterogeneous grouping works well in language arts because students of differing ability levels learn a great deal from each other and stimulate each other.*[9] He does utilize subgrouping within his classes for various aspects of the program. For example, Jeffrey varies the number and type of spelling words assigned according to the instructional and developmental level of the students.

He assesses the readiness level of his students for instruction in specific skills by observing student performance on classroom activities. For example, Jeffrey places an emphasis on composition and he determines which students need specific instruction in various aspects of grammar and usage, spelling, and handwriting *by using the student's actual writing as a diagnostic source.*[10] He feels strongly that students learn to write by writing and that teachers learn the strengths and weaknesses of students by examining their writing carefully. Otherwise, it is like trying to learn to swim by reading a book. Therefore, he teaches grammar and usage, spelling, and handwriting in the context of composition.

Included in the composition instruction is practice in writing complete sentences, writing a good paragraph, writing a three-paragraph report, making and following an outline, writing creatively, preparing a rough draft, editing and proofreading, writing the final draft, and responding to a specific writing prompt. Students follow the writing process and develop their skills as prescribed in the state's basic skills writing program. Writing is an important part of the curriculum and is used to tie together the various components of the language arts program.

In developing listening skills, Jeffrey stresses following oral and written directions. He works to develop good listening habits as he reads to his students regularly.

Jeffrey considers the area of speaking as "one of my things." He uses many activities which encourage oral expression, including some public speaking. All students have the opportunity to participate in some speech contests during the year, and a number of students enter oratorical contests in which they write, memorize, and deliver a speech. This aspect of the curriculum also integrates many language arts skills.

Student progress is reported formally through a six-week report card, the school's standard procedure. In addition, Jeffrey sends student work home for parents to examine

Students need adequate practice in writing.

and he conducts many student and parent conferences. A checklist which shows student progress on skills listed in the curriculum guide is kept for each student and used to assess progress during conferences. He also sends interim reports to parents of students who are having problems during the grading period. Usually when parent conferences are held, all four unit teachers meet with the parents so a complete picture of the child can be presented. The parent can share information with, and ask questions of, all teachers. This method of conferencing seems to work well and is appreciated by the parents.

Jeffrey maintains a file folder for each student in which he keeps samples of the student's writing so that the student, the teacher, and the parents can see progress over a period of time.[11] One can note growth in the student's ability to use language, to express herself or himself clearly and concisely, to use legible handwriting, and to spell accurately. Students are often surprised to see the amount of improvement they have made over a period of time.

Jeffrey stresses that teachers must make the language arts fun if they want to be successful.[12] He says that aspects of the language arts can be dry and the teacher must work to make these as enjoyable and meaningful as possible. "You need to get to know your students well and help them to know that you care about them. The first thing you have to do is get the kids on your side. I find it is important to let the students know that I know my subject well but that I am still learning too. I encourage them to find mistakes that I make and I try to allow for a relaxed atmosphere."

Jeffrey praises his students when it is deserved and he gives them special attention. He writes "Happy Grams" to his students on special occasions. He finds that the students repond very positively to the comments he writes in their journals. Students warm up to the teacher fast and they seem to feel freer to express themselves in class.

Jeffrey provides special help for students at any time it seems to be needed. He has prepared some special packets of material for use in class and at home to provide practice in various skill areas. Jeffrey also helps students during recess and after school as needed. Additional special help is available through learning disability classes, reading resource classes, and Title 1 classes.

The classroom bulletin boards are used for creative and involvement activities.[13] They may focus on writing poetry or developing an ongoing short story. Bulletin boards are used to promote learning and student creativity rather than for displaying trite sayings and/or teacher-made exhibits.

The enthusiasm Jeffrey has for teaching, the fun he has while teaching, the competence he exhibits in his teaching field, and his concern for the development of his students make Jeffrey's classroom a stimulating one for his sixth-graders.

Explanation

1 A team of teachers which plans together daily is likely to know students better and to provide a well-coordinated program. Teams should be selected because their members have abilities and skills that complement each other. In addition, each team should operate under the premise that all members share a joint responsibility for planning and leading the learning activities for a specific group of students. When teachers plan as a team, they can plan for the whole child; they can provide for the cognitive, the affective, and the psychomotor development of the child. Their discussions lead to a constantly increasing knowledge of students, content, and resources. They can plan for units of instruction which are reinforced and enriched in all content areas. Together they can set realistic and comprehensive goals, plan instructional strategies, select appropriate resources, discuss grouping and subgrouping, and determine assessment measures to be used. They can engage in long-term planning, short-term planning, and evaluation of classroom work. The advantages of team planning are numerous and students are the real beneficiaries of the process.

2 When teachers plan together and develop lesson ideas and units together, they are aware of the skills and concepts which are being introduced in the various content areas. The teachers can then reinforce the skills in different content areas. The content for compositions may be selected from social studies or science units. The spelling and vocabulary words may be selected from all the content areas. An emphasis on certain handwriting skills may be included in the instruction and reinforcement provided by all teachers. The team of teachers can plan so that the teachers use fewer fill-in-the-blank types of activities and assign more writing of sentences and paragraphs to help all the students strengthen their composition skills.

3 In previous chapters, we have emphasized the importance of interrelating the various language arts skills. This interrelatedness needs to occur at all grade levels. Students and teachers must be aware that reading, writing, listening, and speaking involve receptive activities (reading and listening) and expressive activities (writing and speaking) and that they are directly related to thinking. The four aspects of language arts should be taught and practiced in an interrelated manner.

In its publication entitled "What Are the Basics in English?", the National Council of Teachers of English (7)

. . . advocates the importance of language arts skills being used to reinforce each other. In this process of reinforcement, students explore a wide range of reading interests, get involved in a variety of related learning activities, and thereby develop a firmer grasp of all of the necessary language competencies (p. 1).

4 Although textbooks play an important part in the instructional program, they should not dictate the curriculum. The teachers in a given school district should be actively involved in developing a K–12 language arts curriculum guide. The skills to be taught and the sequence for their introduction, reinforcement, and practice should be determined as a result of assessing the needs of, and expectations for, students in the school district. Once the curriculum is established, the teachers can select textbooks, commercial materials, and teacher-made materials which will be appropriate for teaching the curriculum. Teachers choose the tool which will best enable them to teach the concepts and skills to the students with whom they are working.

5 Research (11) clearly indicates that students learn to write by writing, with appropriate instruction. Students at all grade levels should write regularly. Teachers should ask students to write short papers, based on varied and interesting stimulations. Student writing should be related to the experiences of the student. Students should be writing sentences and paragraphs rather than filling in the blanks or matching columns or labeling parts of speech. Many duplicated materials, workbook exercises, and textbook drill exercises ask students to do the latter. We strongly recommend that teachers emphasize writing or original responses rather than filling in the blanks, matching, or labeling. As seems to be the case in several aspects of the language arts, our students may be overskilled and underpracticed. In order to become proficient in the skills of composition, students need to have extensive practice in writing. However, this practice must be accompanied by instruction.

6 Research on the teaching of grammar and usage (7, 11) suggests that they should be taught functionally in the same fashion that we teach the language skills of speaking and writing. The research points out that the isolated teaching of skills cannot be justified. We should focus on the functional role and uses of language.

The authorities cited by Haley-James (11) recommend that formal study of grammar should be delayed until grade eight or nine. Until then, revising writing in view of the audience for the writing should be the basis of grammar-related language study. We should continue to teach grammar, but the focus of our teaching should be on the functional use of language instead of the labeling of parts of speech, memorizing definitions, and diagramming sentences. The formal study of grammar is very abstract, and most elementary school students have not reached the developmental stage at which they are able to handle this abstract information. Writing a cinquain, causing students to *use* nouns, verbs, adjectives, synonyms, and possibly adverbs and similes, may accomplish far more than a formal grammar lesson.

7 Journal writing is advocated by many as a means of getting students to express their thoughts and ideas in writing. Some journal writing will be very personal and students will not want the teacher or anyone else to read it. Other students will want the teacher to read their journal entries. Many teachers write comments to the students in the journal, and a correspondence between the student and teacher may develop because of the journal. As Jeffrey testifies, the practice of journal writing becomes an ongoing habit for many students. The teacher may require students to write in their journals daily, weekly, or any other amount of time that seems to be profitable and feasible.

Fader (9) states that journal writing is consistently successful. He recommends that the only criterion for judging journal writing is the amount of writing produced. Since the journal is a place for students to practice their writing, it is not corrected. We also recommend the suggestions Fader provides for initiating and continuing the practice of journal writing. Other excellent ideas relative to journal writing can be found in an article by Elliot, Nowosad, and Samuels (8).

8 Teacher-made and commercially produced games can enrich the instructional program and can provide practice in the skills which have been taught. This can be especially true in the areas of spelling and vocabulary. Hodges (15) advocates that teachers and parents use inquiry-oriented word games to provide practice in spelling. "The value of word games in the teaching of spelling lies not only in the enjoyment they offer young children, but in their potential to promote inquiry and experimentation"' (p. 15). In the second half of his booklet, Hodges explains numerous spelling-oriented word games which can be played by children, teachers, and parents. These games provide an excellent example of how teacher- or parent-made games can enhance and enrich learning.

9 We advocate the use of heterogeneous grouping for language arts so that students can benefit from peer learning experiences as well as from teacher-directed activities. Children need the stimulation and model of children with abilities different from their own. A 1971 study of ability grouping (10) concluded that the homogeneous grouping of students shows conflicting evidence; that it promotes scholastic achievement in high-ability groups but seldom does in average or low-ability students. Homogeneous grouping also reinforces negative self-concepts for students who are placed in low-achievement groups. The latter students become less motivated, especially if they are from lower socioeconomic backgrounds and are minority groups. The study recommends a procedure for a stratified heterogeneous grouping plan, which seems to benefit most students.

10 It would seem advisable for teachers to secure a writing sample from each of their students early in the school year. These writing samples should then be used diagnostically to determine strengths and weaknesses. The teacher can use the information gained to prioritize instructional emphases and to group within the classroom.

Burns (3) provides some charts which teachers could use to record diagnostic information about composition, listening, speaking, and other language arts components. The charts can assist the teacher in grouping for similar instructional needs and for determining those skills which all or most of the children seem to have mastered already.

Teachers can tell what knowledge a child has gained and what that child's ability to apply that knowledge is by examining the child's composition. As Burns (3) points out, "Even though a pupil may be able to give a 'definition' of an adjective, this is no assurance that he can or does make effective use of descriptive words. Only those skills which actually appear in a pupil's daily performance can be considered learned" (p. 80).

11 The best way to note progress in composition is to keep samples of student papers which were written at various times during the year. As you examine papers written in September, November, January, March, and May, you should be able to see improvement in the student's ability to write. Students can see the progress and so can parents. A list of grades in a gradebook does not show growth or progress, but writing samples do. The writing samples are valuable for use in student conferences and in parent conferences. Each teacher should maintain a file folder of writing samples for each student. One or two of the student's best pieces of writing might be kept in the folder and passed on to the student's teacher for the following year.

12 If teachers were to lay the textbooks in the language arts series (grades three to twelve) on a table with the books opened to the table of contents, they would note that they are nearly identical. The same information is presented each year, with a few new items added here and there. This could provide for a very boring program as students progress from grade to grade. The teachers must search for novel and enjoyable ways to provide instruction, enrichment, and practices. More of the same will cause students to lose interest and can make language arts classes boring and the students listless. Teachers should always be seeking ways to involve students so that they apply, analyze, synthesize, and evaluate and learning becomes meaningful.

13 Classroom bulletin boards should be used to list involvement activities for students. Learning station activities may be placed there for practice and/or enrichment. Students should be encouraged to develop learning activities which can be presented on the bulletin board. Bulletin boards can also be an outlet for displaying the creative abilities of students in various forms. Teachers should refrain from purchasing commercially prepared bulletin board materials and should encourage students to prepare bulletin board displays and activities. Bulletin boards are an additional means for providing learning experiences for children.

BIBLIOGRAPHY AND REFERENCES

1 Block, Janet K. "Those Mistakes Tell Us A Lot." *Language Arts,* vol. 5, May 1980, pp. 508–513.

2 Bloom, Benjamin. *Stability and Change in Human Characteristics.* New York: John Wiley and Sons, 1964.

3 Burns, Paul C. *Diagnostic Teaching of the Language Arts.* Itasca, Ill.: F. E. Peacock, 1974.

4 Brookover, Wilbur B., Sailor, Thomas, and Paterson, Ann. "Self-Concept of Ability and School Achievement." *Sociology of Education,* vol. 37, Spring 1964, pp. 271–278.

5 Calkins, Lucy McCormick. "When Children Want to Punctuate: Basic Skills Belong in Context." *Language Arts,* vol. 57, May 1980, p. 568.

6 Clay, Marie. *Reading the Patterning of Complex Behavior*. London: Heinemann Educational Books, 1977, p. 165.

7 Dunning, Steven, and Redd, Virginia. "What Are the Basics in English?" *SLATE Starter Sheets*, vol. 1, no. 2, August 1976, p. 1.

8 Elliott, Sharon, Nowosad, John, and Samuels, Phyllis. " 'Me At School,' 'Me At Home': Using Journals with Preschoolers." *Language Arts*, vol. 58, no. 6, September 1981, pp. 688–691.

9 Fader, Daniel N., and McNeil, Elton B. *Hooked on Books: Program and Proof*. New York: Berkley Publishing Company, 1968, p. 19.

10 Findley, Warren G., and Bryan, Marian M. *Ability Grouping: 1970—Status, Impact, and Alternatives*. Athens, Ga.: University of Georgia Center for Educational Improvement, 1971.

11 Haley-James, Shirley (ed.). *Perspectives on Writing in Grades 1–8*. Urbana, Ill. The National Council of Teachers of English, 1981.

12 Harding, D. W. "Response to Literature." In Margaret Meek, Aidan Warlow, and Griselda Barton (eds.), *The Cool Web: The Pattern of Children's Reading*, New York: Atheneum, 1978, pp. 379–392.

13 Hickman, Janet. "Children's Responses to Literature: What Happens in the Classroom?" *Language Arts*, vol. 57, May 1980, pp. 524–529.

14 Hillman, Judith. "Reading Aloud to Children: A Rationale," Study prepared at St. Michael's College. Ontario: University of Toronto, 1975, 8 pp. (ED 172 152).

15 Hodges, Richard E. *Learning to Spell*. Urbana, Ill.: The National Council of Teachers of English, 1981.

16 Larrick, Nancy. *A Parents' Guide to Children's Reading* (4th ed.) New York: Bantam Books, 1975.

17 Lumpkin, Don. *Relationship of Self-Concept to Reading*. Ph.D. dissertation, University of Southern California, 1959.

18 McCormick, Sandra. "Should You Read Aloud to Your Children?" *Language Arts*, vol. 54, February 1977, pp. 139–143.

19 Olsen, Henry D., and Mangieri, John N. "Self-Concept-of-Academic Ability and Reading Proficiency," *Reading Horizons*, vol. 17, Fall 1976, pp. 28–34.

20 Petty, Walter T., and Jensen, Julie M. *Developing Children's Language*. Boston: Allyn and Bacon, 1980, p. 74.

21 Pilon, A. Barbara. "Culturally Divergent Children and Creative Language Activities." In James L. Laffey and Roger Shuy (eds.), *Language Differences: Do They Interfere?* Newark, Del.: International Reading Association, 1973, pp. 127–146.

22 Prescott, Daniel. "What I Have Learned from Children." In Clarence W. Hunnicutt (ed.), *Education, 2000 A.D.* Syracuse, N.Y.: Syracuse University Press, 1956, pp. 41–62.

23 Purkey, William W. *Self-Concept And School Achievement*. Englewood Cliffs, N.J.: Prentice-Hall, 1970.

24 Quandt, Ivan. *Self-Concept and Reading*. Newark, Del.: International Reading Association, 1972.

25 Smith, Lillian H. *The Unreluctant Years*. Chicago: The American Library Association, 1953, p. 17.

26 Wadsworth, Barry J. *Piaget's Theory of Cognitive Development*. New York: Longman, 1977, p. 9.

27 Winkeljohann, Sister Rosemary. "How Do We Promote Communication Arts?" *Language Arts*, vol. 57, September 1980, pp. 660–663.

28 Glazer, Susan M. *How Can I Help My Child Build Positive Attitudes toward Reading?* Newark, Del.: International Reading Association, 1980.

CHAPTER 8

LANGUAGE ARTS IN THE MIDDLE SCHOOL

OVERVIEW

Only in the last few years have the middle grades (six, seven, and eight) come to be recognized as a separate educational entity. Their programs have often been added on rather than built into the school curriculum, appearing either at the end of the elementary grades or at the beginning of the secondary ones.

In recent years, however, these grades have begun to receive the attention they deserve, for research has shown that students in these grades are unique in their physical, social, psychological, and intellectual development. An effective middle school instructional program must take into account the special attributes and needs of students during these years. At this level the school program must focus on two primary considerations: the *individual* needs and the *societal* needs of the student.

The focus of this chapter will be on the teaching of the language arts in the middle grades. The chapter will begin by discussing the nature of students in these grades. We will then describe the curricular emphases, instructional activities, and assessment measures associated with providing language arts instruction to students in these grades.

Individual Needs During these school years, the responsibility for learning must shift progressively to the learner. Opportunities must be provided for the students to adapt independently to their environment and to secure a better understanding of the world in which they live. Students always vary greatly in interests, aptitudes, and abilities, but this is especially so during the eleven- to fourteen-year-old's accelerated growth and emerging self-realization. This accelerated change dominates every facet of student growth during this period, and the resulting individually patterned development must be accounted for in a program of basically individualized instruction.

Instruction must meet two important challenges from the student: (1) the need to become increasingly independent in his or her thought and actions, and (2) the growing reliance upon the social security offered by the school and the home rather than by any single individual such as a parent. It is incumbent upon the school to provide for the individual needs of this student through a logical, sequential program of instruction based upon relevant skills, values, and understandings.

Societal Needs   Because he or she lives in a dynamic and rapidly changing society, the middle school student, as he or she begins to develop self-realization as a unique individual, needs and deserves a school program which emphasizes human and democratic values in its philosophy, content, and methodology. Such a program must assist this student in understanding the societal expectations to which he or she is or will be subjected. Since change is a prevailing characteristic of today's society, an effective school program will help the student understand and participate in the processes of change. The program should also be cognizant of the pluralistic American society which requires members who understand its varying norms of behavior, life-styles, and cultural and ethnic divergencies.

The middle school years offer varied and challenging experiences and opportunities for students and for teachers. We shall refer to a middle school as a school which contains at least three sequential grade levels and, for our purposes, shall contain grades six, seven, and eight. It would probably include children from ages ten or eleven to about thirteen or fourteen. Students at this level are struggling between the stages of childhood and adolescence, often referred to as the period of *transescence* or the time between ages. "*Transescence* is defined as that period in an individual's development beginning prior to the onset of puberty and continuing through early adolescence. It is characterized by changes in physical development, social interaction, and intellectual functions" (12). Students are quite different during this period and the learning program must provide opportunities which will help them to grow and develop in accordance with their individual abilities and capacities.

The rationale for the middle school is to provide an appropriate school for the boys and girls attending it. This has required a careful study of the middle school age children and their needs, interests, and concerns. These needs, interests, and concerns require a flexible learning environment for the middle school and the establishment of specific goals for the program. The *South Carolina Middle School Guide* states:

> Although many functions of the middle school are shared with elementary and secondary schools, planned opportunities and activities in the middle school must be developed with the following major purposes in mind:
>
> **1** To help each child understand himself as a developing person.
> **2** To prepare each child to understand and accept his new role as a developing adolescent.
> **3** To foster independent learning and self-direction.
> **4** To provide experiences designed to assist each child in clarifying his values and those of others.
> **5** To provide instruction in and application of the decision-making process.
> **6** To permit wide exploration of personal interests.

7 To ensure every child a degree of success in understanding underlying principles and key concepts of the organized disciplines.

8 To build upon basic skills acquired in elementary school.

9 To promote maximum growth in basic communication and computational skills.

10 To make learning exciting.

11 To emphasize learning experiences that will help the child make appropriate choices in the more specialized secondary school.

In order to accomplish these goals, teachers are more important than facilities. The success of the school will be determined more by people than by purse. The middle school concept embraces the premise that education should be concerned with more than the acquisition of knowledge; students do not become functional members of society simply by accumulating information. The pre-adolescent must be exposed to educational experiences that will teach him *how* to learn, *how* to critically evaluate his ideas and values, and *how* to develop interests and attitudes as he relates to individuals, peer groups, and society (50).

Lounsbury and Vars (29) discuss the special qualities needed by a middle school teacher and how these qualities help to accomplish the goals of the middle school. They further delineate the special characteristics which teachers during the middle school years should possess: "Not that they need to be better educated, more intelligent, more experienced, or possess more specialized knowledge. Rather, they need to be special by being secure, open, empathic, positive, and caring individuals who genuinely like middle school students and understand fully the nature of middle school education." As the preceding implies quite clearly, every teacher is not suited to be a middle school teacher.

Teachers of language arts in the middle school usually find themselves in one of two organizational structures. Either they are totally departmentalized and teach language arts (also known as English) for the entire school day or they may teach language arts and one other subject area. In either of these structures, teachers may function as an independent entity or as a member of a team of teachers which provides the total instructional program for a specific group of students. We would recommend the team approach so that teachers can plan together to provide the best learning program for the entire range of children being served by the school. The language arts skills can be interrelated with all content areas and all teachers can help to reinforce the reading, writing, listening, and speaking skills which are needed in all disciplines.

Middle school teachers usually have a set number of minutes per week which are allotted for language arts instruction. Most teachers seem to have one fifty- to sixty-minute period per day with each class and they are expected to teach, use, and practice all the language arts skills during that time period. Some schools allow two periods of language arts per day for each class. When this is the case, one period is usually designated for reading and the other period is for all the other language arts. Sometimes, unfortunately, the two periods are taught by different teachers. The two teachers may not have time for planning together and may have totally independent and incongruent programs.

We recommend that at the middle school level, students have two periods daily for language arts instruction and that the same teacher teach both periods for a specific class of students. We further recommend that the teacher integrate the teaching of the language arts skills into both class periods and that none of the language arts areas be isolated from the others. The reading and/or literature lessons and experiences should lead to writing, listening, and speaking activities. Writing should lead to further reading, listening, and speaking, and so on. Students and teachers need to realize the importance of the interrelationship of the language arts.

Class size and teaching load become important factors for middle school language arts teachers. Teachers will probably have twenty-five to thirty-five students per class and may have five or six different classes per day. Teachers could find themselves with a class load of 150 or more students per day. The more students the teacher is assigned, the more difficult it is to prepare for and teach the language arts effectively. If class loads are high, the tendency is to conduct the classes like mini high school classes rather than to focus on the middle school students' unique learning needs. The National Council of Teachers of English (36) adopted the NCTE Policy Statements of Teachers' Workload in 1976 and in 1977. These statements follow:

Elementary:

1 The elementary classroom teacher should not be responsible for more than 25 pupils per class.

2 One class period or a minimum of thirty minutes should be provided within each school day for each elementary school teacher's planning time.

3 Half day a month should be set aside for each elementary school teacher for long-range planning.

4 The use of additional human resources in the classroom should not be used to increase the pupil teacher ratio.

5 Clerks should be available to teachers on an assigned basis to attend to noninstructional tasks.

6 A library and instructional materials center with proper staff and adequate, varied teaching materials should be provided in every elementary school.

7 Participation in long term continuous inservice programs should be considered a part of teachers' workloads and should involve released time from other duties.

8 Participation in professional meetings and activities at local, state, and national levels should be encouraged and financially supported.

Board of Directors, 1977

Secondary:
RESOLVED, That full time English teachers (in secondary schools) be assigned a daily teaching load of no more than 100 students.

Board of Directors, 1976

Various writings about the middle school curriculum seem to stress the variety of experiences which should be provided and the need for numerous exploratory programs. These experiences and exploratory programs may be provided during the regular curricular activities and as extra opportunities during "nonacademic" class periods. Carl Rogers (40) would seem to be an advocate of teaching more than facts and basics when he says that "The only man who is educated is the man who has learned how to learn; the man who has learned how to adapt and change; the man who has realized that no knowledge is secure, that only the process of seeking knowledge gives a basis for security." Rogers says that educators should rely on the process of learning and not on amassing quantities of static knowledge.

Research conducted by Epstein (13) concludes that there are brain growth spurts in children and adolescents which need to be considered in their educational programs. Epstein's work shows that these brain growth spurts occur almost simultaneously with the classical main stages given in Piaget's period of intellectual development. In summarizing Epstein's research and its implications for education, Toepfer (53) states that "In approximately 85% of all youngsters, the brain ceases to grow between the ages of 12 to 14. This hiatus in brain growth approximates the transescent's pubertal metamorphosis" (p. 1). Toepfer supports Epstein in contending that parents and educators should not "expect continued cognitive growth" during this time and that middle school programs should "focus upon refinement of existing cognitive skills" instead of trying to force students to learn new cognitive skills when "absence of brain growth cannot support this new learning" (p. 2).

The literature about the middle school emphasizes that the focus should be on the learner. The middle school should not be a mini high school and should not be planned primarily to teach "the facts" or "the basics" someone might decide that students should possess before beginning high school. Since the focus should be on the learner, let us look at the middle school learner and try to identify some of the characteristics which are unique to the middle school years.

THE CHILD

"Adolescence is likely to be a challenging and sometimes difficult stage in the young person's struggles toward maturity as well as a period of high hopes, exciting new experiences, and expanded opportunities for personal growth" (33, p. 246). This statement from Mussen, Conger, and Kagan (33) says a great deal about the child during the years of adolescence. It indicates that adolescence is a time of many changes. Physical, social, psychological, sexual, and cognitive changes affect the middle school student. A major point to keep in mind is that those changes occur at various times and for various time periods in different children. The environmental factors which surround the student may have a significant effect on these changes.

Physical Characteristics

The beginning of adolescence is accompanied by increased rates of growth in height and weight. This growth spurt will begin at different times and last different amounts of time within a group of adolescents. There may be considerable differences among children in a given class. Muscular development is also occurring during this time. Adolescents move into and through puberty during the middle school years and are experiencing various levels of sexual maturation. Other physical changes may include a lowering of the voice, changes in rate of energy production, and growth of bones. The adolescent tends to be relatively free from diseases, but often has poor posture and is awkward. The endurance level may be lower during this period.

Social and Emotional Characteristics

During adolescence, students generally try to decrease their dependence on the family, and they become increasingly more cognizant of their peer group. The peer group becomes more important in terms of status, security, language, dress, and behavior. Adolescents want to be independent of older and younger groups but want very much to conform to their age group. Peer pressure is very strong and probably reaches its peak during this period. The differences which occur in adolescents because of physical and sexual changes can cause social and emotional problems for these students. Middle school students sometimes appear to lack control of their emotions, and they may exhibit a wide variety of moods. Anger is common and students may worry a great deal.

Intellectual Characteristics

Learning to understand and work with abstract concepts and entering the stage that Piaget calls formal operations are the major intellectual changes which occur during adolescence. The cognitive changes during this period are important to many facets of the adolescent's life. "Changes in the nature of parent-child relationships, emerging personality characteristics and psychological defense mechanisms, planning for future educational and vocational goals, mounting concerns with social, political, and personal values, even a developing sense of personal identity, all are strongly influenced by these cognitive changes" (33, p. 439). Adolescents are often extremely critical (of parents and social, political, and religious systems) as they attempt to use formal operational thought. They become capable of making judgments and begin to use hypothetical reasoning. Experience is what keeps adolescents from solving many adult problems.

SUMMARY

Georgiady and Romano (17) developed an excellent summary of the characteristics of middle school students and their implications for the middle school curriculum. This summary is shown below.

I PHYSICAL GROWTH CHARACTERISTICS

A BODY GROWTH

The growth pattern is the same for all boys and girls, but there are wide variations in the timing and degree of changes. The sequential order in which they occur is relatively consistent in both sexes.

Each person rapidly accelerates before pubescence and decelerates after pubescence.

During the transition between childhood and adolescence (six months after puberty), the greatest amount of physical (as well as psychological and social) change in an individual will occur.

IMPLICATION FOR THE CURRICULUM

Emphasize self-understanding throughout the curriculum. This can be done by:

1 Providing health and science experiences that will develop an understanding of growth such as: (1) weighing and measuring at regular intervals and charting gains or losses; (2) observing growth of plants and animals; (3) learning about individual differences in growth.

2 Providing guidance at the classroom level and by utilizing school counselor(s) as resource persons.

A BODY GROWTH (*continued*)

1 Growth hormone (anterior lobe of pituitary gland) stimulates overall growth of bones and tissue. This hormone is largely responsible for the growth rate.

2 Gonad-stimulating hormone causes gonads (testes and ovaries) to grow, which produce hormones of their own. When gonads reach maturity they seem to dry up the growth hormone.

3 Changes in thymus, thyroid, and possibly adrenal glands result in changes in rate of energy production (metabolism), blood pressure, and pulse rate.

4 Bones grow fast, muscles slower; legs and arms grow proportionately faster than trunk. Hands and feet mature before arms and legs. This split growth is called *asynchrony*.

IMPLICATION FOR THE CURRICULUM

3 During physical education classes, providing for individual differences by having several groups of differing abilities.

Provide opportunities for interaction among students of multi-ages.

B HEALTH

Continues to enjoy comparative freedom from diseases; however, eyes, ears, and especially teeth may require medical attention. Minor illnesses of short duration are fairly common during early pre-adolescence.

Poor posture and awkwardness become increasingly evident.

Physical education classes should provide health instruction as well as exercise. Periods should be long enough to allow adequate time for showers—which should be required.

C BODY MANAGEMENT

Endurance is usually not high, perhaps because of the rapid growth spurt. Pre-adolescents can overtire themselves in exciting competition.

For many, this is a period of listlessness, possibly of an emotional or physical cause.

Pimples and excessive perspiration become problems as glands produce oily secretion.

Formulate school policy regarding homework assignments to insure adequate play time.

Discuss good health habits such as to bathe regularly. Discuss sales propaganda for beauty aids.

II EMOTIONAL AND SOCIAL CHARACTERISTICS

A EMOTIONAL STATUS (STABILITY)

The comparative serenity of later childhood is left behind and emotions begin to play a more obvious part in their lives. They frequently appear unable to control them and often lose themselves in anger, fear, love. Sometimes no relationship between the importance of situation and violence of reaction. Extreme variance in moods.

Uncertainty may begin and a strict self-criticism. Also strict criticism of others. Tend to suppress feelings later in age and to keep things to themselves in contrast to early part of age when they immediately express all feelings.

Strong positive feelings toward ideals that are effectively presented. Frustrations grow out of conflicts with parents or peers, and awareness of lack of social skills, or in failure to mature as rapidly as others. Anger is common and may grow out of feelings of inadequacy, fatigue, rejections, uncertainty.

IMPLICATION FOR THE CURRICULUM

Discuss values, morality, and what's important. Get children's feeling on these. If consideration emerges, stress this for children to remember in relationships.

Help child find activities at which he excels. Provide for an ample variety of outlets to emotions and for educational learning.

Provide dramatic experiences which allow the child to release tension, to take different roles, and to achieve satisfactions in the eyes of peers.

Encourage youngsters to be critical of their work but in a way that will help them not to feel inferior.

B FEELINGS OF SELF AND OTHERS

Feelings about parents and peers change. View them more realistically. May be quick and vociferous to younger sibling which may cause younger sibling to tease to get a rise out of older child. Later in period, he gets along quite well and may in fact be nice to have around.

Group is all important. Compulsion to dress conformity, language, possessions, and behavior. Tend to look down on less mature. Failure to achieve status or belonging may lead to self-pity. Often fights in group but may make up quickly. By end of stage the gang changes to the crowd.

Begins by boys loathing girls but girls liking boys. Each stay with own sex. Boys later tend to tease girls and to "steal" loose articles of clothing. Late in period both prefer mixed parties.

Learn to accept others for what they are.

Learn behavior necessary to add to the group.

Develop appreciation for individual company as well as group.

Be aware that criticism can be constructive and see the merits of accepting some of it.

Punish the act when necessary. Be firm and fair.

Develop an understanding of the opposite sex through readings, discussions, role playing, etc.

C TENDENCY TO HAVE FEARS

Tends to pooh-pooh fears but is apprehensive in dark. Likes flashlight nearby or light shining into room from without. Not comfortable on dark streets. Will reject baby sitter but is afraid at home alone. Unexplainable noises or objects stir a wild imagination.

Fears are more in form of worries. Worry over non-acceptance primary. Can imagine that report grades and peer criticism are cues of non-acceptance. Worry over school work, exams, promotion. Boys may worry over money, physical ability, facial blemishes. Girls worry about development (too fast or too slow), belonging, and later to acceptance by opposite sex.

Worries because of increasing demands of self as well as of school and home.

D PERSONAL IDEALS AND VALUES

Conscience becomes more apparent at this stage. Exhibits strong feelings about fairness, honesty and values in adults but may "relax" their own. Example: boys cheating in school; girls shoplifting.

This may grow out of greater need for wide variety of articles, greater chance of success in not getting caught, pressure of gang, general emotional instability of age.

Sense of simple justice strong. Want fair teacher and are quick to challenge anyone unfair. May become martyr to include peer left out of crowd. Expect high levels from teachers and parents. Accept drinking and swearing in moderation. Want independence but may feel anxiety when parents' expectations are not met. Want to do what's right. Pressure of crowd strong.

E INDEPENDENCE

Begins to cut loose from parents. May look for an adult other than parent for help in understanding complexities of life. Wants to cut loose from authority and to figure things out for self. Protests he is no longer baby. Gripes when restricted.

IMPLICATION FOR THE CURRICULUM

Discuss worries and fears in class. Encourage freedom of expression of feelings and in communicating problems. Show examples of people who have had problems and have learned to overcome them. Show by illustration peers and adults who have learned to overcome them.

Explain that many adults strive to help this group. Attempt to build faith in home, church, school, with emphasis on parent, clergy, teachers, and counselors and who to consult when necessary.

Find ways to release tensions.

Show how to accept disappointment because there is always another way to seek rewards.

Let the children help develop a method for establishment of some classroom rules. Show the need for rules in a simple society and for a complex society.

Attempt to instill a respect for rules, for law, for school, for all authority.

Discuss that there are pressures on every person of every age and understand what forces these pressures are—parent, gang, friend, etc. Learn that each person is accountable for his own actions and behavior and pays his own price.

Learn to develop a respect for others' feelings, others' rights, others' property.

Develop sense of responsibility, that each of us is responsible to someone or something every minute of our lives.

Expect that they respect each other in everyday courtesies and politeness. Discuss the role of authority in a society.

Understand that it is normal at this age to want to be independent. Provide learning activities which include independent study.

Analyze the behavior of the group and attempt to sort out desirable and undesirable characteristics.

E INDEPENDENCE (*continued*)	IMPLICATION FOR THE CURRICULUM

Much behavior is role playing and cannot be taken at face value. He must respond as the group would expect. May say "The rest of the kids are doing it." Could show lack of concern for family but look out if one is in bad health or needs help. He shows much concern.

Provide role playing activities to understand personal and family problems.

Parents often misunderstand and can cause problems by demanding level of performance far beyond child's ability.

During early stage may need help and rules at parties. Later is able to work alone quite independently. True in school as well. Often when class is left alone teachers may find them creatively employed when returning.

Provide opportunity for the group to plan—such as use of time, group activity, independent activity, projects, other.

Provide opportunity for students to work independently when they desire to.

Wishes to preserve a self-identity. Often wishes to be alone. Often goes to room to read alone or to be alone. Spends time in reflective thinking toward end of age.

Provide a quiet corner for independent study both in the classroom and in the Learning Center.

F RESPONSIBILITY AND SENSITIVENESS

Home hostilities are expanded but if channeled right by giving choice, they are more apt to select an activity to do. Generally hate to work early in period. Especially at home.

Provide opportunities to discuss feelings displayed at home and how to cope with them.

Beginning to accept views of others and to live in harmony with those with whom they disagree.

Provide many situations where he grows in his ability to work with the group or other individuals.

Able to wash car, dishes, babysit and other home responsibilities. The acceptance of work responsibility seems natural at first. Enthusiasm is great then may slack off toward end of period.

Provide activities which help him to work well, complete jobs, and to be increasingly responsible.

G PLAY

At early stages the competitive spirit and the will to excel are primary. One boy in desire to win may ridicule another who makes an error.

Provide opportunities for a variety of activities so that a student may excel in one.

Team play is understood and practiced. They can work reasonably well together but ground rules should have first been established and a supervisor should be in attendance, especially at the earliest stage.

Provide opportunity for all girl, all boy games; for mixed activity; and for activity where the best in it compete against one another to exclusion of poorer ability students.

Provide activity for increasingly difficult coordination in both boys' and girls' interests.

G PLAY (*continued*)

Girls lose interest in dolls and become increasingly more aware of their appearance and of boys. Boys detest girls at earlier age, later tease them, push them in water, steal little articles of clothing and run expecting to be chased. Much chasing of one another in halls of school, on street, or wherever with "wait 'til I get you." Toward end of period boys and girls prefer mixed parties.

Some may collect, other write in diaries. Most prefer to play with others. Those alone may need much individual consideration. An especially good time is summer camp as all enjoy swimming, group activity, and running.

Roller skating, baseball, swimming, jumping rope are favorite activities. Also just chasing one another.

Near end of period, group play is still appreciated, but not for winning. Participants are more concerned about how well each did. Rules not needed as much. Group more able to make up rules as needed.

IMPLICATION FOR THE CURRICULUM

Participate in vigorous exercise but also in the quiet and spectator games.

Learn that on a team, all must contribute.

Learn that criticizing each other on a team can cause internal decay. Building each member is a way to win.

Know that there are many kinds of activities to enjoy throughout life, some active and others more passive. That a truly rounded person will participate and appreciate to some extent all of them or at least to appreciate and understand another's participation.

Provide active and quiet team activities in curricular and noncurricular learnings.

III MENTAL GROWTH CHARACTERISTICS

GENERAL STATEMENT

As the child matures physically, increasing in body size and developing more and more motor skills, there is a concurrent growth in mental skills. His world widens with each succeeding experience, and he can cope more readily with abstract ideas. He develops his ability to generalize and to discover relationships. Because of the great differences in mental and physical characteristics, a single, preconceived standard for all may cause extreme pressure on many.

A INTELLECTUAL DEVELOPMENT

Have already learned to make comparisons and to recognize likenesses and differences. Can meet failure and disappointment and accept criticism. Can face reality as well as admit strength and weaknesses.

IMPLICATION FOR THE CURRICULUM

Provide opportunities for critical reasoning and problem solving.

Use hypothetical situations occasionally in language arts and social studies situations.

A INTELLECTUAL DEVELOPMENT

Is capable of making judgments. Can make generalizations and engage in reflective thinking.

Can carry out concrete operations (7–11 years) dealing with the properties of the present world.

Develops ability to use hypothetical reasoning, formal operations, using objects (12–15 years). This is the final childhood stage preparatory to adult thinking.

Develops concepts of volume (11 or 12 years).

Some will be satisfied in learning the characteristics of electric bell circuits, as one example; others will go on to discover the basic laws of work and apply them to new situations.

While brain and other neural developments are almost complete, experience is lacking to solve adult problems.

Charts, maps, and diagrams are now useful means of communication.

Attention span continues to increase with all activities, with the most striking gains being problem solving.

Reading rates may become adult.

B INTERESTS

Interests are related to accelerating physical growth, increasingly strong emotional reactions, and the awareness of new roles awaiting them in society. Problems of human relations become increasingly important.

There is a wide variety of interests and individual differences become greater.

Reading and collecting equal or exceed the high rates of later childhood.

This is the period of excessive daydreaming.

Girls become more preoccupied with themselves and their appearance.

C CREATIVE ABILITY AND APPRECIATIONS

Individual differences in creative ability are pronounced. Exceptional talent, if given opportunity and training, develops rapidly. Some students are self-conscious and highly critical of themselves.

IMPLICATION FOR THE CURRICULUM

Provide experiences such as in science and social studies where the student must look at the data and arrive at suitable conclusions.

Provide for the full range of intellectual development through the provision of activities to meet the needs of the student.

Provide activities in both the formal and informal situations to improve his reasoning powers.

To provide experiences to challenge each youngster's thinking abilities in the instructional program.

Provide opportunities for a variety of experiences in curricular and co-curricular activities.

Provide experiences which will help the student learn how to read charts, maps, and diagrams effectively.

Recognize that students have varying attention spans and make provisions for this variation in the instructional program, homework, etc.

Keep an adequate number of books at all levels of reading ability.

Provide reading materials which contain examples of emotional problem solving, various occupations, and problems of human relations.

Provide reading instruction which is individualized. This is more effective than level grouping.

Provide opportunities for reading individually and in organizing clubs in various interest areas.

Provide a program of learnings which is exciting and meaningful.

Provide experiences in clothing and textiles, food and nutrition.

Provide experiences for individuals to express themselves by writing and participating in dramatic productions.

C CREATIVE ABILITY AND APPRECIATIONS	IMPLICATION FOR THE CURRICULUM
Writing, dramatizing, and painting are particularly appealing for self-expression and creative expression. Diaries, poetry, and letters are used for expressing thoughts.	Provide experiences in the various arts for all transescents.

Middle school administrators and teachers need to gain a thorough understanding of the growth characteristics of the pre-adolescent, and to provide learning experiences which are consistent with these needs. Without this knowledge, teachers do not have an adequate basis for defining the types of teaching–learning experiences needed. This lack of knowledge made	the junior high school a pale carbon copy of the senior high school. The middle school movement provides a golden opportunity to develop schools truly designed for pre-adolescents. Without a full knowledge of the growth characteristics of the pre-adolescent the dream of a true middle school just cannot be realized.

LANGUAGE ARTS IN THE MIDDLE SCHOOL

As we develop the instructional program for this unique group of middle school students, we need to incorporate the aforementioned considerations into the language arts curriculum.

LISTENING

Listening instruction is generally a neglected area at the middle school level. Teachers, well aware of the importance of careful listening, admonish students to pay attention, but generally have few resources to assist in teaching listening skills. Research in the teaching of listening is limited, although current study is being devoted to this neglected language art.

Devine (11), in summarizing research on listening, has noted that children and adults spend a large amount of time each day listening and that listeners, unlike readers, appear particularly susceptible to influence by the peculiar power of the spoken word. No doubt, listening skill can have a profound impact on an individual's school, professional, and social lives.

Listening is intimately associated with the other language arts and, in effect, forms the basis for development in the other areas. Lundsteen (30), in comparing listening to the other areas, points out that the ability to listen may set limits on the ability to read. Both listening and reading are receptive processes, those in which the individual *receives* information. Among the similarities between listening and reading is the importance of a student's understanding of the particular context of the situation. Listening comprehension and reading comprehension involve similar skills, such as comprehending details, main idea, and inference, and higher-level skills, such as separating fact from opinion or reality from fantasy.

Instructional Emphases The National Institute of Education/CEMREL Task Force, developing a summary of usable research in oral and written communication (25), describes the nature of the listening process. According to this model, listening is both purposive and active. The listener can have a variety of purposes for listening—from trying to remember a set of directions to deriving pleasure from a well-told story. The listener is not passive; interactive demands range from selective attention to verbal response to a speaker. Furthermore, listening is multimodal; numerous nonverbal factors such as body language clues influence the message given and received.

Listening involves a complex of cognitive operations; like reading and writing, listening is a process that builds from the sensory level to the problem-solving level. Listening motivation is inseparable from listening skill; all of the above characteristics are affected by the student's motivation (or lack of it). Finally, and most importantly, listening is a teachable process. A student's ability in certain skills can be improved measurably through proper instruction.

Thus, based on the research, a plan for teaching listening is needed. An instructional focus at the middle school level should be one that permeates the entire curriculum. Teachers of all subject areas have a responsibility for the following goals:

1 *Develop a climate for listening activities.* The teacher should be aware of physical conditions in the classroom, his or her own manner and style of speaking, and opportunities for students to speak and listen to one another.

2 *Determine specific skills of listening that should be incorporated into the curriculum.* Although these skills should always be viewed as part of a broader whole, instruction in such skills as following directions may be required.

3 *Serve as a model for students by striving to develop your own listening ability.* Busy middle school teachers often do not give more than cursory attention to individual students.

4 *Stress listening comprehension.* Read to students, show them films, provide records and tapes. Ask them questions about details, main ideas, and inferences.

5 *Focus on critical and evaluative listening.* With the enormous influence the media have on students, it is imperative that students learn to discern a speaker's purpose and to recognize propaganda.

Instructional Strategies A recurring theme of this text is the interrelatedness of the language arts and the necessity for viewing language instruction in a holistic manner. Thus, the teacher should adopt as a primary strategy the meshing of listening into the total program. However, strategies specifically emphasizing listening should be part of a teacher's repertoire.

Cunningham, Cunningham, and Arthur (9) advocate the use of the Directed Listening Activity at the middle school level. This activity consists of three stages: readiness, listening–reciting, and follow-up. The readiness stage prepares students for listening. The teacher establishes motivation, builds background for new or difficult concepts, introduces new words, and sets a purpose or purposes for listening. In the second stage, students listen to information for the specified purposes. After a student engages in listening, the teacher asks appropriate literal and inferential questions.

Discussion involving interpretive and evaluative comments follows. Students relisten if necessary to clarify understanding. In the follow-up stage, the teacher provides activities that expand on the purposes set and the concepts presented. This directed activity can be used frequently in the classroom.

Smith (46) identifies four types of listening for which skills should be developed:

1 Attentive listening—in which the listener is focusing on one person or one stimulus.

2 Appreciative listening—in which the listener's purpose is purely enjoyment.

3 Analytical listening—to which the listener will respond in some manner.

4 Marginal listening—in which several distractions are present.

With Smith's type of listening as a framework, some activities that are appropriate for fostering listening at the middle school level include:

1 Following directions and sequence activities. Middle school students enjoy "tricky" assignments that require careful attention to draw pictures or carry out an activity correctly.

2 Games. Students in grades five to eight enjoy games such as "literary sleuth." The teacher reads part of a story to students. The class then projects endings for the story, identifying the clues that support those endings.

3 Listening comprehension. Periodic assignments during which students listen to find word meanings from context, remember details, identify main ideas, and make inferences are suggested. The teacher or a student can read selected passages. Tape recordings, radio or television programs, or presentations by resource speakers can be used.

4 Critical thinking. The influence of the mass media cannot be overestimated. Teachers can assign listening and viewing activities, then have class discussions to determine bias and analyze propaganda.

5 Pleasure listening. Students need to listen purely for pleasure. Time should be set aside for the teacher of a student to read good literature to the class with no questioning or discussion. Students need to hear model oral reading.

Problems Teachers should be aware of potential difficulties they may encounter in implementing the previous recommendations.

1 Middle school students are experiencing rapid physical, emotional, and social changes that can affect their attention span, concentration, and motivation for listening.

2 According to Landry (28), listening per se is not likely to be included in the curriculum and in instructional materials. Teachers will have to rely on their own creativity in developing activities in most situations.

3 Measurement of listening is rudimentary. There are few well-designed instruments for testing listening. Furthermore, generally there is little emphasis in state or district basic skills programs on this language art.

4 Growth in listening ability is less evident in many cases than in reading, composition, or handwriting.

5 In essence, knowledge about listening is sketchy. Cazden (8), in assessing what we do not know about teaching language arts, includes effective listening as one concern.

Assessment   Teacher observation and informal diagnosis are the most feasible methods of assessing student needs in listening instruction. Anecdotal records, informal checklists, and selected questions can give a teacher important information about student growth. Lundsteen (30) offers a number of ideas for informal evaluation. One suggestion is to guide the class in developing class standards of desirable listening behaviors. These standards can be put in checklist form. A long-used method of testing listening comprehension is to develop an informal listening inventory. The teacher reads aloud a set of graded paragraphs to a student. The highest level at which the student can answer a series of questions successfully is the student's listening comprehension level.

Published listening skills materials often include assessment devices. These can be useful in giving teachers ideas for informal measures as well as for placing students in the appropriate level of material.

Since teacher assessment can sometimes be inaccurate, standardized tests have been developed. However, standardized tests in listening must be viewed with caution (30). Several tests on the market are designed for the middle school level; before using these, the teacher should read a review of them in Lundsteen's book (30), in the *Diagnostic Teaching of the Language Arts* (6), or in Buros' *Mental Measurements Yearbook* (7).

SPELLING

Spelling, essentially learned as a visual skill, is indeed a basic skill in the mind of the public. Our society in general—including parents, the media, business—places great importance on this ability because correct spelling is necessary to communicate appropriately and clearly in writing.

Often taught in strict isolation, spelling is best learned in relationship with the other language arts as an integral part of vocabulary, reading, and composition instruction. Current research indicates that spelling is not merely a psychomotor skill achieved through memory and practice. Rather, it is a highly sophisticated language learning (24). Hodges (24) reports on studies considering spelling which indicate English has "a writing system that on the surface appears to be erratic and irregular but is at higher and more abstract levels quite logical. Our writing system, in short, is not merely a reflection of speech sounds but of other language elements as well—word-building elements, syntax, and meaning" (p. 7).

Petty, Petty, and Becking (39) state that spelling requires two basic abilities: the ability to recall how words look and, for those words the student cannot recall or has not seen, the ability to associate letters and patterns of letters with specific sounds.

Instructional Emphases   Some general considerations in determining a middle school instructional focus are these:

1 *Spelling instruction should be based on student experiences with words.* Rules or generalizations should evolve from direct experience with words. Some often-taught spelling generalizations have more words that do not comply with them than words that do.

Many activities can help to improve spelling and vocabulary skills.

2 *Efficient study habits should be encouraged.* Middle school students should become increasingly engaged in planning their spelling study approach and in correcting their own attempts.

3 *Increased student responsibility in the program allows for greater individualization.* At the middle school level, there are marked differences in spelling ability. The use of the same spelling list and numbers of words bores good spellers and frustrates poor ones.

4 *Current research strongly indicates that spelling should be taught through meaningful language activity rather than rote drill* (52).

Instructional Strategies Various researchers have determined that about 3000 words make up 95 percent of those most commonly used in writing (16). Students need to focus their attention on high-frequency words that usage and the teacher deem appropriate. Other researchers have compiled lists of words commonly misspelled. Dale, O'Rourke, and Bamman (10) provide an excellent master list of such words that deserve extra attention; they also provide ideas for teaching the words in context.

Learning to spell is a series of impression and recall procedures (39). Middle school students should review the steps for studying new words outlined in Chapter 4 to ensure that they can follow the steps independently.

For students who have extreme difficulty in learning words, an approach such as the Visual Auditory Kinesthetic Tactile (VAKT) method is recommended. This approach requires the student to touch and trace the word while looking at it and saying it. Barbe and Swassing (5) offer a number of suggestions for adjusting spelling instruction to a child's dominant learning mode (visual, auditory, or kinesthetic). Finally, use of the typewriter might assist students failing to learn to spell in other, more traditional ways.

Steps in the VAKT process follow (15):

Step 1   VAKT (large strips of paper)
   a Teacher and student look up chosen word in dictionary to study meaning.
   b Teacher writes word, simultaneously saying syllables.
   c Student traces (actually touching) word with index finger, saying syllables (no distortion of sounds).
   d Student writes word without model. (If incorrect, recycle **c** and **d** until correct.)
   e Student underlines syllables and then whole word.
   f Student writes word twice correctly without model and uses it orally in context.
   g Student files word.
Step 2   VAK (file cards)
   a Teacher and student look up chosen word in dictionary.
   b Teacher writes word, simultaneously saying syllables.
   c Student traces word in the air, saying syllables without distortion.

      d Student writes word without model. (If incorrect, recycle **c** and **d** until correct.)

      e Student underlines syllables and the whole word.

      f Student writes word twice correctly without model and uses in context.

      g Student puts word in meaningful sentence; teacher writes sentence (except for new word) and student fills in learned word.

      h Student files word.

Step 3   Student works completely alone on VAK.

Step 4   Student moves into regular program.

As *good* spellers mature, according to Templeton (52), the visual realm may take on an interesting additional importance. By grade ten, knowledge of orthographic structure (spelling system) appears to influence higher-order phonological skills (sound–symbol analysis) rather than the reverse. As Templeton explains, "*Seeing* a base word, as opposed to hearing it, seems to provide a more direct link with the appropriate phonological rules that apply to derivatives of the base word" (52, p. 91). Thus, the spelling system might alert a student that *equation* and *equanimity* are related more easily than hearing the two words pronounced alone would indicate.

These findings reinforce the importance of tying spelling and vocabulary instruction together at the middle school level, particularly through a study of word structure (prefixes, suffixes, and roots) and a study of etymology (word origins). If research can identify characteristics of good spellers further, educators can attempt to reinforce those characteristics in all students.

Middle school pupils enjoy games and puzzles as a means of reinforcing spelling skills. Some suggestions are anagrams, Password (and other television games), Scrabble, and dictionary games. Also, students like such creative activities as inventing words and definitions by combining prefixes, roots, or suffixes or making compound words. Word games provide enjoyment, but they can also encourage inquiry and experimentation; they further offer challenging settings for practicing spelling, settings which promote the development of generalizations about the written language (24).

A contract system similar to the one refined by Barnes as presented in a book by Wilson and Gambrell (57) can work well for the spelling curriculum at the middle school. The following steps are recommended:

1 Teacher and students develop the spelling list based on words missed in writing and on lists of frequently used words.

2 The class takes a pretest and each student corrects his or her paper.

3 The students contract to learn a certain number of words that week through a variety of interrelated activities.

4 Students decide (with teacher guidance) what process to use to study the words.

5 Before the posttest, each student circles on the test paper the numerals of those words under contract.

6 The teacher and students evaluate progress.

7 If grades must be given for spelling, the teacher might require a certain number of words for a certain number of points.

Spelling instruction for these grades should be a component of the writing program; students should learn how to proofread their own work. Furthermore, spelling ability and reading ability are highly related.

Another area of concern for the middle grades is dictionary use. Direct instruction is necessary to assist students in viewing this reference as a useful spelling tool. Lists of books of frequently misspelled words are quick reference sources.

Again, spelling and vocabulary instruction should always be done in context. Students should learn and reinforce their knowledge of words through reading, writing, speaking, and listening activities. They should not study isolated lists of words, but they can make their own books of words they frequently misspell or misuse.

Problems   One of the biggest problems facing the middle school teacher is the possibility of negative student attitudes toward spelling. Methods such as writing each misspelled word numerous times or spelling orally to excess can contribute to these negative feelings. Also, students who have not developed efficient spelling study practices may have reinforced inappropriate spellings to the extent that they are difficult to correct.

A potential problem is the lack of consistency among content area teachers in their spelling requirements. A consensus among grade-level teachers regarding spelling expectancies can counteract this problem.

Another major concern of the middle school teacher is the issue of time. Often only one class period is available for teaching all the language arts. Interrelating the spelling instruction with reading and writing instruction, as suggested earlier, is probably the best solution to the time problem as well as being sound pedagogically.

Fisher and Terry (16) have categorized the most common student spelling errors into five groups: (1) overdependence on phonetic analysis, (2) selection of incorrect options when there are several alternative ways to represent a sound, (3) not using the English phoneme–grapheme system, (4) reversing letters, and (5) spelling the homonym. Further, student and teacher dialects can affect correct spelling. A student might spell a word phonetically by the dialectical pronunciation rather than the "standard" one.

Assessment   Self-evaluation is a crucial element in spelling programs at the middle school level. Students in these grades enjoy keeping individual progress charts. They can also keep notebooks with a record of words misspelled in their writing. Middle school students need to correct their own practice tests and learn to analyze their errors. They should also proofread and correct their compositions.

The teacher should conduct periodic group evaluations to measure class growth. For more precise diagnostic purposes, useful procedures include the analysis of student compositions for recurring errors and the maintenance of anecdotal records with the various kinds of errors categorized. To compare student growth with a national sample, Greene's *The New Iowa Spelling Scale* (20) is available. This scale yields the percentage of students (through the eighth-grade level) who spelled a particular word correctly.

COMPOSITION

"Reading maketh a full man, conference a ready man, writing an exact man," observed Francis Bacon. An appreciation of composition ability and the precision of thought it demands, then, is not new.

What is new is a national concern over composition. After years of lamentation over reading ability, the attention of the public and the educational community is turning to writing. Yet, according to Graves (19, p. 13), "Although writing is frequently extolled, worried over, and cited as a public priority, it is seldom practiced in schools." A recent extensive survey of secondary schools by Applebee (1) revealed that writing paragraph-length or longer compositions took about 3 percent of the class time observed; furthermore, homework required paragraph-length writing 3 percent of the time.

The National Council of Teachers of English *Standards for Basic Skills Writing Programs* defines writing as "the process of selecting, combining, arranging and developing ideas in effective sentences, paragraphs, and, often, longer units of discourse" (35). This process of composition is a worthwhile pursuit because writing is an inherently satisfying personal activity which offers a release from psychological tension and which meets the basic human need to communicate (25). Composition serves as a means to expand learning, and writing is closely related to the other communication skills of listening, reading, and speaking.

Instructional Emphases   Writing is a process which leads to the development of a variey of products. As stated earlier, this process view should underlie the instructional program. Students should learn the major stages of *prewriting, writing, revision,* and *postwriting* (48).

In the *prewriting stage,* the writer must identify a purpose, select a specific topic, identify the audience, determine the type of information (content) needed, and decide on an organizational plan (48). The prewriting stage is a thinking stage. Students should engage in brainstorming, reading, discussion, and other background-building activities during this stage. Haley-James (21) stresses that oral language activity should both precede and occur during writing. She also observes that students write more effectively when they sense a need to write for a specific purpose or audience; further, a variety of *real* audiences is important to their motivation and their development as writers.

The *writing stage* is the first-draft stage. Using the results of prewriting activity, the student begins putting ideas on paper. The student's concern at this time is the content—selecting and organizing ideas.

During the *revision phase,* students review their papers primarily to make content changes. They may make additions, deletions, changes in sentence structure and transitions, vocabulary substitution, and organizational refinements. Haley-James (21) points out that purpose and audience lead logically to revision of certain pieces of writing. (Not all writing should be revised.) In his summary of findings gleaned from research, Glatthorn (18) includes Bamberg's (2) conclusion that there is strong evidence that the revision process is crucial to improved writing. Teacher and peer conferences are important as the writer revises. Graves (19) advocates the process–conference approach to writing instruction; in this approach, successive brief teacher–pupil conferences during the writing assist the student in developing a polished piece. Peers can be effective evaluators in the revision process (18, 54).

Revision can be a fruitless activity if it is viewed only as a mechanical process of correcting punctuation and spelling (27). Editing is important, but it should come at the end of the revision stage, after content revision has occurred.

Many teachers erroneously believe that teaching isolated grammar helps to improve writing (22). In fact, the formal study of grammar should not begin until grade eight or nine; revising writing in view of its audience should be the means for language study in the middle school (21).

The *postwriting stage* is the follow-up stage. Students can share their compositions to receive feedback on how well they accomplished their purpose. Listening, speaking, and reading activities might be built around the writing. Student writing might be published at this time.

Smith (45) cautions that "The act of writing does not break itself down into neatly identifiable and manageable 'steps', rather it is part of all our existence." Thus, the writing process is a continuous, cyclic process. Awareness of the various stages can assist the teacher and student greatly in writing improvement; however, rigid and inflexible adherence to set procedures and time constraints is not intended.

Applebee (1, p. 100) proposes that students receive more opportunities to use writing as a tool for learning rather than just as a way to indicate learned information. An effective writing program offers students a variety of experiences. Students should write:

1 For a variety of purposes—to tell a story, to describe, to inform, to persuade, to entertain, to express oneself, and to explore a topic.

2 For a variety of audiences—self, peers, teachers, parents, public, and so on.

3 In a variety of forms—poetry, letters, journals, essays, stories, and so on.

Purpose, audience, and form determine the kind of writing students do—narrative, descriptive, expository, or persuasive.

A student's developmental stage greatly influences *how* and *what* is written (27). The best source of writing content is student interest and experience (35). At the middle school level of development, according to Klein (27), the teacher should be especially concerned with structuring writing contexts to expand the range of audiences students address. Students in the intermediate grades and above can more skillfully manipulate features of style and form, grammatical structures, and modes (kinds) of discourse. Middle school students should experience all modes of discourse (narrative, descriptive, expository, and persuasive). Finally, paired writing assignments and projects in which students produce joint compositions are especially effective at the middle school grades (27).

Students should write frequently and regularly on self-selected topics (21). Yet frequency of writing alone does not bring about writing improvement (22). Composition *instruction* should accompany writing assignments.

Students learn to write by writing, but they also learn to write by reading. Good literature should be a part of any composition program (37). There is research evidence to support the contention that increased reading positively affects writing (22).

Finally, the teacher should serve as a model for students (27). Teachers of all subject areas should be writers themselves. Students need to see adults engaged in prewriting, writing, revision, and postwriting activities.

Instructional Strategies   Some specific ideas for implementing the writing process in the middle school classroom follow:

1 Language experience activities based on student experiences.

2 Sentence-building and sentence-combining exercises in which students both expand and synthesize sentences.

3 Sentence frames and paragraph frames in which students fill in partially completed sentences and paragraphs.

4 Patterned writing such as haiku or cinquain poems.

5 Using literature as a motivator for writing.

6 Content area writing—reports, problems, explanations, arguments.

7 Newspaper writing—who?, what?, where?, when?, why?, how?.

8 Varied forms—journals, messages, lists, autobiographies, poems, epitaphs, greeting cards, telegrams, letters to pen pals, plays, tall tales, myths, and legends.

Several recommended sources for activities are:

1 Weehawken Board of Education. *Individualized Language Arts: Diagnosis, Prescription and Evaluation.* Weehawken, N.J.: National Diffusion Network Project, 1974.

2 Stewig, John Warren. *Read To Write: Using Children's Literature as a Springboard for Teaching Writing.* New York: Holt, Rinehart and Winston, 1980.

3 Carter, Candy, and Rashkis, Zora. *Ideas for Teaching English in the Junior High and Middle School* (new ed.). Urbana, Ill.: National Council of Teachers of English, 1980.

4 Cahill, Robert B., and Hrebic, Herbert J. *Cut the Deck.* San Francisco: Perma-Bound, 1977.

Problems   Perhaps the most difficult problem to overcome in the teaching of composition is the relegation of responsibility for this instruction almost exclusively to the language arts teacher. Fader (14), the National Assessment of Educational Progress reports (34), and Applebee (1) all point out the absolute necessity for writing instruction across the curriculum.

Another problem in composition instruction is that most of it has consistently been negative and error based (22). Emphasis has traditionally been placed on mechanical correctness rather than content. It is imperative that composition instruction be a positive experience. Further, growth in composition is a long-term process. Writing requires time and effort. Both students and teachers must realize that writing is not always easy to learn or to teach.

Cazden (8) notes that in classroom practice the abundance of time is spent in listening and reading because of the numbers of students teachers must instruct and because of ever-increasing numbers of standardized tests. In a related observation, she states that sales of lined paper continue to decline as sales of duplicating paper for short-answer dittoed activities rise (8).

A final important problem in composition instruction is the fact that most middle school teachers have received little or no preparation in *how* to teach composition. Consequently, lacking better information, these teachers teach the way they were taught, if they teach writing at all.

Assessment   Assessment of student writing should be based on the mode of writing the teacher has been teaching. Different kinds of composition (narration, description, exposition, and persuasion) make different demands on the student. The teacher should use student writing for diagnosis in determining instructional needs. The writing abilities of the students, for example, should govern which elements of grammar, usage, and style are to be taught. Teachers should employ group evaluation, peer evaluation, self-evaluation, and teacher evaluation. The primary response should not be to what is wrong with a given composition, but rather to what is right (56). In fact, research indicates that intensive correction of errors is ineffective in improving composition (22).

In evaluating individual composition growth, the teacher should attend to complete pieces of student writing and should address clarity and content before spelling, handwriting, punctuation, and usage. The assessment process should include regular responses to student writing over a period of time (35). It is recommended that students keep writing folders to enable teachers, students and parents to view progress.

Many teachers become frustrated by trying to assess analytically every piece of writing students do; consequently, many do not assign writing regularly. To deal with this problem, teachers can focus on one or two elements of composition at a time and rely on frequent peer and self-evaluation. *How to Handle the Paper Load* from the National Council of Teachers of English offers many suggestions along these lines. According to Odell (38), "the purpose of the schools is to improve students' writing, not simply to judge it."

In evaluating groups of students and writing programs, teachers should be aware of procedures such as holistic, primary-trait, and analytic scoring systems. Holistic scoring involves getting an overall impression of a piece of writing; raters are trained in a certain set of criteria and have studied model papers before reading. Primary-trait scoring concentrates on a particular characteristic of composition; this method determines whether or not a specific piece of writing achieves its purpose. For example, if a student is asked to write a letter on an issue, the student work is judged on how effectively it deals with the primary traits of letter writing and addressing the issue. Analytic scoring focuses on specific elements of writing, both content and mechanics. It is probably the most time-consuming scoring system.

Useful references on assessment include Cooper and Odell's *Evaluating Writing:*

Describing, Measuring, Judging and Diederich's *Measuring Growth in English* (both from the National Council of Teachers of English).

HANDWRITING

Penmanship once held a place of high esteem in the American school system. In more recent years, however, minimal time has often been allocated to handwriting because of time constraints and because of the unpopularity of handwriting instruction among teachers and students (51). Yet handwriting instruction is important for communication purposes. Illegible handwriting causes societal problems—undelivered mail, misinterpreted messages, misread business communications. There are signs that the pendulum is swinging again; more educators are concerned about the role of handwriting in communication (3) and its relationship to the other language arts.

Instructional Emphases   At the middle school level, handwriting instruction is important because of the need for reinforcement and maintenance of skills and because of the increased demands on students for written work (39). Handwriting should be taught in the context of composition and content material rather than in practice with isolated sentences. It should be viewed as a means of improving communication.

Specific goals should be set for handwriting instruction, goals which lead to the general objective of legibility in everyday written work (3). Legibility rather than penmanship should be stressed.

Particularly at the middle school level, individualization of instruction should be provided because of the wide range of student ability. Students can participate in a variety of independent activities to improve their handwriting.

Instructional Strategies   The main concern in handwriting facing teachers in the later grades is correction of poor habits (55). Most middle school teachers have little information on how to deal with handwriting problems. Figure 8-1 illustrates twelve common handwriting problems and the corrective techniques to be used for dealing with them (55).

A student's particular modality strength (visual, auditory, kinesthetic, or combination) should be considered in handwriting instruction. Visual learners need consistent visual models; auditory learners need to hear consistent language in descriptions of letters and strokes. Kinesthetic learners have potential for excellent handwriting, since handwriting is primarily a kinesthetic–visual task (4).

Problems   Several problems face the middle school teacher in teaching handwriting. Most teachers at this level have received little training in how to instruct students in this skill.

Often students are surrounded by numerous handwriting models—many of which

Common Handwriting Problems and Corrective Techniques

Problem	Example	Corrective Techniques
Handwriting is so small that it cannot be read easily.	*in adult proportion*	• Use ruled paper on which a midline appears or rule a midline on standard writing paper. Explain that minimum letters touch the midline. • Practice large writing at the chalkboard. • Give correct models of words, have the student copy them, then evaluate for size. • Identify the problem so the student is aware of what must be corrected.
When two maximum undercurves are joined (ll, fl), letter formation suffers.	*parallel*	• Emphasize that the basic undercurve stroke must be made correctly. • Make a wide undercurve to allow room for the loop that follows. • Make slant strokes parallel to each other.
The height of the lower-case letters is not consistent.	*Write freely*	• Use paper that has a midline and a descender space, or rule a midline on standard paper. • Have the student identify maximum, intermediate, and minimum letters. • Evaluate writing for alignment by drawing a horizontal line across the tops of the letters that are supposed to be of the same size. • Shift paper as the writing progresses.
The maximum letters (b, f, h, k, l) are made without loops.	*little*	• Demonstrate and explain proper formation of undercurve that begins loop of letter. • Demonstrate and explain proper formation of the slant stroke. • Point out that the top of the letters is rounded and determines the width of the loops.
The slant of the writing is irregular.	*flight*	• Check for correct paper position. • Pull strokes in the proper direction. • Shift paper as writing progresses. • Shift hand to the right as writing progresses. • Evaluate slant by drawing lines through letters to show the angle at which they are made.
When an undercurve joins an overcurve (in, um), the letters are poorly written.	*instrument*	• Show how the undercurve to overcurve is a smooth, flowing stroke. • Explain that the undercurve ending continues up and then quickly overcurves into the downward slant stroke.
The quality of the writing changes within a single word.	*laboratory*	• Shift both the paper and the hand as the writing progresses. The paper moves toward the student, and the hand moves away. • Write in the same area of the paper, roughly a six-inch diameter circle that is located at the midpoint of the body about ten inches from the edge of the desk. • Do not reach out to write or write very close to the body.
The letters a, d, g, o, q are not closed.	*book amount*	• Stress proper beginning strokes. • Write correctly formed model letters on the student's paper, explaining the strokes while the student watches.
Non-looped letters such as t, p, i, u, w are looped and become difficult to read.	*little*	• Demonstrate that there is a pause at the top of these letters. • Encourage the student to write slower, as speed causes the loops in the letters. • Pause before making the slant stroke in the letters a, d, g, i, j, p, q, t, u, w, and v. • Emphasize the retrace in these strokes.
Checkstroke joinings, for example br, we, are poorly made.	*break weather*	• Demonstrate the letters b, v, o, and w and explain the strokes as you form them. • Use the auditory stroke description "retrace and swing right" as students practice b, v, o, w. • Demonstrate correct joinings in which the first letter has a checkstroke. • Point out the letter forms that change when they are preceded by a checkstroke: br, os.
Handwriting is so slow that there is no smoothness in the individual letters.	*Intermediate*	• Encourage students to write letters with smooth and complete motions. • Engage in relaxation exercises before practicing writing. Excessive muscle tension is the cause of slow writing. • Emphasize rhythm rather than alignment or slant. These qualities can be developed later.
Joinings involving overcurves, such as ga, jo, are not well made.	*baggage job*	• Show how all overcurve connections cross at the baseline, not above or below it. • Make the overcurve motion continuous. Do not change its direction in mid-stroke. • Check letter formation.

FIGURE 8-1
Common handwriting problems and corrective techniques. (Copyright © 1980 Zaner-Bloser, Inc., Columbus, Ohio. Used with permission of the publisher.)

are different. Students may see models on letter strips; on ditto sheets; and in handwriting, spelling, or language books. In addition, the teacher may use still another model. The teacher should be aware of the need for consistency in models, particularly for the visual learner (4).

Some middle school teachers find the frequent embellishment of handwriting a problem. Others see this embellishment as an expression of personality and of individualism. For young adolescents, handwriting may be a safe means of expressing independence.

Further, with the demands on class time in the language arts, many teachers neglect handwriting instruction. Wasylyk and Milone (55) point out that fifteen minutes of teaching three times a week will produce noticeable results in handwriting development.

Another problem is the societal expectation for all students to master both manuscript and cursive writing. Because of this expectation, it is necessary for middle school students to refine their cursive writing. There is, however, no need to require students to use cursive exclusively. It is most important for the student to use his or her most legible handwriting. Many real-world situations demand manuscript; most applications ask you to print.

Assessment   A goal of handwriting instruction at the middle school is guiding students toward self-evaluation. Students should have a clear standard of acceptability against which to compare their handwriting. Students should learn to evaluate the specific elements of their handwriting: letter form, size, slant, proportion, alignment, space, and line quality (55).

Commercial handwriting series may have scales available against which students can compare their own writing. Also available is the Ayers Handwriting Scale (from the Bureau of Educational Research and Service, University of Iowa). Handwriting evaluation can be part of the final-draft stage in composition. Growth in handwriting, as in composition, can be observed by keeping student work in file folders over a period of time.

SPEAKING

Human beings have the capacity for four vocabularies: listening, speaking, reading, and writing. This order is generally that of size—the listening vocabulary is the largest, while the writing vocabulary is the least extensive. The child first learns words through listening; then speaking develops. Smith, Goodman, and Meredith (44) emphasize the primacy of "speech–thought"; the expansion of speech is primary, for it is the foundation for all other verbal communication.

Adults use oral language as their most common means of communication; all peoples have developed a form of oral language (51). Skill and fluency in speaking have dramatic effects upon life in general—on one's social, educational, and vocational success, for example. Rightly or wrongly, we judge and are judged on the basis of speech. Shuy (43) indicates that social stratification studies using language data alone may be the most accurate indexes of socioeconomic status available.

Even the fate of nations can depend on effective diplomacy, which demands precision in oral language. In an electronic, interactive world, speaking often takes precedence over written communication.

Instructional Emphases   Focus in oral communication at the middle school level should include as goals improving fluency, clarity, and precision in speech (25). Middle school students have acquired the basic language elements; they are involved in refining their speech.

Standards for Effective Oral Communication Programs, from the Speech Communication Association (49), outline the characteristics of a model program. Oral communication instruction, according to these standards, should provide a wide range of experiences to stimulate effective speaking skills appropriate to (1) different situations (from informal to formal), (2) different purposes (from informing to creative expression), (3) different audiences (from peers to community), (4) different communication forms (from conversation to public speaking), and (5) different speaking styles (from impromptu speaking to formal reading).

At the middle school, students are capable of expanding their repertoire of communication behaviors. They need purposeful, organized instruction in speaking and ample opportunities to practice the behaviors introduced. They need encouragement to experiment with oral language in a comfortable environment.

Students need ample opportunities to practice speaking skills.

Instructional Strategies   To provide the necessary variety of experiences, teachers must offer an array of activities in the speaking curriculum. Ideas for recommended experiences follow:

1 *Informal conversation.* Certainly informal conversation goes on among students without teacher encouragement; however, teacher sanction of any informal conversation in the middle school classroom is rare. Informal conversation, in a controlled situation, can enable the teacher to interact positively with students on a given subject.

2 *Oral descriptions of pictures, objects, scenes.* Students at this age enjoy giving a description and having peers guess the object or place. This kind of oral practice is an excellent prewriting activity.

3 *Language experience stories at an appropriate level of maturity.* Language experience involves the development of reading material based on student experiences and oral vocabulary; students become authors. The first stage in a language experience activity (either individual or group) is discussion of an experience and oral composition of a story about that experience.

4 *Discussion (small group to panel).* Fisher and Terry (16) caution that discussions must have a distinct purpose and must be structured in some manner. Standards for the discussion must be set, time for student preparation provided, and instruction given in asking questions, answering questions in a relevant manner, and learning to share the conversation (25).

5 *Oral reading.* Round-robin reading is not advocated. Paired students might read to each other for oral reading practice. Students and teacher might read orally to prove a point, to answer a question, or to entertain and appreciate. Oral reading of dialogue and selected poetry enhances growth in literary appreciation.

6 *Oral reviews of books and movies.* For middle school students, reviews might be given in small groups rather than on a whole class basis. Further, reviewers might use charts, slides, or other aids to shift the focus of attention from themselves (16).

7 *Questioning by students and teachers.* Attention should be given to the various levels of comprehension in formulating questions: literal, inferential–interpretive, and critical–evaluative. Also, attention is needed on *how* to answer questions. For example, on what evidence is a conclusion based? The teacher might model aloud his or her thinking process in formulating the answer to a question.

8 *Announcements, directions, phone usage, social conventions.* Students can make announcements and can give directions for classmates to follow. Telephone companies often have educational consultants and materials with information on proper telephone usage. In addition to phone usage, students can practice other social conventions such as making introductions.

9 *Reporting.* Reports should be rather brief and basically of an informal nature. An oral reporting exercise is an excellent way to help students learn to summarize. At this age, perhaps group presentations are preferable to help students become more comfortable speaking before others.

10 *Beginning parliamentary procedure.* Middle school pupils enjoy clubs based on common interests. Teacher sponsors can introduce rudiments of parliamentary procedure during club business meetings.

11 *Interviewing*. A one-to-one experience, interviewing an older adult, civic leader, or another student, provides needed experience in oral communication. Students should be well prepared by the teacher before attempting an interview.

12 *Storytelling*. Listening to an expert storyteller can enchant all ages. After such an occasion, opportunities can be provided to emulate the model by telling simple stories in the classroom.

13 *Choral reading*. This speaking of poetry is an excellent vehicle for involving a whole group in meaningful oral expression and in learning to appreciate poetry.

14 *Role playing*. Playing various roles can allow the middle school student to try out, in a nonthreatening manner, oral language appropriate to a variety of situations and for a variety of audiences and purposes.

15 *Pantomime*. This art accentuates the importance of nonverbal communication. Learning to pantomime also points up how much we depend on the spoken word in common communication.

16 *Creative dramatics*. Improvisational activities can foster oral language growth as students develop dialogue to respond to the stimulus provided.

17 *Audiotaping and videotaping*. Interest in the equipment itself and in radio and television celebrities can motivate interest in making tapes. The need to rewrite and edit a script promotes clarity and precision in speaking and writing.

18 *Elementary debate*. The principles of setting up an argument can be introduced at the middle school level. As a parallel, persuasive writing might be initiated.

19 *Performances for younger children*. Middle school pupils might take some of Smith's (46) suggestions for oral activities with younger children—chalk talks, flannel board stories, shadow plays—and prepare and give them.

20 *Sentence expansion, combining, and rearrangement*. The teacher can guide pupils through a series of oral exercises to expand short sentences into longer, more complex ones, to combine several short sentences into one, and to rearrange parts of sentences to change emphasis or meaning.

It must be emphasized that all these speaking activities interrelate with listening, reading, and writing. Speaking and listening serve as the basis for reading and writing. Once the student learns to read and write, all four language arts continually reinforce one another in a circular fashion. At the middle school level, it is crucial that oral language receive direct attention.

Problems A major problem is the lack of instructional emphasis on speaking. Fisher and Terry (16, p. 144) observe that often *talk* is not viewed as "a significant vehicle for learning." In many cases, silence in a classroom is interpreted as a desirable state. Reading and writing may be considered the teachable language arts, with speaking and listening skill assumed. De-emphasis on oral communication instruction probably is due to the "common belief that children learn to speak and to listen without the benefits of concerted teaching . . . what students may lack in the absence of deliberate oral communication instruction, however, are communication behaviors which are flexible and effective" (25, p. 25).

Also, at the middle school level, students are undergoing changes that can affect their willingness to participate in some oral language development activities. Often self-conscious and shy or, at the other extreme, inappropriately aggressive, students may be reluctant to participate at all or may participate in an unacceptable manner. Also, peer pressure dictates what kind of speech is appropriate, and what kind is not "school English." Teachers must structure activities carefully to deal with these characteristics.

Finally, dialect is an issue teachers should consider. All speakers use some form of dialect, "any variety of language shared by a group of speakers" (25, p. 94). Students should never be made to feel their language is wrong. Rather, the teacher has a responsibility to accept the student's language while guiding the student toward facility with the usage the community accepts as standard English. Students need to learn that different forms of language are acceptable in different situations; that is, the concept of audience determines whether formal or informal language is appropriate.

Assessment   Cazden, reviewing what educators do *not* know about the language arts, asks: "How should we evaluate oral language competencies? Apart from the time-consuming nature of such evaluation, we simply don't know yet how to do it well, validly and reliably" (8, p. 596).

Because of the lack of other tools for measuring oral language, teachers must rely on and must improve their own observational skills. Informal oral communication assessment should occur within specific contexts for communication, such as reading aloud, small group discussion, or formal reports. Standards for evaluation of communication should be designed for the particular situation. For example, slang might be appropriate in a peer group discussion but unacceptable in a formal speech (25).

Peer evaluation and self-evaluation are also important areas to develop at the middle school level. Students should work with the teacher in establishing criteria for oral language performance and in devising rating scales and checklists. The teacher should exercise great care to ensure that evaluation is constructive and unobtrusive; particularly at middle school age, students are sensitive to any comments that might be construed as criticism. Evaluation should encourage rather than inhibit growth in oral expression.

READING APPLICATION

In an era of concern about "the basics," a crucial goal of the language arts program is establishing literature as a "basic." The public must become cognizant that literature is a powerful device, one which has enormous practical, personal, and social effects. Practically, students who read are ones who use language effectively and efficiently. They develop vocabulary skill and a feel for written language. Personally, readers participate vicariously in many lives and learn to think about the choices made in those lives. Socially, the American experience, our nation's common purpose, is expressed in literature (41).

A major goal of an effective reading-application program is the nurturing of lifelong readers. As Montebello (32, p. 101) asserts, "the teaching of literature is part of a planned program for which the main object is enjoyment of literature and continued interest in reading through developing a sensitivity to literary elements as well as to content."

Judy (26) advocates breaking down the traditional distinction between the terms *reading* and *literature*. The two are not separate; rather, they are indefinably bound together.

Instructional Emphases   John Stewig (51, pp. 325–326) identifies three distinct functions of literature: "(1) to provide a literary experience, (2) to impart information, and (3) to provide a vehicle for developing language-related skills of memory, sequence, description, expression, comprehension, interpretation, analysis, synthesis, and evaluation." The *only* objective of the literary experience is enjoyment; the ultimate result of daily literary experience is a lifelong positive attitude toward reading. The information experience provides a foundation of factual knowledge about a particular topic for a specific purpose. The language-related experience focuses on development of specific language skills.

According to Stewig, a major instructional problem has been failure to view these three functions as separate and distinct. For example, using the literary experiences as a means for the language-related experience (such as interrupting the reading of a story with skills teaching) is a great abuse. The literary experience should not be confused with the other two functions of literature. Each has its place; each is important. National Assessment of Education Progress data (34) indicate that older students tend to view reading mainly in terms of its second function; they view reading more as a source of information than as a source of enjoyment or of self-understanding.

Implementing the functions of literature, as stated earlier, requires a planned program. The middle school teacher must develop strategies for motivating and encouraging students to read and strategies for guiding students in responding to literature and building literary skills.

Instructional Strategies   Motivating and encouraging reading are the foundations of an effective program. Fader (14) proposes the concepts of *saturation* and *diffusion* in his book, *Hooked on Books* and in its revisions. *Saturation* refers to the dispersal of paperback books, magazines, and newspapers throughout the curriculum. *Diffusion* refers to the belief that every teacher in every subject area must be involved in fostering literacy.

Content-area teachers can serve as models by letting students see them read and by encouraging free reading in their classes. Also, content-area teachers are best qualified for teaching the reading skills important to their subject. They must teach vocabulary and comprehension skills and can provide necessary reinforcement for composition, listening, speaking, spelling, and handwriting skills growth.

The librarian–media specialist plays a central role in cultivating lifetime readers. A media-center staff attuned to the interests of students can be a major force in the literature program. The staff can assist the teacher by citing sources of recommended books for middle school students and criteria for choosing them. Three such sources are *Reading Ladders for Human Relations, High Interest–Easy Reading,* and *Your Reading,* all available from the National Council of Teachers of English. *Easy Reading: Book Series and Periodicals for Less Able Readers* is available from the International Reading Association. Some states also sponsor book award contests in which students select their favorite books.

An important factor in motivation is a student's particular reading interests. The teacher can develop a familiarity with the usual middle school preferences while becoming attuned to the divergent choices of individuals. An interest inventory is a tool for identifying individual reading interests. An example is included in Chapter 6.

A crucial element in motivating students to read is the provision of free reading experiences as part of the regular curriculum. Equally important is the teacher's reading aloud periodically; students need to hear model oral reading.

Scheduled schoolwide reading gives importance to pleasure reading. Sustained silent reading (SSR), sometimes referred to as uninterrupted sustained silent reading (USSR), involves the entire school in reading for a given period of time either daily or weekly. Each classroom should have a wide selection of reading materials; students may bring their own materials to be read by them. Basic procedures include:

1 Students choose materials and read silently for the allotted period of time.

2 Teachers, principals, custodians, and the entire staff read recreationally to set an example.

3 Everything else stops during this activity. *Everyone,* including visitors, reads.

4 No records, no reports are involved (31).

Other motivational techniques encourage student reading. Some of these strategies follow:

1 Book clubs and discussion groups. The Junior Great Books Program for able readers is effective in extending student interest.

2 Paperback collections. Students can be encouraged to begin a personal collection. *Fifty Creative Ways to Use Paperbacks in the Middle Grades* (23) offers classroom-tested ideas for stimulating reading.

3 Classroom libraries or reading corners.

4 Newspaper activities.

5 Media motivators (television, film, filmstrips, records, cassettes).

6 "Top ten" or "most wanted" lists from fellow students.

7 Varied reading materials (magazines, brochures, maps, comics, cookbooks, pamphlets, reference books).

Student response to literature can take a variety of forms. Relating personally to a selection is part of the process of appreciating literature. In addition to reacting through written and oral expression, students can react to books through drama, art, music, and multimedia projects.

Some specific techniques for encouraging thoughtful student response follow:

1 *Language experience approach.* Having students become authors themselves and then using their original work as reading material are foundational activities in the response process.

2 *Writing activities.* Writing letters to characters or from characters, eulogies for characters, advertisements for books, and reviews for newspapers interest many middle school students (47).

3 *Oral activities.* Storytelling to younger children, "selling" the book to classmates, or talking about favorite books in small groups can build student enthusiasm.

4 *Drama.* Role playing, dressing up like characters and acting out a scene is appropriate.

5 *Approach through other arts.* Art, music, multimedia presentations, collages, mobiles, illustrations, posters, murals, selection of appropriate music for a setting, and slide-tape presentations incorporate the other arts into literature.

6 *Vocabulary development activities.* Montebello (32) presents a number of resources for teaching students about words and language using literature.

7 *Communicating with authors.* Authors enjoy correspondence from students and will often answer letters. The Dial-an-Author brochure from Bantam Books (42) offers suggestions for developing a successful reader–writer interview program.

8 *Bibliotherapy.* Bibliotherapy is exploring materials with students that deal with problems similar to their own. Students can discover how a fictional or real character handled a particular situation.

Problems   The thoughts of youth may be long, long thoughts, but as far as literature is concerned, their thoughts are evidently lacking in depth and sophistication. For many American 17-year-olds, thinking about what they have read and expressing their thoughts coherently appear to be difficult and unfamiliar tasks (34, p. 1).

The report on the last National Assessment of Educational Progress reading and literature assessment concludes that although young Americans seem to agree reading is important in the present world, reading is not necessarily a top priority. Thus, middle school teachers face an important challenge in promoting positive attitudes toward reading and in teaching students to read inferentially and evaluatively. In teaching students to analyze literature, however, teachers must guard against killing the work through overanalysis. Dissection of literature is not the goal; analysis should be placed in the context of student engagement with the reading (26).

Another challenge language arts teachers face is eliciting cooperation from content area teachers in incorporating the appropriate reading skills into their subject area programs and in promoting pleasure reading. Many states now require reading courses of all middle school teachers, thus providing them with information to help them carry out their responsibilities in the application of reading.

A final potential problem is censorship. With an increased realism in literature for young people, parental or community objections might be forthcoming. Each school should have a definite policy for dealing with such objections.

Teachers should also be cognizant of cultural, racial, or sexual stereotyping in some literature. Students should have the opportunity to read positive portrayals of all groups.

Assessment   In assessing the reading and literature program, one should keep in mind Stewig's (51) distinct functions of literature explained earlier. The literary experience has *one* purpose and only one purpose—enjoyment. Under no circumstances should assessment activities interfere with that objective. Requiring students to answer questions or make reports on books read for pleasure is not recommended.

The teacher might want to evaluate his or her program to see that it provides maximum experiences for fostering enjoyment. Questions that might guide the teacher include these:

Have I introduced students to a wide variety of literature?
Is there planned time in the curriculum for enjoyment activities?
Are my students becoming more interested in reading for pleasure?

The teacher might also want to use interest inventories to determine the reading likes and dislikes of students.

The other two functions of literature Stewig (51) identifies are to impart information and to provide a vehicle for language-related skills. Informal observation, teacher-made essay and multiple-choice tests, standardized assessments of reading and language skills checklists, and informal reading inventories might all be appropriate for evaluating progress in achieving the purposes of these two functions. Numerous books on diagnosis and evaluation offer suggestions for assessing reading and language skills.

The main thrust of this section, however, is on motivating students to read for enjoyment. To that end, assessment should focus on providing appropriate literary experiences, not on testing.

CONCLUDING COMMENTS

Throughout this chapter, we have discussed the uniquenesses of students in the middle school grades. These students clearly need a very special type of instruction and program to continue their acquisition of skills and competence in the language arts. Implementation of this chapter's content will help to make this end a reality.

BIBLIOGRAPHY AND REFERENCES

1 Applebee, Arthur N. *Writing in the Secondary School.* Urbana, Ill.: National Council of Teachers of English, 1981.
2 Bamberg, Betty. "Composition Instruction Does Make a Difference." *Research in the Teaching of English,* vol. 12, February 1978, pp. 47–59.
3 Barbe, Walter B., and Lucas, Virginia H. "Instruction in Handwriting: A New Look." *Childhood Education,* vol. 50, no. 4, February 1974, pp. 207–209.
4 Barbe, Walter B., and Milone, Michael N., Jr. *Teaching Handwriting Through Modality Strengths.* Columbus, Ohio: Zaner-Bloser, 1980.
5 Barbe, Walter B., and Swassing, Raymond H. *Teaching through Modality Strengths: Concepts and Practices.* Columbus, Ohio: Zaner-Bloser, 1979.
6 Burns, Paul C. *Diagnostic Teaching of the Language Arts.* Itasca, Ill.: Peacock Publishers, 1974.

7 Buros, Oscar K. *Mental Measurements Yearbook.* Highland Park, N.J.: Gryphon Press, 1978.

8 Cazden, Courtney B. "What We Don't Know about Teaching the Language Arts." *Phi Delta Kappan,* 1980, vol. 61, no. 9, 1980, pp. 595–596.

9 Cunningham, James W., Cunningham, Patricia M., and Arthur, Sharon V. *Middle and Secondary School Reading.* New York: Longman, Inc., 1981.

10 Dale, Edgar, O'Rourke, Joseph, and Bamman, Henry A. *Techniques of Teaching Vocabulary.* Palo Alto, Calif.: Field Educational Publications, 1971.

11 Devine, Thomas G. "Listening: What Do We Know after Fifty Years of Research and Theorizing?" *Journal of Reading,* vol. 21, 1978, pp. 296–304.

12 Eichhorn, Donald. *The Middle School.* New York: The Center for Applied Research in Education, 1966, p. 3.

13 Epstein, Herman. "A Neuroscience Framework for Restructuring Middle School Curricula." *Transescence: The Journal of Emerging Adolescence,* vol. 5, pp. 6–11, July 1977.

14 Fader, Daniel. *The New Hooked On Books.* New York: Berkley, 1976.

15 Fernald, G. M. *Remedial Techniques in Basic School Subjects.* New York: McGraw-Hill, 1943. Revised by Byron Callaway and Susan J. Smith in *Teaching Reading in South Carolina Secondary Schools.* Columbia, S.C.: South Carolina Department of Education, 1978.

16 Fisher, Carol J., and Terry, C. Ann. *Children's Language and the Language Arts.* New York: McGraw-Hill, 1977.

17 Georgiady, Nicholas P., and Romano, Louis G. "Growth Characteristics of Middle School Children: Curriculum Implications." *Middle School Journal,* vol. 8, February 1977, pp. 12–15, 22–23.

18 Glatthorn, Allan A. "Curriculum Change in Loosely Coupled Systems." *Educational Leadership* vol. 39, no. 2, November 1981, pp. 110–113.

19 Graves, Donald H. *Balance the Basics: Let Them Write.* New York: Ford Foundation, 1978.

20 Greene, Harry A. *The New Iowa Spelling Scale.* Iowa City: State University of Iowa, 1954.

21 Haley-James, Shirley (eds). *Perspectives on Writing in Grades 1–8.* Urbana, Ill.: National Council of Teachers of English, 1981.

22 Haynes, Elizabeth. "Using Research in Preparing to Teach Writing." *English Journal,* vol. 66, January 1978, pp. 82–88.

23 Hellriegel, Diane (compiler). *Fifty Creative Ways to Use Paperbacks in the Middle Grades.* New York: Scholastic Book Services, 1980.

24 Hodges, Richard E. *Learning to Spell.* Urbana, Ill.: ERIC Clearinghouse on Reading and Communication Skills and National Council of Teachers of English, 1981.

25 Holdzkom, David, et al. *Research within Reach: Oral and Written Communication.* St. Louis, Mo.: Research and Development Interpretation Service, CEMREL, 1983.

26 Judy, Stephen N. *Explorations in the Teaching of English* (2d ed.). New York: Harper and Row, 1981.

27 Klein, Marvin L. "Teaching Writing in the Elementary Grades." *The Elementary School Journal,* vol. 81, no. 5, May 1981, pp. 319–326.

28 Landry, D. L. "The Neglect of Listening." *Elementary English,* vol. 46, 1969, pp. 599–605.

29 Lounsbury, John H., and Vars, Gordon E. *A Curriculum for the Middle School Years.* New York: Harper and Row, 1978, p. 1.

30 Lundsteen, Sara W. *Listening: Its Impact on Reading and the Other Language Arts.* Urbana, Ill.: National Council of Teachers of English, 1979.

31 McCracken, Robert A. "Initiating Sustained Silent Reading." *Journal of Reading,* vol. 14, May 1971, pp. 521–522, 582–583.

32 Montebello, Mary S. *Children's Literature in the Curriculum.* Dubuque, Iowa: William C. Brown, 1972.

33 Mussen, Paul H., Conger, John J., and Kagan, Jerome. *Child Development and Personality* (5th ed.). New York: Harper and Row, 1979.

34 National Assessment of Education Progress *Bulletin*. Denver, Colo.: National Assessment of Educational Progress, 1981.

35 National Council of Teachers of English/SLATE. *Standards for Basic Skills Writing Programs*. Urbana, Ill.: National Council of Teachers of English, 1979, p. 1.

36 National Council of Teachers of English/SLATE. *What Happens in Smaller Classes?* Urbana, Ill.: National Council of Teachers of English, 1980, p. 2.

37 National Council of Teachers of English. *How to Help Your Child Become a Better Writer*. Urbana, Ill.: National Council of Teachers of English, 1980.

38 Odell, Lee. *Evaluating Writing*. Urbana, Ill.: National Council of Teachers of English/ SLATE, 1979, p. 1.

39 Petty, Walter T., Petty, Dorothy C., and Becking, Marjorie F. *Experiences in Language: Tools and Techniques for Language Arts Methods* (3d ed.). Boston: Allyn and Bacon, 1981.

40 Rogers, Carl. *Freedom To Learn*. Columbus, Ohio: Charles E. Merrill, 1979, p. 104.

41 Rouse, John. *Literature as a Basic*. Urbana, Ill.: National Council of Teachers of English/ SLATE, 1980.

42 Scales, Pat. *Dial-an-Author*. New York: Bantam Books, 1981.

43 Shuy, Roger. "Sociolinguistics." In Roger Shuy (ed.), *Linguistic Theory: What Can It Say About Reading?* Newark, Del.: International Reading Association, 1977, pp. 80–94.

44 Smith, E. Brooks, Goodman, Kenneth S., and Meredith, Robert. *Language and Thinking in School* (2d ed.). New York: Holt, Rinehart and Winston, 1976, p. 209.

45 Smith, Frank. "Myths of Writing." *Language Arts*. vol. 58, no. 7, October 1981, p. 796.

46 Smith, James A. *Creative Teaching of the Language Arts in the Elementary School* (2d ed.). Boston: Allyn and Bacon, 1973.

47 Smith, Susan J. (ed.). *Teaching Reading in South Carolina Secondary Schools*. Columbia, S.C.: South Carolina Department of Education, 1978.

48 South Carolina Department of Education. *Teaching and Testing Our Basic Skills Objectives— Writing*. Columbia, S.C.: South Carolina Department of Education, 1981.

49 Speech Communication Association. *Standards for Effective Oral Communication Programs*. Falls Church, Va.: Speech Communication Association, circa 1978.

50 South Carolina Department of Education. *South Carolina Middle School Guide*. Columbia, S.C.: South Carolina Department of Education, 1975, pp. 20–21.

51 Stewig, John Warren. *Exploring Language with Children*. Columbus, Ohio: Charles E. Merrill, 1974.

52 Templeton, Shane. "Spelling, Phonology, and the Older Student." In Edmund H. Henderson and James W. Beers (eds.), *Developmental and Cognitive Aspects of Learning to Spell: A Reflection of Word Knowledge*. Newark, Del.: International Reading Association, 1980, pp. 85–96.

53 Toepfer, Conrad F., Jr. *A Realistic Expectation for Cognitive Growth during Transescence*. Speech presented at the Association for Supervision and Curriculum Development National Convention, Houston, Tex., March 21, 1977.

54 Van De Weghe, Richard. *Research in Written Composition: Fifteen Years of Investigation*. Las Cruces, N. Mex.: New Mexico State University, 1978.

55 Wasylyk, Thomas M., and Milone, Michael N., Jr. *Corrective Techniques in Handwriting: Cursive*. Columbus, Ohio: Zaner-Bloser, 1980.

56 Wilhide, Jim. *Building Composition Skills*. Columbia, S.C.: South Carolina Department of Education, 1981.

57 Wilson, Robert M., and Gambrell, Linda B. *Contract Teaching . . . for Academic Success!* Silver Spring, Md.: Reading Education, 1975.

CHAPTER 9

THE TEACHER'S ROLE IN LANGUAGE ARTS INSTRUCTION

Thus far in this book, we have shared with you various definitions and principles related to the language arts; we have provided you with some theoretical background about children's development and we have described classroom situations in which exemplary teachers work with students. We believe that your vicarious visits to these classrooms will enable you to begin to attain an understanding of teaching as well as an understanding of the ways in which the language arts can be taught at a particular grade level.

In this chapter, the emphasis is directly upon the teacher. As you prepare to become a teacher, the thought of working with twenty or thirty children can be an intimidating one. Not only will you be responsible for facilitating students' learning, you must handle discipline problems, and you will be expected to develop and maintain an environment which is conducive to children's intellectual and emotional growth. You will need to find answers to questions such as "What is a good teacher?" "What is a good school?" "Are there any specific characteristics which set apart effective language arts teachers from those who are not as effective?" As you search for answers to these questions, you will begin to formulate a philosophy which will help you become a teacher who is capable of making sound educational decisions.

WHAT TEACHING CHARACTERISTICS SHOULD BE AVOIDED?

No one sets out to be a poor teacher. When people enter the teaching profession they hope to have positive effects on the students with whom they work. Yet many do not succeed.

Many go into classrooms and assume authoritarian roles in which they control the activities and events that take place. They are the decision makers, they initiate all the activities, and they do most, if not all, of the talking. In other instances, they go to the opposite extreme. In their classrooms, they exercise no authority. Students are free to do as they please. Any activities, talk, or experiences which occur are initiated and carried out by the students.

It is a paradox that teachers who want to help students learn may choose leadership roles which militate against their learning. Many of the authoritarian teachers do not possess authoritarian personalities, just as many who perform at the other end of the continuum are not passive individuals. Their reasons for behaving in ways which are inconsistent with their personalities have to do with their preconceived ideas of what constitutes good teaching, and it is probable that they are not consciously aware of the ways in which they formed these ideas.

Most people have a cultural stereotype as well as an idealized version of what constitutes a good teacher. We have all had experience with many teachers as we have gone through the elementary grades and the secondary school, and we have also been influenced by the teachers portrayed in literature, on television, and, for those old enough to remember, on the radio. Such characters as Miss Dove, Our Miss Brooks, and Miss Jean Brodie have influenced our conception of teachers. Many people incorporate these stereotyped actions into their notions of how teachers should perform.

In order to get college students to look at the cultural stereotype of teachers, one of the writers asked students enrolled in a language arts methods class to pretend they were television directors. Their task was to cast the part of a teacher for a television situation comedy. The audience was to know that the person was a teacher just from the character's outward appearance. Only later was the actor to be permitted to act in such a way that the audience could see teacher characteristics.

The students had no difficulty in completing the assignment. First, they listed such physical attributes as a female teacher with hair pulled back in a bun, wearing glasses and dowdy clothes. For personality characteristics they listed such traits as rigid and strict disciplinarian. When the students were asked to compare themselves with the description which evolved from the listed attributes, they were unanimous in their agreement that none of them fit the description. They believed this was an old-fashioned portrayal of the way teachers used to be. They seemed to believe that when teachers exchanged their dowdy clothes for blue jeans and restyled their hair so they could blow-dry it, they exchanged the old personality attributes for new ones. As a continuation of the exercise, the students were asked to list the characteristics of an ideal teacher. They named such traits as knowledgeable, understanding, and sensitive. When asked to compare themselves with this ideal teacher, most agreed this was the model they would strive to become.

A case can be made that many people graduate from teacher training institutions and venture into classrooms with their stereotype of teacher still intact. They have not thought through such issues as classroom management, discipline problems, and student and teacher roles. In short order they find that it is not enough for a teacher to be a dedicated, nice person who loves children. Teachers who are faced with troublesome teaching situations often act in one of two ways. Either they revert to what was done to them and adopt the role based on their stereotype of teachers or they go the other way—they react to this stereotyped teacher model by becoming the opposite of it. If their stereotype of teacher is that of an authoritarian personality, they try to lessen their power and delegate decision making to their students.

Research indicates that neither the authoritarian dictator nor the powerless teacher promotes student achievement (26). The authoritarian encourages children to become dependent learners—they do what they are told and nothing more. On the other hand, the teacher who relinquishes all power and expects students to function in a laissez-faire atmosphere causes students to experience anxiety. Lack of teacher direction leads to student confusion and confusion evokes anxiety.

It is important for persons who plan to become teachers to reconceptualize the role of the teacher so that their choice of leadership style will be consonant with good teaching. In order to do this it is helpful to look at teaching in its larger context—in the institution in which it is performed, the school.

HOW DOES A TEACHER'S VIEW ABOUT SCHOOLS AFFECT TEACHING STYLE?

In Webster's dictionary, school is defined as "a place or establishment for teaching and learning." This definition is too simplistic for teachers whose perception of the school will determine their teaching practices. Molnar (16, p. 63) provides a more complex definition when he writes: "All schools, regardless of their organization, represent contrived environments which reflect certain value priorities, as well as implicit or explicit assumptions about how teaching and learning are most effectively facilitated."

Molnar sees the school as having three functions: the training function, a process through which students acquire a set of externally verifiable skills; a schooling function, which is concerned with the socialization of students; and an education function in which the emphasis is on the individual and his or her interaction with the environment. While all these functions occur in all schools, each is not given the same priority in any one school.

A teacher's concept of a school's function will determine to a large extent his or her perception of the ideal teacher. If he or she believes the first two functions to be of primary importance, the language arts teacher will approach teaching from the point of view of skills acquisition. Reading, writing, speaking, listening, spelling, and handwriting will be seen as being composed of essential skills to be mastered, and instruction will take place in a highly organized manner.

Teaching materials will provide an opportunity for students to acquire and practice certain well-defined skills, while test results coupled with teacher observation will provide evidence that these skills have been learned. The emphasis will be on learning for the future. Children may not enjoy the process of skills acquisition, but in the long run they will be happy that they have mastered these skills. Children who become competent in the language arts will eventually get good jobs and take their places in society.

If the teacher's concept of the school's function is that the school is for education, his or her teaching philosophy will reflect this belief. Rather than thinking that the knowledge needed for children to develop communication skills comes from outside the learner and that teachers impart knowledge, he or she will believe that children learn communication skills by interacting with their environment. The teacher will believe that the child will gain proficiency in the language arts by reading, by listening, by writing, and by talking. Teaching materials will be varied (for example, trade books will be valued not only for reading skills practice but also for the opportunities they provide for independent learning). Attaining language arts skills will be a goal for the here and now. It will be seen as both a pleasurable and worthwhile pursuit.

It is an oversimplification to suggest that teaching is an either/or proposition—that teachers believe either in the primacy of the first two functions or in the third function. In actual practice, teachers have many beliefs and many options for exercising them. The point to remember is that beliefs determine behaviors.

Roy (20) describes six different patterns of adaptation which teachers use to react to institutionalized goals (such as the teaching of language arts) and institutionalized means for accomplishing these goals (such as teaching manuals and instructional grouping).

Conforming teachers represent the predominant form of adaptation. They conform to the aims of the school because they agree with both the goals and the means which the school selects to achieve the goals. These teachers accept "the reward–punishment model, competition, the giving of grades, testing, and the need for efficiency and for preserving the system" (20, p. 43).

A second pattern is embraced by *innovative teachers* who accept the goal—the teaching of language arts—but not the means for achieving that end. These teachers may feel that grouping is inappropriate or the textbooks are inhibiting. They search for new ways to teach language arts, even at the risk of alienating their principals or fellow teachers.

Teachers who reject the goal but accept the prescribed means are called *ritualists*. To these people the means become the goal. Roy describes this teacher as being "the proponent of the 'keep busy rule'. He may relish the 'ditto method' of teaching. . . . He uses certain materials, texts, and methods because they are there" (20, p. 44). Teaching to the ritualists is controlling children's behavior. Such control mechanisms as standing in line, raising hands, and passing out seat work are confused with the business of learning. Carefully devised lesson plans and attractive bulletin boards are synonymous with good teaching to the ritualists.

Another teacher type is the *retreatist*. At one time these teachers accepted both the means and the goal, but after unsuccessfully attempting to facilitate students' learning, they reject not only the goal but the means as well. These teachers lament that "No one can be expected to teach these kids anything!" In today's parlance, they might be called victims of teacher burnout.

A fifth pattern of adaptation is used by *rebellious* teachers who also reject the goal and the means sanctioned by the school system for attaining it. They differ from retreatists in that they substitute another goal and choose other means for attaining the new goal. Rebels would not be convinced that schools need so much emphasis on the language arts. They would point to successful people who could neither read nor write. These teachers would believe that the school should emphasize other goals (such as becoming one's own person and getting along with others). Rebellious teachers usually operate outside of public schools; often they are found in alternative schools.

The last type, the *censorious* teacher, comes closest to Roy's ideal teacher. Censorious teachers are highly critical of the school. Their value systems are attuned to the ideals which they believe are achievable rather than the real world of the school system. They ask that schools live up to their stated philosophies. In most schools, lip service is given to meeting individual needs, but in actual practice these frequently are not met. The need for children to experience success is touted, yet in most schools many children experience failure. If the censorious teachers have to choose between becoming advocates of the child or of the school, they will side with the child. These teachers would support the goal of language arts teaching and they would accept the means as at least one option for attaining the goal; however, they would consider the goal as secondary in importance to the children involved.

Prospective teachers can learn a great deal about possible leadership styles by a careful analysis of Roy's six teacher types. These styles of behavior not only develop as a reaction to perceived school goals and school-sanctioned means for goal attainment, but they also are an outgrowth of the teacher's perceived function of the school.

It is a useful exercise to attempt to predict teacher success or failure predicated on these teacher styles. It would seem logical that the conformist, the innovator, and the censorious teachers would have positive effects on the language arts learning of at least some of the children in their classes, while it is doubtful that the ritualist, the retreatist, or the rebel would fare so well. The odds are that the latter three teacher types would have negative effects. Since they do not believe in the goal—the instruction of language arts—it is likely that children would not show much growth in this area while under their tutelage. Without research data based on careful studies of these teaching behaviors and their effects on student learning, we can only speculate on probable successes or failures of particular teaching styles.

WHAT DOES RESEARCH HAVE TO SAY ABOUT TEACHER EFFECTIVENESS?

Research is a systematic attempt to provide answers to questions. The quest to identify the effective teacher has been occurring for a long time, yet research in this area is still not definitive. Teacher effectiveness research explores relationships between what the teacher does and what the pupil learns. Researchers look at actual teaching behaviors that can be observed in classroom settings (such as teacher talk, pupil talk, time spent on an instructional task). They carefully observe a particular behavior and then they measure its effect on the achievement of students. Observation and measurement are integral parts of this research. Teacher behavior is most often measured by trained observers who record their observations on rating scales, while student learning outcomes are usually measured as achievement gain on standardized tests.

Some problems inherent in this type of research have not yet been mastered. You must have at least some knowledge of these limitations if you are to be able to take advantage of what research can tell you about effective teachers.

Teacher observation may be a questionable procedure for gathering data about teacher behavior. There is a growing body of literature which indicates that the presence of an observer in the classroom has an influence on the teacher's behavior. A study by Samph (22) indicated that teachers criticized students more when no observer was in the room; that when an observer was present, teachers praised students more. An investigation by DiMartino (5) showed teachers' verbal behavior became "warmer" in the presence of an observer. McIntyre's (13) work suggests that when teachers are observed they tend to exhibit more positive behaviors toward their students then they ordinarily would.

Hursh (10) conducted a study which utilized not only an overt classroom observer but also a covert observer stationed behind a one-way mirror who examined what took place when an observer was not present. The subjects of this study were two college students working with eight preschool children. It was found that the students complied with the observer's request that they increase their physical contact with the children more when the observer was present than when he was not present. The data indicate that "if teachers know what an observer wants to see they will perform that behavior."

The results of studies such as these cause some educators to question the validity of data collected during teacher observation. Others (11, 15) believe this is not a serious limitation because the information derived through observation relative to teaching behavior is better than none at all.

There are several additional cautionary notes for you to keep in mind as you read results of effective teacher studies. The teacher behaviors, called process variables, must interact with the students' backgrounds. Students differ in terms of age and grade levels, experiential backgrounds, language development, and learning styles. Because of this no teaching strategy will work for all students all the time.

Students also differ in their reactions to various process variables. For example, if a researcher is investigating the effect of teacher praise on the learning of children, the results may show some students reacting to praise from their teacher by increasing their efforts while others negate its effect by believing the teacher is "sugar-coating" the assessment of their work.

In a similar vein, the process variable of time spent on an instructional task will interact with student behaviors. A teacher may spend twenty minutes teaching a certain skill. Some members of the class may pay close attention, while others tune in and out of the learning experience and some children pay little or no attention. The teacher behavior is the same for all but the effects of the learning will differ.

An additional problem arises with the product dimension in teacher effectiveness studies. Achievement test gain is only one aspect of the possible learning outcomes of language arts instruction. Standardized tests measure information which was covered or skills that were taught, but it is difficult to measure such things as the appreciation of literature or creative writing using such tests. It is important to keep in mind that while skills mastery is an important part of a teacher's responsibility, it is only part of the learning process which leads to language arts proficiency.

It would be convenient if research could show that teachers who do certain things or act in certain ways cause children to learn more than others who act differently. This is not the case. Research cannot specify instructional strategies which *cause* learning; it can only provide some implications for practice. Nonetheless, language arts teachers can learn about practices which have a positive effect on students' achievement by a careful analysis of research results.

As Medley (14) stated in his review of 289 teacher effectiveness studies, we should ". . . forget about the cause-and-effect inferences the researchers worry about and examine their findings for information about competent teacher performance" (p. 6). Even though all the answers are not known and, given the complexity of the task, may never be known, we can formulate some tentative guidelines for good teaching. Even in the absence of complete information, teachers can take advantage of what is known about effective instruction. The following section discusses research findings which have implications for teachers of elementary and middle school language arts.

For more than fifty years, major research efforts have emphasized the importance of the teacher. Beginning in the 1920s and continuing for many years, research focused

Teachers plan together to meet student needs.

on trying to discover the best method or the best materials for teaching a particular subject. The thought was that if a best method could be identified and proper materials developed, anyone could be a good teacher. Methods and materials would be teacher-proof. The results of studies of this sort were not encouraging; no best method or material was identified. Repeatedly it was found that it is the teacher who plays a major part in determining the success or failure of a particular course of study.

The results of recent investigations not only support this conclusion, they take it a step further. There is a growing body of literature which suggests that individual teachers can and do have a significant effect upon student achievement. It has also been shown that some teachers are more successful than others in producing achievement gains in children.

Although studies about teacher behaviors have been reported for many years, the modern era of teacher effectiveness research has produced a relatively small number of studies. Rosenshine (19), a recognized authority in teacher effectiveness research, states that "Fewer than 25 studies have been conducted on any specific variable such as teacher praise or teacher questions, and these studies are spread across all grade levels, subject areas and student backgrounds" (p. 61).

Research dealing specifically with language arts teaching is almost nonexistent. One of the few exceptions is the work of Brophy (2), who studied teaching behaviors which foster language arts improvement. To do this, he observed second- and third-grade teachers whose students were doing well not only in the language arts but in mathematics as well. He found that good teaching behaviors differed according to the socioeconomic status (SES) of the children.

In schools where the children were predominantly high SES, the more successful teachers were more likely to teach in traditional ways, to be critical and demanding, to have high expectations for the students, and to keep them involved in their instructional tasks. Successful teachers in low-SES schools also had high expectations, but their interactions with the children were different. They were more feelings oriented, more supportive and encouraging, and they were willing to help children with personal matters. In addition, these teachers were interested in finding the best teaching materials with which to work with these children. Brophy concludes from his study that successful language arts teachers tailor their teaching methods to the ways in which students learn best.

Smith (24) conducted an investigation to see the effects of organizational structure on the language arts learning of 552 sixth- and seventh-grade students. Her purpose was to determine whether test scores increase more for students in a language arts block or in a departmentalized organization. She found that sixth-grade children who were taught in the language arts block demonstrated greater academic gain in language than children who were instructed in the departmentalized organizational structure.

Although there is a paucity of language arts research, there are many teacher effectiveness studies which include reading achievement as a variable of interest. This is because students' reading gains can be measured and the researcher can often find a relationship between particular process variables and students' achievement gains. The results of these studies have some implications for language arts teachers as they look for effective teaching practices for the skills components of the language arts.

McDonald (12) studied effective reading instruction at the second- and fifth-grade levels. He found once again that teachers do exert differential effects upon student achievement. He also found that a teacher's pattern of performance is more likely to be related to achievement than a single teaching practice and that effective teaching practices will differ by subject matter and grade level.

McDonald concluded that an effective teaching pattern in second grade was one in which (1) considerable time is devoted to explaining, discussion, and questioning; (2) considerable time is spent on independent work; and (3) the teacher uses a variety of teaching techniques. An effective teacher practice in fifth grade was one in which the teacher used thought-provoking questions to help children participate in a sustained interaction about ideas.

Heilman, Blair, and Rupley (8) cite research from five studies which offer evidence that competent teachers' classrooms are characterized by less deviant or disruptive pupil behavior. Teachers relied on task-related comments rather than on the use of criticism to direct student behavior. The classrooms were not strictly regimented nor were they always quiet, but students were kept busy with instructional tasks which had the effect of lessening disruptive behavior. Effective teachers were able to prepare the environment so that learning took place.

Teachers who possess good managerial skills have positive effects on children in their classes. Research (7) has shown that teachers who lack managerial abilities can be identified during the first few days of school, that these problems generally continue throughout the school year, and that teachers' managerial skills have a relationship to levels of student involvement. When Wade (25) constructed a test of teacher skills used in reading instruction, he included several measures of teacher diagnostic skills which can be classed as managerial skills (such as grouping students for instruction, diagnosing reading difficulties, and identifying word recognition errors). The results of the test showed that teachers who scored well on the skill measures had students who performed at a higher reading level than did teachers who did not score as well.

Research studies show that diagnosis is an important part of effective skills instruction. Weber (26) found that successful teachers used more ongoing diagnostic evaluation than did their less successful counterparts. The results of a two-year longitudinal investigation with reading teachers at third-grade levels showed that there was a difference in the diagnostic procedures employed by successful and unsuccessful teachers. Effective teachers used a test–teach–test strategy to determine the reasons students were having problems in skills areas.

Diagnosis itself is not a teaching strategy. It is what the teacher does with the information gleaned from diagnostic procedures which have an effect on student learning. Studies of the more effective teachers of basic skills have begun to establish a pattern of learning behaviors, labeled *direct instruction* by researchers, which has a positive relationship to students' achievement.

The concept of direct instruction is defined by Good (6) as active teaching. It is perceived as an instructional program in which a teacher identifies and sets specific learning goals, uses diagnostic procedures to monitor student progress, and frequently shows children how to do assigned work. Rosenshine (18) conceptualized direct instruction as academic activities which are structured so that: (1) students understand the teaching goals, (2) sufficient time is allocated for instruction, (3) there is extensive content coverage, (4) student performance is monitored, (5) teachers' questions are at a low enough cognitive level so that students can correctly answer them, and (6) students are provided with immediate feedback.

In his summary of recent research, Rosenshine reported the results of three investigations into primary-grade reading and mathematics for low-SES children. All three researchers looked for relationships between certain instructional variables and the achievement of students. They found that the amount of time spent directly on academic activities was positively related to achievement, while time spent on nonacademic activities (games, dramatic play, discussion of home and family) was negatively related to achievement in reading and mathematics.

The reader should not jump to erroneous conclusions on the basis of these studies. The results of this research do not provide evidence to support the idea that teachers should not use games or dramatic play; rather, the reader must be aware that the effects of children taking part in these activities are not measured on achievement tests which are designed to measure basic skills. The results of these studies imply that if teachers want children to demonstrate their competency in basic skill areas by doing well on achievement tests, the children must spend time practicing the competencies on which they will be tested.

McDonald's (12) research adds support to the importance of academically engaged time. The results of his research cause him to believe that the teacher's method of organizing instruction is crucial to effective teaching. He concludes that the teacher who spends an inordinate amount of time on classroom management activities is depriving students of the direct instructional time they need in order to acquire and practice necessary skills.

Content covered, a process variable which is included in the concept of direct instruction, has been called a commonsense factor which has an effect on students' achievement levels. *Content covered* refers to whether or not students have had the chance to learn the particular concepts or skills which are treated on achievement tests. Simply stated, if students' competence is to be demonstrated by performance on a test and if teachers have not emphasized the particular skills to be tested, it is unlikely that the students will score well enough to appear competent. For example, children who are proficient in the use of dictionaries because they have used them repeatedly in their creative writing activities might not have scored well on a test of dictionary skills if their teachers had not emphasized the discrete skills which are to be tested.

WHAT ARE SOME RESEARCH IMPLICATIONS FOR THE LANGUAGE ARTS TEACHER?

Because of the limited number of studies concerning teaching strategies and organizational patterns and because these studies are affected by such factors as learning styles, student attention, and socioeconomic status, conclusions about techniques and organization must be tenuous. Yet the studies do provide food for thought for teachers and tentative guidelines and implications for practice can be derived from them.

The research findings presented in the preceding section imply that (1) elementary

Language arts teachers must be instructional leaders.

and middle school teachers have differing effects on the learning of children; (2) classroom management skills are very important; and (3) effective teachers employ a pattern of teaching strategies, labeled *direct instruction,* which are positively related to student achievement. These implications can aid teachers in becoming more effective in language arts instruction. The research indicates that language arts teachers must be the instructional leaders; methods and materials must not be permitted to dictate the curriculum. Effective teachers will tailor their methods and apply the materials they use to the idiosyncratic needs of the students. Shuy (23), an educator who writes teachers' manuals for a basal reading series, agrees with this position. He writes: "The simple and unvarnished truth is that we who develop manuals do not know your children at all. Even clearer is the fact that you do. We can do no better than to provide a menu and it is up to you to determine what to order for your students" (p. 920).

Effective language arts teachers must develop good managerial skills. Classrooms will not be strictly regimented nor will they be overly quiet; rather, students will know what is expected of them, they will be involved in sufficient instructional tasks, and the environment will be one that is conducive to learning. Teachers will rely on task-related comments rather than on the use of criticism or scolding to keep children focused on learning tasks.

The direct instructional variables, which research findings suggest are associated with effective language arts teaching, are presented in Figure 9-1. The major characteristics of effective instruction based on the results of process–product research include a systematic and meaningful development of language arts skills, well-established purposes for learning opportunities for application of skills, and maximum time for contact with students. The research suggests that it is also important for teachers to use different strategies and organizational patterns when they work with children in the primary grades from the ones they use with children in the intermediate grades.

Berliner (1) uses a one-sentence statement to summarize what he believes teachers can learn from the results of process–product research. He writes: "If the tests they use are matched to the curriculum they teach, then elementary school teachers who find ways to put students into contact with the academic curriculum, and keep them in contact with that curriculum while maintaining a convivial classroom atmosphere, are successful in promoting . . . achievement" (p. 306).

Educational researchers use scientific inquiry into the nature of teaching effectiveness in an effort to pinpoint some characteristics associated with effective teaching. They acknowledge that this field is still in its infancy and that it will be a long time before definitive answers can be given, but many believe with Cruickshank (4) that as educators develop a research data base, the teaching profession will be deemed more scientific.

Other members of the teaching profession look at teaching from a different perspective. They see teaching as more of an art than a science. Cook (3) speaks for this school of thought as she urges teachers to go beyond technique. Cook examined the principles inherent in the National Council of the Teachers of English (NCTE) Statement on the Preparation of Teachers of Language Arts.

Cook (3) defines two concepts, *teaching* and *language arts,* in terms of the Statement's philosophy. She states that it is no longer enough for a teacher to be one who is "skilled at manipulating the tools of the trade, assisted by skills lists, pre-packaged 'teacher-proof' materials, and modern technology" (p. 51). The teacher for the 1980s must be a well-trained professional "who can facilitate children's healthy growth and development in ways that will enable them to live successfully in our complex, modern society" (p. 51). The term *language arts* is no longer defined as merely an academic discipline but in a broader sense, as "a means by which students grow emotionally; students respond to their experiences and learn about their worlds, their feelings, their attitudes and themselves by using language about these subjects" (17, p. 197).

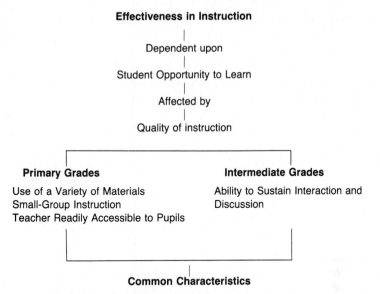

Effectiveness in Instruction

Dependent upon

Student Opportunity to Learn

Affected by

Quality of instruction

Primary Grades

Use of a Variety of Materials
Small-Group Instruction
Teacher Readily Accessible to Pupils

Intermediate Grades

Ability to Sustain Interaction and
Discussion

Common Characteristics

- High teacher expectations for students.
- Teachers attempt to match their teaching methods with individual learning styles of students.
- Teacher knowledge and preparation time for a lesson.
- Lesson presentation geared to student level.
- Development of effective record-keeping system.
- Proper use of materials for instruction.
- Development of ongoing diagnostic techniques.
- Maximum time for contact with students.
- Well-established purposes for learning.
- Opportunities for application of skills learned.
- Systematic and meaningful development of language arts skills.

Adapted from William H. Rupley and Timothy R. Blair. *Reading Diagnosis and Remediation: A Primer for Classroom and Clinic,* 2nd edition, p. 39. Copyright © 1983 by Houghton Mifflin Company. Used by permission.

FIGURE 9-1
Instructional variables associated with effective language arts teaching.

Griffiths (7), president of the New York State Teacher Education Conference Board (TECB), calls on teachers themselves to determine the marks of the effective teacher and how effectiveness can be increased. He believes teaching is too complex "to limit effectiveness to the transmission of knowledge and the development of intellectual abilities" and to limit it in this way "is to overlook contributions to other educational goals, such as socialization, character development, zeal for continued learning, full realization of unique potential, . . . and practical competence."

Griffiths, speaking for members of the teaching profession, delineates ten characteristics which he thinks mark the effective teacher:

1 Diligence in keeping oneself current and increasing one's mastery with respect to the body of knowledge and skill taught.

2 Commitment to continual personal growth through intellectual activity.

3 Awareness of societal expectations, institutional goals, and professional responsibilities.

4 Receptivity to advances in pedagogical practices.

5 Conscientiousness and proficiency in planning and preparation for teaching encounters, based on knowledge of the outcomes to be sought and the most efficient means of achieving them.

6 Artistry in managing and performing instructional functions effectively.

7 Concern for students as individuals, based on mutual respect.

8 Dependability as participant in faculty planning and decision making.

9 Dedication to furthering the effectiveness of the teaching profession.

10 Generosity in contributing talents to community welfare and improvement.

CONCLUDING COMMENTS

The emphasis in this chapter has been on the teacher. We have looked at complex issues involved in finding answers to questions such as: "What is a good teacher?" "What is a good school?" and "Are there any specific characteristics which set apart effective language arts teachers from those who are not as effective?" While we have not been able to provide you with the definitive answers to each question, you have been given information to think about as you search for answers. As you reflect on these questions, you will begin to formulate a teaching philosophy which will help you become a teacher who is capable of making sound educational decisions.

BIBLIOGRAPHY AND REFERENCES

1 Berliner, David C. "Using Research on Teaching for the Improvement of Classroom Practice." *Theory into Practice,* vol. 19, Autumn 1980, p. 306.

2 Brophy, Jere E. "Teacher Behavior and Student Learning." *Educational Leadership,* vol. 37, October 1979, pp. 33–38.

3 Cook, Gillian E. "Artisans or Education? The NCTE Statement on the Preparation of Teachers of Language Arts." *Language Arts,* vol. 58, January 1981, pp. 51–57.

4 Cruickshank, Donald R. "Synthesis of Selected Recent Research on Teacher Effects." *Journal of Teacher Education,* vol. 27, Spring 1976, pp. 57–60.

5 DiMartino, C. J. "Observer Effects on Teacher Verbal Behavior as Perceived by Students." Ph.D. dissertation, University of Georgia, 1974.

6 Good, Thomas L. "Teacher Effectiveness in the Elementary School." *Journal of Teacher Education,* vol. 30, March–April 1979, pp. 52–64.

7 Griffiths, Daniel E. "The Effective Teacher." New York: Teacher Education Conference Board. Position Paper, October 1981.

8 Heilman, Arthur W., Blair, Timothy R., and Rupley, William H. *Principles and Practices of Teaching Reading* (5th ed.). Columbus, Ohio: Charles E. Merrill, 1981.

9 Heyns, R., and Lippett, A. "Observation of Group Behavior." In Leon Festinger and Daniel Katz (eds.), *Research Methods in the Behavioral Sciences.* New York: Dryden Press, 1953, pp. 380–417.

10 Hursh, H. "A Pilot Project to Examine Whether Teachers 'Turn on' Only When Observers are Present." Paper presented at the annual meeting of the American Psychological Association, New Orleans, Aug. 30–Sept. 3, 1974.

11 Jersild, A., and Meigs, M. "Direct Observation as a Research Method." *Review of Educational Research,* vol. 9, December 1939, pp. 472–482.

12 McDonald, Frederick J. "Report on Phase II of the Beginning Teacher Evaluation Study." *Journal of Teacher Education,* vol. 27, Spring 1976, pp. 39–42.

13 McIntyre, D. John. "Administrator's Dilemma: Teacher Evaluation and the Observer Effect." NASSP Bulletin, vol. 64, March 1980, pp. 36–40.

14 Medley, Donald M. *Teacher Competence and Teacher Effectiveness, A Review of Process–Product Research.* Washington, D.C.: American Association of Colleges of Teacher Education, 1977, p. 6.

15 Medley, D. M., and Mitzel, H. E. "Measuring Classroom Behavior by Systematic Observation." In N. L. Gage (ed.), *Handbook of Research on Teaching,* vol. 1. Chicago: Rand McNally, 1963, pp. 247–328.

16 Molnar, Alex. "Reading and Values." In James B. Macdonald (compiler and ed.), *Social Perspectives on Reading: Social Influences and Reading Achievement.* Newark, Del.: International Reading Association, 1973, pp. 62–74.

17 NCTE Committee on Teacher Preparation and Certification. "A Statement on the Preparation of Teachers of English." *English Education,* vol. 7, Summer 1976, pp. 195–210.

18 Rosenshine, Barak V. "Academic Engaged Time, Content Covered, and Direct Instruction." Paper presented at the American Education Research Association annual meeting, New York, 1977.

19 Rosenshine, Barak V. "Recent Research on Teaching Behaviors and Student Achievement." *Journal of Teacher Education,* vol. 27, Spring 1976, p. 61.

20 Roy, Will. "Reading, Bureaucracy, and Individual Adaptation. In James B. Macdonald (compiler and ed.), *Social Perspectives on Reading: Social Influences and Reading Achievement."* Newark, Del.: International Reading Association, 1973, pp. 40–52.

21 Rupley, William H., and Blair, Timothy R. "Characteristics of Effective Reading Instruction." *Educational Leadership,* vol. 29, December 1978, pp. 171–173.

22 Samph, T. "Observer Effects on Teacher Behavior." Ph.D. dissertation, University of Michigan, 1968.

23 Shuy, Roger W. "What the Teacher Knows Is More Important Than Text or Test." *Language Arts,* vol. 58, November–December 1981, pp. 919–929.

24 Smith, Nancy M. "A Comparison of the Language Arts Block with the Departmentalized Organization for Language Arts in Grades Six and Seven in Aiken County, South Carolina." Ed.D. dissertation, University of South Carolina, 1981.

25 Wade, Eugene W. "The Construction and Validation of Ten Teacher Skills Used in Reading Instruction, Grades 2–5." Ph.D. dissertation, Indiana University, 1960.

26 Weber, G. "Inner-City Children Can Be Taught to Read: Four Successful Schools." Council for Basic Education, Washington, D.C., Occasional Paper 18, 1971.

27 Zahorik, John. "Reading The Impact of Classroom Interaction." In James B. Macdonald (compiler and ed.), *Social Perspectives on Reading: Social Influences and Reading Achievement.* Newark, Del.: International Reading Association, 1973, pp. 55–61.

CHAPTER 10

THE LANGUAGE ARTS PROGRAM

One of us recently conducted an inservice meeting for teachers in a rather large school district. At the culmination of the session, an attempt was made to have a discussion focusing on language arts programs. The majority of those in attendance showed virtually no interest in the topic. Finally, one brave individual said: "Programs don't mean much to me. Most of these programs are light years removed from what I teach." While that teacher's forthrightness may be commendable, we strongly disagree with his viewpoint.

Language arts programs and classroom instruction are not islands unto themselves. The development and implementation of an effective language arts program is dependent upon teachers and quality classroom instruction. Similarly, a language arts program should serve as a statement of the intended learning outcomes toward which teaching should be directed and the knowledge, attitudes, and skills which should be acquired by students. Thus, language arts programs and classroom teaching are *dependent on,* not independent of, one another.

PROGRAM ANALYSIS

Does your school have an effective language arts program? If you are presently teaching and have answered the preceding question, write down what led you to respond as you did. If you are preparing to become a teacher, we suggest you visit an elementary or middle school and pose our question to teachers and/or administrators in the school. Find out why they answered as they did.

For a reader of this chapter who is preparing to become a teacher, a discussion of a language arts program may seem somewhat removed from your role as a teacher.

Such is not the case. A language arts program represents the end to which your daily classroom efforts will be directed. Materials will be selected on the basis of it, teaching processes will be advocated in order to attain its objectives, and evaluations of language arts instruction will be based upon it. In essence, knowledge of language arts programs in general (as well as the one in the school in which you will teach) is quite important to your subsequent success as a teacher of the language arts.

In working with several schools, we find that dissatisfaction with a set of language arts materials is frequently the reason some have negative perceptions about "a program." Although the language arts series used in a school may represent the language arts program to many teachers and administrators, a series should not represent the program in toto. A language arts series should represent a *component* of a program.

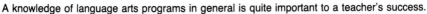

A knowledge of language arts programs in general is quite important to a teacher's success.

As such, it should serve as a vehicle for aiding teachers in their efforts to provide instruction for certain aspects of a program.

If the merit of a language arts series is not a legitimate criterion for deciding whether or not a language arts program is effective, you may be wondering what the correct measures for making this judgment are. Principally, there are two major factors: testing and perceptions. An explanation of these follows.

Testing

At present, there is great emphasis upon achievement test results in our nation's schools. Particularly in the so-called basic subjects—reading, language arts, and mathematics— the performance of each child is closely monitored to determine the amount of progress being made in the respective area. Parents wish to know if their children are above grade level, local school officials compare their students' achievement with that of adjacent districts, and states supply legislators with reports on how their students stack up against regional and national standards. In each of the aforementioned instances, the pressure is great to exceed "the average" standard of achievement.

The merits of this emphasis is a subject of conjecture. Some contend that achievement tests provide a school with extremely valuable information. For schools whose students perform well on such measures, it could be argued that data derived from such tests give the schools concrete evidence that their language arts programs are quality ones and are satisfying their aims.

Standardized language arts achievement tests have received criticism from numerous educators. For example, in discussing standardized testing in language arts, Petty and Jensen (12) state: "Many aspects of language use are difficult to measure, however. In fact, at the present time, some aspects are impossible to measure objectively, as standardized tests seek to do." In addition to this deficiency, the validity and interpretation of standardized achievement tests in the language arts have been areas of criticism.

Should testing be used to assess the effectiveness of a school's language arts program? Our answer to that question is *yes*. However, we may need to clarify our response. First, it should be remembered that there are myriad types of tests—essay, diagnostic, informal, and others—which can be used in schools. Standardized tests, of course, are merely one of the entire array of assessment measures.

Second, it is generally conceded that standardized tests measure mechanical aspects, such as spelling and capitalization, adequately, but are relatively ineffective in assessing the language usage abilities of children. Clearly, then, if a comprehensive assessment of a program is to occur, standardized tests will have to be supplemented by other types of devices in areas standardized tests alone do not measure adequately. In many schools, another excellent resource for evaluation exists. The classroom records maintained by teachers will indicate the students' progress made relative to the attainment of specific language arts objectives. Therefore, an evaluation should utilize informal measures such as worksheets, interviews, checklists, and classroom and cumulative records, as well as standardized language arts measures.

Finally, a program should not be revised in order to conform to the components of a battery of tests. Cronbach (3) reminds us that testing "should fit the content of the curriculum."

Testing can provide teachers and school officials with valuable information about the strengths and deficiencies of their language arts program. Care should be taken to choose the best types of tests from the entire range available. These devices should "match" the major programmatic objectives. If properly selected, implemented, and interpreted, testing can serve as a yardstick for measuring *what is* against *what is desired* in student achievement in the language arts.

Perceptions

Tests do not constitute the sole basis upon which judgments about a language arts program are made. Frequently, testing occurs to "prove" that a program is "bad." Care should be taken to ensure that an evaluation of a program does not become a witch hunt. When performance is less than expected, it should be approached in a positive manner—consideration of circumstances, past achievement, and so forth—so that proper revisions will be made in the future. This will serve the public's demand for accountability while fostering programmatic quality.

How does the viewpoint that a program needs revision develop? Frequently it materializes, officially or by word of mouth, from one or more of the following groups: parents, teachers, administrators, or community members.

Are the viewpoints of the group advocating programmatic revision valid? Is the negative perception widely held, or is it the opinion of a vocal minority? What *specific* aspects of the language arts program need revision? These and other comparable questions must be posed—and answered—in order to make *correct* judgments about the current language arts program.

As part of a language arts program's regular evaluation process, mechanisms should be built in to ensure that *responsible* groups (such as teachers and parents) have the opportunity to express their views about the program. The perceptions of these groups can serve at least two purposes. First, their reactions can help school personnel decide if there are problems with the current program. Second, their perceptions can be looked at to see if there are areas within the program that can be changed or strengthened to make it even better. This may entail the use of simple and/or complex reporting measures.

For example, a question may be posed, verbally or in writing, to a group, such as: Do you feel our school's language arts program is an effective one? If the overwhelming majority of those questioned respond with a "yes," your job may be completed. However, should the majority respond with a "no" to this question, an attempt should be made to ascertain the reason(s) for the dissatisfaction with the present program.

From a time usage standpoint, a follow-up questionnaire should be constructed and administered. Numerous books have been written on the subject of the construction of questionnaires and their interpretation, so we will not dwell on this subject here. However, the following may aid in designing a questionnaire (13):

1 Are the forms simple and easy to understand? Are directions and items clear?
2 Does the questionnaire cover pertinent information?

3 Is it easy to compile information from the instrument for a final report?
4 Does the instrument collect different types of data in a similar format?
5 Is it a positive instrument? Are the statements conveyed positively?
6 Will resulting data be useful for program revision and future planning?

If properly done, a questionnaire or interview focusing upon the major goals and elements of a language arts program can yield valuable information. Such data frequently will point out serious deficiencies in a program, and/or confirm or refute the suppositions some entertained about a program.

Analysis

Now let us return to the question asked at the beginning of this section. Does the school have an effective language arts program? As you will recall, we requested that the previous question be answered and the reasons which led you to your response be given.

In most instances, an assessment of a language arts program was probably based upon a single factor. For example, the response may have been predicated upon student scores on an achievement test or what was "heard" from others about the program. While one's answer may be correct, the basis upon which the question was answered was not.

Decisions about a program should be made as a result of a *comprehensive* evaluation process. Robinson and Rauch (14) contend that there are two purposes for evaluating a program: (1) "to ensure the adopted objectives of the program are being met;" and (2) "to ascertain the progress of students." In order to achieve these results, an evaluation should employ a variety of standardized as well as informal measures which assess the salient features of a program. More will be said about these devices later in this chapter.

Program evaluation also involves the collection of subjective information about a program. Data derived from this form of assessment may confirm a hypothesis about a program or suggest facets of the program which need to be analyzed further.

Testing and the perceptions held about a program are both important. At times, both will indicate that a program is effective or that revision is needed. At other times, the results from one will improve the other. For example, knowledge of test results may make teachers feel more positively about their language arts program. Similarly, after dissatisfaction is expressed with composition practices in a school, more comprehensive testing may take place and results may show that the present program is inadequate in this respect.

Let us assume that an analysis of a program indicates that it needs to be revised. In the next section of this chapter, we will discuss how to make these modifications.

PROGRAM DEVELOPMENT

Determining that a language arts program needs modification is an important decision. Deciding who will be responsible for making these revisions is equally important. As for who should participate in this phase, it is recommended that "individuals who are to be involved in a reorganization directly affecting them, and upon whom the ultimate reorganization depends, should actively participate in the process of change" (2). Clearly, then, this programmatic revision should include teacher, administrator, and community member representation.

After determining who will play a primary role in shaping the program's revision, the precise nature of the programmatic improvement must be delineated. Specifically, the committee must decide whether the entire language arts program is to be studied or merely segments of it, such as grades four through six, or the composition skills to be acquired. There is no magic formula to be followed, but the guidelines offered by Mangieri, Bader, and Walker (10) for revising a reading program also seem applicable to the task of altering a language arts program:

1 A program should not be revised merely for the sake of change or for punitive purposes. The program should not be implemented in order to punish teachers or to focus publicly on their deficiencies. Rather, improvement should be the reason for programmatic change. Remember that individuals are more likely to support a change when they understand why it is being proposed.

2 The committee responsible for planning revisions in a reading program should have adequate teacher representation. The teachers selected or elected for the committee should be chosen on the basis of their professional competence and the contributions which they can make to the committee.

3 Since teachers are responsible for the implementation of the changes being planned, the differences among teachers should be kept in mind. Teachers differ in their experience, expertise, intelligence, and motivation and in the types of positions they occupy. Programmatic changes that are being considered should be realistically evaluated in terms of whether the teachers have the skill and the desire necessary to implement them.

4 As programmatic changes are being considered, care must be taken to ensure that the modifications will not conflict with the other goals and programs within the school. Such potential conflicts should be resolved *prior* to the implementation of the revised program. In addition, the program should not become so extensive that a teacher has little time for other aspects of the curriculum.

5 A committee to revise a reading program must be afforded enough time to accomplish the job. Revising a reading program is an arduous task that can consume as much time as is needed to plan a program. Given normal conditions, a reading program cannot be significantly revised by a committee after one hour's work or after a single meeting. Usually, several meetings, held over numerous weeks time, will be needed to accomplish this task.

Some of the committee's activities may be conducted after school, but released time from regular teaching or administrative duties must be given to the committee's members. Incentives such as release from certain duties or remuneration for service can be effective in getting maximum effort from the committee.

6 As many persons as possible should be involved in the process of revising an elementary school reading program. This is not meant to imply that all should have an equal amount of responsibility. Some teachers will have a greater role in the change process than others. Every teacher who will be affected by the revised program should be part of the process of revision. There will then be a greater likelihood that a sense of ownership of the new program will develop and that teachers will support the revised program.

7 Remember that evaluation is an integral part of programmatic change. Evaluation makes the need for specific changes apparent. The question of how revised parts of the program will later be evaluated should be considered. The committee responsible for revising the program should answer the question: How will we be able to show whether or not the changes improved our school's reading program?

Two additional cautions should be offered at this time. First, *do not examine instructional materials until after the program revision is completed.* A school or district should determine the objectives of its language arts program and then find teaching materials compatible with the program. In other words, the program precedes materials. Unfortunately, in many instances, the commercial language arts materials determine what the program is to be.

Second, *remember that the process of program revision is a complex task.* Visits should be made to schools considered to have quality language arts programs. While these visits can provide program developers with excellent ideas about their own program, schools should not attempt to emulate another district's language arts program exactly. Although it may be effective at that site, the entire program will probably be inappropriate for another setting. Mangieri and Corboy (9) say: "Among the reasons for the mismatch may be deficiencies in: personnel training and motivation; student population; instructional setting; available fiscal and programmatic resources; and, community socioeconomic constituency."

Resources

In revising or developing a language arts program, there are several legitimate sources to aid individuals in their efforts. We have previously discussed school visitations to see other quality language arts programs in operation. There are other resources available such as professional literature, professional organization guidelines, and school curriculum guides. Each of these will be subsequently discussed.

Professional Literature At the present time, people interested in the language arts have a plethora of professional literature available to them. There are many fine textbooks which deal with pedagogical, philosophical, and curricular aspects of the language arts. The National Council of Teachers of English regularly publishes materials of significance to the field of language arts. These materials are in addition to its fine, regularly published professional journals: *Language Arts* and the *English Journal.* Also, articles dealing with the language arts regularly appear in publications such as *The Reading Teacher,* the *Journal of Reading,* the *Elementary School Journal,* and the *National Association of School Principals' Bulletin.*

Professional research which focuses directly or implicitly on the language arts should also be read. While it would be almost impossible to cite each available source, many

Visiting other classrooms may help teachers in revising their own programs.

current research investigations in the language arts can be located in *The Education Index, The Reading Research Quarterly,* and *The Journal of Educational Research.* Significant research is also being conducted in curricular and instructional areas which affect the language arts. For example, learning modality research (4), learning investigations (7), and studies of effective schooling (16) should be examined by those seeking programmatic improvement. We also suggest you examine books which deal totally or partially with the areas of curriculum planning (6), evaluation (17), and language arts instruction (5, 11).

Professional Bodies   Currently numerous publications are available from professional associations at the state and national levels as well as from state departments of education which pertain to the language arts. These materials focus upon curricular planning and ingredients, teaching approaches and techniques, instructional materials, evaluations, and many other comparable topics.

At the state level, probably the best sources from which to seek assistance in order to identify available publications would be your state chapter of the National Council of Teachers of English and of the International Reading Association. In addition, the language arts division or consultant from your state department of education is likely to be able to provide you with assistance.

Illustrative of the type of material available from professional organizations is the National Council of Teachers of English's "Criteria for Planning and Evaluation of English Language Arts Curriculum Guides (Revised)" (18). These criteria are shown in Appendix 10-1.

Schools   Earlier in this chapter, we recommended that visiting other school districts may foster ideas about a school's own language arts program. In addition, professionals responsible for program revision may also wish to consult with individuals from other school districts. They may wish to "pick their brains" about how the program was developed, programmatic ingredients, problems encountered or anticipated, evaluation, or any of the 1001 other matters which seem to arise during this phase. The ideas offered by these persons are merely that; they should represent *possible* courses of action. What is best for a district must be determined by those within that district.

School districts can aid program development efforts in yet another way. Since these agencies are daily involved in the implementation of programs in classrooms, they can provide excellent examples of the type(s) of written matter which must be formulated for that to occur.

In the appendixes to this chapter, you will find a rationale of a language arts curriculum (Appendix 10-2), a course of studies for a language arts program at the third-grade level (Appendix 10-3), and a language arts checklist for grade eight (Appendix 10-4). These materials were developed by the Norfolk (Virginia) Public Schools, the Muskingum (Ohio) County Public Schools, and the Prince George's County (Maryland) Public Schools, respectively.

Devices such as the checklist shown in Appendix 10-4 typically serve one or more of the following purposes: (1) to provide a teacher with a record of the objectives a student has attained, (2) to serve as a reporting instrument to parents of their childrens' achievements, (3) to engage students in self-evaluation of their language arts efforts. Checklists also can aid in coordinating the language arts program from grade to grade and from the elementary school to middle and secondary school levels.

IMPLEMENTATION

After deciding how a language arts program is to be revised and what its new constituents will be, it is time to implement it in classrooms. The planned changes will not occur on their own. In order for them to make a positive difference in classroom instruction and learning, certain steps must be followed.

Of paramount importance to the revised program's future success is the awareness of the district's or school's faculty, administrators, and community members of the precise nature of the "new" program. Although Mangieri (8) is speaking here about secondary reading programs, his words also hold true for revised language arts programs:

> It is imperative that information about a secondary school reading program be shared with the entire faculty. Teachers should be apprised about what the program encompasses, what it hopes to accomplish, and what, if any, role they can, or are expected to, play in the program. The author cannot overemphasize the importance of a well-informed faculty if a secondary school reading program is to be successful. The degree to which they are knowledgeable may very well determine whether faculty members are valuable allies of the program or fierce adversaries of it (8).

Knowledge of the program on the part of teachers, administrators, and faculty is the first step to making its implementation successful. After teachers are made cognizant of the revised program, it is also quite likely that they will need to receive additional training in order to employ the program with students. Usually, this training occurs as part of a school district's inservice efforts.

Anyone familiar with education knows that inservice programs can either make a meaningful contribution to a district or be a waste of time, energy, and money. We recommend adherence, to the degree possible, to the following six principles for effective inservice education:

1 Teachers are more likely to benefit from inservice programs in which they can choose goals and activities, as contrasted with programs in which the goals and activities are preplanned for them.

2 Teachers are more likely to be influenced in school-based training programs than in those taking place on college campuses.

3 The objectives of an inservice program should be specific teaching performances or outcomes.

4 Training programs that have different training experiences are more likely to accomplish their objectives than programs that have common activities required for all participants.

5 The teacher's personal goals and needs and those of the school should be congruent if training is to improve school system operations significantly.

6 Training related to job assignments is most effective if adequate time is provided within the current work schedule for each activity (1).

The preceding generalizations can aid in planning an inservice program. A caution should also be offered. Inservice customarily takes place prior to a program's inception. Sometimes forgotten, however, is that inservice and opportunities for dialogue about a program should be planned *while* the program is being implemented. Such sessions will go a long way in helping the revised program to be a success.

FINAL COMMENTS

In this chapter, several points have been made about language arts programs. Hopefully, the relevance of a program to classroom instruction has been established. Also, although some may perceive of program revision as merely changing a language arts series, we hope you realize that this is a shortsighted and erroneous approach to program development. The process of analyzing and improving a school's language arts program can bring the positive results which a school district desires for its students.

A school would be abdicating its responsibility if it did not offer the best possible language arts program for its students. As Savage (15) correctly contends: "Language is crucial to living and learning in all areas. Children's effectiveness in dealing with language will largely determine their effectiveness in dealing with their entire school experience. The key subject, the core, the foundation, of the elementary school curriculum is language arts."

APPENDIX 10-1: CRITERIA FOR PLANNING AND EVALUATION OF ENGLISH LANGUAGE ARTS CURRICULUM GUIDES (REVISED)

INTRODUCTION

To perform the task of curriculum evaluating, the Committee on Curriculum Bulletins has developed and repeatedly revised its "Criteria for Planning and Evaluation of Curriculum Guides," trying to keep up with trends set by the best curriculum practitioners. These criteria were established with several objectives in mind. First, with these criteria each member of the Committee has a uniform tool which he can use to evaluate the curriculum guide. In line with this first objective, the subcommittee that developed the criteria felt that each guide should be evaluated as a unique guide, not directly compared to other guides throughout the United States. Secondly, the criteria serve to help schools and other educational agencies develop and evaluate curricula designed to guide teachers. The Committee also hopes that the criteria will be a possible change agent. The evaluation instrument was designed to apply to many different content emphases within the field of English-language studies, along with the learning process, organization, methodology, and language versatility. The criteria and the annotation are a kind of synthesis set of Utopian standards with definite biases that the Committee readily acknowledges. So far no single guide has "met" the standards for the criteria.

School districts wishing to have guides evaluated should mail one copy to the NCTE Committee on Curriculum Bulletins, 1111 Kenyon Road, Urbana, Illinois 61801. It would help the Committee to have in addition a statement containing information about the development of the guide, the nature of the school population and community, and the guide's relationship to other curriculum materials in use. The evaluation process normally takes from four to eight weeks. There is no charge for this service.

PHILOSOPHY: WHAT WE SUBSCRIBE TO

This guide . . .

1 has a statement of philosophy that coherently explores the beliefs of teachers about students and subject matter.

Philosophy is what we believe, and it's a good thing to get out in the open.

2 has content that follows logically and consistently from its statement of philosophy.
If a philosophy doesn't guide decision-making, it's largely useless.
3 promotes a natural, organic integration of language arts experiences.
Things ought to go together.
4 encourages teachers to view language both as a subject and as a communicative process central to all human life and learning.
Language is primarily a living process, not an artifact.
5 stipulates that individual processes of language development and concept development take precedence over arbitrary grade level expectancies or requirements.
The best chance for stimulating learning is to start where the kids are.
6 expresses the belief that the English program should aid students in planning, executing, and evaluating their learning experiences both individually and in groups.
Who's it for anyway? Complete involvement in the process is ideal.
7 suggests that teaching and learning are cooperative, not competitive, activities in the classroom.
Nobody ever really wins. The business of the classroom is cooperation: between teachers and students, and students and students.
8 indicates that successful experiences in language development are essential for all students.
Success comes in all colors, shapes, and sizes. All kids need to succeed in school.

POLICIES AND PROCEDURES: HOW WE OPERATE

This plan . . .

1 helps free teachers by explaining their responsibilities and by suggesting the possibilities open to them.
School systems usually have expectations and it's a good thing for teachers to know their options.
2 states procedures for both individual and group decision-making on such matters as selecting and ordering materials, equipment, and services.
The nuts and bolts ought to be specified, not just guessed at.
3 supports the view that curriculum building is an ongoing process.
Curriculum, like kids, keeps changing—or at least it should. There ought to be a plan and somebody to make sure it happens.
4 reflects the interaction and cooperation of members of the total educational community.
Everybody should have a say, and they ought to be listened to.
5 encourages continual inservice training and professional improvement for all teachers.
Change is continuous, as is the learning process.

OBJECTIVES: WHAT WE HOPE WILL HAPPEN

This guide . . .

1 has objectives that follow directly from the philosophy.
"What you see is what you get!"
2 sets clear objectives for all the major components of the English curriculum.
Say what you want to happen so that it makes sense to you and anybody who reads it.
3 states objectives in a manner which facilitates recognition and description of progress.
An objective can be a useful thing if it helps you to focus on what kids do.

4 distinguishes teacher objectives from student objectives.

What teachers do should be differentiated from what students do.

5 recognizes that many objectives are desirable even though progress toward them may not be conveniently observed nor accurately measured.

Restriction to a limited set of precise objectives can unduly inhibit learning and teaching. Some goals are reached only very gradually, almost imperceptibly, and some processes are not easily broken into steps or levels of achievement.

6 recognizes that cognitive and affective behavior are inseparable in actual experience.

Thoughts and feelings interact continuously.

7 contains objectives for improving language performance, as well as perceiving more clearly what others do with language.

Language is a game for playing as well as watching. You learn to do something by doing it, not by sitting on the sidelines.

ORGANIZATION: HOW WE CHANNEL THE FLOW OF ENERGY

This plan . . .

1 makes clear how particular units, lessons, and/or procedures are related to the total English program.

Connections need to be made now and then. It helps if you have some idea how things might fit together and make sense.

2 suggests a possible workable sequence of basic communication skills.

A suggested logical order is helpful even if it can't always be followed by particular children.

3 organizes major aspects of the language arts to provide directions for planning.

Themes are a pretty good way to organize a curriculum but not the only way.

4 regards textbook materials, if used, as resources rather than courses of study.

Textbooks don't equal the curriculum—at least not in the best programs. Teachers and kids and parents are the real resources.

5 suggests a variety of classroom organizations and activities to accommodate various kinds of learning.

Classrooms are not conveyor belts in the factory of learning. It's the things that happen on the way that count.

6 supplies specific procedures which will enable teachers to help their students to become increasingly independent.

Dependency is learned, but so is independence.

7 reflects the principle that the students themselves should often generate learning activities.

Kids are natural learners who sometimes learn to be uncurious and unquestioning. They learn when we let them.

PROCESS AS CONTENT:
THE WAYS THAT STUDENTS EXPERIENCE

This guide . . .

1 distinguishes between conventional "expository" teaching methods and "discovery," "inductive," or "inquiry" methods.

No method is sacred; each is useful for a different purpose. In many schools, however, more emphasis needs to be placed on inquiry.

2 contains activities that have a "problems" or "questions" focus.

Documents from the past or problems from the present or future should often be used to promote training in inquiry.

3 arranges its inquiry approach so that students gain confidence in their problem-solving abilities.

An "inquiry attitude" is learned through successive and successful encounters with problems that can be solved.

4 indicates methods to promote cooperative interaction among students.

Classroom experiences should provide guided practice in group dynamics.

5 has strategies to encourage each student to discover and extend his own ways of perceiving and learning.

Because each student has a unique perception of experience, it is essential for him to develop his own growing analytic and creative powers.

6 stipulates ways to focus conscious attention on the processes of inquiry and learning.

Inquiry processes—learning how to learn—are probably the most important activities that students and their teachers can engage in.

LANGUAGE

This guide . . .

1 suggests that the content of language study often comes from real life.

Language is as real and personal as each individual.

2 provides for study of conventional areas of linguistics.

Linguistics, as usually taken up in schools, includes semantics, history of language, grammars, regional dialects, social dialects, lexicography, and kinesics (body language).

3 suggests study of unique customs of specific language areas.

The "languages" of advertising, politics, religion, and many other human activities are worth studying. Teachers need to ask the right questions about the ways these languages work.

4 provides for frequent imaginative use of language in student-created and student-moderated groups.

Improvised drama, role-playing, task groups, and brainstorming are ways that kids can explore language. Imagine what it would be like if. . . . Then talk it out.

5 reflects knowledge of current or recent developments in modern language theory.

Some of the new grammars work better than the old ones because they describe our language more precisely.

6 suggests activities that help students learn the difference between grammar and usage.

Grammar is primarily the study of language structure; usage is the study of the values we attach to pronunciations, vocabulary, and particular conventions.

7 recognizes that analysis of language, as in grammar study, does not necessarily improve performance in composing.

The analysis of grammar is different from processes of composing.

8 recognizes the assets of bidialectal, bilingual, and non-English-speaking children in exploring language concepts.

We live in a pluralistic society.

9 suggests activities that help students acquire or expand their facility to understand and use the English language.

The basis for all language is experience.

10 recognizes the importance of children accepting their "home-rooted" language, as well as that of others.

Positive self-concepts help kids to become more "open" people.

COMPOSITION: HOW WE SHAPE LANGUAGE AND OURSELVES

This guide . . .

1 perceives composing as occurring in four ways: speaking, writing, acting, and filming.
Composing requires an orchestration of experience. There are different ways to say things, and all are worthy of investigation.
2 emphasizes the significance of composing as a means of self-discovery.
E. M. Forster said, "How can I know what I think 'til I hear what I say?"
3 recognizes the importance of the composing processes as ways of bringing order to human experience.
Composing is a way to make sense of our world.
4 has activities designed to stimulate composing.
Precomposing experiences, if important to kids, can help stimulate more worthwhile writing.
5 recommends that composing should often occur in small groups.
Kids can help each other shape their thinking.
6 affirms that composing is always creative.
7 suggests that composing stems from meaningful precomposing experiences.
The better the input, the better the output. Creation requires stimulation.
8 recommends that composition should occur for different purposes and usually for audiences other than the teacher.
Decisions about communication ought to be determined by something more than the teacher's grade book. Authenticity is a function of knowing whom you're talking to and why.
9 recommends that composing should occur in an atmosphere of maximum sharing.
Let kids help each other.

MEDIA: "THE MEDIUM IS THE MESSAGE"

This guide . . .

1 promotes audiovisual as well as verbal literacy.
Students need to explore the relationships among visual, verbal, and kinesthetic communication.
2 acquaints teachers with the characteristics and potential use of various media.
The electronic age is with us. Are we with it?
3 suggests ways of involving students in using media.
A pen and ink is just one voice. Kids need the options of communicating with color, motion, and sound.
4 suggests specific media supplements for learning activities.
The media are like extension cords; they plug into a wider world.
5 lists media resources available to teachers, and specifies procurement procedures.
What's available and how do you get it? Media doesn't get used unless it's accessible.

READING AND LITERATURE: THE WORLDS STUDENTS EXPERIENCE

This guide . . .

1 provides ways for the teacher to determine individual degrees of readiness.
Shakespeare said, "The readiness is all."

2 suggests procedures to help teachers develop student reading skills.

The "teaching of reading" means more than having a few books around.

3 recognizes that a total reading program reaches beyond the developing of basic reading skills.

A person really never stops learning how to read. There are always new skills to learn.

4 relates the skills of reading to a total language program.

Reading, writing, listening, and speaking are more like a web than like four peas in a pod. You touch one strand of language experience, and the whole thing vibrates and responds.

5 makes provisions for a comprehensive literature program.

Get a lot of books of all kinds in kids' hands.

6 recognizes that it is more important to "engage in" literature than to talk about terms.

Literary terms, conventions, and systems of classification are inventions of the profession. If talk about these externals is substituted for experience with literature, we "murder to dissect," as Wordsworth put it.

7 recommends that teachers allow and encourage students to select and read all types of literature, especially contemporary.

Take the lid off the reading list, and let kids explore.

8 helps teachers to identify, accept, and explore all varieties of affective and cognitive response.

What kids say about literature is important, and so is how they feel about it. Our efforts should be devoted to helping kids extend and deepen their responses.

9 suggests acting and role playing as a means of exploring literature.

Literature is frozen drama. Whenever you get your body into the language of a poem or story, you're interpreting it.

EVALUATION: DISCOVERING AND DESCRIBING WHERE WE ARE

This guide . . .

1 has a coherent and useful rationale for evaluation.

The rationale should be related to philosophy and objectives. The reporting policy should be explicit.

2 stipulates that reporting procedures describe pupil progress, including growth beyond the scope of stated objectives.

Teachers and students should not feel inhibited by narrowly specified objectives. "The asides are essential to the insides."

3 makes clear that grades and standardized tests, if used, do not constitute the major purpose of evaluation.

Marks and scores are not ends; the end of evaluation should be information useful for furthering achievement.

4 suggests methods of evaluation which help to encourage a pupil, not to discourage him.

Teachers should encourage and respect any progress a pupil makes rather than punish or badger him for any apparent lack of progress.

5 helps teachers diagnose individual learning progress and suggests methods and material to accomplish this.

Each pupil learns in a different way at a differing rate from other pupils.

6 suggests that most evaluation be tailored to the students' ability, age, and personality.

Evaluation should be adapted to people, not vice versa. If evaluation is primarily for helping individuals learn, and if differences are at least acknowledged, then evaluation should be individualized.

7 recognizes that the student must be involved in all evaluation.

Self-evaluation is crucial to learning.

8 suggests ways that teachers and students can use the results of evaluation to change the program as often as necessary.

The ideal curriculum is tentative, flexible, and responsive to the results of continual evaluation.

DESIGN: FORM, FUNCTION, AND FLAVOR

This guide . . .

1 is easy to read; the language is clear and effective.

Guide writers should set a good example in communicating; our medium has a message.

2 exhibits an appealing form and style.

An attractive and creative guide will stimulate use.

3 has a format which makes revision convenient.

A looseleaf format makes a guide more amenable to change.

4 states its relationship to any other curriculum guides published by the school system.

Sometimes new teachers have a better idea of what's going on when curriculum relationships are explicit.

5 suggests as resources a large variety of specific background materials and school services.

A guide, to be useful, has got to have useable things in it.

6 identifies people and procedures which will promote interdisciplinary activities.

We can build walls around ourselves with labels like English, social studies, and science.

APPENDIX 10-2: RATIONALE OF A LANGUAGE ARTS CURRICULUM

The Norfolk Public Schools Language Arts Curriculum incorporates the following goals:

1 Use of a positive approach to language processes, both oral and written.

2 Presentation of language in context rather than in isolation.

3 Continuation of successful learning strategies mastered by children before formal schooling: association, patternings, experimentation.

4 Application of understandings related to the interaction of language and thought.

5 Development of students' thought processes rather than knowledge of arbitrary labels.

6 Development of students' understanding of their own intuitive language processes.

7 Enhancement of oral language competence as an important aid to reading and writing proficiency.

8 Use of cognitive stages which stress the systematic elements of language.

9 Promotion of teachers' understanding of syntax, semantics, and phonology developing in sequential and spiral processes.

10 Utilization of each component of the language arts—listening, speaking, reading, and writing—as a complement and reinforcement.

Reprinted with the permission of the Norfolk Public Schools, Norfolk, Va.

APPENDIX 10-3: LANGUAGE ARTS COURSE OF STUDIES FOR THIRD GRADE

INTRODUCTION

This Language Arts Course of Study has been prepared to provide quality educational programs for students. The course of study identifies the skills and concepts teachers are responsible for teaching, gives parents and teachers a picture of what will be covered, and assures continuity to the educational program.

Serving as a working guide to give direction for lesson planning and selection of instructional materials, it is not intended to define or limit the teaching style or approach. That opportunity of choice is left to individual teachers.

This course of study reflects a set of agreements of what is essential to an effective language arts program and communicates those objectives to administrators, teachers, students and the community.

DEFINITION OF SYMBOLS USED

I Introduce—exposure/awareness of skill
D Develop—practice/use of skill
M Master—knowledge of skill at level of application
R Reinforce—reapplication and maintenance

THIRD-GRADE READING

Program Objectives

The student will demonstrate an ability to read with comprehension, discrimination, enjoyment and continued interest and learning.

The student will develop an awareness that reading creates a positive self-concept and understanding of others.

Word Attack   The student will be able to:

M   recognize final consonant sounds of words.
M   identify short vowels and short vowel rules.
M   recognize and read all Dolch words.
M   identify and write consonant blends and diagraphs.
M   apply medial sounds to the printed word.
M   pronounce r-controlled vowel sounds.
M   apply the final e generalization to the printed word.
M   identify and apply compound words.
D/M recognize and identify assigned sight words.
D   identify and apply contractions.

Reprinted with the permission of the Muskingum County Public Schools, Zanesville, Ohio.

D   recognize, identify and apply plurals.
D   classify words and phrases.
D   identify consonant variant sounds.
D   develop and recognize diphthongs.
D   recognize silent letters.
D   identify and use base words and endings.
D   identify and apply abbreviations.
D   use multiple meanings of words.
D   use context clues within a reading selection.
D   recognize and use homonyms, synonyms, and antonyms.
D   recognize and use syllables and apply to word structure.
D   understand and use possessive forms of words.

Comprehension   The student will be able to:

Literal
D describe and explain an illustration.
D recognize and interpret punctuation and special print in context.
D follow oral and written directions.
D determine correct order of sequence.
D recognize and recall specific information.
D identify key words and thought units.
D locate the main idea and details of a paragraph or a selection.
D recognize the importance of reading for a specific purpose.

Interpretative
D formulate supporting details from given information and past experience.
D generalize the main idea which is not clearly stated in a selection.
D identify likenesses, differences in characters, time, or places.
D recognize and explain cause and effect in a selection.
D predict outcomes for a given selection.
D recognize whether the author's general purpose is to inform or to entertain.
D identify simple character traits.
D summarize given information using direct or paraphrased statements.
D draw a conclusion and support it with factual information stated in the material.
D relate own experience to the material.
I generalize sequence not stated.
I determine author's meanings from author's figurative use of language/colloquial speech.
I use (synthesize) given information and other sources.

Evaluative/Applicative
D recognize and differentiate between reality and fantasy.
I recognize the difference between fact and opinion.

Appreciative
D verbalize own feelings and attitudes about a selection.
D identify with characters and happenings in a given selection.
D demonstrate personal preferences in selection of reading.

THIRD-GRADE READING

Program Objectives

The student will demonstrate an ability to read with comprehension, discrimination, enjoyment and continued interest and learning.

The student will develop an awareness that reading creates a positive self-concept and understanding of others.

The student will develop an awareness of major literary concepts through the study of American and world literature, interpreting literature as a reflection of life and the ideas of diverse cultures.

Reading Experiences   The student will be able to:

D read silently for enjoyment for a sustained period of fifteen minutes.
D read orally for appropriate reasons such as choral reading, scripts, announcements.
D read silently at his/her instructional level for learning and enjoyment.
I alter his/her rate of reading related to the task.

Literature   The student will be able to:

D become familiar with many good books and stories.
D retell stories in his/her own words.
D develop concepts of people, places and things outside his/her immediate environment.
D compare stories.
D respond creatively to stories through art, music, drama, writing and dance.
D define a short story.
D demonstrate a knowledge of myths, legends, fantasies and parables.
D define drama.
D recognize various forms of poetry as rhyming or free verse.
I recognize the plot of a story.
I recognize and explain the setting of a story.
I recognize specific characterizations of a story.
I recognize a biography.

THIRD-GRADE WRITING

Program Objectives

The student will demonstrate the ability to write creatively and competently.
The student will adapt his/her writing to different purposes and audiences.

Composing   The student will be able to:

M recognize various forms of writing as communication processes.
M know that thoughts written down comprise the language experience stories.
D expand writing vocabulary.
D recognize that words work together in meaningful thought units (phrase and clauses) within a sentence.

D vary their sentences by adding and rearranging words, phrases and clauses.
D proofread own work.
D write original story showing simple plot.
D write in first and third person.
D write a poem that follows a pattern such as a couplet (two lines with an end rhyme).
D develop creative forms of writing.
I demonstrate the ability to deal with one topic per paragraph.
I write a friendly letter such as an invitation or thank-you letter.
I write narrative in logical sequence.

Handwriting   The student will be able to:

Manuscript

M demonstrate muscle control and eye–hand coordination for writing.
M use appropriate letter-size relationship.
M use appropriate spacing of letters and words.
M use the base line as a guide.
M write upper and lower case letters in manuscript.
M write letters and numerals from memory.
D copy from near and far.
D use headings and indentations appropriately.
I use margins appropriately.

Cursive

D/M read cursive writing.
I/D use correct beginning, connecting and ending strokes for cursive writing.
I/D apply uniform slant and pressure for cursive writing.
I/D use appropriate size and proportion for all letters in cursive writing.
I/D use headings, indentations, and margins appropriately.
I/D use correct position of body, hand, pencil, and paper.
I analyze own handwriting for neatness and legibility.

Spelling   The student will be able to:

D transfer speech to print.
D use correct spelling and word meaning in all forms of writing.
D use phonics as a *tool* in spelling.
D use the dictionary to verify spelling and syllabication of words.
D proofread written work.
D use affixes correctly.
D recognize and use abbreviations and contractions.

Grammar   The student will be able to:

M write sentences.
M use action verbs.
D recognize and use four types of sentences.
D use appropriate end punctuation and capitalization.
D recognize and use commas and apostrophes.
D use common and proper nouns.

I identify and use two parts (subject and verb) of a sentence.
I use singular, plural and possessive forms of noun and pronoun.
I use verbs of being.
I identify and use tense of verbs (past, present and future).
I learn and correctly use principal parts of common regular and irregular verbs.
I identify and use pronouns.
I use adjectives correctly.

Study Skills   The student will be able to:

D use the external organization of a book as an aid in book use.
D use alphabetical order to locate words.
D use a dictionary.
D use an encyclopedia.
I recognize the use of visual aids in written materials.
I follow a teacher-made study schedule.

Research Skills   The student will be able to:

M know the proper care of books.
D recognize and differentiate between various types of literature through the text, illustrations, artistic style and subject matter.
D share favorite books by written oral reports.
D know where the public library is and how to get a card.
D locate the sections of the library (easy, fiction, nonfiction, biography, reference, etc., and library tools (card catalog, pamphlet file, etc.).
D retrieve fiction and easy books which are arranged alphabetically on the shelves by author's last name.
D realize that fiction stories provide an account of imaginary happenings and nonfiction provide factual or "real" information.
D realize that fantasy is an imaginary happening which is highly fanciful or supernatural while fiction is imaginary happenings which are plausible.
D identify the title, author, and illustrator of any book.
I be acquainted with the Dewey decimal system.
I know that one can find a book in the card catalog by looking up the title, author or subject and then retrieve it from the shelf.
I be acquainted with standard subject headings used in the card catalog.

THIRD-GRADE LISTENING

Program Objective

The student will be able to listen with attentiveness, discrimination and empathy.
    The student will be able to:

M follow detailed directions.
M identify and discriminate sounds.
M identify rhyming words.
D recognize and describe the main idea in a story.

D retell story in correct sequence.

D memorize material appropriate to level.

D give objective reasons for agreeing and disagreeing with what someone says.

D differentiate between fact and opinion in oral presentation.

D react to the speaker's message and give reason for those reactions.

D associate past learning experiences to a new situation to provide meaning to the new situation.

I summarize the main ideas from an oral presentation.

THIRD-GRADE SPEAKING

Program Objective

The student will acquire the language ability to communicate his/her ideas and feelings effectively.

The student will be able to:

Mechanics

D speak in a clear and distinct voice at appropriate volume.

D make use of facial expressions and voice to make one's presentation more interesting.

Oral Presentation

D relate and share experiences.

D tell a story, fact or fiction.

D participate in role-playing activities, puppetry, and other forms of dramatization.

D present a prepared book report.

Discussion

D use common courtesy in speaking to others.

D contribute by reacting responsibly in a small group.

D think through his/her ideas before speaking.

THIRD-GRADE VISUAL LITERACY

Program Objective

The student will be able to view on literal, interpretive, and critical levels.

The student will be able to:

M group pictures into a sequence.

D appreciate visual communications.

D recognize the main idea from visual presentations.

D recognize details within visual presentations.

D translate a picture or series of pictures into a verbal story.

D identify models and heroes in visual programs.

D recognize the difference between fact and fantasy in presentations.

D personally evaluate the worth of visual presentations.

D recognize that one views visual presentations for specific purposes.

D associate and integrate pictures and other visuals with past experiences.

D identify the use of line, shape, color, texture, and music to communicate moods in visual and/or audiovisual presentations.

D recognize the effect of television commercials on his/her life.

D be exposed to the pressures associated with commercials for products.

I recognize news programming.

THIRD-GRADE CAREER EDUCATION

Program Objective

The student is able to discover and learn the knowledge, skills, attitudes and values necessary to carry out career decisions related to language arts.

The student will be able to:

D know various vocational opportunities in language arts and communication fields.

D know that a wide range of careers relate to communication by printed media: writer, editor, proofreader, typist, publisher, literary agent, etc.

D know that a wide range of careers relate to communication by visual media: announcer, actor, cameraman, director, producer, script writer, etc.

D know that communication skills are necessary in all careers.

D know that listening skills are vital to safety, accuracy, efficiency, and effectiveness in the world of work.

APPENDIX 10-4: ENGLISH LANGUAGE ARTS CHECKLIST (ELAC)

NOTE: This checklist is a ready reference of objectives collated from current curriculum guides and from the Declared Competencies Index of the Maryland State Department of Education. For your own reference, you may wish to check those items completed in your classes. All students are not expected to master every behavior, nor are students limited to this list: they will go further. Since most of the objectives are sequential, reviewing items from previous grades may be necessary.

Continuing Objectives, introduced in previous years, are appropriate for all students at each grade. Continuing Objectives should be reviewed and reinforced each year as necessary.

EIGHT
LANGUAGE

Usage

— Use case forms of pronouns correctly.
— Form the past tense of regular and irregular verbs.
— Differentiate among homonyms commonly confused.
— Use correct forms of commonly confused verbs (ex: teach/learn).

Grammar

— Distinguish between dependent and independent clauses.
— Classify conjunctions according to type.
— Classify pronouns according to type.
— Conjugate verbs in the present, past, and future tenses.
— Diagram compound sentences.

Mechanics

— Set off words in apposition with commas.
— Place a comma in a compound sentence to set off independent clauses joined by a conjunction.
— Insert a comma to separate a direct quotation from the rest of the sentence.
— Use a comma to set off nonrestrictive phrases or clauses.
— Use quotation marks correctly.
— Capitalize words indicating family relationships when used specifically and without a possessive pronoun.
— Capitalize the names of streets and avenues.
— Capitalize the names of buildings, schools, and parks.
— Capitalize the names of specific organizations.
— Capitalize the names of important historical periods or events.
— Capitalize the first word in each item of an outline.

LITERATURE

— State the main idea in a given selection.
— List supporting details of a topic sentence.
— Distinguish between fact and opinion.
— State cause and effect relationships.
— List the elements of drama that make it a distinct literary type.
— Define commonly used terms that come from folklore: folktale, myth, legend, ballad, riddle, anecdote, tall tale.
— State the theme of a short story.
— Identify character traits from context clues.
— List at least five similarities and differences between poetry and prose.
— Distinguish between the denotative and connotative meanings of words.

COMPOSITION

— Prepare minutes of a meeting.
— Write a recipe card.
— Take notes from spoken material.
— Write a note giving directions about items to be delivered.
— Write an invitation.
— Reply in writing to an invitation.
— Write a note of apology.
— Prepare a treasurer's report.
— Construct a paragraph in response to a question.
— Write a paragraph that develops an idea through reasons.
— State a main idea in a topic sentence.
— Develop sentences that will support a topic sentence.
— Write a concluding sentence.
— Proofread work for errors in mechanics, usage, and spelling.
— Develop appropriate titles for paragraphs.
— Follow proper manuscript form.
— Prepare all papers accurately and legibly.

SPELLING

— Use final **e** rule with suffixes beginning with a vowel.
— Use final **e** rule with suffixes beginning with a consonant.

___ Form the plural of nouns ending in **y**.
___ Form the plural of nouns ending in **f** and **o**.
___ Apply syllabication rule for **vc/cv** pattern (ex: ac-cept).
___ Apply syllabication rule for **v/cv** pattern (ex: a-head).

___ Apply syllabication rule for **vce** pattern (ex: re-ceive).
___ Apply syllabication rule for **/cle** pattern (ex: ta-ble).

BIBLIOGRAPHY AND REFERENCES

1 *A Planning Process for Inservice Education, Western Washington State College.* Washington, D.C.: Teacher Corps, U.S. Office of Education, Department of Health, Education and Welfare. Contract no. 300-76-0302, pp. 4–5.

2 Burg, Leslie A., Kaufman, Maurice, Korngold, Blanche, and Kovner, Albert. *The Complete Reading Supervisor: Tasks And Roles.* Columbus, Ohio: Merrill, 1978, p. 27.

3 Cronbach, Lee J. In Arno A. Bellack and Herbert M. Kliebard (eds.), *Curriculum And Evaluation.* Berkeley, Calif.: McCutchan Publishing Corporation, 1977, p. 320.

4 Dunn, Rita K., and Dunn, Kenneth J. "Learning Styles/Teaching Styles: Should They . . . Can They . . . Be Matched?" *Educational Leadership,* vol. 36, no. 4, January 1979, pp. 238–243.

5 Fisher, Carol J., and Terry, C. Ann. *Children's Language and the Language Arts.* New York: McGraw-Hill, 1977.

6 Hass, Glen. *Curriculum Planning: A New Approach:* Boston: Allyn and Bacon, 1977.

7 Kniker, Charles R., and Naylor, Natalie A. *Teaching Today and Tomorrow.* Columbus, Ohio: Merrill, 1981, ch. 6.

8 Mangieri, John N. "Reading Programs: Suggestions for Principals." *NASSP Bulletin,* vol. 63, no. 425, March 1979, p. 61.

9 Mangieri, John N., and Corboy, Margaret. "Quality Reading Programs—What Are Their Ingredients?" *NASSP Bulletin,* vol. 65, no. 449, December 1981, p. 62.

10 Mangieri, John N., Bader, Lois A., and Walker, James E. *Elementary Reading: A Comprehensive Approach.* New York: McGraw-Hill, 1982, pp. 255–257.

11 Marcus, Marie. *Diagnostic Teaching of the Language Arts.* New York: John Wiley & Sons, 1977.

12 Petty, Walter T., and Jensen, Julie M. *Developing Children's Language.* Boston: Allyn and Bacon, 1980, p. 119.

13 *Resource Guide for Inservice Teacher Education, Washington West School District, Vermont.* Washington, D.C.: Teacher Corps, U.S. Office of Education, Department of Health, Education and Welfare. Contract no. 300-76-0303, p. 150.

14 Robinson, H. Alan, and Rauch, Sidney J. *Guiding the Reading Program.* Chicago: Science Research Associates, 1965, p. 64.

15 Savage, John F. *Effective Communication.* Chicago: Science Research Associates, 1977, p. 29.

16 Shoemaker, Joan, and Fraser, Hugh W. "What Principals Can Do: Some Implications from Studies of Effective Schooling." *Phi Delta Kappan,* November 1981, vol. 63, no. 3, pp. 178–82.

17 Smith, Richard J., Otto, Wayne, and Hanson, Lee H. *The School Reading Program.* Boston: Houghton Mifflin Company, 1978, ch. 7.

18 Winkeljohann, Sister Rosemary. *English Language Arts Curriculum Guides K–12.* Urbana, Ill.: National Council of Teachers of English, 1977, pp. 17–26.

LIST OF APPENDIXES

APPENDIX A: LITERATURE

APPENDIX B: ORAL EXPRESSION

APPENDIX C: WRITTEN EXPRESSION

APPENDIX D: SPELLING AND HANDWRITING

APPENDIX E: PROFESSIONAL DEVELOPMENT

APPENDIX F: DEALING WITH PARENTS

APPENDIX G: NAMES AND ADDRESSES OF PUBLISHERS

APPENDIX **A**

LITERATURE

A-1. SOME IDEAS FOR INTRODUCING BOOKS TO CHILDREN

A-2. THE NEWBERY AWARD-WINNING BOOKS AND THEIR GRADE EQUIVALENTS

A-3. THE CALDECOTT AWARD-WINNING BOOKS

A-4. BIBLIOTHERAPY: HELPING CHILDREN COPE

A-5. REFERENCES TO CHILDREN'S BOOKS

A-6. CHILDREN'S BOOK CLUBS

A-7. GRAPH FOR ESTIMATING READABILITY

A-8. FIVE FINGERS: A STUDENT TECHNIQUE FOR ASSESSING AND AVOIDING DIFFICULT READING MATERIALS

A-9. A PROCEDURE FOR DEVELOPING AN INVENTORY OF STUDENT LITERATURE SELECTIONS

A-10. CHIDREN'S MAGAZINES

A-11. HIGH-INTEREST LOW-VOCABULARY MAGAZINES

A-1. SOME IDEAS FOR INTRODUCING BOOKS TO CHILDREN

1 Read the first few lines of each book aloud. You will be surprised at how revealing these can be. Not every book will work for this; you will have to do a little preliminary checking and mark how many lines to read.

2 Ask the children to guess what the book might be about by showing the picture on the cover and talking about it. Select books with cover pictures that lend themselves to suggesting a story.

3 Select books with chapter headings that are revealing. Do not read all the chapter titles; choose the most intriguing.

4 Read about the author from the jacket. What kind of books do you think this person would write? Some authors have written a number of books and have interesting lives to hear about.

5 Show the illustrations in the book and ask the children to guess what the book might be about, where it takes place, whether it is funny and so on. Be sure to check on the pictures to see how revealing of the story they are.

6 Select books with the main character's name in the title. There are lots of these, and the jackets invariably start off describing this person, so it is easy to introduce them this way.

7 Find odd titles and ask what the class thinks the book might be about. The covers will give some clues also.

8 Read the first lines of several chapters to show how the story moves along.

9 Read a segment of conversation from the first chapter.

A-2. THE NEWBERY AWARD-WINNING BOOKS AND THEIR GRADE EQUIVALENTS*

The Newbery award is presented to the author of the most outstanding contribution to American children's literature published during the previous year. This award is sponsored by the Children's Services Division of the American Library Association.

1922 *The Story of Mankind* by Hendrik Willem van Loon. Liveright.
1923 *The Voyages of Doctor Dolittle* by Hugh Lofting. Lippincott.
1924 *The Dark Frigate* by Charles Hawes. Little, Brown.
1925 *Tales from Silver Lands* by Charles Finger. Doubleday.
1926 *Shen of the Sea* by Arthur Bowie. Dutton.
1927 *Smokey, the Cowhorse* by Will James. Scribner.
1928 *Gayneck, the Story of a Pigeon* by Dhan Gopal Mukerju. Dutton.
1929 *The Trumpeter of Krakow* by Eric P. Kelly. Macmillan.
1930 *Hitty, Her First Hundred Years* by Rachel Field. Macmillan.
1931 *The Cat Who Went to Heaven* by Elizabeth Coatsworth. Macmillan.
1932 *Waterless Mountain* by Laura Adams Armer. Longmans.
1933 *Young Fu of the Upper Yangtze* by Elizabeth Lewis. Winston.
1934 *Invincible Louisa* by Cornelia Meigs. Little, Brown.
1935 *Dobry* by Monica Shannon. Viking.
1936 *Caddie Woodlawn* by Carol Brink. Macmillan.
1937 *Roller Skates* by Ruth Sawyer. Viking.
1938 *The White Stag* by Kate Seredy. Viking.
1939 *Thimble Summer* by Elizabeth Enright. Rinehart.
1940 *Daniel Boone* by James Daugherty. Viking.

*Leonard, Charlotte. *Tied Together Topics and Thoughts for Introducing Children's Books*. Metuchen, N.J.: Scarecrow Press, 1980, pp. 2–5.

1941 *Call it Courage* by Armstrong Sperry. Macmillan.
1942 *The Matchlock Gun* by Walter D. Edmonds. Dodd, Mead.
1943 *Adam of the Road* by Elizabeth Janet Gray. Viking.
1944 *Johnny Tremain* by Esther Forbes. Houghton Mifflin.
1945 *Rabbit Hill* by Robert Lawson. Viking.
1946 *Strawberry Girl* by Lois Lenski. Lippincott.
1947 *Miss Hickory* by Carolyn Sherwin Bailey. Viking.
1948 *The Twenty-One Balloons* by William Pene du Bois. Viking.
1949 *King of the Wind* by Marguerite Henry. Rand McNally.
1950 *The Door in the Wall* by Marguerite de Angeli. Doubleday.
1951 *Amos Fortune, Free Man* by Elizabeth Yates. Aladdin.
1952 *Ginger Pye* by Eleanor Estes. Harcourt.
1953 *Secret of the Andes* by Ann Nolan Clark. Viking.
1954 *. . . and Now Miguel* by Joseph Krumgold. Crowell.
1955 *The Wheel on the School* by Meindert DeJong. Harper.
1956 *Carry On, Mr. Bowditch* by Jean Lee Latham. Houghton Mifflin.
1957 *The Miracles of Maple Hill* by Virginia Corensen. Harcourt.
1958 *Rifles for Watie* by Harold Keith. Crowell.
1959 *The Witch of Blackbird Pond* by Elizabeth George Speare. Houghton Mifflin.
1960 *Onion John* by Joseph Krumgold. Crowell.
1961 *Island of the Blue Dolphins* by Scott O'Dell. Houghton Mifflin.
1962 *The Bronze Bow* by Elizabeth George Speare. Houghton Mifflin.
1963 *A Wrinkle in Time* by Madeleine L'Engle. Farrer, Straus.
1964 *It's Like This, Cat* by Emily Neville. Harper.
1965 *Shadow of a Bull* by Maia Wojciechowska. Atheneum.
1966 *I, Juan De Pareja* by Elizabeth Borton De Trevino. Farrar, Straus & Giroux.
1967 *Up a Road Slowly* by Irene Hunt. Follett.
1968 *From the Mixed-Up Files of Mrs. Basil E. Frankweiler* by E. L. Konigsburg. Atheneum.
1969 *The High King* by Lloyd Alexander. Holt.
1970 *Sounder* by William Armstrong. Harper.
1971 *The Summer of the Swans* by Betsy Byars. Viking.
1972 *Mrs. Frisby and the Rats of Nimh* by Robert C. O'Brien. Atheneum.
1973 *Julie of the Wolves* by Jean Craighead George. Harper.
1974 *The Slave Dancer* by Paula Fox. Bradbury.
1975 *M.C. Higgins, The Great* by Virginia Hamilton. Macmillan.
1976 *The Grey King* by Susan Cooper. Atheneum.
1977 *Roll of Thunder, Hear My Cry* by Mildred D. Taylor. Dial.
1978 *Bridge to Terabithia* by Katherine Paterson. Crowell.
1979 *The Westing Game* by Ellen Raskin. Dutton.
1980 *A Gathering of Days: A New England Girl's Journal, 1830–32* by Joan Blos. Scribner.
1981 *Jacob Have I Loved* by Katherine Paterson. Crowell.
1982 *A Visit to William Blake's Inn: Poems for Innocent and Experienced Travelers* by Nancy Willard. Harcourt.
1983 *Dicey's Song* by Cynthia Voight. Atheneum.

A-3. THE CALDECOTT AWARD-WINNING BOOKS

The Caldecott award is presented annually to the illustrator of the most outstanding picture book published during the previous year. This award is sponsored by the Children's Services Division of the American Library Association.

1938 *Animals of the Bible, A Picture Book*. Illustrated by Dorothy P. Lathrop. Text selected by Helen Dean Fish. Lippincott.
1939 *Mei Li*. Illustrated and written by Thomas Handforth. Doubleday.
1940 *Abraham Lincoln*. Illustrated and written by Ingri and Edgar d'Aulaire. Doubleday.
1941 *They Were Strong and Good*. Illustrated and written by Robert Lawson. Viking.
1942 *Make Way for Ducklings*. Illustrated and written by Robert McCloskey. Viking.
1943 *The Little House*. Illustrated and written by Virginia Lee Burtan. Houghton Mifflin.
1944 *Many Moons*. Illustrated by Louis Slobodkin. Written by James Thurber. Harcourt.
1945 *Prayer for a Child*. Illustrated by Elizabeth Orton Jones. Written by Rachel Field. MacMillan.
1946 *The Rooster Crows . . .* Illustrated by Maud and Miska Petersham. Macmillan.
1947 *The Little Island*. Illustrated by Leonard Weisgard. Written by Golden MacDonald, pseud. (Margaret Wise Brown). Doubleday.
1948 *White Snow, Bright Snow*. Illustrated by Roger Duvoisin. Written by Alvin Tresselt. Lothrop.
1949 *The Big Snow*. Illustrated and written by Berta and Elmer Hader. Macmillan.
1950 *Song of the Swallows*. Illustrated and written by Leo Politi. Scribner.
1951 *The Egg Tree*. Illustrated and written by Katherine Milhous. Scribner.
1952 *Finders Keepers*. Illustrated by Nicholas, pseud. (Nicolas Mordvinoff). Written by Will, pseud. (William Lipkind). Harcourt.
1953 *The Biggest Bear*. Illustrated and written by Lynd Ward. Houghton Mifflin.
1954 *Madeline's Rescue*. Illustrated and written by Ludwig Bemelmans. Viking.
1955 *Cinderella, or the Little Glass Slipper*. Illustrated and translated from Charles Perrault by Marcia Brown. Scribner.
1956 *Frog Went A-Courtin'*. Illustrated by Feodor Rojankovsky. Text retold by John Langstaff. Harcourt.
1957 *A Tree Is Nice*. Illustrated by Marc Simont. Written by Janice May Udry. Harper.
1958 *Time of Wonder*. Illustrated and written by Robert McCloskey. Viking.
1959 *Chanticleer and the Fox*. Illustrated by Barbara Cooney. Adapted from *The Canterbury Tales*. Crowell.
1960 *Nine Days to Christmas*. Illustrated by Marie Hall Ets. Written by Marie Hall Ets and Aurora Labastida. Viking.
1961 *Baboushka and the Three Kings*. Illustrated by Nicholas Sidjakov. Written by Ruth Robbins. Parnassus Press.
1962 *Once a Mouse*. Illustrated and retold by Marcia Brown. Scribner.
1963 *The Snowy Day*. Illustrated and written by Ezra Jack Keats. Viking.
1964 *Where the Wild Things Are*. Illustrated and written by Maurice Sendak. Harper.
1965 *May I Bring a Friend?* Illustrated by Beni Montresor. Written by Beatrice Schenk de Regniers. Atheneum.
1966 *Always Room for One More*. Illustrated by Nonny Hogrogian. Retold by Sorche Nic Leodhas. Holt.
1967 *Sam, Bangs & Moonshine*. Illustrated and written by Evaline Ness. Holt.
1968 *Drummer Hof*. Illustrated by Ed Emberley. Adapted by Barbara Emberley. Prentice-Hall.
1969 *The Fool of the World and the Flying Ship*. Illustrated by Uri Shulevitz. Retold by Arthur Ransome. Farrar, Straus & Giroux.
1970 *Sylvester and the Magic Pebble*. Illustrated and written by William Steig. Windmill/Simon.
1971 *A Story, A Story*. Illustrated by Gail E. Haley. Retold by Gail E. Haley from an African folktale. Atheneum.

1972   *One Fine Day*. Illustrated by Nonny Hogrogian. Adapted by Nonny Hogrogian from an Armenian folktale. Macmillan.

1973   *The Funny Little Woman*. Illustrated by Blair Lent. Retold by Arlene Mosel. Dutton.

1974   *Duffy and the Devil*. Illustrated by Margot Zemach. Retold by Harve Zemach from a Cornish tale. Farrar, Straus & Giroux.

1975   *Arrow to the Sun*. Illustrated by Gerald McDermott. Adapted by Gerald McDermott from a Pueblo Indian tale. Viking.

1976   *Why Mosquitoes Buzz in People's Ears*. Illustrated by Leo and Diane Dillon. Retold by Verna Aardema from a West African tale. Dial.

1977   *Ashanti to Zulu: African Traditions*. Illustrated by Leo and Diane Dillon. Written by Margaret Musgrove. Dial.

1978   *Noah's Ark*. Illustrated and written by Peter Spier. Doubleday.

1979   *The Girl Who Loved Wild Horses* Illustrated and written by Paul Goble. Bradbury.

1980   *Ox-Cart Man*. Illustrated by Barbara Cooney. Written by Donald Hall. Viking.

1981   *Fables*. Illustrated and written by Arnold Lober. Holt.

1982   *Jumanji*. Illustrated and written by Chris Van Allsburg. Houghton Mifflin.

1983   *Shadow*. Illustrated and translated by Marcia Brown. Scribners.

A-4. BIBLIOTHERAPY: HELPING CHILDREN COPE

In recent times, a number of children's books have been published which deal with life problems. Some educators believe that reading about characters with similar problems helps children to cope with their own life situations. The following pages list titles of recommended picture books for the primary-age student and books for the intermediate-age student.

Author Illustrator	Title	Publisher	Appropriate grade level†	Theme
	Picture books (primary)			
Alexander, M.*	Nobody Asked Me If I Wanted a Babysitter	Dial	PS–1	Sibling rivalry
Arnold A. McCully, E. A.*	Black Is Brown Is Tan	Harper	K–3	Interracial family
Babbitt, N.*	The Something	Farrar	PS–3	Fear of the dark
Baylor, B. Marshall, J.	Plink, Plink, Plink	Houghton	K–3	Fear of night sounds
Bernstein, J. E. Gullo, S. V.	When People Die	Dutton	K–3	Death
Blaine, M. Walner, J.	The Terrible Thing That Happened at Our House	Parents	K–2	Working mother
Brandenberg, J. Aliki	I Wish I Was Sick Too!	Greenwillow	K–3	Sibling conflict
Bunin, C.* Bunin, S.*	Is That Your Sister? A True Story of Adoption	Pantheon	K–3	Interracial adoption
Caines, J. F. Kellogg, S.	Abby	Harper	PS–1	Adoption
Carrick, C. Carrick, D.	The Accident	Scabury	K–3	Death of a pet
Clifton, L. Grifalconi, A.	Everette Anderson's 1–2–3	Holt	K–3	New father
Clifton, B. Barnett, M.	My Brother—Fine with Me	Holt	K–3	Running away
De Paola, T.*	Andy: (That's My Name)	Prentice-Hall	PS–K	Teasing
De Paola, T.*	Nana Upstairs and Nana Downstairs	Putnam	PS–K	Death of a grandparent
Dragon Wagon, C.	Will I Be Okay?	Harper	K–2	Fears
Fassler, J. Lasker, J.	Howie Helps Himself	Whitman	1–3	Handicapped child
Genevieve, G. Shimin, S.	Send Wendell	McGraw-Hill	K–3	Sibling conflict

Author	Title	Publisher	Level	Topic
Goffstein, M. B.*	My Crazy Sister	Dial	K–3	Sibling conflict
Greenfield, E.	She Came Bringing Me That Little Baby Girl	Lippincott	K–2	Sibling conflict
Steptoe, J.				
Hutchins, P.*	Titch	Macmillan	K–3	Sibling conflict
Jerrold, B.	The Smallest Boy in the Class	Morrow	1–3	Being the smallest
Wohlberg, M.				
Keats, E. J.*	Peter's Chair	Harper	PS–1	Sibling conflict
Lapsley, S.	I Am Adopted	Bradbury	PS–K	Adoption
Charlton, M.				
Lexau, J. M.	Me Day	Dial	K–3	Divorce
Weaver, R.				
Peterson, J. W.	I Have a Sister: My Sister Is Deaf	Harper	PS–2	Deaf sister
Ray, D.				
Schick, E.*	Peggy's New Brother	Macmillan	K–2	Sibling conflict
Sharmat, M. W.	I Want Mama	Harper	K–2	Mother's trip to hospital
Hoban, L.				
Shortall, L.*	Tony's First Dive	Morrow	1–3	Fear of the water
Simon, N.	I Was So Mad!	Whitman	K–3	Anger
Leder, D.				
Tobias, T.	Moving Day	Knopf	PS–K	Moving
du Bois, W. P.				
Viorst, J.	Alexander and the Terrible, Horrible, No Good, Very Bad Day	Atheneum	K–3	Having an off day
Cruz, R.				
Viorst, J.	The Tenth Good Thing about Barney	Atheneum	K–2	Death of a pet
Bleguad, I.				
Waber, B.*	But Names Will Never Hurt Me	Houghton	PS–1	Teasing
Wasson, V. P.	The Chosen Baby	Lippincott	PS–K	Adoption
Coalson, G.				
Zolotow, C.	A Father Like That	Harper	K–2	Not having a father
Shecter, B.				
Zolotow, C.	If It Weren't for You	Harper	1–3	Sibling conflict
Shecter, B.				
Zolotow, C.	My Grandson Lew	Harper	K–3	Death of a grandparent
du Bois, W. P.				

(continued)

Author illustrator	Title	Publisher	Appropriate grade level†	Theme
Zolotow, C. Lobel, A.	The Quarreling Book	Harper	K–2	Family conflicts
Zolotow, C. du Bois, W. P.	William's Doll	Harper	PS–3	Sex roles
Books (intermediate)				
Aaron, C.	Better than Laughter	Harcourt	5–7	Running away
Albert, L.	But I'm Ready to Go	Bradbury	6–9	Learning disabilities
Alcock, G.	Run, Westy, Run	Lothrop	4–6	Running away
Alexander, A.	To Live a Lie	Atheneum	4–6	Runaway mother
Bauer, M. D.	Foster Child	Seabury	5–7	Foster child
Blue, R.	Grandma Didn't Wave Back	Watts	3–5	Senility
Blue, R.	A Month of Sundays	Watts	3–4	Divorce
Blume, J.	Are You There God? It's Me, Margaret	Bradbury	4–6	Religious identity
Blume, J.	Blubber	Bradbury	4–6	Defending a friend
Blume, J.	Deenie	Bradbury	5–7	Sclerosis
Blume, J.	It's Not the End of the World	Bradbury	4–7	Divorce
Blume, J.	Tales of a Fourth Grade Nothing	Dell	3–4	Sibling conflicts
Blume, J.	Then Again, Maybe I Won't	Bradbury	5–7	Moving
Brandon, B.	Luther Raps	Eriksson	2–4	Black awareness
Branfield, J.	Why Me?	Harper	5–7	Diabetes
Brooks, J.	Uncle Mike's Boy	Harper	5–7	Divorce
Byars, B.	The Summer of the Swans	Avon	5–7	Death of a sister
Cameron, E.	A Room Made of Windows	Dell	5–7	Mentally retarded brother
Carlson, N. S.	Marchers for the Dream	Harper	4–5	Poor and black
Cavanna, B.	Going on Sixteen	Scholastic	6–9	Motherless girl

Cleaver, V. Cleaver, B.	Grover	Lippincott	4–6	Mother's suicide
Cleaver, V. Cleaver, B.	Me Too	Lippincott	5–7	Father's nervous breakdown Mentally retarded twin
Cohen, B.	Bitter Herbs and Honey	Lothrop	6–9	Jewish prejudice
Coles, R.	Dead-End School	Dell	4–6	Busing
Conford, E.	Dreams of Victory	Dell	4–6	Shy, social misfit
Corcoran, B.	A Dance to Still Music	Atheneum	6–9	Deafness
Corcoran, B.	Make No Sound	Atheneum	5–7	Guilt
Donovan, J.	Wild in the World	Avon	6–9	Death of family
Duncan, L.	A Gift of Magic	Little	5–8	ESP Divorce
Ellis, E. T.	Celebrate the Morning	Atheneum	5–9	Mentally ill mother
Ewing, K.	A Private Matter	Harcourt	4–5	Divorce
Farley, C.	The Garden Is Doing Fine	Atheneum	5–7	Death of father
Fassler, J.	Howie Helps Himself	Whitman	2–4	Cerebral Palsy
Gardam, J.	The Summer after the Funeral	Macmillan	6–9	Death of father
Gersten, I. F.	Ecidujerp, Prejudice: Either Way, It Doesn't Make Sense	Watts	5–7	Prejudice
Gordon, S.	Girls Are Girls and Boys Are Boys: So What's the Difference?	Day	3–4	Sex roles
Greene, C. C.	Beat the Turtle Drum	Viking	4–6	Death of sister
Greenwald, S.	The Secret in Miranda's Closet	Houghton	3–5	Sex roles
Griffin, J. H.	A Time to Be Human	Macmillan	5–7	Prejudice
Hooks, W. H.	Doug Meets the Nutcracker	Warne	4–6	Sex roles
Hunt, Irene	Lottery Rose	Scribner	6–8	Child abuse
Karp, N. J.	Turning Point	Harcourt	5–8	Jewish prejudice
Kelley, S.	Trouble with Explosives	Bradbury	5–7	Stuttering
Klein, N.	Taking Sides	Pantheon	5–7	Divorce
Le Shan, E.	Learning to Say Good-by: When a Parent Dies	Macmillan	5–7	Death of parents

(continued)

Author illustrator	Title	Publisher	Appropriate grade level†	Theme
Little, J.	*Home from Far*	Little	4–6	Death of brother Foster siblings
Little, J.	*Kate*	Harper	5–8	Jewish prejudice
Little, J.	*Mine for Keeps*	Little	4–6	Cerebral palsy
Little, J.	*Take Wing*	Little	5–7	Mentally retarded brother
Madison, W.	*Maria Luisa*	Lippincott	4–6	Chicano prejudice
Mann, P.	*There Are Two Kinds of Terrible*	Doubleday	5–7	Illness and death of mother
Mathis, S. B.	*Sidewalk Story*	Viking	3–5	Eviction
Mathis, S. B.	*Teacup Full of Roses*	Viking	6–9	Drug addiction
Newfield, M.	*A Book for Jodan*	Atheneum	3–4	Divorce
Orgel, D.	*The Mulberry Music*	Harper	4–6	Death of grandparent
Parker, R.	*He Is Your Brother*	Scholastic	5–6	Autistic brother
Perl, L.	*Dumb Like Me, Olivia Potts*	Seabury	4–6	Super intelligent siblings
Pollowitz, M.	*Cinnamon Cane*	Harper	5–7	Death of grandfather
Reynolds, P.	*Different Kind of Sister*	Lothrop	5–6	Mentally retarded sister
Richards, A. Willis, I.	*How to Get It Together When Your Parents Are Coming Apart*	McKay	6–9	Divorce
Roberts, W. D.	*Don't Hurt Laurie*	Atheneum	4–6	Child abuse
Rodowsky, C. F.	*What about Me?*	Watts	6–9	Death of Mongoloid brother
Sachs, M. A.	*A December Tale*	Doubleday	5–7	Child abuse
Slote, A.	*Hang Tough, Paul Mather*	Lippincott	4–7	Leukemia
Smith, D.	*A Taste of Blackberries*	Crowell	4–6	Death of a friend
Snyder, A.	*First Step*	Holt	5–8	Divorce Alcoholic parent
Sobol, H. L.	*My Brother Stephen Is Retarded*	Macmillan	2–4	Mentally retarded brother
Spence, E.	*The Devil Hole*	Lothrop	6–9	Autistic brother
Stolz, M.	*The Edge of Next Year*	Harper	5–8	Death of mother
Stolz, M.	*Leap before You Look*	Harper	6–9	Divorce
Vogel, I.	*My Twin Sister Erika*	Harper	5–7	Death of twin

*Illustrated by author.
†PS = preschool; K = kindergarten.

A-5. REFERENCES TO CHILDREN'S BOOKS

Arbuthnot, May Hill. *The Arbuthnot Anthology of Children's Literature*. New York: Lothrop, 1976.

Arbuthnot, May Hill, et al. (eds.). *Children's Books Too Good to Miss*. Bloomington, Ind. Indiana University Press, 1980.

Arbuthnot, May Hill, and Sutherland, Zena. *Children and Books*. Glenview, Ill.: Scott Foresman & Company, 1977.

Baskin, Barbara H. and Harris, Karen H. *Books for the Gifted Child*. New York: R.R. Bowker, 1980.

Baskins, Barbara. *Notes from a Different Drummer: A Guide to Juvenile Fiction Portraying the Handicapped*. New York: R.R. Bowker, 1977.

Bernstein, Joanne. *Books to Help Children Cope with Separation and Loss*. New York: R.R. Bowker, 1977.

Children's Book Council. *Children's Books: Awards and Prizes*. New York: Children's Book Council, 1977.

Children's Books in Print. New York: R.R. Bowker, published annually.

Cianciolo, Patricia. *Adventuring with Books: A Booklist for Pre-K–Grade 8*. Urbana, Ill.: National Council of Teachers of English, 1977.

Cianciolo, Patricia (ed.). *Picture Books for Children*. Chicago: American Library Association, 1973.

Davis, Enid. *The Liberty Cap: A Catalog of Non-Sexist Materials for Children*. Chicago: Academy Press Limited, 1977.

Dreyer, Sharon. *The Bookfinder*. Circle Pines, Minn.: American Guidance Service, 1977.

Gillespie, John T. *Paperback Books for Young People: An Annotated Guide to Publishers and Distributors*. Chicago: American Library Association, 1977.

Gillespie, John T., and Gilbert, Christine (eds.). *Best Books for Children*. New York: R.R. Bowker, 1981.

Greene, Ellin and Schoenfeld, Madalynne (eds.). *A Multimedia Approach to Children's Literature: A Selective List of Films: Filmstrips, and Recordings Based on Children's Books*. Chicago: American Library Association, 1977.

Huck, Charlotte. *Children's Literature in the Elementary School*. New York: Holt, Rinehart and Winston, 1979.

Isaacson, Richard H., and Bogurt, Gory (eds.). *The Children's Catalog*. H.W. Wilson Company, 1981.

Kujoth, Jean. *Best Selling Children's Books*. Metuchen. N.J.: Scarecrow Press, 1973.

Spache, George. *Good Reading for Poor Readers*. Champaign, Ill.: Garrard Publishing Company, 1974.

Spache, George. *Good Reading for the Disadvantaged Reader: Multiethnic Resources*. Champaign, Ill.: Garrard Publishing Company, 1975.

Sunderlin, Sylvia (ed.). *Bibliography of Books for Children*. Washington, D.C.: Association for Childhood Education International, 1974.

Sutherland, Zena (ed.). *The Best in Children's Books*. Chicago: University of Chicago Press, 1980.

The WEB (Wonderfully Exciting Books). Columbus, Ohio: The Ohio State University. Periodical, published four times per year.

A-6. CHILDREN'S BOOK CLUBS

Publisher and address	Name of book club	Recommended for ages
Book-of-the-Month Club 345 Hudson Street New York, N.Y. 10014	Young Readers of America	9–14
Grolier Enterprises Inc. 575 Lexington Avenue New York, N.Y. 10021	Beginning Reader's Program	5–8
	Disney's Wonderful World of Reading	5–10
Junior Literary Guild 501 Franklin Avenue Garden City, N.Y. 11530	Preschool Level (K Group)	2–5
	Primary Level (P Group)	5–8
	Easy-reading Level (E Group)	5–8
	Intermediate Level (A Group)	9–12
	Upper Elementary and Junior High Level (B Group)	12–15
Parents Magazine Press 52 Vanderbilt Avenue New York, N.Y. 10017	Parents Magazine's Read Aloud and Easy Reading Program	3–8
Scholastic Book Services 904 Sylvan Avenue Englewood Cliffs, N.J. 07632	See Saw Book Club	5–7
	Lucky Book Club	7–9
	Arrow Book Club	9–11
	Teenage Book Club	12–14
Xerox Education Publications 1250 Fairwood Avenue Columbus, Ohio 43206	Primary	5–7
	Intermediate	8–9
	Senior	10–11
	Buddy Books Paperback Book Club	5–7
	Goodtime Books Paperback Books	7–9
	Discovering Books Paperback Book Club	9–12

A-7. GRAPH FOR ESTIMATING READABILITY—EXTENDED*

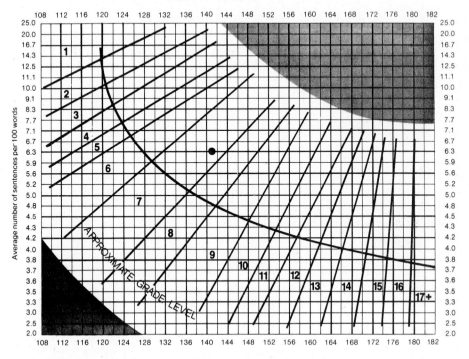

Average number of syllables per 100 words

Expanded Directions for Working Readability Graph

1 Randomly select three (3) sample passages and count out exactly 100 words each, beginning with the beginning of a sentence. Do count proper nouns, initializations, and numerals.

2 Count the number of sentences in the hundred words, estimating length of the fraction of the last sentence to the nearest one-tenth.

3 Count the total number of syllables in the 100-word passage. If you don't have a hand counter available, an easy way is to simply put a mark above every syllable over one in each word, then when you get to the end of the passage, count the number of marks and add 100. Small calculators can also be used as counters by pushing numeral 1, then push the + sign for each word or syllable when counting.

4 Enter graph with *average* sentence length and *average* number of syllables; plot dot where the two lines intersect. Area where dot is plotted will give you the approximate grade level.

5 If a great deal of variability is found in syllable count or sentence count, putting more samples into the average is desirable.

*This "extended graph" does not outmode or render the earlier (1968) version inoperative or inaccurate; it is an extension. (Reproduction permitted—no copyright.)

Fry, E. "Fry's Readability Graph: Clarifications, Validity, and Extension to level 17," vol. 21, no. 3, 1977, pp. 242–252.

6 A word is defined as a group of symbols with a space on either side; thus, *Joe, IRA, 1945* and & are each one word.

7 A syllable is defined as a phonetic syllable. Generally, there are as many syllables as vowel sounds. For example, stopped is one syllable and wanted is two syllables. When counting syllables for numerals and initializations, count one syllable for each symbol. For example, *1945* is four syllables, *IRA* is three syllables, and & is one syllable.

A-8. FIVE FINGERS: A STUDENT TECHNIQUE FOR ASSESSING AND AVOIDING DIFFICULT READING MATERIALS

Most measures of readability are designed to be performed by the teacher. Since the teacher is not always available to monitor student recreational reading selections, it is helpful if the student can assess the difficulty level of the material himself. For years, teachers have directed intermediate-level students to use the "five finger method" in order to avoid books that are too difficult.

Using this technique, the student is directed to read one page of a book, putting a finger up each time that he comes to a word he does not recognize. If all five fingers go up before he finishes reading a page, the book is too difficult and another book should be selected. For beginning readers, the same procedure may be followed. However, only two or three fingers per page would be sufficient to determine that a book is too difficult.

A-9. A PROCEDURE FOR DEVELOPING AN INVENTORY OF STUDENT LITERATURE SELECTIONS

Frequently, the books which are most popular among students are those recommended by their peers rather than those recommended by teachers, parents, and librarians. The following procedure was designed to allow students the opportunity to share titles of favorite books.

Step 1: Ask students to write down the titles of several of their favorite books.

Step 2: Compile their selections and list the book titles on a worksheet using a format similar to the following. Note: These titles were some of the favorites listed by a group of sixth-graders.

Recreational Reading Survey: Student Selections

In the first column, put a check next to any books you have read. If you have not read a book but you have heard of it, place a check in the second column. In the third column, put a check next to any books you would like to read.

Book titles	Books I have read	Books I recognize	Books I would like to read
Star Wars			
UFO			
Cars Against the Clock			
Riddles and Jokes			
Martin L. King Jr.			
The Army Bear			
Little House in the Big Woods			

Step 3: Collect the surveys and direct a committee of students to tally the results.

Step 4: Provide feedback on the results of the survey in one of the following ways:

Distribute a duplicated copy of the results to the class. For example:

20 percent of the class has read *Star Wars*.

100 percent of the class is familiar with it.

Direct the students in constructing posters and bulletin boards publicizing the results of the study.

Provide students with graph paper and assist them in plotting the number of students who read each book and the other results.

Submit the information for publication in the school newspaper.

Step 5: Obtain from the library those books which the students indicated that they would like to read.

Step 6: Apply your findings to future book orders. Share the results with the librarian and other teachers.

A-10. CHILDREN'S MAGAZINES*

Title	Audience	No. of issues per year	Publisher	Comments
Boys' Life	Boys, ages 11–16	12	Boy Scouts of America	Minimum 15 subscriptions to one address; free teacher's edition
Career World I	Ages 9–13	9	Curriculum Innovations, Inc.	
Child Life	Ages 7–14	10	Saturday Evening Post Company	
Children's Digest	Ages 7–12	10	Parents' Magazine Enterprises, Inc.	
Children's Express	Ages 7–14	12	Cheshire Communications Company	Written by children 13 years and younger; assistant editors 14–17 years.
Children's Playcraft	Ages 7–12	10	Parents' Magazine Enterprises, Inc.	
Children's Playmate	Ages 3–8	10	Saturday Evening Post Company	
Cricket	Ages 6–12	12	Open Court Publishing Company	
The Curious Naturalist	Ages 6–12	4	Massachusetts Audubon Society	
Current Health	Ages 9–13	9	Curriculum Innovations, Inc.	Minimum 15 subscriptions to one address; free teachers edition
Daisy	Age 9	9	Girl Scouts of U.S.A.	Intended for Brownie Girl Scouts
Dynamite	Ages 9–14	12	Scholastic Book Services	
Ebony Jr.	Ages 6–12	10	Johnson Publishing Company, Inc.	

Magazine	Audience		Publisher	Notes
Electric Company Magazine	Graduates of Sesame Street	12	Children's Television Workshop	
Highlights for Children	Preschool and elementary school child	11	Highlights for Children, Inc.	
Humpty Dumpty's Magazine for Little Children	Ages 3–7	10	Parents' Magazine Enterprises, Inc.	
Jack and Jill Magazine	Ages 5–12	10	Saturday Evening Post Company	
Pack-O-Fun	Ages 7–12	10	Clapper Publishing Company	"The only scrapcraft magazine"
Pizzazz	Ages 10–14	12	Marvel Comics Group	
Ranger Rick's Nature Magazine	Ages 5–12	12	National Wildlife Federation	
Sesame Street	Preschool children	10	Children's Television Workshop	Spanish edition available
Stone Soup	Ages 6–12	5	Children's Art Foundation	Composed of children's work
World, National Geographic	Ages 8–12	12	National Geographic Society	
Wow	Ages 4–8	9	Scholastic Book Services	
Young World Magazine	Ages 10–14	10	Saturday Evening Post Company	Formerly Golden Magazine

*For additional information on children's magazines consult Katz, B., and Richards, B. G. *Magazines for Libraries* (3d ed.). New York: R.R. Bowker Company, 1978.

A-11. HIGH-INTEREST LOW-VOCABULARY MAGAZINES

The following magazines were designed for intermediate-age students reading at the primary-grade levels.

Title	Interest level	Reading level	No. of issues per year	Publisher	Comments
Action	Grades 7–9	Grades 2.0–2.9	14	Scholastic Book Services	Minimum 10 subscriptions to one address; free teacher's edition
Know Your World	Grades 4–10	Grades 2–3	28	Xerox Education Publications	Minimum 10 subscriptions to one address; free teacher's edition
Sprint	Grades 4–6	Grades 2.0–2.9	14	Scholastic Book Services	Minimum 10 subscriptions to one address; free teacher's edition

ORAL EXPRESSION

B-1. A LIST OF POETRY BOOKS FOR PRIMARY AND INTERMEDIATE-GRADE STUDENTS

B-2. SUGGESTIONS FOR SELECTING AND PREPARING MATERIAL FOR CHORAL READINGS

B-3. PUPPETRY BOOKS FOR CHILDREN

B-4. MAKING PUPPETS

B-5. SOURCES OF CHILDREN'S PLAYS

B-6. WEBBING

B-7. CRITERIA FOR SELECTING LITERATURE TO READ TO CHILDREN*

B-1. A LIST OF POETRY BOOKS FOR PRIMARY- AND INTERMEDIATE-GRADE STUDENTS

In order to be enjoyed thoroughly, poetry should be presented orally. Listed below are books of poetry suggested for use with primary- and intermediate-grade students. Those books marked with a + would be appropriate for both the primary and intermediate grades.

Although poetry is presented under the section termed "Oral Expression," it can also be a stimulus for written expression.

Poetry for Primary-Grade Levels

Aldis, Dorothy. *All Together: A Child's Treasury of Verse*. New York: Putnam's Sons, 1952.

Association for Childhood Education International. *Sung under the Silver Umbrella*. New York: Macmillan, 1972.

Behn, Harry. *Little Hill*. New York: Harcourt Brace Jovanovich, 1949.

+ Blishen, Edward (ed.). *Oxford Book of Poetry for Children*. New York: Watts Franklin, 1964.

+ Bogan, Louise, and Smith, William (eds.). *The Golden Journey: Poems for Young People*. Chicago: Contemporary Books, 1976.

Brooks, Gwendolyn. *Bronzeville Boys and Girls*. New York: Harper and Row, 1956.

Ciardi, John. *I Met a Man*. Boston: Houghton Mifflin, 1961.

Ciardi, John. *Fast and Slow: Poems for Advanced Children and Beginning Parents*. Boston: Houghton Mifflin, 1978.

Foster, John L. (ed.). *A First Poetry Book*. New York: Oxford University Press, 1980.

+ Frost, Robert. *Stopping by Woods on a Snowy Evening*. New York: Dutton, 1978.

Geismer, Barbara, and Suter, Antoinette. *Very Young Verses*. Boston: Houghton Mifflin, 1945.

Hillert, Margaret. *Farther than Far*. Chicago: Follet, 1969.

Kherdian, David (ed.). *The Dog Writes on the Window with His Nose: and Other Poems*. New York: Scholastic Book Services, 1977.

Kuskin, Karla. *Dogs and Dragons, Trees and Dreams*. New York: Harper & Row, 1980.

+ Love, Katherine (ed.). *Little Laughter*. New York: Thomas Crowell, 1957.

O'Neill, Mary. *Hailstones and Halibut Bones*. New York: Doubleday, 1961.

Pomerantz, Charlotte. *The Tamarindo Puppy and Other Poems*. New York: Greenwillow Books, 1980.

Prelutsky, Jack. *The Headless Horseman Rides Tonight*. New York: Greenwillow Books, 1980.

Prelutsky, Jack. *The Queen of Eene*. New York: Greenwillow Books, 1978.

Prelutsky, Jack. *Rolling Harvey Down the Hill*. New York: Greenwillow Books, 1980.

+ Silverstein, Shel. *Where the Sidewalk Ends*. New York: Harper & Row, 1974.

+ Thurman, Judith. *Flashlight and Other Poems*. New York: Atheneum, 1976.

+ Tudor, Tasha (ed.). *Wings from the Wind: An Anthology of Poetry*. Philadelphia: Lippincott Company, 1964.

+ Wallace, Daisy (ed.). *Fairy Poems*. New York: Holiday House, 1980.

+ Wallace, Daisy. *Witch Poems*. New York: Holiday House, 1976.

Poetry for Intermediate-Grade Levels

Adoff, Arnold (ed.). *Black Out Loud: An Anthology of Modern Poems by Black Americans*. New York: Macmillan, 1970.

Arbuthnot, May Hill, and Root, Shelton (eds.). *Time for Poetry*. Holyoke, Mass.: Scott Education Division, 1967.

Brewton, John (ed.). *Under the Tent of the Sky*. New York: Macmillan, 1937.

Brewton, Sara, Brewton, John E., and Blackburn, John Brewton. *Of Quarks, Quasars and Other Quirks: Quizzical Poems for the Supersonic Age*. New York: Crowell, 1977.

Carroll, Lewis. *Poems of Lewis Carroll*. New York: Crowell, 1973.

Cole, William. *Beastly Boys and Ghastly Girls*. New York: Dell, 1977.

Cole, William. *Oh, What Nonsense*. New York: Viking Press, 1966.

Farjeon, Eleanor. *Eleanor Farjeon's Poems for Children*. Philadelphia: Lippincott, 1951.

Hughes, Langston. *Don't You Turn Back; Poems*. New York: Knopf, 1969.

Larrick, Nancy. *Crazy to Be Alive in Such a Strange World*. New York: M. Evans, 1977.

Larrick, Nancy (ed.). *Piper, Pipe That Song Again*. New York: Random House, 1965.

Lear, Edward. *A Book of Nonsense*. New York: Metropolitan Museum of Art, 1980.

Livingston, Myra C. *The Way Things Are and Other Poems*. New York: Atheneum, 1974.

McCord, David. *Speak Up: More Rhymes of the Never Was and Always Is*. Boston: Little, Brown, 1962.

Mayer, Mercer (ed.). *The Poison Tree and Other Poems*. New York: Scribner, 1977.

Morrison, Lillian. *Who Would Marry a Mineral? Riddles, Runes, and Love Tunes*. New York: Lothrop, 1978.

Morrison, Lillian (ed.). *Sprints and Distances: Sports in Poetry and the Poetry in Sport*. New York: Crowell, 1965.

Nash, Ogden. *Custard and Company*. Boston: Little, Brown, 1980.

Norris, Leslie. *Merlin and the Snake's Egg: Poems*. New York: Viking Press, 1978.

Plotz, Helen (ed.). *Life Hungers to Abound: Poems of the Family*. New York: Greenwillow Books, 1978.

Prelutsky, Jack. *Nightmares: Poems to Trouble Your Sleep*. New York: Greenwillow Books, 1976.

Prelutsky, Jack. *Pack Rat's Day and Other Poems*. New York: Macmillan, 1974.

Prelutsky, Jack. *The Snoop on the Sidewalk and Other Poems*. New York: Greenwillow Books, 1977.

Sandburg, Carl. *Wind Song*. New York: Harcourt Brace Jovanovich, 1960.

Saunders, Dennis (ed.). *Magic Lights and Streets of Shining Jet*. New York: Greenwillow Books, 1978.

Starbird, Kaye. *The Covered Bridge House and Other Poems*. New York: Scholastic Book Services, 1979.

Teasdale, Sara. *Stars To-Night*. New York: Macmillan, 1930.

Untermeyer, Louis. *A Galaxy of Verse*. New York: M. Evans, 1978.

Worth, Valerie. *Still More Poems*. New York: Farrar, Straus & Giroux, 1978.

B-2. SUGGESTIONS FOR SELECTING AND PREPARING MATERIAL FOR CHORAL READINGS

Four principles for selecting a poem to be read in chorus are sufficient:

1 Make it relatively short.

2 Keep it simple. The reading level should be no higher than that of the poorer readers in your group, preferably somewhat below the group's instructional level. Choose material at the independent reading level.

3 Look for something with a catchy title that will put imaginations to work.

4 Select a poem that will come alive when read aloud—words with fascinating sounds, contrast of some sort that can be interpreted, mood that can be enhanced through oral interpretation, or dialogue that bears the stamp of personality.

Preparation for choral reading can be guided by one principle—contrast. Your medium is a group of voices. Therefore it's useful to have one or two simple classi-

Woodbury, Jean. "Choral Reading and Readers Theatre: Oral Interpretation of Literature in the Classroom." In Dianne Monson and Dayann McClenathan (eds.), *Developing Active Readers: Ideas for Parents, Teachers, and Librarians*. Newark, Del.: International Reading Association, 1979, p. 67.

fications for the voices in your class—high and low, for instance, as well as strong and soft. Of course, these basic voice tendencies can and should be extended, but it may be wise to begin with what the children produce naturally and work gradually for more range.

Some elements of contrast you may choose to work with are

1 Low voice versus high voice
2 One voice versus two or more voices
3 Small group versus large group
4 Mixed voices versus high or low voices
5 Fast delivery versus slow or moderate delivery
6 Smooth flowing versus punctuated or choppy delivery
7 Aggressive versus unctuous delivery
8 One line versus many lines

B-3. PUPPETRY BOOKS FOR CHILDREN

For additional information on puppetry, refer your students to the following sources.

Ackley, Edith F. *Marionettes: Easy to Make, Fun to Use*. Philadelphia: Lippincott, 1939.
Cochrane, Louise. *Shadow Puppets in Color*. Boston: Plays, Inc., 1972.
Cochrane, Louise. *Tabletop Theatres*. Boston: Plays, Inc., 1974.
Currell, David. *The Complete Book of Puppetry*. Boston: Plays, Inc., 1975.
Jagendorf, Moritz. *Puppets for Beginners*. Boston: Plays, Inc., 1952.
Luckin, Joyce. *Easy to Make Puppets*. Boston: Plays, Inc., 1975.
Mahlmann, Lewis, and Jones, David C. *Puppet Plays for Young Players*. Boston: Plays, Inc., 1974.
Mertin, George. *Plays for Puppet Performance*. Boston: Plays, Inc., 1979.
Pels, Gertrude. *Easy Puppets*. New York: Crowell, 1951.
Reiniger, Lotte. *Shadow Puppets, Shadow Theatres and Shadow Films*. Boston: Plays, Inc., 1975.
Ross, Laura. *Finger Puppets: Easy to Make, Fun to Use*. New York: Lothrop, 1971.
Ross, Laura. *Hand Puppets: How to Make and Use Them*. New York: Lothrop, 1969.
Ross, Laura. *Scrap Puppets: How to Make and Move Them*. New York: Holt, Rinehart and Winston, 1978.

B-4. MAKING PUPPETS*

Some Paper Bag Puppets
Stand-up/Square Bottom Lunch Bags
crayons; magic-markers; all kinds of paper, scissors, and glue; felt or wool; any other materials; or any combination imaginable.

*Weiger, M. "Puppetry." *Elementary English*, 1974, *51*, pp. 59–64.

1.
Fist in bag.
Middle finger
may be tongue,
making
mouth move.

Bottom

2.

Paste the chin on
the side of the bag
under the bottom
flap. Paste the top
of the puppet's
face on the
bottom of the
bag. Bend four
fingers to fit in
the folded flap.

3.

Thumb   Pinkie

4.

Paper Plate

Paste a
paper body
on the
puppet's
head.

Knife-edged Paper Bags

Stuff head with crushed paper. Insert tagboard tube for index finger. Put thumb and middle finger through holes in the front of bag.

Fist Puppets

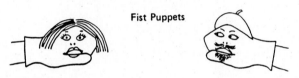

The bare hand may be used, with features painted on by magic-marker or equivalent. If gloves are used, the features may be applied in any media.

Some Stick Puppets

Oaktag and sticks are usually used, but even a light doll or other type puppet may be supported by a stick. The puppet may be one-piece, or arms and/or legs may be attached with paper clasps and thin rods attached to the limbs to make them move. Every front-facing puppet should have a back. Every side-facing puppet should have two sides and be able to travel in either direction. The puppet may be extremely simple or complex, depending upon the ability of the puppeteer.

Finger Puppets

May be constructed in many ways of many things.

Pointing up!

bare fingers

scooped-out small potatoes

peanut shells

paper

felt (The back of the hand faces the audience and characters not performing disappear into the palm of the hand.)

Pointing down!

With glove.

Spider –
dark glove.

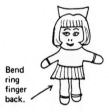

Bend
ring
finger
back.

Sew face on back of glove.
Add skirt and color buttons,
shoes, and cuffs.

Felt head, on middle finger.
Stuff nose. Remaining fingers
legs. Could add saddle.

Finger
holes

← Elastic-
fit over
fingers
and
upper
body.

 Short
pants.

Paper or tag board.
Elastic at waist of
pants or skirt
should hold top
of puppet in place.

Back
View

Stuff head, body, and toes with
soft paper toweling. Front of
pants are attached to body. Insert fingers through back of
pants to manipulate the feet.
Stuffed cloth body may have
skirt, and bare fingers are legs
and feet with fingertips painted
as shoes.

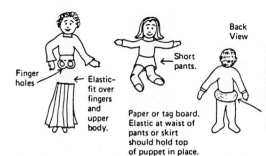

1. Pipe cleaners.

2. Crepe paper over tube, and
wire to fasten to
pipe-cleaner body.

5. Put fingers through round
pipe cleaner and then through
pants. Shoes can be made and
put on fingertips.

3. Stuff and cover
body with crepe
paper.

4. Costume.

Bend ring-finger back.

Draw features on the back of the hand. Color
tips of the first two fingers for shoes. Attach
clothing of paper or material with sticky
tape. Attach hair to wrist.

Sock Puppets

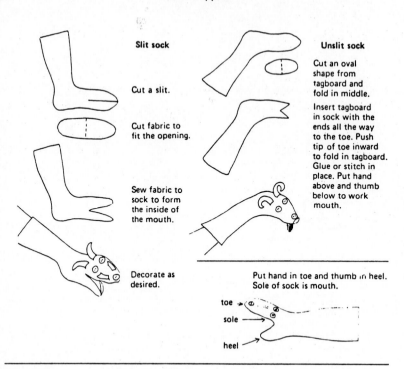

Slit sock

Cut a slit.

Cut fabric to
fit the opening.

Sew fabric to
sock to form
the inside of
the mouth.

Decorate as
desired.

Unslit sock

Cut an oval
shape from
tagboard and
fold in middle.

Insert tagboard
in sock with the
ends all the way
to the toe. Push
tip of toe inward
to fold in tagboard.
Glue or stitch in
place. Put hand
above and thumb
below to work
mouth.

Put hand in toe and thumb in heel.
Sole of sock is mouth.

toe →
sole →
heel →

Stuffed sock

slits →

Make same.
Swing toe of
sock over head
without cutting
to form hat.

Stuff heel. Insert tube for finger. Cut off toe to make arms,
or use bare fingers as arms through slits.

Hand Puppets

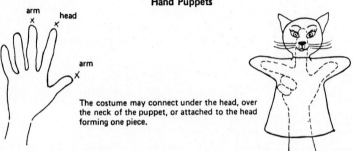

arm
×
head
×

arm
×

The costume may connect under the head, over
the neck of the puppet, or attached to the head
forming one piece.

The head may be: a ball, clay, a potato or other vegetable, a toilet-soap box or other boxes, sponge, paper, cloth, papier-mache, tubing, sawdust, and paste, kitchen tools (spoon, potato masher, gourds, styrofoam, a balloon, dividers of egg cartons). Animal features: wood, plaster, etc.

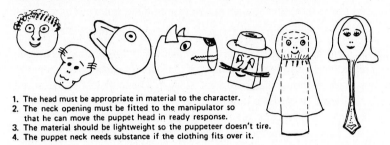

1. The head must be appropriate in material to the character.
2. The neck opening must be fitted to the manipulator so that he can move the puppet head in ready response.
3. The material should be lightweight so the puppeteer doesn't tire.
4. The puppet neck needs substance if the clothing fits over it.

The puppet body must fit the puppeteer's hand and the puppet head. It must be lightweight and the material must suit the character. Padding, stuffing, or wiring may be used if desired to give the body substance. A wad of tissue clutched between the two bent fingers helps.

Other Puppets

Marionettes
Balloon
Broom
Shadow
Rod
Doll

B-5. SOURCES OF CHILDREN'S PLAYS

Alexander, Sue. *Small Plays for Special Days*. New York: Houghton Mifflin, 1977.

Bradley, Virginia. *Is There an Actor in the House? Dramatic Material from Pantomime to Play*. New York: Dodd, Mead and Co., 1975.

Henderson, Nancy. *Celebrate America: A Baker's Dozen of Plays*. New York: Julian Messner, 1978.

Hughes, Ted. *The Tiger's Bones and Other Plays for Children*. New York: Viking Press, 1974.

Kamerman, Sylvia E. (ed.). *Children's Plays from Favorite Stories*. Boston: Plays, Inc., 1970.

Kamerman, Sylvia E. (ed.). *Fifty Plays for Holidays*. Boston: Plays, Inc., 1975.

Korty, Carol. *Plays from African Folktales: With Ideas for Acting, Dance, Costumes, and Music*. New York: Scribners, 1969.

Korty, Carol. *Silly Soup: Ten Zany Plays*. New York: Scribners, 1977.

Laurie, Rona. *Children's Plays from Beatrix Potter*. New York: Frederick Warne & Co., 1980.

Miller, Helen. *First Plays for Children*. Boston: Plays, Inc., 1971.

Miller, Helen. *Short Plays for Children*. Boston: Plays, Inc., 1969.

Rockwell, Thomas. *How to Eat Fried Worms and Other Plays*. New York: Delacorte Press, 1980.

B-6. WEBBING*

Just as a spider attaches the lines of its web to many points and projections before strengthening those lines with further strands and reinforcing the web with intersecting lines, so can the classroom teacher develop a web of possibilities with children.

1 Begin with an idea, a concept, or a topic and using a brainstorming technique have children suggest all the possible ramifications of that topic, no matter how remote. Perhaps the stimulus for webbing came from a story read aloud to the class and generated interest in a topic or raised a question.

2 Write down on the chalkboard or chart all of the suggested topics, ideas, activities, and questions that are generated. Just as the spider swings out on long lines to catch the web on a projection, so may the ideas elicited from children catch on to a slim thread of thought that can later be reinforced by further discussion.

3 The next stage of webbing is categorizing the ideas into pockets of interest that are related to each other in some way. There may be four or five main categories or as many as ten to fifteen.

4 Once the separate categories have been identified, then books, both fiction and nonfiction, may be listed from which children can gain additional input, activities may be suggested, and additional materials such as filmstrip, film, recordings, or real objects may be identified.

5 The final stage is drawing the web. Children may assist the classroom teacher in "webbing" all the possible strands, or, after experiences with webbing, they can create their own webs. Their involvement in the webbing focuses their attention on the concept with which they began and provides the opportunity for many activities reaching out from the center of the web.

*From a publication prepared by the Ohio Department of Education, Division of Inservice Education, *Motivation, Unleashing the Learning Power,* 1978, pp. 64–65.

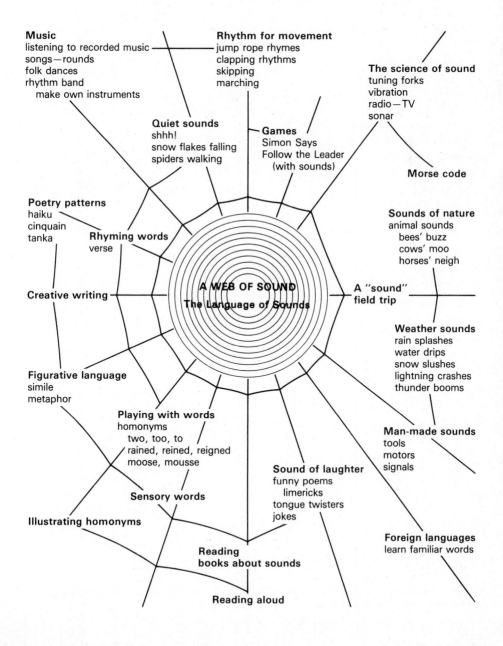

Music
listening to recorded music
songs—rounds
folk dances
rhythm band
    make own instruments

Rhythm for movement
jump rope rhymes
clapping rhythms
skipping
marching

The science of sound
tuning forks
vibration
radio—TV
sonar

Quiet sounds
shhh!
snow flakes falling
spiders walking

Games
Simon Says
Follow the Leader
(with sounds)

Morse code

Poetry patterns
haiku
cinquain
tanka

Rhyming words
verse

Sounds of nature
animal sounds
    bees' buzz
    cows' moo
    horses' neigh

Creative writing

A WEB OF SOUND
The Language of Sounds

**A "sound"
field trip**

Weather sounds
rain splashes
water drips
snow slushes
lightning crashes
thunder booms

Figurative language
simile
metaphor

Playing with words
homonyms
    two, too, to
    rained, reined, reigned
    moose, mousse

Man-made sounds
tools
motors
signals

Sound of laughter
funny poems
    limericks
tongue twisters
jokes

Sensory words

Illustrating homonyms

Foreign languages
learn familiar words

**Reading
books about sounds**

Reading aloud

B-7. CRITERIA FOR SELECTING LITERATURE TO READ TO CHILDREN*

1 Is each book quality literature? Does it contain a meaningful message, consistent characterization, a plausible plot, and superlative style? If the book is nonfiction, is the content accurate, logical, and well-written?

2 Does the book make a significant contribution to the child's world today? Does it offer him something for future use: an idea, a value, a nugget of knowledge? Does the book give enjoyment to the listener? Does it promote appreciation?

3 Does the book spark the imaginations of the children? Does it contain genuine emotion?

4 Does the book itself gain from being shared orally because of its humor, its thought-provoking qualities, its colorful phrases, or its truths? Is it a book that children could or would not be likely to read for themselves?

5 Is the book suitable to the ages and stages of development of the students? Are the children psychologically ready for it?

6 What piece of literature is most suitable to the various class groups from the standpoint of length? If the book is for preschool or first-grade children, can it be completed in one reading? Does the longer book for older children have chapters of the proper length so that natural stopping-places may be readily identified? Does the book provide natural and stimulating "launching pads" for the next reading without necessitating undue review of what has gone before?

*Robert Whitehead, *Children's Literature: Strategies of Teaching,* © 1968, pp. 93–94. Reprinted by permission of Prentice-Hall, Inc., Englewood Cliffs, N.J.

WRITTEN EXPRESSION

C-1. THE 100 MOST FREQUENTLY USED WORDS IN THE WRITTEN WORK OF CHILDREN IN THE UNITED STATES

C-2. DICTATION—A LANGUAGE EXPERIENCE PROCESS

C-3. SOME WAYS TO MAKE BOOKS

C-4. SHARE YOUR STUDENTS: WHERE AND HOW TO PUBLISH CHILDREN'S WORK

C-5. PATTERN WRITING AND PREDICTIVE LANGUAGE

C-6. PUBLICATION OF SIMPLE HARD-COVER BOOKS

C-7. PUBLICATION OF THE ULTIMATE IN HARD-COVER BOOK BINDING

C-8. A BIBLIOGRAPHY OF PREDICTABLE BOOKS

C-9. EVALUATING WRITING

C-10. STANDARDS FOR BASIC SKILLS WRITING PROGRAMS

C-1. THE 100 WORDS MOST FREQUENTLY USED IN THE WRITTEN WORK OF CHILDREN IN THE UNITED STATES*

1 the	**4** to	**7** we	**10** of	**13** have
2 I	**5** a	**8** in	**11** is	**14** my
3 and	**6** you	**9** it	**12** was	**15** are

(continued)

*Folger, Sigmund, "The Case for a Basic Written Vocabulary," *The Elementary School Journal*, vol. 47, no. 1, 1946, p. 47. Copyright © 1946 by The University of Chicago. All rights reserved. Reprinted by permission of the University of Chicago Press.

C-1 (Continued)

16 he	33 your	50 get	67 come	84 put
17 for	34 got	51 would	68 can	85 two
18 on	35 there	52 our	69 day	86 house
19 they	36 went	53 were	70 good	87 us
20 that	37 not	54 little	71 what	88 because
21 had	38 at	55 how	72 said	89 over
22 she	39 like	56 he	73 him	90 saw
23 very	40 out	57 do	74 home	91 their
24 will	41 go	58 about	75 did	92 well
25 when	42 but	59 from	76 now	93 here
26 school	43 this	60 her	77 has	94 by
27 me	44 dear	61 them	78 down	95 just
28 with	45 some	62 as	79 if	96 make
29 am	46 then	63 his	80 write	97 back
30 all	47 going	64 mother	81 after	98 an
31 one	48 up	65 see	82 play	99 could
32 so	49 time	66 friend	83 came	100 or

C-2. DICTATION—A LANGUAGE EXPERIENCE PROCESS*

Verbal Expression

Expressive writing is predicated upon a confident and articulate use of language. Proficiency in verbal expression develops only through frequent opportunity to hear good language and to practice it. Therefore, both in and out of school pupils should be given frequent and ample opportunity to express themselves verbally. The ability to speak with clarity and precision facilitates a willingness on the part of the pupil to try to write, may stimulate enthusiasm in the effort, and will more likely spark enjoyment which supports persistence in the writing effort.

Dictation

The creation of good writing is not an easy task. For elementary-age children the initial physical and mental difficulties may be distracting to the point that an organized presentation of their thoughts is prohibitive. A proven way to reduce this tension during the early stages of creative writing is to provide pupils with opportunities to dictate their thoughts while others write them. Dictation can be taken by the teacher, by paraprofessionals, volunteers, peers, student tutors, and by parents at home. The writer should be able to transcribe the pupil's story rapidly and legibly at the appropriate

*Booth, Philip, Fort Jackson Elementary Schools, Fort Jackson, S.C.

level of the child's handwriting development. (If the pupil recognizes letters only in manuscript, dictation should be taken in manuscript.)

For this process to be successful in a classroom, the teacher's management system must allow time and location for dictation. At first a pupil's dictated story should be taken word for word and need not be long. Due to the time-consuming nature of the process, pupils should understand that others deserve time for dictating their stories.

Topics

Topics for writing span the gamut of an individual's interests. Pupils should be encouraged to use their imagination fully and reassured that no right or wrong or limits are imposed on their creativity. Stories may evolve from other stories, from television programs, from personal experiences, and from topics of personal interest. Dreams are a wonderful source of ideas and encourage children to remember portions of their lives which are most often disregarded. Retelling dream experiences also acts as a psychological catharsis, releasing tensions and creative ideas.

Children will often enjoy inserting the names of friends in their stories which adds relevance and an enjoyable personal touch. Story titles relating to the topic can be generated prior to, in the middle of, and after the completion of the story. When the impetus for a story is generated by the pupil, there usually is little difficulty in selecting an appropriate title.

Imposing a writing topic upon a child is not advised, though suggestion of ideas can be helpful.

Rereading, Rewriting, and Sharing

As soon as the finished product has been dictated, pupils should be encouraged to reread their stories to themselves. Difficult words can be rediscovered through the help of classmates or others in the classroom. A time for pupils to share their stories with others should be provided. The more consistent this time, the better. An excellent way to handle this sharing time is to allow a portion of each day's class meeting or show-and-tell time for the presentation of pupils' creative work. In this way pupils know that there is a time each day that they may use to present their stories and can organize their time and efforts accordingly.

In preparation for this, pupils may want to rewrite their story in their own handwriting. This may seem more important to them if they choose to display their stories. Effort should be made by the teacher to display all pupils' work—in the classroom, in the hallways, in the cafeteria, in the principal's office, etc. If the children choose to bind their stories into book form and illustrate them, these can be placed in the class library, in the school library, or wherever seems appropriate for others to enjoy.

Recording their stories on audio and/or videotape increases the fun and pleasure of writing and provides subtle feedback regarding the presentation of their work.

Polishing

Little if any emphasis should be placed upon form and structure during the initial phases of learning to write creatively. Premature imposition of technicalities may inhibit the feeling of enjoyment and confidence that must be established before the pupil is acquainted with elements that lend polish to the written word.

A gradual transition into "polish" should evolve naturally. Elements of good form are modeled by the person taking dictation. Titles, capitalization, paragraph form, margins, should be mentioned fairly casually at first. Punctuation should evolve and be inserted relative to the natural pauses of the pupil's voice while dictating. After a few stories have been dictated and pupils have been touched by the enjoyment and excitement of seeing their verbal expression in written form, they should be encouraged to watch carefully the actual writing of the story as they dictate it.

Their train of thought will not be disrupted at this stage if the person taking dictation says, "I am going to change paragraphs and indent this next sentence because you are changing such and such a subject to another" or "Since we are starting a new sentence, I am placing a capital letter here and a question mark here because you are asking a question," etc. Matching verb tenses to subjects, writing good sentences (minimal use of the word "and"), use of quotation marks, can all be taught in this manner. The process is relevant to pupils' needs and provides immediate and practical learning.

On Their Own

After pupils are confidently writing on their own without the need for dictation, a serious and more intense effort can safely be placed on "final form" without discouragement. No creative effort should be presented to the teacher for constructive criticism before the student has completed personal proofreading. Pupils should be encouraged to proofread their efforts aloud to themselves. If the writing flows, if punctuation matches natural pauses, proofreading is accomplishing its intended purpose. Asking classmates to proofread the story is a wonderful way to teach others while stimulating socialization and group interaction.

At the right time pupils should read their stories in private to the teacher. The teacher should not disfigure the story with corrections but should mark areas where a correction is needed or a clearer statement is required with an erasable mark and allow the pupil to determine the correction. A small eighth of an inch line underneath a correction area is sufficient. The teacher can either facilitate the corrections during the time that the pupil is reading the story or permit the pupil to make the total correction effort. Pupils may solicit help from their classmates if they cannot on their own determine what corrections are necessary. Of course, the teacher should be available for this as well. Rewriting is tedious, especially at the lower elementary levels where the physical effort of writing is maximum. However, the element of rewriting should be emphasized and balanced to the particular capabilities of each child.

The more advanced elements of the writing process such as topic sentences, main ideas, organization, and concluding statements should be addressed gradually. These elements are usually the most abstract and difficult to implement. An important point to remember is that each child's effort is valid and good relative to his or her current level of accomplishment and ability.

C-3. SOME WAYS TO MAKE BOOKS*

Basic Materials

Papers and containers	Fasteners	Tools
heavy cardboard (boxes)	metal rings	scissors
oaktag	yarn, thread	glue
newspaper	ribbon, twine	1″ and 2″ tape
construction paper	staples	paper punch
newsprint	brass fasteners	paper cutter
manila paper	nuts, bolts, washers	needles
wallpaper sample	shoelaces	stapler
books	elastic bands	
flat boxes		
paper towel tubes		

Decorative Materials

crayons, paints, magic markers
contact paper scraps, used gift paper
cloth oddments—burlap, felt cottons

Large Class Books

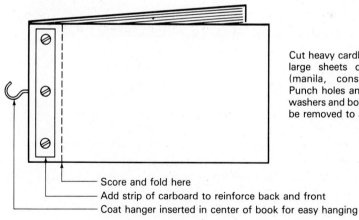

Cut heavy cardboard covers to suit large sheets of assorted papers (manila, construction, oaktag). Punch holes and fasten with nuts, washers and bolts. These can easily be removed to add pages.

————— Score and fold here
————— Add strip of carboard to reinforce back and front
————— Coat hanger inserted in center of book for easy hanging

Protect the book covers with clear contact paper or by brushing with a solution of Elmer's glue and water (consistency of cream).

*Sealey, Leonard, Sealey, Nancy, and Millmore, Marcia. *Children's Writing: An Approach for the Primary Grades*. Newark, Del.: International Reading Association, 1979, pp. 31–34.

Small Books for Individual Use

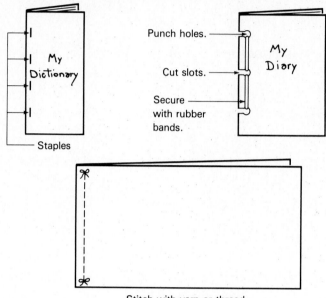

Punch holes.

Cut slots.

Secure with rubber bands.

Staples

Stitch with yarn or thread.

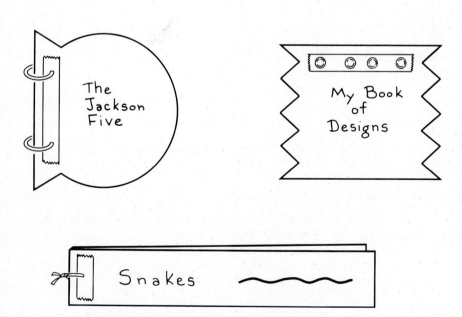

Apply Scotch tape to front and back covers.
Punch holes through tape and fasten with rings, brass
fasteners, twists from plastic bags, or shoelaces.

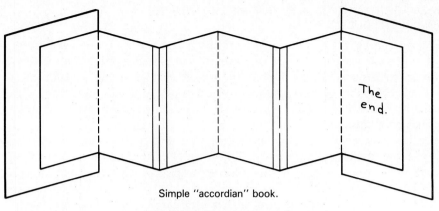

Simple "accordian" book.

Fold sheets of heavy paper and
tape several sheets together.
Paste first and last folded pages
to heavy card covers.

Small Books for Individual Use (unconventional)

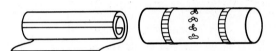

Tape several sheets of paper together. Roll up the sheets of paper
and insert them into a decorated
paper towel tube.

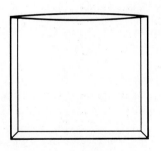

Tape two pieces of cardboard together on three sides only to make
an "envelope." Slip pages inside.

Use flat boxes decorated by individual children to protect the pages
of their stories (One box for each
story).

Roll up pages of writing inside
scrap pieces of felt, oaktag, or
leather and tie into a "scroll" with
ribbon.

C-4. SHARE YOUR STUDENTS: WHERE AND HOW TO PUBLISH CHILDREN'S WORK*

How many times, paging through magazines for children, have you lamented the missed opportunities to have your own students' work shared in print? While we don't want our students to consider publishing the primary goal for writing, submitting their work for publication can be suggested to children as one worthwhile way to share their ideas. Through publishing, not only do young writers share their ideas with a large audience, they gain pride and satisfaction in a job well done.

For those students interested in publishing, this article provides teachers with suggestions, and an alphabetical, annotated list of child magazines that publish writing and art by children. Each listing describes the magazine, types of children's work published, guidelines, and addresses for submitting work. This is not a comprehensive list. It is limited to various secular children's magazines that welcome children's contributions.

Suggestions for Publishing

These general guidelines should be followed when submitting children's work to any publisher.

1 Before submitting material the teacher and student should become familiar with prospective magazines to get a feel for the type of material accepted.

2 Magazine editors work months in advance. Seasonal material should usually be submitted at least four or five months beforehand. Consult specific guidelines and deadlines.

3 Submit work to only one publisher at a time. Publishers don't generally accept simultaneous submissions. You may also want to include a letter with the work stating that it has not been submitted elsewhere. If the work is returned, then resubmit it to another publisher.

4 Keep a file copy of any work submitted. Papers can get lost or misplaced. Some publishers will return the material if it is accompanied by a stamped, self-addressed envelope, others will not. Even those who attempt to return materials cannot be held responsible.

5 Label each contribution securely with child's name, age, and address. Some editors want additional information, such as name of school, parent's consent slip, and a note signed by parent or teacher stating that the child did the work.

6 For the most part editors want original work from children. Don't try to embellish it with adult skill. To do so may actually blemish it. Much of the charm of children's art and writing stems from their style.

7 Follow editors' guidelines explicitly, and send the type of children's work that they encourage.

*Copeland, Kathleen. "Share Your Students: Where and How to Publish Children's Work." *Language Arts,* vol. 57, 1980, pp. 635–638.

Magazines for Children

Child Life is a monthly (except bimonthly in June–July and August–September) magazine, for children ages nine through fourteen. It is published by the Benjamin Franklin Literary Medical Society, Inc., which also publishes *Children's Playmate* and *Jack and Jill.* Young writers, poets, and artists may participate in an annual contest. For rules and guidelines consult one of the magazines. The address is *Child Life,* P.O. Box 567B, Indianapolis, IN 46206.

Children's Playmate is issued monthly (except bimonthly in June–July and August–September) for ages five through eight. Regular features for child writers include "Lines that Rhyme" (original poems with titles), "Jokes and Riddles," and "Pictures by our Playmates." The publisher sponsors an annual contest for young writers, poets, and artists. If you want your material returned, be sure to include a stamped, self-addressed envelope. Send contributions to the appropriate department (e.g., "Lines that Rhyme"), *Children's Playmate,* P.O. Box 567B, Indianapolis, IN 46206.

Cricket, appearing monthly for children ages six through twelve, welcomes letters which are published in "The Letterbox" section. Children may write about something which appeared in *Cricket,* or about something in their own lives. Each month this magazine sponsors story, poetry, and drawing contests, which are described in the "Cricket League" section. Entries must be the original work of children not over twelve years of age, and must pertain to the theme specified in the issue. They must be submitted with the parent's permission and a signed statement by a teacher or parent that no help was given. If entries are typed, they need to be accompanied by the original work. Entries cannot be returned. Mail entries to either "Cricket Letterbox" or "Cricket League," P.O. Box 100, LaSalle, IL 61301.

Dynamite is published monthly by Scholastic Magazines, Inc., for intermediate grade students and older. Readers' comments and bits of verse are published in "Pssssst . . . Pass It On." Send your gags, jokes, tricks, and funny ideas to "Hot Stuff," If you have a pet peeve or gripe (like "Don't you hate when a visitor comes over and you have to turn off the TV show you waited a week to see!"), send it to "Bummers," and it may be published in a cartoon. Look over the contents of *Dynamite* to inspire ideas of your own. The mailing address is *Dynamite,* 50 West 44th Street, New York, NY 10036.

Daisy is a monthly magazine (except for one issue for June through September), from the Girl Scouts of U.S.A. It invites all readers to send original art and writing for possible use in "Show-case" and other pages of the magazine. Along with name, age, and address contributors should include their troop number if they are Girl Scouts. If you want material returned you must send a stamped, self-addressed envelope. Materials should be sent to *Daisy* Art and Writing, 830 Third Avenue, New York, NY 10022.

Ebony Jr! is a monthly magazine (except bimonthly June–July and August–September), for children, especially black children, ages six through twelve. Bea Julian, editorial assistant, writes that *Ebony Jr!* welcomes creative submissions from young readers. This magazine has regular features that focus on children's work: "The Art Gallery" (pictures), "From Our Readers" (letters to the editor), and "Writing Readers" (one-page short stories, as well as poems, jokes, and riddles). *Ebony Jr!*

also sponsors an annual writing contest for children ages six through twelve, which is announced in the April and May issues. *Ebony Jr!* will answer queries from teachers and children, explaining how they can submit work. Contributors will receive responses in three weeks to three months. Mail contributions to *Ebony Jr!,* 820 S. Michigan Avenue, Chicago, IL 60605.

The Electric Company Magazine is published monthly (except bimonthly December–January and April–May) by the Children's Television Workshop, to interest beginning readers. In mailing contributions, mark on the address the department for which the material is intended (e.g., children are invited to send in their favorite jokes or riddles to Dept. EC4B). Other features include a monthly contest for imaginative drawings (e.g., a super dog that you dream up), to be marked for Dept. EC4C, and other "red, hot and burning" ideas to be marked for "Hot Lines," Dept. EC4D. The address for all materials is *The Electric Company Magazine,* P.O. Box 2926, Boulder, CO 80322.

Highlights for Children, published eleven times a year for ages two through eleven, features "Our Own Pages," a section devoted to children's stories, poems, and drawings. The drawings should be black pencil or crayon on white $8\frac{1}{2}$-by-11-inch paper. Entries must be accompanied by a signed note from teacher or parent stating that the child did the work submitted. Each issue also has a "Letters to the Editor" section. From time to time readers are asked to send in limericks, Haiku, tongue twisters, and story endings which are responses to a story-starter picture or unfinished story that has appeared in a previous issue. Other occasional features include "Scissorettes," with children using specified-shaped cutouts to create original pictures; and "Creatures Nobody Has Ever Seen," in which the student must draw, name, and describe an original creature. Riddles and jokes, which need not be original, also are accepted. This magazine does not return contributions. Send entries to *Highlights for Children,* 803 Church Street, Honesdale, PA 18431.

Jack and Jill is published monthly (except bimonthly in June–July and August–September) for ages eight through twelve. A regular feature is "From Our Readers" which includes letters to the editor, poetry, and drawings. Materials should be original and should bear the child's name, age, and address, along with the name of the school. Send letters to "Our Readers Write," pictures to "Picture Exhibition," and poems to "Poetry by Our Readers." The publisher sponsors an annual contest for young writers, poets, and artists. If you want your material returned, be sure to send a stamped, self-addressed envelope. Address all material to *Jack and Jill,* P.O. Box 567B, Indianapolis, IN 46206.

National Geographic World is published monthly by the Special Publications and School Services Division of the National Geographic Society, for students ages eight to fourteen. Features include a mailbag column for letters from readers, games, puzzles, and photo-journalism. The editor suggests that you query in advance about any photography work proposed. The address is *National Geographic World,* 17th and M Streets, N.W., Washington, D.C. 20036.

Odyssey, published monthly, emphasizes astronomy and outer space for children ages eight to twelve. It has an "Input" column for letters to the editor, and a quiz page for contributors (e.g., "Q1: Did a planet explode where the asteroid belt is?"). The

Odyssey Club pages feature imaginative drawings in full colors. Put your drawings on 8½-by-11-inch paper, and print your name, address, and other information on the back. A free sample copy and further information may be obtained by writing *Odyssey,* 411 E. Mason Street, P.O. Box 92788, Milwaukee, WI 53202.

Stone Soup, a literary magazine by children up to age fourteen, is published five times a year, in September, November, January, March, and May. The editors will consider for publication any original artwork and any story or poem written by a child, regardless of the child's writing skills (spelling, grammar, handwriting) as long as the work is not based on obvious formula or cliché. They state they have no length limitations and, in fact, like to receive long stories. There is no need to type the manuscript before sending it in. Pictures may be paintings or pen drawings, and may be any size, color, or any combination of colors. Contributors who want material returned should enclose a stamped, self-addressed envelope. Within six weeks of receipt, editors will notify you of intention. Accepted work is usually published three months to a year after acceptance. Send all work to *Stone Soup,* P.O. Box 83, Santa Cruz, CA 95063.

Remember that your young authors will be competing with many other contributors. If one publisher does not select an entry, that effort may still be acceptable elsewhere. Often work is returned not for lack of quality, but for lack of space. Other outlets for children's work include school district publications, school newspapers, classroom publications, and professional journals. Some local newspapers and broadcasters use students' art and commentary.

Emphasize to your students that whether or not a submission is accepted, writing remains an exciting and worthwhile adventure.

C-5. PATTERN WRITING AND PREDICTIVE LANGUAGE

One of the ways in which teachers can involve all children in writing is to use the technique of pattern writing. Teachers can select stories with recurring patterns, read the stories to the children, engage in language development and language expanding activities, and involve the children in writing activities using the story pattern.

Phyllis Crawford (Crawford, Phyllis. *Pattern Writing* [handout], 11434 Robin Hood, Baton Rouge, LA 70815) states that "From the structured, repeated language pattern, children are able to easily anticipate the sequence of what comes next. The patterns provide a natural and enjoyable stimulus for children to write their own variations. These writings then become a motivational source for reading by the child author and others."

Sources for pattern writing may be found in prose, poetry, songs, language games, the various Japanese poetry forms, etc. Stories with predictive language are especially useful. Some suggested resources for use in the classroom are:

Brown, Margaret Wise. *The Important Book.* New York: Harper & Row, 1949.
Charlip, Remy. *What Good Luck! What Bad Luck!* New York: Scholastic Book Services, 1969.
Clapp, Ouida H. (ed.). *On Righting Writing.* Urbana, Ill.: National Council of Teachers of English, 1977.
Einsel, Walter. *Did You Ever See?* New York: Scholastic Book Services, 1962.

D. C. Heath & Company Bookshop Programs. *That Awful Cinderella & The Poor Old Troll.* Stories by Alvin Granowsky and Morton Botel. Lexington, Mass., 1973.

Kipling, Rudyard. *Selections from Just So Stories,* New York: Scholastic Book Services, 1975.

Martin, Bill, Jr., and Brogan, Peggy. *Sounds of Language Series. New York: Holt, Rinehart & Winston, 1972.*

Martin, Bill, Jr. *The Instant Readers.* New York: Holt, Rinehart & Winston, 1970.

O'Neill, Mary. *Hailstones and Halibut Bones.* New York: Doubleday, 1961.

C-6. PUBLICATION OF SIMPLE HARD-COVER BOOKS*

These publications most often represent the efforts of a single child or of two working together, perhaps as author and illustrator. The author may choose to include dictated materials, writing done independently, or both. If teachers prepare some hard-cover books in advance, with blank pages in them, children may have a clearer idea of what *hard-cover* means.

Published materials in this form may be included in the classroom library or in the school library where they may be catalogued and placed on the shelves with commercially published books, or shelved as a special collection.

From Cover to Cover: Publishing in Your Classroom, Joy Hebert, ed. Chicago, Ill.: Encyclopaedia Brittanica Educational Corporation, February 1970, pp. 5–11.

If hard-cover bindings are to be made, children and teachers need to keep an eye open for sources of cardboard (noncorrugated) and cover materials. Shirt cardboard, gift boxes, and tablet backs are sources. Paper companies in your community may be able to provide access to their scrap containers. Cover materials, including fabric scraps, wrapping paper, contact paper, and wallpaper, may be available from parents who sew, remnant counters in fabric stores, and out-of-date wallpaper sample books.

Steps for making covers follow on the next pages.

Step 1 Stack the completed pages and add two extra pages, one before the title page and one after the final page.

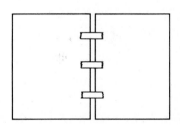

Step 2 Fasten the pages together along the left edge or at the top, depending on the way the book is to open. Staples will be adequate for books of a few pages, but sewing is more durable. Sewing may be done by hand and can be done on a sewing machine using the longest stitch.

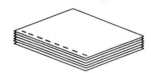

Step 3 Cut two pieces of cardboard one-fourth inch larger in each direction than the page size. If shirt cardboard is used, a double thickness may be desired.

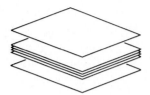

Step 4 Tape the two pieces of cardboard together with a one-fourth inch separation between them so that the cover is hinged.

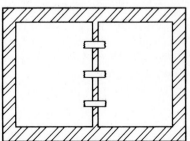

Step 5 Place the cardboard on the cover material and cut a piece large enough to extend one full inch around the outer edge of the cardboard.

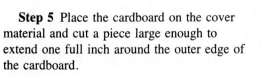

Step 6 Remove the cardboard and coat the reverse side of the cover material with glue. An easy formula is three parts Elmer's glue and one part water. This can be spread easily. Replace the hinged cardboard and fold the edges of the cover material around the cardboard. Pull the cover edges tightly to remove puckers and bubbles.

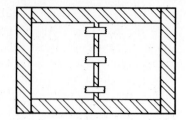

Step 7 Cut a piece of colored construction paper large enough to cover the inside of the book cover and paste it in place over the edges of the cover material.

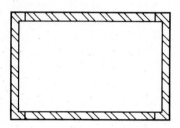

Step 8 Fasten the bound pages into the book with tape. Construction paper the same color as the inside of the cover can be cut and pasted in place to cover the tape.

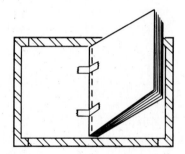

C-7. PUBLICATION OF THE ULTIMATE IN HARD-COVER BOOK BINDING*

This technique requires some materials that may not be available in school supply houses, and it is a more expensive and more complex process. However, the resulting publications are much like commercially bound volumes in appearance and durability. The essential material is dry mounting tissue. This may be purchased at most camera stores and is commonly used for mounting photographs. The most useful is Fotoflat Removable Dry Mounting Tissue, available from Seal, Incorporated, Derby, Conn. This comes precut and packaged in many sizes and can be removed by reheating. To utilize the dry mounting tissue, a domestic iron is necessary, or a dry mounting press

*From *Cover to Cover: Publishing in Your Classroom,* Joy Hebert, ed. Chicago, Ill.: Encyclopaedia Brittanica Educational Corporation, February 1970, pp. 5–11.

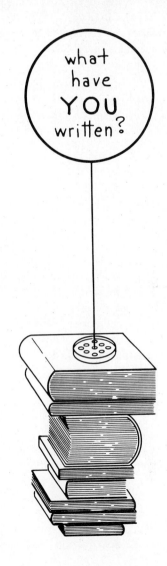

may be used. With these specialized materials, the binding procedure is not too different from that for simple hard-cover books.

Steps for binding follow:

Step 1 Stack the completed pages and add an extra page each, front and back.

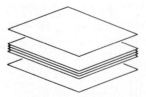

Step 2 Sew the pages together. Sewing by machine creates a more durable binding than hand sewing.

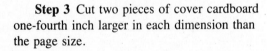

Step 3 Cut two pieces of cover cardboard one-fourth inch larger in each dimension than the page size.

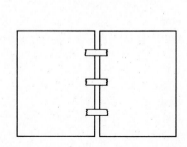

Step 4 Tape the two pieces of cardboard together with a one-fourth inch separation in the hinge.

Step 5 Place the cardboard on the cover material and cut the material to extend one inch beyond each edge of the cardboard. Though many cover materials may be used, fabric is successful and durable.

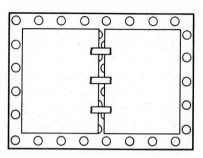

Step 6 Insert dry mounting tissue between the cardboard and the cover material and cut the dry mounting tissue the size of the material. Press the cloth side or the cardboard side with a warm iron (synthetic setting). Under heat the dry mounting tissue becomes a bond between the material and cardboard.

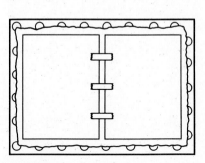

Step 7 Fold the edges of the cover material around the cardboard by ironing the corners down first and then the sides.

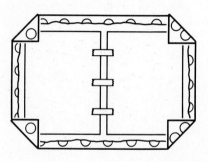

Step 8 Tape the bound pages of the book into the cover. Masking tape is durable

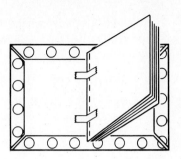

Step 9 Cut two pieces of colored construction paper the height of the pages and more than twice the width of the pages.

Step 10 Cut two pieces of dry mounting tissue slightly less than the height of the book and two inches wider than the page width.

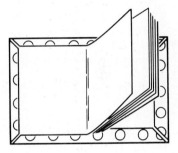

Step 11 Use one piece of dry mounting tissue and one piece of construction paper and lay them in place inside the front cover. Iron the construction paper so that the dry mounting tissue bonds it to the inside of the cover and overlaps to cover the tape in the hinge and adheres to the extra page sewn into the front of the book.

Step 12 Turn the pages of the book until the back cover is exposed. With dry mounting tissue bond the construction paper in place as in the front.

Step 13 Turn the book pages one by one and gently crease them to lie flat.

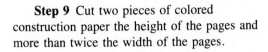
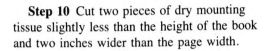

Step 14 Use dry mounting tissue and the iron to adhere a title to the outside front cover.

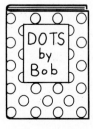

Should a book cover made with dry mounting tissue begin to come apart with use, scraps of the tissue and an iron can be used to make repairs.

C-8. A BIBLIOGRAPHY OF PREDICTABLE BOOKS*

Adams, Pam. *This Old Man*. New York: Grossett and Dunlap, 1974.

Alain. *One, Two, Three, Going to Sea*. New York: Scholastic, 1964.

Aliki. *Go Tell Aunt Rhody*. New York: Macmillan, 1974.

Aliki. *Hush Little Baby*. Englewood Cliffs, N.J.: Prentice-Hall, 1968.

Aliki. *My Five Senses*. New York: Thomas Y. Crowell, 1962.

Asch, Frank. *Monkey Face*. New York: Parents' Magazine Press, 1977.

Balian, Lorna. *The Animal*. Nashville, Tenn.: Abingdon Press, 1972.

Balian, Lorna. *Where in the World Is Henry?* Scarsdale, N.Y.: Bradbury Press, 1972.

Barohas, Sarah E. *I Was Walking Down the Road*. New York: Scholastic, 1975.

Baum, Arline, and Baum, Joseph. *One Bright Monday Morning*. New York: Random House, 1962.

Becker, John. *Seven Little Rabbits*. New York: Scholastic, 1973.

Beckman, Kaj. *Lisa Cannot Sleep*. New York: Franklin Watts, 1969.

Bellah, Melanie. *A First Book of Sounds*. Racine, Wis.: Golden Press, 1963.

Bonne, Rose, and Mills, Alan. *I Know an Old Lady*. New York: Rand McNally, 1961.

Brand, Oscar. *When I First Came to This Land*. New York: Putnam's Sons, 1974.

Brandenberg, Franz. *I Once Knew a Man*. New York: Macmillan, 1970.

Brown, Marcia. *The Three Billy Goats Gruff*. New York: Harcourt Brace Jovanovich, 1957.

Brown, Margaret Wise. *Four Fur Feet*. New York: William R. Scott, 1961.

Brown, Margaret Wise. *Goodnight Moon*. New York: Harper and Row, 1947.

Brown, Margaret Wise. *Home for a Bunny*. Racine, Wis.: Golden Press, 1956.

Brown, Margaret Wise. *Where Have You Been?* New York: Scholastic, 952.

The Bus Ride (illustrated by Justin Wager). Part of a basal reading series (text), Level 2, Book A. New York: Scott, Foresman, 1971.

Carle, Eric. *The Grouchy Ladybug*. New York: Thomas Y. Crowell, 1977.

Carle, Eric. *The Mixed Up Chameleon*. New York: Thomas Y. Crowell, 1975.

Carle, Eric. *The Very Hungry Caterpillar*. Cleveland, Ohio: Collins World, 1969.

Charlip, Remy. *Fortunately*. New York: Parents' Magazine Press, 1964.

Charlip, Remy. *What Good Luck! What Bad Luck!* New York: Scholastic, 1969.

Cook, Bernadine. *The Little Fish that Got Away*. Reading, Mass.: Addison-Wesley, 1976.

de Regniers, Beatrice Schenk. *Catch a Little Fox*. New York: Seabury Press, 1970.

de Regniers, Beatrice Schenk. *The Day Everybody Cried*. New York: The Viking Press, 1967.

de Regniers, Beatrice Schenk. *How Joe the Bear and Sam the Mouse Got Together*. New York: Parents' Magazine Press, 1965.

de Regniers, Beatrice Schenk. *The Little Book*. New York: Henry Z. Walck, 1961.

de Regniers, Beatrice Schenk. *May I Bring a Friend?* New York: Atheneum, 1972.

de Regniers, Beatrice Schenk. *Willy O'Dwyer Jumped in the Fire*. New York: Atheneum, 1968.

Domanska, Janina. *If All the Seas Were One Sea*. New York: Macmillan, 1971.

Duff, Maggie. *Jonny and His Drum*. New York: Henry Z. Walck, 1972.

Duff, Maggie. *Rum Pum Pum*. New York: Macmillan, 1978.

---

*Lynn K. Rhodes, "I Can Read! Predictable Books as Resources for Reading and Writing Instruction," *The Reading Teacher*, February 1981, vol. 34, no. 5, pp. 511–518.

Emberley, Barbara. *Simon's Song*. Englewood Cliffs, N.J.: Prentice-Hall, 1969.

Emberly, Ed. *Klippity Klop*. Boston, Mass.: Little, Brown, 1974.

Ets, Marie Hall. *Elephant in a Well*. New York: The Viking Press, 1972.

Ets, Marie Hall. *Play with Me*. New York: The Viking Press, 1955.

Flack, Majorie. *Ask Mr. Bear*. New York: Macmillan, 1932.

Galdone, Paul. *Henny Penny*. New York: Scholastic, 1968.

Galdone, Paul. *The Little Red Hen,* New York: Scholastic, 1973.

Galdone, Paul. *The Three Bears*. New York: Scholastic, 1972.

Galdone, Paul. *The Three Billy Goats Gruff*. New York: Seabury Press, 1973.

Galdone, Paul. *The Three Little Pigs*. New York: Seabury Press, 1970.

Ginsburg, Mirra. *The Chick and the Duckling*. New York: Macmillan, 1972.

Greenberg, Polly. *Oh Lord, I Wish I Was a Buzzard*. New York: Macmillan, 1968.

Hoffman, Hilde. *The Green Grass Grows All Around*. New York: Macmillan, 1968.

Hutchins, Pat. *Good-night Owl*. New York: Macmillan, 1972.

Hutchins, Pat. *Rosie's Walk*. New York: Macmillan, 1968.

Hutchins, Pat. *Titch*. New York: Collier Books, 1971.

Keats, Ezra Jack. *Over in the Meadow*. New York: Scholastic, 1971.

Kent, Jack. *The Fat Cat*. New York: Scholastic, 1971.

Klein, Lenore. *Brave Daniel*. New York: Scholastic, 1958.

Kraus, Robert. *Whose Mouse Are You?* New York: Collier Books, 1970.

Langstaff, John. *Frog Went A-Courtin'*. New York: Harcourt Brace Jovanovich, 1955.

Langstaff, John. *Gather My Gold Together: Four Songs for Four Seasons*. Garden City, N.Y.: Doubleday, 1971.

Langstaff, John. *Oh, A-Hunting We Will Go*. New York: Atheneum, 1974.

Langstaff, John. *Over in the Meadow*. New York: Harcourt Brace Jovanovich, 1957.

Laurence, Ester. *We're Off to Catch a Dragon*. Nashville, Tenn.: Abingdon Press, 1969.

Lexau, Joan. *Crocodile and Hen*. New York: Harper and Row, 1969.

Lobel, Anita. *King Rooster, Queen Hen*. New York: Greenwillow, 1979.

Lobel, Arnold. *A Treeful of Pigs*. New York: Greenwillow, 1979.

Mack, Stan. *10 Bears in My Bed*. New York: Pantheon, 1974.

Martin, Bill. *Brown Bear, Brown Bear*. New York: Holt, Rinehart and Winston, 1970.

Martin, Bill. *Fire! Fire! Said Mrs. McGuire*. New York: Holt, Rinehart and Winston, 1970.

Mayer, Mercer. *If I Had. . . .* New York: Dial Press, 1968.

Mayer, Mercer. *Just for You*. New York: Golden Press, 1975.

McGovern, Ann. *Too Much Noise*. New York: Scholastic, 1967.

Memling, Carl. *Ten Little Animals*. Racine, Wis.: Golden Press, 1961.

Moffett, Martha. *A Flower Pot Is Not a Hat*. New York: E.P. Dutton, 1972.

Peppe, Rodney. *The House that Jack Built*. New York: Delacorte, 1970.

Polushkin, Maria. *Mother, Mother, I Want Another*. New York: Crown Publishers, 1978.

Preston, Edna Mitchell. *Where Did My Mother Go?* New York: Four Winds Press, 1978.

Quackenbush, Robert. *She'll Be Comin' Round the Mountain*. Philadelphia: Lippincott, 1973.

Quackenbush, Robert. *Skip to My Lou*. Philadelphia: Lippincott, 1975.

Rokoff, Sandra. *Here Is a Cat*. Singapore: Hallmark Children's Editions, no date.

Scheer, Julian, and Bileck, Marvin. *Rain Makes Applesauce*. New York: Holiday House, 1964.

Scheer, Julian, and Bileck, Marvin. *Upside Down Day*. New York: Holiday House, 1968.

Sendak, Maurice. *Where the Wild Things Are*. New York: Scholastic, 1963.

Shaw, Charles B. *It Looked Like Spilt Milk*. New York: Harper and Row, 1947.

Shulevitz, Uri. *One Monday Morning*. New York: Scribner's, 1967.

Skaar, Grace. *What Do the Animals Say?* New York: Scholastic, 1972.

Sonneborn, Ruth A. *Someone Is Eating the Sun.* New York: Random House, 1974.
Spier, Peter. *The Fox Went Out on a Chilly Night.* Garden City, N.Y.: Doubleday, 1961.
Stover, JoAnn. *If Everybody Did.* New York: David McKay, 1960.
Tolstoy, Alexei. *The Great Big Enormous Turnip.* New York: Franklin Watts, 1968.
Welber, Robert. *Goodbye, Hello.* New York: Pantheon, 1974.
Wildsmith, Brian. *The Twelve Days of Christmas.* New York: Franklin Watts, 1972.
Wolkstein, Diane. *The Visit.* New York: Alfred A. Knopf, 1977.
Wondriska, William. *All the Animals Were Angry.* New York: Holt, Rinehart and Winston, 1970.
Zaid, Barry. *Chicken Little.* New York: Random House, no date.
Zemach, Harve. *The Judge.* New York: Farrar, Straus & Giroux, 1969.
Zemach, Margot. *Hush, Little Baby.* New York: E.P. Dutton, 1976.
Zemach, Margot. *The Teeny Tiny Woman.* New York: Scholastic, 1965.
Zolotow, Charlotte. *Do You Know What I'll Do?* New York: Harper and Row, 1958.

C-9. EVALUATING WRITING*

The Issues

Any practical discussion of the evaluation of writing has to answer one basic sort of question: What do we *have* to do to obtain reliable, informative judgments about students' writing? Which evaluation procedures are really essential and which would be nice to try if we lived in the best of all possible worlds? Are there any respectable shortcuts?

In order to answer these questions, we will have to consider two additional questions:

1 What are our purposes for evaluating students' writing? What do we hope to learn and how do we plan to use what we learn?
2 What do we expect student writers to be able to do? What kinds of skills do we want them to develop?

These latter questions may seem to lead us into a quagmire of speculation and pointless theorizing. But they won't. Current information about writing and the writing process provides direct answers to these questions. And these answers, in turn, let us make informed, responsible decisions about what we must do in order to evaluate student writing.

Professional Viewpoints

Purposes for Evaluating Writing. One reason we need to evaluate students' writing is to find out what students need to do in order to become better writers; this involves diagnosing problems students must overcome and identifying strengths teachers may help students utilize. Another purpose for evaluation is to make predictions about students' chances of doing well in subsequent writing courses. An advisor at a college, for example, may want to counsel students about their chances of succeeding in a

*National Council of Teachers of English, *Slate* newsletter, vol. 5, no. 1, February 1979.

particular college writing course. A third purpose for evaluation is to find out how well students are currently doing. This may mean that we want to find out which students in a group (in a particular twelfth grade class, for example) are the best writers and which are the poorest; it may also mean that we want to compare the writing of one group of students with that of another. Or it may be that we want to find out whether a particular composition program is, in fact, helping students to improve their writing.

This third purpose may be the one we most often associate with evaluation. When students come to the end of a semester or a year or a high school career, we are greatly concerned about whether they have learned to write with a reasonable degree of skill. Indeed, this concern may be so strong that it leads us to overlook the first purpose I mentioned, that of diagnosing students' strengths and weaknesses as writers. Such an oversight is a serious mistake. The purpose of the schools is to improve students' writing, not simply to judge it. And, of course, it is hard to improve students' writing unless one has a good idea of the areas in which students need help. Fortunately, we can both judge and diagnose through a single evaluation procedure. But we have to be careful. Not all procedures will allow us to accomplish both goals.

Of course, we might decide to have two or more separate evaluations, one to accomplish each of our purposes. But that seems inefficient. Or, we might decide that diagnosis is the exclusive responsibility of classroom teachers. Such a decision seems reasonable since classroom teachers are continually engaged in diagnosis. The only difficulty here is that diagnosis by individual teachers may not let us identify problems that are common to, say, many of the tenth grade students in a given school.

Expectations for Student Writers. From reading newspaper articles and listening to television commentators, one gets the impression that teachers primarily expect students to learn to observe certain conventions of usage, spelling, punctuation, and sentence structure. That expectation is just reasonable enough to be seriously misleading. Certainly writers must be able to spell and punctuate correctly. They must also be able to write in complete sentences and avoid double negatives. But we must also expect writers to have other basic skills which have almost no relation to the ability to spell, etc. These other skills are *basic* in that, without them, one cannot communicate effectively in writing.

For one thing, we must expect writers to be able to determine what they wish to say. That is, they must be able to explore a topic, to think about their ideas, feelings, and values in order to decide what they want to communicate through their writing. If a writer has previously given a great deal of thought to a topic or has frequently encountered the problem that he or she is writing about, ideas may come very quickly; the writer may decide almost immediately what needs to be said. In other situations, one may have to deliberate for a while, perhaps doing some background reading, perhaps discussing the topic with a friend, or perhaps just sorting out one's own ideas, experiences, or feelings. In any case, writers have to formulate the point they wish to communicate through their writing.

We must also expect writers to be able to choose the language, sentence structure, organization, and information that will enable them to achieve a particular purpose with their intended audience. In writing letters, reports, memos—even in filling out forms—writers have to answer such questions as these: What does my audience already know about this topic? What additional information do I need to provide my audience? Will my audience appreciate my attempts to be casual or humorous, or should I maintain a formal tone? Have I used phrases that my audience is likely to misconstrue?

In summary, we must certainly expect students to observe certain conventions of spelling, punctuation, and so on. But, equally as important, we must also expect them to discover what they wish to communicate and to express their message in a way that is appropriate to their audience and purpose.

Strategies for Action

Thus far, I have been laying the groundwork for answers to the practical questions of how we should evaluate student writing. I'll begin by giving an answer to the most practical of these questions: *Are there any respectable shortcuts?* More specifically, can we rely on standardized "objective" tests? With only one exception, the answer must be no.

Standardized tests are only useful for making reliable predictions about a student's chances of success in subsequent writing courses. For other purposes, these tests are virtually useless. They do not ask students to engage in the activities they have to engage in when they write. Standardized tests do not ask students to decide on a message they wish to communicate, nor to choose the information, language, and sentence structure that will communicate that message to a particular audience so as to achieve a particular purpose. At best, standardized tests determine whether students can perform only one of the basic activities of a competent writer—observing conventions of spelling, etc. Because of this limitation, standardized tests can give us very little information about students' strengths and weaknesses as writers; they cannot help us much with the problem of diagnosis. Our first "strategy for action," then, is to give up the notion that standardized tests can provide a respectable shortcut in the diagnosis and judgment of students' writing ability.

The question "What do we *have* to do?" leads us to other strategies for action.

1 We have to ask students to write. More specifically, we have to pose tasks that give students the chance to determine their audience and purpose, and we have to allow them enough time to formulate their ideas, write a draft, revise it, and check their spelling, punctuation, and sentence structure.

2 We have to ask readers to make judgments about the quality of students' writing. That is, we cannot evaluate by counting specific features of writing—the number of errors, the length of sentences, the use of relatively rare words. We have to ask a reader to decide whether a writer has discussed the assigned topic in ways that are appropriate for his or her intended audience and purpose.

3 We must demonstrate that these judgments are reliable. We must show that a single reader is consistent in his or her use of a particular set of criteria for judging writing. Or we must show that two or more judges, working independently, can use a particular set of criteria to come to similar conclusions about the quality of a particular piece of writing.

4 If we want to make reliable judgments about the writing of an individual student (rather than judgments about groups of students) we must examine more than one piece of writing. There is some evidence that an individual student's writing performance will vary from day to day or from topic to topic. To ensure that we have a fair sample of what an individual student can do, we must base our judgment on at least two pieces of that student's writing.

5 We must remember that the schools' primary obligation is to improve student writing, not merely to evaluate it. Thus, we must choose evaluatory procedures that will help us diagnose students' strengths and weaknesses as writers.

6 We must have a good program for *teaching* writing. We must give students regular instruction in doing the sort of writing tasks which we will use in our evaluation. This instruction cannot be limited to a single course or a single year.

Thus far, I have talked about only the most basic requirements for an evaluation of writing. Space will not permit me to consider specific procedures that will vary depending on whether the evaluation is done by an individual teacher who wants to measure student progress, a school that wants to measure the effectiveness of its writing program, or a state department of education that is obliged to determine which students in a given state are minimally competent and which are not. Fortunately, these procedures are spelled out in great detail in the list of resources at the bottom of this page. The point with which I must conclude is that we can do a responsible job of evaluating student writing and meet the criteria suggested above. And we can ensure that evaluation not only lets us make judgments about student writing but also enables schools to get on with their basic job of improving that writing.

Resources

Cooper, Charles R. "Measuring Growth in Writing." *English Journal* 64 (March, 1975): 111–120.
Cooper, Charles R., and Odell, Lee. *Evaluating Writing: Describing, Measuring, Judging.* Urbana, Ill.: NCTE, 1977.
Diederich, Paul. *Measuring Growth in English.* Urbana, Ill.: NCTE, 1974.

> Lee Odell
> (For the NCTE/SLATE Steering Committee
> on Social and Political Concerns)

C-10. STANDARDS FOR BASIC SKILLS WRITING PROGRAMS*

The following standards were developed by a specially selected committee of teachers, supervisors, and writing specialists for use by states and school districts establishing comprehensive literacy plans. The National Council of Teachers of English urges study of these standards as a means of determining that plans attend not only to effective practice within the classroom but also to the environment of support for writing instruction throughout the school and the community. If effective instruction in writing

*National Council of Teachers of English, *Slate* newsletter, vol. 4, no. 2, April 1979.

is to be achieved, all the standards need to be studied and provided for in shaping comprehensive literacy plans.

At a time of growing concern for the quality of writing in the society, it is important to take the most effective approaches to quality in school writing programs. These standards will help states and school districts assure that efforts to be undertaken will indeed lead to improvement.

Planners must begin with an adequate concept of what writing is. To serve this purpose, we offer the following:

Operational Definition of Writing

Writing is the process of selecting, combining, arranging, and developing ideas in effective sentences, paragraphs, and, often, longer units of discourse. The process requires the writer to cope with a number of variables: *method of development* (narrating, explaining, describing, reporting, persuading); *tone* (from very personal to quite formal); *form* (from a limerick to a formal letter to a long research report); *purpose* (from discovering and expressing personal feelings and values to conducting the impersonal "business" of everyday life); *possible audiences* (oneself, classmates, a teacher, "the world"). Learning to write and to write increasingly well involves developing increasing skill and sensitivity in selecting from and combining these variables to shape particular messages. It also involves learning to conform to conventions of the printed language appropriate to the age of the writer and to the form, purpose, and tone of the message.

Beyond the pragmatic purpose of shaping messages to others, writing can be a means of self-discovery, of finding out what we believe, know, and cannot find words or circumstances to say to others. Writing can be a deeply personal act of shaping our perception of the world and our relationships to people and things in that world. Thus, writing serves both public and personal needs of students, and it warrants the full, generous, and continuing effort of all teachers.

Standards for Basic Skills Writing Programs

An effective basic skills program in writing has the following characteristics:

Teaching and Learning

1 There is evidence that knowledge of current theory and research in writing has been sought and applied in developing the writing program.

2 Writing instruction is a substantial and clearly identified part of an integrated English language arts curriculum.

3 Writing is called for in other subject matters across the curriculum.

4 The subject matter of writing has its richest source in the students' personal, social, and academic interests and experiences.

5 Students write in many forms (e.g., essays, notes, summaries, poems, letters, stories, reports, scripts, journals)

6 Students write for a variety of audiences (e.g., self, classmates, the community, the teacher) to learn that approaches vary as audiences vary.

7 Students write for a wide range of purposes (e.g., to inform, to persuade, to express the self, to explore, to clarify thinking).

8 Class time is devoted to all aspects of the writing process: generating ideas, drafting, revising, and editing.

9 All students receive instruction in both (a) developing and expressing ideas and (b) using the conventions of edited American English.

10 Control of the conventions of edited American English (supporting skills such as spelling, handwriting, punctuation, and grammatical usage) is developed primarily during the writing process and secondarily through related exercises.

11 Students receive constructive responses—from teachers and from others—at various stages in the writing process.

12 Evaluation of individual writing growth:

    a is based on complete pieces of writing;

    b reflects informed judgments, first, about clarity and content and then about conventions of spelling, mechanics, and usage;

    c includes regular responses to individual pieces of student writing as well as periodic assessment measuring growth over a period of time.

Support

13 Teachers with major responsibility for writing instruction receive continuing education reflecting current knowledge about the teaching of writing.

14 Teachers of other subjects receive information and training in ways to make use of and respond to writing in their classes.

15 Parent and community groups are informed about the writing program and about ways in which they can support it.

16 School and class schedules provide sufficient time to assure that the writing process is thoroughly pursued.

17 Teachers and students have access to and make regular use of a wide range of resources (e.g., library services, media, teaching materials, duplicating facilities, supplies) for support of the writing program.

Program Evaluation

18 Evaluation of the writing program focuses on pre- and post-program sampling of complete pieces of writing, utilizing a recognized procedure (e.g., holistic rating, the Diederich scale, primary trait scoring) to arrive at reliable judgments about the quality of the program.

19 Evaluation of the program might also include assessment of a sample of student attitudes; gathering of pertinent quantitative data (e.g., frequency of student writing, time devoted to writing activities); and observational data (evidence of prewriting activities, class anthologies, writing folders, and student writing displays).

Prepared by the NCTE Committee on Standards for Basic Skills Writing Programs

Gary Tate, Chair.
Marjorie Farmer
Richard Gebhardt
Martha L. King
Barbara Lieb-Brilhart
Betty Murray
Lee Odell
Eileen Tway

SPELLING AND HANDWRITING

D-1. 222 SPELLING DEMONS FOR SECOND, THIRD, FOURTH, FIFTH, AND SIXTH GRADES

D-2. WORDS ALL AUTHORS USE

D-3. WORDS WITH IRREGULAR SPELLING AND PRONUNCIATION

D-4. ELEMENTARY SCHOOL DICTIONARIES

D-5. PICTURE DICTIONARIES

D-6. HANDWRITING EVALUATION SCALE

D-1. 222 SPELLING DEMONS FOR SECOND, THIRD, FOURTH, FIFTH, AND SIXTH GRADES*

about	and	balloon	brought
address	answer	basketball	can
afternoon	anything	because	cannot
again	anyway	been	can't
all right	April	before	children
along	are	birthday	Christmas
already	arithmetic	bought	close
always	aunt	boy	come
am	awhile	boys	coming
an	baby	brother	couldn't

(continued)

*Fitzgerald, James A. *A Basic Life Spelling Vocabulary*. Milwaukee, Wis.: The Bruce Publishing Company, 1951, pp. 144–150. Reprinted by permission of the Glencoe Press.

APPENDIX D-1 (*Continued*)

cousin	here	now	studying
daddy	him	nowadays	summer
day	his	o'clock	Sunday
Dec.	home	Oct.	suppose
didn't	hope	off	sure
dog	hospital	on	surely
don't	house	once	swimming
down	how	one	teacher
Easter	how's	our	teacher's
every	I	out	Thanksgiving
everybody	I'll	outside	that's
father	I'm	party	the
Feb.	in	people	their
fine	isn't	play	them
first	it	played	then
football	it's	plays	there
for	I've	please	there's
fourth	Jan.	pretty	they
Friday	just	quit	they're
friend	know	quite	think
friends	lessons	receive	thought
from	letter	received	through
fun	like	remember	time
getting	likes	right	to
goes	little	said	today
going	lots	Santa Claus	together
good	loving	Saturday	tomorrow
good-by	made	saw	tonight
got	make	school	too
grade	Mar.	schoolhouse	toys
guess	maybe	send	train
had	me	sent	truly
Halloween	Miss	sincerely	two
handkerchiefs	morning	snow	until
has	mother	snowman	vacation
have	Mr.	some	very
haven't	Mrs.	something	want
having	much	sometime	was
he	my	sometimes	we
hear	name	soon	weather
hello	nice	stationery	well
her	Nov.	store	went

(*continued*)

APPENDIX D-1 *(Continued)*

were	will	write	you're
we're	with	writing	yours
when	won't	you	
white	would	your	

D-2. WORDS ALL AUTHORS USE*

a	best	cow	few	happy
about	better	cut	find	hard
after	big	daddy	fine	has
again	black	day	fire	hat
all	blue	dear	first	have
along	book	did	five	he
also	both	didn't	fly	head
always	boy	do	for	heard
am	box	does	found	help
an	bring	dog	four	her
and	brother	done	friend	here
animal	brown	don't	from	him
another	but	door	full	his
any	buy	down	fun	hold
are	by	draw	funny	home
around	call	dress		hope
as	came	drink	game	hot
ask	can		gave	house
asked	car	each	get	how
at	cat	eat	girl	hurt
ate	chair	egg	give	
away	children	eight	glad	I
	Christmas	end	go	if
baby	city	enough	goes	in
back	clean	ever	good	into
ball	coat	every	got	is
be	cold	eye	grade	it
beautiful	come		green	its
because	coming	fall	grow	
bed	could	far		jump
been	country	fast	had	just
before		father	hand	

(continued)

*Allen, Roach Van, and Allen, Claryce, "Pupil Book," *Language Experiences in Reading, Level III.* Chicago: Encyclopaedia Britannica Press, 1967, p. 2.

APPENDIX D-2 (Continued)

keep	night	rain	take	very
kind	no	ran	talk	
know	nobody	read	teacher	walk
	none	ready	tell	want
large	not	red	ten	warm
last	now	ride	than	was
laugh		right	thank	wash
left	of	room	that	water
let	off	round	the	way
letter	often	run	their	we
light	old		them	week
like	on	said	then	well
little	once	saw	there	went
live	one	say	these	were
long	only	school	they	what
look	open	see	thing	when
	or	seven	think	where
made	other	shall	this	which
make	our	she	those	while
man	out	should	thought	white
many	outside	show	three	who
may	over	side	through	why
me	own	sing	time	will
men		sister	to	winter
milk	paper	sit	today	wish
money	party	six	together	with
more	pass	sleep	told	work
morning	past	small	too	would
most	pay	so	took	write
mother	people	some	town	
much	pet	something	try	yard
must	pick	soon	two	year
my	pig	start		yellow
myself	place	stay		yes
	play	stop	under	you
name	pretty	story	until	your
never	pull	street	up	
new	put	summer	us	zipper
next		sun	use	zoo
nice	quick	sure	used	
	quiet			

D-3. WORDS WITH IRREGULAR SPELLING AND PRONUNCIATION*

above	could	give	machine	ranger
across	couple	gives	many	ready
again	cousin	gloves	measure	really
against	cruel	gone	might	right
aisle	curve	great	mild	rough
already		guard	million	
another	dead	guess	mind	said
answer	deaf	guest	minute	says
anxious	debt	guide	mischief	school
any	desire		mother	science
	do	have	move	scissors
bear	does	head	Mr.	sew
beautiful	done	heart	Mrs.	shoe
beauty	don't	heaven		should
because	double	heavy	neighbor	sign
been	doubt	here	neither	snow
behind	dove	high	night	soften
believe	dozen		none	soldier
bind		idea		some
both	early	Indian	ocean	someone
bough	earn	instead	of	something
bread	eight	isle	office	sometime
break	enough		often	son
bright	eye	key	oh	soul
brought	eyes	kind	once	special
build		knee	one	spread
built	father	knew	onion	square
bury	fence	knife	only	steak
busy	field	know	other	straight
buy	fight		ought	sure
	find	language		sword
calf	folks	laugh	patient	
captain	four	laughed	piece	their
caught	freight	leather	pretty	there
chief	friend	library	pull	they
child	front	light	purpose	though
clothes		lion	push	thought
colt	garage	live	put	to
coming	get	lived		together
cough	getting	love	quiet	ton
	ghost			

(continued)

*Allen, Roach Van, and Allen, Claryce. "Pupil Book," *Language Experiences in Reading, Level III.* Chicago: Encyclopaedia Britannica Press, 1967, p. 18.

APPENDIX D-3 *(Continued)*

tongue	vein	weather	whose	would
too	very	weight	wild	wrong
touch	view	were	wind	
two		what	wolf	
		where	woman	you
use	was	who	women	young
usual	wash	whom	won	your

D-4. ELEMENTARY SCHOOL DICTIONARIES

Title	Grade level	Copyright	Publisher
The Charlie Brown Dictionary	K–3	1973	Random House (hardcover) Scholastic Paperbacks (paper)
The Children's Dictionary	3–6	1970	A. Wheaton & Co., distributed by British Book Centre
The Ginn Beginning Dictionary	2–4	1973	Ginn & Co.
The Ginn Intermediate Dictionary	3–8	1974	Ginn & Co.
My First Dictionary	1–3	1980	Houghton Mifflin
Beginning Dictionary	3–6	1979	Houghton Mifflin
Macmillan Beginning Dictionary	3–8	1976	Macmillan
Macmillan Dictionary for Children	3–8	1976	Macmillan
The New Horizon Ladder Dictionary of the English Language	2–6	1970	New American Library
The Oxford Children's Dictionary in Colour	1–3	1976	Oxford University Press
The Picture Dictionary for Children	K–3	1977	Grosset & Dunlap
Pyramid Primary Dictionary Series (Books 1–4)	1–6	1971	Pyramid Publications
Scott, Foresman Beginning Dictionary	3–8	1976	Scott, Foresman
The Super Dictionary	3–8	1978	Holt, Rinehart and Winston
Thorndike-Barnhart Beginning Dictionary	3–8	1974	Scott, Foresman
Troll Talking Picture Dictionary	K–3	1974	Troll Associates
Webster's New Elementary Dictionary	3–8	1975	G. and C. Merriam Co. (trade edition) American Book Company (text edition)

(continued)

D-4 (Continued)

Title	Grade level	Copyright	Publisher
Webster's New World Dictionary for Young Readers	3–8	1976	Collins & World
The Weekly Reader Beginning Dictionary	2–4	1973	Grosset & Dunlap
Word Wonder Dictionary	2–4	1966	Holt, Rinehart and Winston
The Xerox Intermediate Dictionary	3–6	1974	Xerox Family Education Services, distributed by Grosset & Dunlap

D-5. PICTURE DICTIONARIES*

Title	Appropriate grade level	Copyright	Publisher
The Cat in the Hat Beginner Book Dictionary	K–1	1964	Beginner Books
The Golden Picture Dictionary	K–1	1976	Western Publishing Co.
Grosset Starter Picture Dictionary	K–1	1976	Grosset & Dunlap
International Visual Dictionary	K–1	1973	Distributed by Carroll Book Service
My First Golden Dictionary	K–1	1957	Western Publishing Co.
My First Picture Dictionary	K–1	1977	Lothrop, Lee & Shepard (library edition) Scott, Foresman (text edition)
My Pictionary	K–1	1970	Lothrop, Lee & Shepard (library edition) Scott, Foresman (text edition)
My Second Picture Dictionary	K–3	1971	Lothrop, Lee & Shepard (library edition) Scott, Foresman (text edition)
The New Golden Dictionary	K–1	1972	Western Publishing Co.
Storybook Dictionary	K–3	1966	Western Publishing Co.
The Strawberry Picture Dictionary	K–1	1974	Strawberry Books distributed by Larousse & Co.
Two Thousand Plus Index and Glossary	K–3	1977	Raintree Publishers, Ltd. distributed by Macdonald-Raintree

*For further information on children's dictionaries the reader is referred to Kister, K. F. *Dictionary Buying Guide*. New York: R. R. Bowker Company, 1977.

D-6. HANDWRITING EVALUATION SCALE*

Presented below are samples of a scale designed for the evaluation of handwriting. Although only excerpts of grade-level one (manuscript) and grade-level four (cursive) are presented here, the complete scale evaluates grade levels one through eight and is available from Zaner-Bloser, 823 Church Street, Honesdale, PA 18431. Directions are given within the scale for evaluating handwriting according to the following criteria:

Satisfactory	Criteria	Needs improvement
	Letter formation	
	Vertical strokes	
	Spacing	
	Alignment and proportion	
	Line quality	

Example 1 -- Excellent for Grade One

I wrote my name
upon the sand.

Example 2 — Good for Grade One

I wrote my name
upon the sand.

Handwriting Evaluation Scale. Columbus, Ohio: Zaner-Bloser, 1979.

Example 3 — Average for Grade One

I wrote my name
upon the sand.

Example 4 — Fair for Grade One

I wrote my name
upon the sand.

Example 5 — Poor for Grade One

I Wrote My name
uponthesand

Example 1 — Excellent for Grade Four

Once I climbed a mountain,
once I sailed the sea
once I flew across the sky
swifter than a bee.

Example 2 — Good for Grade Four

*Once I climbed a mountain,
once I sailed the sea,
once I flew across the sky,
swifter than a bee.*

Example 3 — Average for Grade Four

*Once I climbed a mountain,
once I sailed the sea,
once I flew across the sky
swifter than a bee.*

Example 4 — Fair for Grade Four

*Once I climbed a mountain,
once I sailed the sea,
once I flew across the sky,
swifter than a bee.*

Example 5 — Poor for Grade Four

*Once I climbed a mountain,
once I sailed the sea,
once I flew across the sky
swifter than a bee.*

E

PROFESSIONAL DEVELOPMENT

E-1. A STATEMENT ON THE PREPARATION OF TEACHERS OF ENGLISH AND THE LANGUAGE ARTS

E-2. EIGHT PROFESSIONAL BOOKS TOO GOOD TO MISS

E-3. KEEPING CURRENT: A LIST OF SUGGESTED PERIODICALS FOR TEACHERS OF THE LANGUAGE ARTS

E-4. A LIST OF IDEA BOOKS FOR TEACHERS OF THE LANGUAGE ARTS

E-5. WHAT IS YOUR T.L.Q. (TEACHING LITERATURE QUOTIENT)?

E-6. CRITERIA OF EXCELLENCE IN TEACHING THE LANGUAGE ARTS

E-1. A STATEMENT ON THE PREPARATION OF TEACHERS OF ENGLISH AND THE LANGUAGE ARTS*

In 1976, *A Statement on the Preparation of Teachers of English and the Language Arts* was issued by the National Council of Teachers of English. This statement cited forty-three qualifications considered necessary for teachers of the language arts. This list is reprinted below and it is recommended as a measure with which teachers and teachers-in-training can evaluate their own qualifications.

---

*National Council of Teachers of English. *A Statement on the Preparation of Teachers of English and the Language Arts*. Urbana, Ill.: National Council of Teachers of English, 1976.

KNOWLEDGE: Teachers of English need to know, and know how to draw on for their teaching, according to the needs and interests of their students:

1 processes by which children develop in their ability to acquire, understand, and use language, both oral and written, from early childhood onward;

2 the relations between students' learning of language and the social, cultural, and economic conditions within which they are reared;

3 the workings (phonological, grammatical, semantic) and uses of the language in general and of the English language in particular; and the processes of development and change in language;

4 linguistic, rhetorical, and stylistic concepts that furnish useful ways of understanding and talking about the substance, structure, development, and manner of expression in written and oral discourse;

5 the activities that make up the process of oral and written composing (these activities may differ among different students);

6 processes by which one learns to read, from initial exposure to language in early childhood, through the first stages of readiness-to-read, through more advanced stages by which the reader comes increasingly to understand and respond to details of meaning and nuances of expression;

7 an extensive body of literature in English (including literature for children and adolescents, popular literature, oral literature, nonwestern literature, and literature by women and minority groups);

8 varied ways of responding to, discussing, and understanding works of literature in all forms;

9 ways in which nonprint and nonverbal media differ from print and verbal media, and ways of discussing works in nonprint and nonverbal media;

10 ways in which nonprint and nonverbal media can supplement and extend the experiences of print and verbal media;

11 instructional resources (including educational technology) and varied sources of information (books, magazines, newspapers, tapes, recordings, films, pictures, and other nonprint and nonverbal materials) that will help students understand—through both intellect and imagination—the subjects and issues they are studying;

12 the uses and abuses of language in our society, particularly the ways in which language is manipulated by various interests for varied purposes;

13 problems faced and procedures used by teachers and educational leaders in designing curricula in English for students of different ages, abilities, and linguistic backgrounds;

14 the uses and abuses of testing procedures and other evaluative techniques for describing students' progress in the handling and understanding of language;

15 major research studies on acquisition and growth of language in children and adults, on reading, on response to literature, on the processes of composing, and on the building of curricula for different kinds of students in different settings.

ABILITIES: Teachers of English must be able:

16 to identify, assess, and interpret student progress in listening, reading, speaking, and writing;

17 to take appropriate steps to help students improve their skill in responding to and using language;

18 to work effectively with students of different ethnic groups, including those who do not speak English as their native language;

19 to organize groups of learners for a variety of purposes appropriate to the English classroom, e.g., discussion, creative problem solving, composing, and commenting on compositions;

20 to engage both the intellect and the imagination of students in their listening, reading, speaking, and writing;

21 to ask questions (at varying levels of abstraction) that elicit facts, opinions, and judgments that are appropriate to the subject and occasion;

22 to respond specifically and constructively to student discourse;

23 to communicate to students, parents, administrators, and officials the conclusions that can be legitimately inferred from results of tests purporting to measure progress in using and understanding language;

24 to set professional goals for themselves and evaluate their progress toward them;

25 to guide students in producing discourse that satisfies their own distinctive needs;

26 to help students distinguish between effective and ineffective discourse;

27 to help students experience the connection between the experience of reading and the experience of writing;

28 to help students learn to observe and report accurately;

29 to help students distinguish among the language options (such as registers and levels of usage) open to them in various social and cultural settings;

30 to help students respond appropriately to the differing demands made on speech and writing by different contexts, audiences, and purposes;

31 to help both beginning and maturing readers apply varied techniques to improve reading comprehension;

32 to help students learn to listen effectively for information, for understanding, and for pleasure;

33 to help students develop satisfying ways of responding to, and productive ways of talking about, works of literature;

34 to help students identify and weigh facts, implications, inferences, and judgments in both spoken and written discourse;

35 to help students develop the ability to respond appropriately to and create nonprint and nonverbal forms of communication, including both symbolic forms and other visual and aural forms (including film, videotape, photography, dramatic performance, song, and other art forms).

ATTITUDES: Teachers of English at all levels need to reveal in their classes and in their work with individual students:

36 a conviction that by helping students increase their power to use and respond to language both creatively and responsibly they are helping those students to grow as human beings;

37 a respect for the individual language and dialect of each student;

38 a willingness to respond and help students respond to work in all the different media of communication;

39 a desire to help students become familiar with the diverse cultures and their art;

40 a recognition that, whatever their rate of growth and progress, all children are worthy of a teacher's sympathetic attention;

41 a sensitivity to the impact that events and developments in the world outside the school may have on themselves and their students;

42 a flexibility in teaching strategies and a willingness to seek a match between students' needs and the teacher's objectives, methods, and materials;

43 a commitment to continued professional growth.

E-2. EIGHT PROFESSIONAL BOOKS TOO GOOD TO MISS*

The National Council of Teachers of English asked the following question of 10 percent of its membership. "If you could recommend a book no elementary teacher should miss, what would you suggest?" The eight books most frequently cited are listed below.

Ashton-Warner, Sylvia. *Teacher*. Bantam Books, 1971.

Fader, Daniel, and McNeill, Elton. *Hooked on Books: Program and Proof*. New York: Berkley Publishing, 1977.

Koch, Kenneth. *Wishes, Lies and Dreams*. New York: Harper & Row, 1980.

Moffett, James. *A Student-Centered Language Arts Curriculum*. Boston: Houghton Mifflin, 1976.

Petty, Walter, et al. *Experiences in Language*. Boston: Allyn & Bacon, 1976.

Postman, Neil, and Weingartner, Charles. *Teaching as a Subversive Activity*. New York: Delacorte Press, 1969.

Smith, Frank. *Understanding Reading*. New York: Holt, Rinehart and Winston, 1978.

Smith, James A. *Creative Teaching of the Language Arts in the Elementary School*. Boston: Allyn & Bacon, 1973.

E-3. KEEPING CURRENT: A LIST OF SUGGESTED PERIODICALS FOR TEACHERS OF THE LANGUAGE ARTS

It is the teacher's professional responsibility to keep abreast of new developments in the field of education. Each elementary teacher should establish the habit of reading regularly from some of the following sources.

The International Reading Association and the National Council of Teachers of English publish a number of other excellent materials teachers of the language arts will find pertinent. In addition, membership in these organizations provides an excellent opportunity to attend workshops and seminars at the local, state, and national levels. Information about publications and memberships may be obtained by writing to each of these organizations.

*National Council of Teachers of English. Urbana, Ill.

Periodical & no. of issues per year	Publisher and address
Educational Leadership 5/yr.	Association for Supervision and Curriculum Development 225 N. Washington St. Alexandria, Virginia 22314
The Elementary School Journal 5/yr.	University of Chicago Press 5801 Ellis Ave. Chicago, Illinois 60637
English Journal 8/yr.	National Council of Teachers of English 1111 Kenyon Rd. Urbana, Illinois 61801
The Horn Book Magazine 6/yr.	The Horn Book, Inc. Park Square Bldg. 31 St. James Ave. Boston, Massachusetts 02116
Instructor 10/yr.	The Instructor Publications, Inc. P.O. Box 6098 Duluth, Minnesota 55806
Language Arts 8/yr.	National Council of Teachers of English 1111 Kenyon Rd. Urbana, Illinois 61801
Learning 9/yr.	Education Today Company, Inc. 1255 Portland Place Boulder, Colorado 80302
Phi Delta Kappan 10/yr.	Phi Delta Kappa Eighth and Union Box 789 Bloomington, Indiana 47402
The Reading Teacher 9/yr.	International Reading Association 800 Bardsdale Rd. P.O. Box 8139 Newark, Delaware 19711
Teacher 9/yr.	Macmillan Professional Magazines, Inc. 677 Schoolcrest Dr. Marion, Ohio 43302
Today's Education 4/yr.	National Education Association of the United States 1201 16th St. N.W. Washington, D.C. 20036
The Web 4/yr.	Wonderfully Exciting Books The Ohio State University Room 200, Ramseyer Hall 29 West Woodruff Columbus, Ohio 43210

E-4. A LIST OF IDEA BOOKS FOR TEACHERS OF THE LANGUAGE ARTS

Carson, Ruth Kearney. *Sparkling Words Three Hundred and Fifteen Practical and Creative Writing Ideas*. Urbana, Ill.: National Council of Teachers of English, 1979.

Carter, Candy, and Rashkis, Zora M. *Ideas for Teaching English in Junior High and Middle School*. Urbana, Ill.: National Council of Teachers of English, 1980.

Gallo, Donald R. (ed.). *A Gaggle of Gimmicks*. Urbana, Ill.: National Council of Teachers of English, 1978.

Gallo, Donald R. (ed.). *Gaggle II*. Urbana, Ill.: National Council of Teachers of English, 1981.

Gerbrandt, Gary L. *An Idea Book for Acting Out and Writing Language K–8*. Urbana, Ill.: National Council of Teachers of English, 1974.

Monson, Dianne L., and McClenathan, Dayann (eds.). *Developing Active Readers: Ideas for Parents, Teachers, and Librarians*. Urbana, Ill.: National Council of Teachers of English, 1979.

Sealey, Leonard, Sealey, Nancy, and Millmore, Marcia. *Children's Writing: An Approach for the Primary Grades*. Newark, Del.: International Reading Association, 1979.

Spache, Evelyn B. *Reading Activities for Child Involvement*. Boston: Allyn & Bacon, 1976.

Spache, George D. *Good Reading for Poor Readers*. Champaign, Ill.: Garrard Publishing Co., 1974.

Spencer, Zane A. *Flair Writing Techniques for the Elementary School Teacher*. Stevensville, Mich.: Educational Service, 1972.

Tiedt, Iris M. *Individualizing Writing in the Elementary Classroom*. Urbana, Ill.: National Council of Teachers of English, 1975.

E-5. WHAT IS YOUR T.L.Q. (TEACHING LITERATURE QUOTIENT)?*

	Yes	No
1 Do you read to children regularly and at least once a week?	_____	_____
2 Do you use storytelling when appropriate?	_____	_____
3 Do you relate content areas of the curriculum to literature?	_____	_____
4 Do you read children's books?	_____	_____
5 Do you help in the selection of children's books for your school?	_____	_____

*Elementary English, vol. 51, no. 4, 1974, p. 581.

	Yes	No
6 Do you teach literature as a regular part of the curriculum?	_____	_____
7 Do you try in several ways to evaluate your literature teaching?	_____	_____
8 Do you encourage students to talk about books they have read?	_____	_____
9 Do you have in your classroom a variety of children's books—a changing but balanced collection?	_____	_____
10 Do your plans for the day include time for teaching literature?	_____	_____
11 Do you read regularly at least one publication devoted to articles about and/or reviews of children's books?	_____	_____
12 Do you encourage the use of the public library?	_____	_____
13 Do the students you teach read and like to read?	_____	_____

Score = Number of yes answers

 13 - You have arrived. The students you teach are fortunate, indeed!
 10 - 11 - 12 - You are well on your way.
 5 - 6 - 7 - 8 - 9 - Changes are in order.
 0 - 1 - 2 - 3 - 4 - What are you waiting for?

NCTE Committee, Teaching Children's Literature

 Tony Amato
 Bernice Cullinan
 Claudia Lewis
 Claire Morris
 Norine Odland, Chairman
 E. Jane Porter
 Carman Richardson

E-6. CRITERIA OF EXCELLENCE IN TEACHING THE LANGUAGE ARTS*

Category I Interactions with Pupils Applying Knowledge of Child Development and Individual Differences

> Seeks to understand each learner's background—social, cultural, linguistic—in relation to established sequences of child development.

1 Respects immaturity, demonstrating concern for and personal interest in each child; treats pupils as competent children, not defective adults; helps children grow through maturational processes at their own pace.

2 Observes and reacts to children's responses in order to know them as individuals—what they need, what they can do, and what they are ready to learn.

3 Realizes that the varying behaviors of children express differing needs; accepts variant responses and channels disruptive activity positively whenever possible.

4 Knows that a pupil needs to be aware of himself as a successful learner, both as an individual functioning independently and as a cooperating member of a group.

5 Observes child's motor and perceptual abilities and plans curriculum experiences accordingly.

Category II Interactions with Pupils Applying Knowledge of Teaching and Learning

> Seeks to unify cognitive and affective learnings through action and reflection.

1 Differentiates between immediate and long-term growth of children in cognitive and affective learnings.

2 Fosters an inquiry approach to learning; emphasizes thinking rather than rote memory of facts and details; asks open-ended questions, involving children in problem situations.

3 Arranges many opportunities for appreciative and aesthetic learnings and emphasizes their values.

4 With the help of pupils identifies curricular goals and plans learning activities; provides for individuals and groups to make many decisions about their learning.

*Robinson, A., and Burrows, A. *Teacher Effectiveness in Elementary Language Arts: A Progress Report*. Urbana, Ill.: National Council of Teachers of English, 1974, pp. 71–80.

5 Analyzes learning activities so that readiness is realistically appraised; provides experiences to develop needed readiness; guides acquisition of new learnings; reinforces learnings as needed by individuals and groups.

6 Uses various approaches in appropriate ways to individualize many learning–teaching activities through multimedia, realia, teacher-made exercises, pupils helping each other, individual conferences, and small, flexible groupings.

7 Uses diagnostic techniques and classroom observation to help choose appropriate teaching–learning procedures; recognizes lack of validity of most standard tests for certain linguistic groups.

8 Evaluates learnings by choosing from a variety of suitable techniques, both formal and informal; uses such evaluations to help each child develop a positive self-image.

9 Adjusts procedures to individual variations in rate and kinds of growth.

10 Keeps appropriate records for each child: learnings attained and those needed, changes of interests, and attitudes toward self, peers, and adults; test scores.

11 Seeks aid of different specialists for individuals in need of special help, but avoids excessive number to whom a child needs to relate.

Category III Interactions with Pupils Showing Awareness of Societal Needs and Values

> Acts upon knowledge that communication springs from, is supported by, and contributes to social interaction; utilizes children's language to capitalize on such interaction.

1 Makes language learning in school functional and natural so that children see its relation to life needs; provides experiences in genuine communication both in the classroom and in the community to help children become selective, flexible readers, writers, speakers, and listeners.

2 Develops understanding of and compassion toward others as part of language attitudes and knowledge; demonstrates awareness that dialects express inherent values of different cultures; builds respect for language of peers, teachers, administrators, parents, and others in school and community.

3 Engages in reading and writing, and stimulates other adults to make such activities visible to children.

4 Leads children toward clarity and constructive use of language in making decisions.

5 Provides opportunities at appropriate times for children who need to add "standard dialect" to their repertoire of dialects.

6 Helps children learn some of the language conventions and community expectations for literate behavior.

Category IV Interactions with Pupils Showing Maturity as a Person and as a Professional

> Sees self as guide, listener, questioner, re-actor, and, in general, as facilitator of language learning.

1 Demonstrates enough personal–professional security through spontaneous use of language to create rapport with children rather than defensiveness about themselves and their language.

2 Shows concern for making himself (herself) understood by pupils and others.

3 Demonstrates that positive expectations are likely to elicit positive results in both oral and written language.

4 Gives visible evidence of support to children through varied expressions of approval; shows neutral or negative reactions when essential.

5 Does not feel threatened by child's use of "four-letter words" for aggressive purposes or because of inadequate vocabulary, but "negotiates" with children concerning appropriate language for different social contexts.

6 Listens to each child attentively, giving needed verbal support in fortifying or changing feelings about a personal or social conflict.

7 Listens to each child attentively and helps with a need for clarification or reinforces child's ideas and their expression.

8 Takes pride in children's linguistic progress and lets them know it.

9 Encourages pupils' initiative and responsibility for their own language learning rather than overdependence upon the teacher.

10 Continues to study: individuals and their languages, their needs and strengths, the developmental sequences of growth, the teaching–learning processes.

Category V Interaction with Pupils Demonstrating Knowledge of the Language Arts

> Builds language on experience and experi-ence on language; fosters genuine, purposeful, enjoyable communication among pupils and with others; shows appreciation for pupils' unique-ness and growth in the use of language.

Language—Basic Concepts

1 Is knowledgeable about ways of assessing oral language development and those language deviations that make a difference to communication, for example, listening and reading comprehension.

2 Applies psycho-socio-linguistic principles to all facets of the language arts.

3 Knows about and respects the variety of dialects in the locality as well as the people who speak those dialects.

4 Understands the roles of various dialects and the problems of communication and attitude involved.

5 Relates language learning to the entire curriculum.

6 Demonstrates and develops an appreciation for the values of language in thinking and feeling.

7 Fosters pupils' sensitivity to and appreciation for the beauty of language.

Listening

1 Helps learners focus attention on the meaning of a message; demonstrates use of phonological, syntactic, and semantic clues rather than teaching abstractions about them.

2 Develops appreciation for the many kinds of listening responses and for the complexity of meaningful listening.

3 Assists pupils in developing special skills needed for the variety of listening situations in our technological society.

4 Helps individuals evaluate and use what is heard in solving problems and coping with realistic situations.

5 Honestly listens to what pupils have to say and demonstrates reception of the messages.

6 Provides opportunities to be sure that what the speaker has said is understood by the listeners—peers, teachers, and others.

7 Opens up experiences in listening to and appreciating the diverse language styles used by peers as well as adults.

8 Attends to the difficulties involved in following oral directions by rephrasing, repeating, explaining, providing examples when necessary; helps individuals learn these techniques for clarifying their messages to others.

9 Places emphasis on purposes for listening strategies appropriate to the solving of particular problems; seeks and guides transfer to many in-school and out-of-school activities.

10 Assists children toward conscious and selective listening and nonlistening when the situation warrants.

Speaking

1 Creates a class climate of respect for each individual's speech as unique and valuable; provides opportunity for pupil talk to exceed teacher talk by a substantial amount of time.

2 Lifts to consciousness the original, unique language used spontaneously by children and adults both for its communication value and for its contribution to creative expression.

3 Reinforces child's natural style of talking, helping him avoid artificial, stilted, imitative expression.

4 Develops appreciation for oral language—listening as well as speaking—in pupils' own lives and in the affairs of people everywhere.

5 Accepts speech within the dialect framework of the speaker as well as hybrid usages which demonstrate that the learner is accepting alternative usages from another dialect.

6 Facilitates acquisition of standard American English through exposure to literature and much free oral response to it; uses other positive techniques, such as brief sentence repetition practice when appropriate, without denigrating speech forms used by the child and his family.

7 Helps pupils plan and present oral communications in different ways for different social situations and different audiences.

8 Assists pupils in identifying kinds of problems to be alert to in oral presentations and to apply techniques for clarifying confusion when it occurs.

9 Uses many kinds of stimuli for informal conversion, formal talks, explanations, descriptions, role playing, mime, plays, group discussions, structured panels.

10 Provides opportunities for pupils to learn to use contemporary media for central as well as supporting presentations—tapes, discs, audio-visual devices; develops criteria for and encourages constructive and critical evaluation of media productions.

Reading

1 Considers reading an act of searching for the author's message; recognizes that reading does not take place unless understanding takes place.

2 In addition, considers reading a dialogue between the author and the reader in which the reader interacts with the author, interprets what the author says, evaluates the message, and uses, stores, or even discards the information and ideas obtained.

3 Recognizes that each child brings a somewhat different cultural, social, emotional, intellectual, and language background to reading and uses that knowledge in the teaching–learning situation.

4 Evaluates the strengths and weaknesses of pupils' language development and relates the knowledge gained to their reading progress.

5 Evaluates individual needs in the skills of reading and continually plans suitable instruction.

6 Helps pupils assess their own reading achievement.

7 Uses oral reading as one evaluation technique without constant interference from the teacher and without an audience.

8 Involves children in reading for a multitude of purposes in a variety of materials.

9 Selects from many organizational plans according to purpose(s) of instruction: flexible groupings, individual pupils, pupil teams, whole class.

10 Has children read orally in purposeful audience situations, with material well-prepared in advance, so as to enhance the experience of the listener.

11 Permits children to read orally in their own dialects without correction unless the message is unclear to the listeners; works toward long-term development of reading orally in standard English.

12 Often reads to pupils, involving and encouraging their responses and their interactions.

13 Serves as an adult model by sharing some of his or her reading interests and experiences with children.

14 Uses appropriate opportunities to stimulate wide reading leading to lifetime reading habits.

Literature

1 Selects literature to read to children and helps them select literature for themselves within their levels of conceptual maturity and language sophistication.

2 Reads appropriate literature to children revealing his or her own satisfaction in the experience without forcing agreement with adult tastes and interpretations.

3 Exposes children to varied models of literary merit and discusses qualities of writing with them without extensive analysis; uses open-ended as well as specific questions to focus attention on style, characterization, plot, setting, point-of-view, theme.

4 Provides much unstructured exploration of literature and exchange of responses based upon knowledge that this free experience leads to favorable reading attitudes and ability to read critically and creatively.

5 Keeps rotating classroom library collection readily accessible to pupils; arranges for class and informal individual use of school library and visits to community library.

6 Suggests books of both prose and verse to individuals and groups appropriate to their personal interests as well as to topics in various curriculum areas.

7 Arranges for deepening and intensifying literary experience through free conversation, discussions, dramatics, graphic arts, and written expression.

Written Composition

1 Encourages each child as a writer whose individual and personal expression is worthy of respect.

2 Values ideas, originality, precision, and vividness of language above technical competence of spelling, sentence form, and mechanics.

3 Provides for children's sharing their stories and verse as a valid and essential part of the communication program; often reads aloud the writing of those children whose oral reading is ineffective.

4 Involves children in genuine communication through practical, informational writing and sees that such writing is shared through oral reading and visual display.

5 Helps children edit work that is to be visually shared in order to facilitate accurate reading and to build pride in correct form.

6 Encourages constructive peer criticism; channels critical evaluation toward finding meaning and clarity.

7 Helps children constructively evaluate their own writing, avoiding risk of destructive self-consciousness.

8 Fosters peer enjoyment of narrative imaginative writing, both prose and verse, for its originality, honesty, and uniqueness.

9 Helps child acquire some of the vocabulary needed to discuss or improve his or her writing through individual conferences; uses common needs as basis for group or class teaching.

10 Shares his writing experience with children on occasion.

Spelling and Handwriting—Skills Related to Writing

1 Demonstrates need for correct spelling in writing for purposeful communication, not only for tests; uses test correction as teaching–learning experience.

2 Organizes spelling instruction around facts of individual spelling needs.

3 Emphasizes, through economical study techniques, mastery of high frequency words rather than words rarely used.

4 Provides various study techniques and encourages pupils' experimenting so as to find dependable methods of achieving success.

5 Fosters pride in achievement of individual goals of independence and use of checking procedures.

6 Sees that pupils develop habits of proofreading as part of "spelling conscience" for writing that is to be read by others.

7 Helps children begin to understand the writing system by using language clues and information about sound–symbol relationships rather than merely memorizing abstractions.

8 Immediately provides the spelling of words needed by children as they write in order to avoid loss of ideas.

9 Develops independence in spelling-for-writing by use of word banks in primary grades, and by use of alphabetized individual lists of needed words in middle grades.

10 Teaches use of dictionary to check spelling when children are mature enough to project variant spellings and to find them quickly in the dictionary; is aware of developmental sequence of such skills.

11 Helps pupils realize necessity of legible handwriting in written communication.

12 Provides appropriate practice for specific handwriting problems; demonstrates cognizance of psycho-physical act of handwriting.

Integration of Language Arts

1 Plans for interaction of reading, writing, listening, and speaking and relates them to cognitive and affective learnings.

2 Develops concepts through use of all the language arts, drawing upon first-hand experience and the media.

3 Involves children in activities that show the relationship of simultaneous use of the language arts—viewing and listening (television), writing and listening (questions

and notes after a speaker or interview), reading and dramatizing; demonstrates the unique contribution of each when used separately and together.

4 Provides isolated practice in needed skills in each of the language arts but makes sure that they are applied in meaningful, purposeful situations throughout the total school curriculum.

F

DEALING WITH PARENTS

F-1. SUGGESTIONS FOR CONDUCTING PARENT–TEACHER CONFERENCES

F-2. POLISHING YOUR TEACHER COMMENTS

F-3. PARENT CHECKLIST FOR ENCOURAGING DEVELOPMENT IN THE LANGUAGE ARTS

F-4. REFERENCES FOR PARENTS

F-5. PARENT EDUCATIONAL MATERIALS

F-6. HOW TO HELP YOUR CHILD BECOME A BETTER WRITER

F-1. SUGGESTIONS FOR CONDUCTING PARENT–TEACHER CONFERENCES

1 Review your files prior to the conference in order to avoid asking unnecessary questions.

2 Arrange to meet in a private place where parents will feel comfortable in talking freely.

3 Avoid questions that encourage yes–no answers. Open-ended questions will provide you with more information.

4 Emphasize the positive. Rather than reporting that a student missed 40 percent of the words on a spelling test, report that the child spelled 60 percent correctly.

5 Limit your discussion to the performance of the child and avoid discussion in which the student is compared to siblings, neighbors, and classmates.

6 Give a realistic assessment of the student's progress in relationship to his or her ability.

7 Share with parents any notes taken during the conference.

8 Invite parents to the classroom to observe the student's performance during the school day.

9 If a problem requires additional professional assistance, refer the parents to the appropriate personnel.

10 Provide examples of the student's work.

11 Avoid the use of terms which may be unfamiliar to parents.

12 If needed, provide in writing specific suggestions of things parents can do to foster learning.

13 Maintain confidentiality of all matters discussed.

F-2. POLISHING YOUR TEACHER COMMENTS*

Although teachers try to emphasize a child's positive behaviors in communicating with the student's parents, there are times when negative behaviors need to be discussed. The following list provides some diplomatic ways of describing a student's negative behaviors. Teachers may want to consult this list in preparing for parent–teacher conferences and in writing comments on report cards.

Somewhat harsh expressions	Euphemisms
Awkward and clumsy	Has difficulty with motor control and coordination
Does all right if pushed	Completes tasks only when interest is stimulated
Fights	Uses physical means to win a point or attract attention
Dirty/bad odor	Needs help in developing good hygiene
Lies	Has trouble distinguishing between what is imaginary and what is real
Cheats	Needs help in following rules and playing fairly
Insolent	Needs help in learning to express himself or herself in a respectful manner
Lazy	Needs constant supervision in order to complete work
Rude	Needs to develop a respectful attitude toward others
Dishonest	(See either Lies or Steals)
Selfish	Needs help in learning to share with others
Coarse	Needs help in learning to develop social skills
Noisy	Needs to develop quieter habits of communicating with others
Disgusting eating habits	Needs help in improving table manners
A bully	Has the ability to lead but needs help in learning to be more democratic

*Jehlen, Genie, Fort Jackson Elementary Schools, Fort Jackson, S.C.

Somewhat harsh expressions	Euphemisms
Babyish	Shows lack of maturity
A gang member	Seems to feel secure only in a group—needs to develop a sense of independence
Disliked by other children	Needs help to learn to make friends and form lasting friendships
Frequently late	Needs help to develop habits of punctuality
Truant	Needs to develop a sense of responsibility in regard to school attendance
Steals	Needs to learn to respect the property and rights of others

F-3. PARENT CHECKLIST FOR ENCOURAGING DEVELOPMENT IN THE LANGUAGE ARTS

Oral Expression

_____ Do you set aside time each day to listen to your child?

_____ Do you develop your child's background by taking him on trips to the zoo, park, airport, museum, post office, and so on?

_____ Do you discuss his or her experiences on such trips with your child?

_____ Do you watch television and movies with your child and discuss what he or she views?

_____ Do you play informal word games such as "What word rhymes with _____?" and "I'm thinking of a word . . . ."?

_____ Do you provide and encourage your child's use of commercially prepared word games as well as the word scrambles and crossword puzzles which are designed for children?

_____ Do you ask your child to retell a story you have read to him or her?

Written Expression

_____ Do you provide a comfortable well-lighted place for your child to write in?

_____ Do you encourage your child to write thank-you letters, greeting cards,

_____ Do you encourage your child to proofread his or her work?

_____ Do you provide your child with crayons, markers, scissors, paper, and other materials and encourage their use?

_____ Do you assist your child in holding a pencil and scissors correctly?

_____ Do you set a good example by letting your child see you consulting a dictionary for correct spellings?

_____ Do you have a children's dictionary in your home?

Reading

_____ Do you have children's books and magazines available in your home?

_____ Do you set aside a quiet time each day in which you and your child read?

_____ Do you have a library card and use it?

_____ Do you take your child to the library frequently and assist the child in locating books relating to his or her interests?

_____ Do you share sections of the newspaper (weather, comics, sports, and so on) with your child?

_____ Do you provide your child with a place to keep her or his books? A bookcase, bookshelf, or cardboard box will do.

_____ Do you give books and magazines to your child on special occasions?

_____ Do you provide your child with a comfortable well-lighted place for reading?

F-4. REFERENCES FOR PARENTS

Books

Arbuthnot, M. H. _Children's Reading in the Home_. Glenview, Ill.: Scott Foresman, 1969.
Buskin, M. _Parent Power: How to Deal with Your Child's School_. New York: Walker, 1975.
Chess, S. _How to Help Your Child Get the Most Out of School_. New York: Doubleday, 1974.
Larrick, N. _A Parent's Guide to Children's Reading_. New York: Doubleday, 1975.
Smith, C. _Parents and Reading_. Newark, Del.: International Reading Association, 1971.

Micromonographs

For a charge of 50¢ each, the following micromonographs may be obtained from the

International Reading Association
800 Barksdale Rd.
Newark, DL 19711

Baghban, M. *How Can I Help My Child Learn to Read English as a Second Language?* (also available in Spanish).
Chan, J. *Why Read Aloud to Children?*
Eberly, D. D. *How Does My Child's Vision Affect His Reading?*
Ransbury, M. K. *How Can I Encourage My Primary-Grade Child to Read?*
Rogers, N. *How Can I Help My Child Get Ready to Read?*
Rogers, N. *What Books and Records Should I Get for My Preschooler?*
Rogers, N. *What Is Reading Readiness?*

The following brochures may be purchased from the International Reading Association in quantities of 100 at a cost of $4.00 per 100, prepaid only. Individual copies are free.

Good Books Make Reading Fun for Your Child
Reading and Pre-First Grade
Studying: A Key to Success—Ways Parents Can Help
Summer Reading Is Important
You Can Encourage Your Child to Read
You Can Use Television to Stimulate Your Child's Reading Habits
Your Home Is Your Child's First School

F-5. PARENT EDUCATIONAL MATERIALS

The following is a list of references which parents may find helpful in working with their children. These materials are available by writing:

South Carolina State Department of Education
Parent Education
706 Rutledge Building
Columbia, South Carolina 29201

Parents are advised to check also with the department of education within their own state for similar publications.

Individual Booklet Titles

Biscuits and Band-Aids—A Booklet about Cooking and Safety
Children Learn by Watching and Helping
Expect the Best from Your Children
Good Feelings between You and Me
Help Your Children Cope with Frustration
How and What Your Child Learns through Play

How to Help Your Child Think and Reason
How Your Child Learns about Math
How Your Child Learns to Read
How Your Child Learns to Talk
Nutritional Needs for Young Children
Parent and Child
Pay Attention to Your Children
Practice What You Teach
Read to Your Child
Recipes for Fun
Talking with Children
Your Child and the Daily Newspaper

F-6. HOW TO HELP YOUR CHILD BECOME A BETTER WRITER*

Dear Parent:

We're pleased you want to know how to help the NCTE effort to improve the writing of young people. Parents and teachers working together are the best means for assuring that children and youth will become skillful writers.

Because the situation in every home is different, we can't say when the best time is to pursue each of the following suggestions. In any case, please be aware that writing skill develops slowly. For some, it comes early; for others it comes late. Occasionally a child's skill may even seem to go backwards. Nonetheless, with your help and encouragement, the child will certainly progress.

The members of the National Council of Teachers of English welcome your involvement in your child's education in writing. We hope you will enjoy following these suggestions for helping your child become a better writer, both at home and at school.

Things to Do at Home

1 Build a climate of words at home. Go places and see things with your child, then talk about what has been seen, heard, smelled, tasted, touched. The basis of good writing is good talk, and younger children especially grow into stronger control of language when loving adults—particularly parents—share experiences and rich talk about those experiences.

2 Let children see you write often. You're both a model and a teacher. If children never see adults write, they gain an impression that writing occurs only at school. What you *do* is as important as what you say. Have children see you writing notes to friends, letters to business firms, perhaps stories to share with the children. From time to time, read aloud what you have written and ask the children their opinion of what you've said. If it's not perfect, so much the better. Making changes in what you write confirms for the child that revision is a natural part of writing, which it is.

*Brochure published by the National Council of Teachers of English.

3 Be as helpful as you can in helping children write. Talk through their ideas with them; help them discover what they want to say. When they ask for help with spelling, punctuation, and usage, supply that help. Your most effective role is not as a critic but as a helper. Rejoice in effort, delight in ideas, and resist the temptation to be critical.

4 Provide a suitable place for children to write. A quiet corner is best, the child's own place, if possible. If not, any flat surface with elbow room, a comfortable chair, and a good light will do.

5 Give, and encourage others to give, the child gifts associated with writing.

pens of several kinds
pencils of appropriate size and hardness
a desk lamp
pads of paper, stationery, and envelopes—even stamps
a booklet for a diary or daily journal (Make sure that the booklet is the child's private property; when children want to share, they will.)
a dictionary appropriate to the child's age and needs. Most dictionary use is for checking spelling, but a good dictionary contains fascinating information on word origins, synonyms, pronunciation, and so forth.
a thesaurus for older children. This will help in the search for the "right" word.
a typewriter, even a battered portable will do, allowing for occasional public messages, like neighborhood newspapers, play scripts
erasers or "white-out" liquid for correcting errors that the child wants to repair without rewriting.

6 Encourage (but do not demand) frequent writing. Be patient with reluctance to write. "I have nothing to say" is a perfect excuse. Recognize that the desire to write is a sometime thing. There will be times when a child "burns" to write, others when the need is cool. But frequency of writing is important to develop the habit of writing.

7 Praise the child's efforts at writing. Forget what happened to you in school, and resist the tendency to focus on errors of spelling, punctuation, and other mechanical parts of writing. Emphasize the child's successes. For every error the child makes, there are dozens of things he or she has done well.

8 Share letters from friends and relatives. Treat such letters as special events. Urge relatives and friends to write notes and letters to the child, no matter how brief. Writing is especially rewarding when the child gets a response. When thank-you notes are in order, after a holiday especially, sit with the child and write your own notes at the same time. Writing ten letters (for ten gifts) is a heavy burden for the child; space the work and be supportive.

9 Encourage the child to write away for information, free samples, travel brochures. For a great many suggestions about where to write and how to write, purchase a copy of the helpful U.S. Postal Service booklet. *All About Letters* (available from NCTE @ $1.50 per copy).

10 Be alert to occasions when the child can be involved in writing. For example, helping with grocery lists; adding notes at the end of parents' letters; sending holiday and birthday cards; taking down telephone messages; writing notes to friends; helping plan trips by writing for information; drafting notes to school for parental signature; writing notes to letter carriers and other service persons; preparing invitations to family get-togethers.

Writing for real purposes is rewarding, and the daily activities of families present many opportunities for purposeful writing. Involving your child may take some coaxing, but it will be worth your patient effort.

Things to Do for School Writing Programs

1 Ask to see the child's writing, either the writing brought home or the writing kept in folders at school. Encourage the use of writing folders, both at home and at school. Most writing should be kept, not thrown away. Folders are important means for helping both teachers and children see progress in writing skill.

2 Be affirmative about the child's efforts in school writing. Recognize that for every error a child makes, he or she will do many things right. Applaud the good things you see. The willingness to write is fragile. Your optimistic attitude toward the child's efforts is vital to strengthening the writing habit.

3 Be primarily interested in the content, not the mechanics of expression. It's easy for many adults to spot misspellings, faulty word usage, and shaky punctuation. Perfection in these escapes most adults, so don't demand it of children. Sometimes teachers—for these same reasons—will mark only a few mechanical errors, leaving others for another time. What matters most in writing is words, sentences, and ideas. Perfection in mechanics develops slowly. Be patient.

4 Find out if children are given writing instruction and practice in writing on a regular basis. Daily writing is the ideal; once a week is not often enough. If classes are too large in your school, understand that it may not be possible for teachers to ask for as much writing practice as they or you would like. Insist on smaller classes—no more than 25 in elementary schools and no more than four classes of 25 for secondary school English teachers.

5 Ask if *every* teacher is involved in helping youngsters write better. Worksheets, blank-filling exercises, multiple choice tests, and similar materials are sometimes used to *avoid* having children write. If children and youth are not being asked to write sentences and paragraphs about science, history, geography, and the other school subjects, they are not being helped to become better writers. *All* teachers have responsibility to help children improve their writing skills.

6 See if youngsters are being asked to write in a variety of forms (letters, essays, stories, etc.) for a variety of purposes (to inform, persuade, describe, etc.), and for a variety of audiences (other students, teachers, friends, strangers, relatives, business firms). Each form, purpose, and audience demands differences of style, tone, approach, and choice of words. A wide variety of writing experiences is critical to developing effective writing.

7 Check to see if there is continuing contact with the imaginative writing of skilled authors. While it's true we learn to write by writing, we also learn to write by reading. The works of talented authors should be studied not only for ideas but also for the writing skills involved. Good literature is an essential part of any effective writing program.

8 Watch out for "the grammar trap." Some people may try to persuade you that a full understanding of English grammar is needed before students can express themselves well. Some knowledge of grammar *is* useful, but too much time spent on study of grammar steals time from the study of writing. Time is much better spent in writing and conferring with the teacher or other students about each attempt to communicate in writing.

9 Encourage administrators to see that teachers of writing have plenty of supplies— writing paper, teaching materials, duplicating and copying machines, dictionaries, books about writing, and classroom libraries of good books.

10 Work through your PTA and your school board to make writing a high priority. Learn about writing and the ways youngsters learn to write. Encourage publication of good student writing in school newspapers, literary journals, local newspapers, and magazines. See that the high school's best writers are entered into the NCTE Achievement Awards in Writing Program or the Scholastic Writing Awards or other writing contests. Let everyone know that writing matters to you.

By becoming an active participant in your child's education as a writer, you will serve not only your child but other children and youth as well. You have an important role to play, and we encourage your involvement.

NAMES AND ADDRESSES
OF PUBLISHERS

Academic Press, Inc.
111 Fifth Avenue
New York, NY 10003

Academic Therapy Publications
20 Commercial Boulevard
Novato, CA 94947

Addison-Wesley Publishing Co., Inc.
2725 Sand Hill Road
Menlo Park, CA 94025

Aladdin Books
Atheneum Publishers
597 Fifth Avenue
New York, NY 10017

Allyn and Bacon, Inc.
470 Atlantic Avenue
Boston, MA 02210

American Book Company
450 W. 33rd Street
New York, NY 10001

American Guidance Service, Inc.
Publishers' Building
Circle Pines, MN 55014

American Library Association
50 East Huron Street
Chicago, IL 60611

Ann Arbor Publishers
611 Church Street
Ann Arbor, MI 48104

Atheneum Publishers
597 Fifth Avenue
New York, NY 10017

Association for Childhood
Education International
3615 Wisconsin Avenue
Washington, DC 20016

Avon Books
959 Eighth Avenue
New York, NY 10019

Bantam Books, Inc.
666 Fifth Avenue
New York, NY 10019

Barnell Loft, Ltd.
958 Church Street
Baldwin, NY 11510

Beginner Books
Div. of Random House, Inc.
201 E. 50th Street
New York, NY 10022

Bell and Howell Co.
7100 McCormick Road
Lincolnwood, IL 60645

Benefic Press
1900 N. Narragansett Avenue
Chicago, IL 60639

Bobbs-Merrill Co.
4300 W. 62nd Street
Indianapolis, IN 46268

Book-of-the-Month Club
345 Hudson Street
New York, NY 10014

R. R. Bowker Co.
1180 Ave. of the Americas
New York, NY 10036

Bowmar Publishing Co.
622 Rodier Drive
Glendale, CA 91202

Boy Scouts of America
U.S. Hwy No. 1
New Brunswick, NJ 08903

Bradbury Press, Inc.
2 Overhill Road
Scarsdale, NY 10538

Wm. C. Brown Co.
2460 Kerper Blvd.
Dubuque, IA 52003

Cambridge Book Co., Inc.
Div. of N.Y. Times Media Co.
488 Madison Avenue
New York, NY 10022

Carroll Book Service, Inc.
Box 1776
North Tarrytown, NY 10591

Center for Applied Research in
Education, Inc.
521 Fifth Avenue
New York, NY 10017

Chandler Publishing Co.
124 Spear Street
San Francisco, CA 94105

Cheshire Communications Co.
257 Park Avenue S.
New York, NY 10022

Childcraft Education Corp.
150 E. 58th Street
New York, NY 10022

Children's Art Foundation
P.O. Box 83
Santa Cruz, CA 95063

Children's Book Council
67 Irving Place
New York, NY 10003

Children's Press, Inc.
1224 W. Van Buren Street
Chicago, IL 60607

Children's Television Workshop
1 Lincoln Plaza
New York, NY 10023

Citation Press
50 W. 31st Street
New York, NY 10001

Clapper Publishing Co.
14 Main Street
Park Ridge, IL 60068

William Collins Sons & Co., Ltd.
2080 W. 117th Street
Cleveland, OH 44111

Contemporary Books, Inc.
180 N. Michigan Avenue
Chicago, IL 60601

Continental Press, Inc.
520 E. Bainbridge Street
Elizabethtown, PA 17022

Coronet Instructional Media
65 E.S. Water Street
Chicago, IL 60601

Crestwood House
515 N. Front Street
P.O. Box 3427
Mankato, MN 56001

Thomas Crowell
201 Park Avenue S.
New York, NY 10003

Crown Publishers, Inc.
1 Park Avenue
New York, NY 10016

Curriculum Associates, Inc.
5 Esquire Road
North Billerica, MA 01862

Curriculum Innovations, Inc.
501 Lake Forest Avenue
Highwood, IL 60040

Delacourte Press
c/o Dell Publishing Co.
1 Dag Hammarskjold Plaza
245 E. 47th Street
New York, NY 10017

Dell Publishing Co.
1 Dag Hammarskjold Plaza
245 E. 47th Street
New York, NY 10017

Developmental Learning Materials
7440 Natchez Avenue
Niles, IL 60648

Dial Press
Subs. of Dell Publishing Co.
1 Dag Hammarskjold Plaza
245 E. 47th Street
New York, NY 10017

Doubleday and Co., Inc.
277 Park Avenue
New York, NY 10017

E. P. Dutton and Co.
201 Park Avenue S.
New York, NY 10003

The Economy Co.
Box 25308
1901 W. Walnut Street
Oklahoma City, OK 73125

Educational Services, Inc.
P.O. Box 219
Stevensville, MI 49127

Educational Developmental
Laboratories, Inc.
Div. of McGraw-Hill Book Co.
1221 Ave. of the Americas
New York, NY 10020

Encyclopaedia Britannica Educational
Corp.
425 North Michigan Avenue
Chicago, IL 60611

Eriksson, Paul S., Pubs.
Battell Building
Middlebury, VT 05753

M. Evans & Co. Inc.
216 E. 49th Street
New York, NY 10017

Farrar, Straus & Giroux, Inc.
19 Union Sq. W.
New York, NY 10003

Fearon–Pitman Publishers, Inc.
6 Davis Drive
Belmont, CA 94002

Follett Educational Corp.
1010 W. Washington Blvd.
Chicago, IL 60607

Four Winds Press
Scholastic Book Service
50 W. 44th Street
New York, NY 10036

Garrard Publishing Co.
1607 N. Market Street
Champaign, IL 61820

Ginn and Co.
Div. of Xerox
191 Spring Street
Lexington, MA 02173

Girl Scouts of USA
830 Third Avenue
New York, NY 10022

Greenwillow Books
Div. of William Morrow & Co., Inc.
105 Madison Avenue
New York, NY 10016

Grolier Educational Corp.
845 Third Avenue
New York, NY 10022

Grosset and Dunlap, Inc.
51 Madison Avenue
New York, NY 10010

Grune and Stratton, Inc.
381 Park Avenue S.
New York, NY 10016

Harcourt Brace Jovanovich
757 Third Avenue
New York, NY 10017

Harper & Row, Inc.
10 E. 53rd Street
New York, NY 10022

Highlights for Children, Inc.
2300 West Fifth Avenue
P.O. Box 269
Columbus, OH 43216

Holiday House, Inc.
18 E. 53rd Street
New York, NY 14304

Holt, Rinehart and Winston
383 Madison Avenue
New York, NY 10017

Houghton Mifflin Co.
Pennington-Hopewell Road
Hopewell, NJ 08525

Ideal School Supply Co.
11000 S. Lavergne
Oak Lawn, IL 08525

Indiana University Press
Tenth and Morton Streets
Bloomington, IN 47405

Instructo Corp.
200 Cedar Hollow Road
Paoli, PA 19301

International Reading Association
800 Barksdale Road
Newark, DE 19711

Jamestown Publishers
Box 6743
Providence, RI 02940

Jastak Associates, Inc.
1526 Gilpin Avenue
Wilmington, DE 19806

Johnson Publishing Co., Inc.
820 S. Michigan Avenue
Chicago, IL 60605

Judy Publishing Co.
Box 5270, Main Post Office
Chicago, IL 60608

Junior Literary Guild
501 Franklin Avenue
Garden City, NY 11530

Kendall/Hunt Publishing Co.
Subs. of William C. Brown Co.
2460 Kerper Boulevard
Dubuque, IA 52001

Alfred A. Knopf
Subs. of Random House, Inc.
201 E. 50th Street
New York, NY 10022

Laidlaw Bros.
Thatcher and Madison Streets
River Forest, IL 60305

Larousse & Co., Inc.
572 Fifth Avenue
New York, NY 10036

Learning Tree Filmstrips
934 Pearl Street
P.O. Box 1590, Dept. 75
Boulder, CO 80306

J. B. Lippincott Co.
227–31 S. 6th St.
E. Washington Square
Philadelphia, PA 19105

Little, Brown & Co.
34 Beacon Street
Boston, MA 02106

Longman, Inc.
19 W. 42nd Street
New York, NY 10036

Lothrop, Lee & Shepard Co.
Div. of William Morrow & Co., Inc.
105 Madison Avenue
New York, NY 10016

Lyons & Carnahan Educational
Publishers
407 E. 25th Street
Chicago, IL 60616

Macmillan Publishing Co.
866 Third Avenue
New York, NY 10022

Marvel Comics Group
Cadence Industries
666 Fifth Avenue
New York, NY 10019

McGraw-Hill Book Co.
1221 Ave. of the Americas
New York, NY 10020

G. & C. Merriam Co.
Subs. of Encyclopaedia Britannica,
Inc.
47 Federal Street
Springfield, MA 01101

Julian Messner
1230 Ave. of the Americas
New York, NY 10020

Metropolitan Museum of Art
Fifth Avenue and 82nd Street
New York, NY 10028

Milton Bradley Co.
74 Park Street
Springfield, MA 01101

William Morrow & Co.
105 Madison Avenue
New York, NY 10016

National Geographic Society
Educational Services
Dept. 01075
17th and M Streets NW
Washington, DC 20036

National Council of Teachers of
English
1111 Kenyon Road
Urbana, IL 61801

National Wildlife Federation
1412 16th Street NW
Washington, DC 20036

New American Library, Inc.
Subs. of The Times Mirror Co.,
Inc.
1301 Ave. of the Americas
New York, NY 10019

Open Court Publishing Co.
P.O. Box 100
LaSalle, IL 61301

Oxford University Press
200 Madison Avenue
New York, NY 10016

Pantheon Books
Div. of Random House, Inc.
201 E. 50th Street
New York, NY 10022

Parents' Magazine Enterprises, Inc.
52 Vanderbuilt Avenue
New York, NY 10017

Parnassus Press
4080 Halleck Street
Emeryville, CA 94608

Penguin Books, Inc.
7110 Ambassador Road
Baltimore, MD 21207

Plays, Inc., Publishers
8 Arlington Street
Boston, MA 02116

Prentice-Hall, Inc.
U.S. Hwy. No. 9
Englewood Cliffs, NJ 07632

G. P. Putnam's Sons
200 Madison Avenue
New York, NY 10016

Rand McNally & Co.
Box 7600
Chicago, IL 60680

Random House
201 E. 50th Street
New York, NY 10022

Saturday Evening Post Co.
1100 Waterway Blvd.
P.O. Box 567B
Indianapolis, IN 46206

Scarecrow Press, Inc.
Subs. of Grolier Educational Corp.
52 Liberty Street
Box 656
Metuchen, NJ 08840

Scholastic Magazines & Book Services
50 W. 44th Street
New York, NY 10036

Science Research Associates
259 E. Erie Street
Chicago, IL 60611

Scott Education Division
35 Lower Westfield Road
Holyoke, MA 01040

Scott, Foresman & Co.
1900 E. Lake Avenue
Glenview, IL 60025

Charles Scribner's Sons
597 Fifth Avenue
New York, NY 10017

The Seabury Press, Inc.
815 2nd Avenue
New York, NY 10017

Strawberry Books
Div. of Larousse & Co., Inc.
572 Fifth Ave.
New York, NY 10036

Troll Associates
320 Rte. 17
Mahwah, NJ 07430

University of Chicago Press
5801 Ellis Avenue
Chicago, IL 60637

The Viking Press
625 Madison Avenue
New York, NY 10022

Walker Publishing Co., Inc.
720 Fifth Avenue
New York, NY 10019

Frederick Warne & Co., Inc.
101 Fifth Avenue
New York, NY 10003

Watts Franklin, Inc.
845 Third Avenue
New York, NY 10022

Western Publishing Co., Inc.
850 Third Ave.
New York, NY 10022

Albert Whitman & Co.
560 W Lake Street
Chicago, IL 60606

H. W. Wilson Co.
950 University Avenue
Bronx, NY 10452

Windmill Books, Inc.
1230 Ave. of the Americas
New York, NY 10020

Xerox Education Publications
245 Long Hill Road
Middletown, CN 06457

Zaner-Bloser
823 Church Street
Honesdale, PA 18431

INDEX

Achievement tests, 117, 119, 124, 127, 128, 130, 132, 257–260
Activities:
  enrichment, 75
  handwriting practice: for home, 59, 64
    for language arts programs, 129, 133
    for library use, 126, 181–182, 186
  listening, 68, 86–90, 129, 131, 133, 141–146, 213–217
  reading, 48, 67–69, 181–182, 186, 190, 235–236
  for spelling, 45, 46, 149, 221
  vocabulary building, 95, 98, 99
  writing, 38, 39, 127–129, 151–156, 192, 194, 197–198, 224
Adolescence, 207
Adventuring with Books (National Council of Teachers of English), 172
Affective domain, 73
Allington, R. L., 135
American Association of School Librarians, 172
American Council on Education, 111
Applebee, A. W., 220, 224, 225
Arbuthnot, M. H., 125
Attitude:
  toward language arts, 66, 70, 74
  toward school, 66, 70
  of teachers, 119, 128
Audience-speaker rapport, 168
Auditory perception and discrimination, 22, 23, 29
Ayres Handwriting Scale, 166, 229

Bader, L., 133, 262
Baker, D., 135
Bamberg, B., 224
Bamman, H. A., 220
Barbe, W. B., 220
Basal Language Arts program, 75, 76
Basic skills, 3
Battenberg, A., 181–182, 186
Bear Named Paddington, A (Bond), 182, 186
Beauchamp, M., 76
Becking, M. F., 218
Beers, J. W., 148
Berlinger, D. C., 252
Best Books for Children (R. R. Bowker Company), 172

Bibliotherapy, 236
Biehler, R. F., 84, 112
Bishop, C., 118, 122
Blair, T. R., 249, 253
Bloom, B. S., 187
Blume, J., 181, 186
Body expression:
  games, 59, 64
  language and, 68, 71
Book Center, 55, 60
Book clubs for children, 109, 235
Book collections, 235
Booklists, 125
Books:
  helping children select, 70, 71, 109, 110
  lists of, 108
  in room, 116, 120
  (*See also* Library)
Brookover, W. B., 73
Brophy, J. E., 248
Brown, R., 6
Bulletin board, 193, 195–196, 200
Bulletin of the Center of Children's Books, The, 125
Burns, P. C., 68, 70, 133, 169, 200
Buros, O. K., 218

Cahill, R. B., 225
Calkins, L. N., 190
Caps for Sale (Slobodkina), 68, 71
Carlson, R. K., 98
Carter, C., 225
Castallo, R., 171
Cazden, C. C., 9, 11, 218, 226, 233
Censorship, 111, 237
Charlotte's Web (White), 127
Children:
  differences among, that affect learning, 1
  emotional characteristics of, 208, 210–215
  expression of thoughts by, 101
  intellectual characteristics of, 24, 25, 85, 141, 208, 213–215
  left-handed, 103
  motivating, to write, 97
    and peer groups, 140
  physical characteristics of, 54, 60, 83, 84, 139, 140, 208–209
  physical development of, 54, 60, 83, 84, 208–209

Children (*Cont.*):
  social characteristics of, 23, 24, 54, 55, 60, 61, 140, 179–180, 183, 208, 210–213
  teaching, to listen, 141–144
  vocabulary development in, 98
Children and Books (Sutherland), 108, 125
Children's Literature for the Elementary School (Huck), 66, 108, 125
Children's Writing: An Approach for the Primary Grades (Sealey, Sealey and Millmore), 38, 39
Chomsky, N., 9
Choral reading, 167, 232
Class sizes, 206
Classroom:
  environment of, 10, 66, 116, 120, 125, 179, 182, 184, 187
  help for speech in, 65, 127
  library in, 116, 120, 125, 126
  management of, 116, 120, 125, 126, 260–261
  organization of, 70
  records in, 260–261
Clay, M., 38, 187
Cognitive development, 25, 141
Cohen, L., 8
Communication, 14, 69, 70, 73, 151, 231–232
Composition, 94–101, 151–163, 223–226
  for communication, 151
  instruction in, 96–98, 197, 225
  interest in, 224
  in listening, 142
  objectives of: affective, 96–97
    cognitive, 95–96
  problems in, 98, 161, 225–226
  proofreading, 99, 154
  punctuation in, 95–96, 156–157
  readiness for, 95
  skill development in, 95–96, 152
  (*See also* Writing)
Concentration games, 59, 64
Conferences, 127, 129, 161–162
Conger, J. J., 207
Content areas, 190, 191, 193–194, 196–197
  reading in, 169–170, 205, 236, 237
  spelling in, 219, 222
Conversation, 117, 122–123
  informal, 231
Cook, G. E., 65, 252
Cooking Center, 55, 60
Cooper, C., 226
Cooperative Primary Test, 90
Corboy, M., 7, 263
Creative play, 105
Creative writing:
  evaluation of, 127, 128

Creative writing (*Cont.*):
  opportunities for, 164
  (*See also* Writing)
Criteria for Planning and Evaluation of English Language Arts Curriculum Guides, 267–273
Critical reading (*see* Reading)
Cronback, L. J., 260
Cruickshank, D. R., 252
Crystallization period, 83
Cullinan, B., 66
Cunningham, J. W., 216
Cunningham, P. M., 216
Curriculum, 3, 58, 59, 63, 64, 216, 217
  middle school, 206
  and reading, 169
  and teachers, 252
Curriculum guides, 192, 194, 196
Cursive writing, 102–103, 164, 166, 229
Cut the Deck, 225

Dale, E., 220
Deardon, R. F., 6, 18
Debating, 231
DeHaven, G. P., 93, 96, 97, 102, 107, 111, 112
DeStefano, J. S., 13, 25, 135
Devine, T. G., 215
Dewey, J., 2
Diagnostic Teaching of Language Arts (Burns), 169, 218
Diagnostic testing, 127, 129
Dialects, 169, 233
  defined, 13
  variations in, 13, 35
  (*See also* Language)
Dictionaries, 91, 93, 222
  homemade, 45
Diederich, P. B., 227
DiMartino, C. J., 246
Directed Listening Activity, 216
Discourse, modes of, 224
D'Nealian writing system, 41
Donoghue, M. R., 75
Downing, J., 25, 49
Dramatization:
  of conversation, 168
  puppets and, 118, 122, 127, 129
  of stories, 127, 168, 236
Durkin, D., 133
Durrell Listening-Reading Series, 90, 147

Easy Reading (International Reading Association), 235
Education Index, The, 264

Educational development, 179, 182, 184, 187
Elementary School Journal, The, 263
Elementary and Secondary Education Act
    (ESEA), 2
Elliot, S., 198
Emerson, R. W., 1
Emotion, 27
Emotional characteristics, 208, 210–215
*Encyclopedia of Activities for Teaching
    Grades K–3* (Malehorn), 68, 70
English Journal, 263
Environment, classroom, 10, 67, 116, 120,
    125, 179, 182, 184, 187
Epstein, H., 207
Erikson, E., 24, 84
ESEA (Elementary and Secondary Education
    Act), 2
Evaluation:
    of creative writing, 127, 128
    of handwriting, 129, 131
        scales for, 164–165, 230
    of listening, 34, 35, 89–90, 147, 218
    of objectives, 126
    of progress, 121–122, 124, 127–128, 134,
        192, 195, 260
    of weekly work, 124, 131, 192
    of writing, 226

Fader, D. N., 199, 225, 234
Federal funding, 2
Ferris, S. R., 168
Field trips, 57, 62
*Fifty Creative Ways to Use Paperbacks in the
    Middle Grades* (Hellriegel), 235
Fisher, C. J., 78, 87, 222, 232
Five Chinese Brothers (Bishop), 118, 122
Fogelberg, D. D., 170
Folders for writing, 161–162
Forester, A. D., 43, 44, 46
Fox, S. E., 135
*From The Mixed-Up Files of Mrs. Basil E.
    Frankweiler* (Konigsburg), 181, 186, 190
Fylemon, R., 57, 62

Gag, W., 68, 71
Gambrell, L. B., 221
Games:
    for concentration, 59, 64
    as interaction, 191, 194, 199
    listening, 29
    spelling, 45, 92–93, 198–199, 220, 221
Gazda, G., 136
Georgiady, N. P., 208–215
Good, T. L., 249

Goodman, K. S., 6, 38
Goodman, Y., 38
Gorman, A. H., 73
Grading (*see* Evaluation)
Grammar, 155–160
    and composition, 156
    defined, 156
    functional usage, 197
    teaching, 155–160, 191, 194, 198
    and writing, 155–157, 191, 194, 198, 224
    (*See also* Language)
Graves, D. H., 223
Green Eggs and Ham (Seuss), 55, 61
Greene, H., 222
Griffiths, D. E., 253
Groups, 117, 118, 121–122, 126, 128–132,
    192, 194, 199
    ability, 117, 132

Haley-James, S., 152, 198, 223
Handedness, 23
Handwriting, 40–42, 101–104, 163–166,227–229
    assessment of, 43, 104, 166, 229, 230
    common errors in, 165
    cursive, 102–103, 164, 166, 229
        transition from manuscript to, 102–103,164
    developing prewriting skills, 37, 38, 41
    developing skill in, 41, 129, 131
    O'Nealian system, 41
    evaluating, 129, 131
        scales for, 103, 165, 166, 229
    instruction in: beginning, 41–42, 101
        in context, 227
        continuing, 129, 131, 164–165
        forms of, 41, 42
        goals for, 227
        individualized, 67, 70, 129, 130, 131, 164,
            193, 196, 227
    for left-handed child, 42, 103
    legibility, 227
    letter form models, 164, 165
    manuscript writing, 42, 101, 162–164
    and modalities, 227
    muscular control, 164
    objectives, 101
    periods for, 67, 68
    problems, 42, 103, 165, 166, 227–228
    position and movement in, 41, 42, 102
    for speed, 103, 165
integration of, 103
logs, 166
models, 103
practice, 42, 103
    (*See also* Activities, handwriting practice)
readiness for, 42, 101, 102

Hansen-Krening, N., 104
"Happy Grams," 129, 131, 193, 196
Harding, D. W., 190
Hearing, 142, 143
Heilman, A. W., 249
Henderson, E. H., 148
Henry, C., 3
Hickman, J., 190
High Interest—Easy Reading (National
    Council of Teachers of English), 235
Hillman, J., 190
Hirsch, E., 103
Hobson, C. F., 73
Hodges, R. E., 148, 150, 165, 199, 218
Holdzkom, D., 154, 156
Holt, Rinehart and Winston, 76
Homework, 69, 72
Horn Book, The, 125
*How Can I Help My Child Build Positive
    Attitudes Towards Reading?* (Glazer),
    191
How To Handle the Paper Load (National
    Council of Teachers of English), 226
Huck, C. S., 9, 10, 30, 47, 66, 110, 125
Hunt, L., 12
Hursh, H., 246

*Ideas for Teaching English in the Junior High
    and Middle School* (Carter and Rashkis),
    225
Identity, building child's, 140
*Individualized Language Arts: Diagnosis,
    Prescription, and Evaluation* (Weehawken
    Board of Education), 225
Instruction (*see* Teaching)
Instructional groups, 117, 118, 121–122, 126,
    128–132
Integrated approach, 3–5
Integration:
    of language arts, 3, 121, 130, 197
    of school and home, 63, 70
    of subjects and skills, 67, 70, 74, 75
Intellectual characteristics, 24, 25, 85, 141,
    208, 213–215
Interaction, games as, 191, 194, 199
International Reading Association, 173

Jacobs, L. B., 151
Jacobson, L., 124
Jensen, J. M., 189, 259
Joplin Plan, 131
Journal of Educational Research, 264
Journal of Reading, 263
Journals, use of, 39, 192, 195, 199, 264

Kagan, J., 83, 85, 207
Kean, J. M., 104
Keats, E. J., 39
Kellogg, R. E., 86
Kindergarten, 21–49, 53–67
Klein, M. L., 224
Konigsburg, E. L., 181, 186

Laird, C., 1
Landry, D. L., 217
Lane, H., 76
Langer, S. K., 65
Language:
    and body expression, 59, 64
    cognitive experiences, 86
    development (*see* Language development)
    enrichment activities, 68, 70
    observation of, 74, 79
    and thought, 3, 5
    (*See also* Language arts; Listening; Speech;
        Speech skills)
Language activities:
    experience stories, 129, 131, 133
    materials and expression, 129, 131, 133
    story telling, 129, 131, 133
    (*See also* Language)
Language arts:
    activities, 196, 199, 200
    and content areas, 191, 193–194, 196–197
    curriculum guides for, 192, 194, 196
    defined, 3
    as foundation of school curriculum, 3
    growth and development in, 188–189
    importance of, 1, 2
    instructional periods in, 205–206
    integration of, 133, 191, 194, 197, 206
    and listening (*see* Listening)
    needs assessment in, 197
    scheduling, 128, 129, 130
    and teaching, 202, 205, 206
    (*See also* Language; Language arts
        program)
Language arts program:
    analysis of, 257, 260–261, 262–263
        comprehensive, 262, 263
        with questionnaires, 261
    basal instruction, 117, 121–122
    beliefs of, 6–14
    content of, 257, 258
    development of, 263–282
        guidelines, 263, 264
        professional journals, 263, 264
        resources for, 263–282
        suggestions for, 265–282

Language arts program (*Cont.*):
  evaluation of, 262–263
    criteria for, 263–265
  integration of, 5, 117, 121, 257–263
  language development and, 68
  modifications in, 259, 261, 262
  perceptions of, 260–261
  process of, 3
  reading in, 107
  reporting progress in, 119, 124, 129, 134
  systematic instruction of, 58, 63
  testing in, 259, 260
    achievement, 257–259
    assessing effectiveness, 261
    matching to needs, 259–260
  (*See also* Language; Language arts)
Language development, 65
  and classroom environment, 66, 125
  importance of teacher's role, 75
  and language arts program, 68
Language Instruction Register, 25
Larrick, N., 191
Learning centers, 55, 56, 61, 65, 66, 116–117, 121
Learning modalities, 68, 77
Lee, J. M., 135
Left-handedness, 42, 103
Letter writing, 57, 58, 62, 63
Librarian, 117, 118, 125, 126, 235
  helping children with books, 68, 70, 71, 108–111
Library, 117, 118, 125, 126, 181, 186
  and books, 235
  learning to use, 126
  and reading, 235
  in room, 116, 120, 125
  skills, introducing, 126
Lickteig, M. J., 7
Listening:
  activities, 68, 86–89, 129, 131, 133, 141–146, 213–217
  affective characteristics of, 87
  assessment of, 34, 35, 89–90, 147, 218
  cognitive characteristics of, 87
  curriculum and, 216, 217
  to develop listening habits, 86, 87
  discrimination in, 142
  environment and, 29, 34
  to follow directions, 217
  games, 29
  goals for, 217
  guidelines for teaching, 87–88
  guides for, 171
  importance of, 86, 129, 131, 215–216
  integration of, 217

Listening (*Cont.*):
  levels of, 143, 144
  for main idea, 87, 216
  planning for, 87
  problems in, 32–34, 89, 147, 217, 218
  purposes for, 87, 142–144, 215, 217
  questioning and, 217
  and reading, 28, 87, 216
  to records and cassettes, 68
  in school program, 141–142
  skills, 28, 87, 144, 192, 195, 216–217
  standards for, 89–90
  tape recorder activities, 106, 109
  teaching of, 55, 61, 87–89
  testing for, 90
Listening Centers, 145
Listening Skills Assessment, 147
Literature:
  appreciation of, 126, 133, 181–182, 186
  assessment of, 111
  attitudes towards, 108
  book lists of, 108
  censorship of, 111
  choosing, 108–109
  functions of, 234
  logs, 182, 186
  materials, selecting, 108–109
  problems with, 110–111
  program in, 125–127
    instruction in, 108–109
    objectives, 107, 234
    planning of, 66
  reading aloud, 66, 68, 127
  and reading programs, 107, 233
  in school program, 68, 125
  and stereotyping, 110
  teacher and, 66
  values of, 68
  written activities with, 109–110
  (*See also* Books)
Literature and The Child (Cullinan), 66
Lounsbury, J. H., 205
Lunsteen, S. W., 144, 215, 218

McCloskey, R., 57
McCormick, S., 190
McCracken, R. A., 13
McIntyre, O. J., 246
Maxwell, J., 2
Measuring Growth in English (Cooper and Odell), 227
Medley, D. H., 247
Mehrabian, A., 168
Mellecker, J., 65

Memorization, 36, 37
Memory, 26, 27
Mental Measurements Yearbook (Buros),
  218
Meredith, R., 229
"Mice" (Fyleman), 57, 62
Middle School, 203–207
  curriculum in, 206
  goals of, 204–205
  organization of, 206, 207
  teachers in, 205, 206
Millmore, M., 38
Milone, M. N., 165
Milz, V. E., 40
Models, 140
Molnar, A., 243
Moody, K., 173
Moss, H. A., 83
Motivation, 116, 119
Music, 29, 30
Mussen, P. H., 207

National Assessment of Educational Progress,
  225
National Association of Librarians, 173
*National Association of School Principals'
  Bulletin*, 263
National Council of Teachers of English, 3,
  172, 197, 206, 223, 226, 252, 267–270
National First and Second Grade Studies, 132
New Hampshire Department of Education,
  142
New Iowa Spelling Scale, The, 222
Niedermeyer, F. C., 103
Nonverbal expressions, 168
Norton, D. E., 101, 102, 103, 132
Notetaking, 171

Objectives:
  evaluation of, 126
  in handwriting, 101
  in language arts, 70, 71
  of reading program, 237
Odell, L., 226
Ollila, L. C., 34
Olsen, H., 73
One Morning in Maine (McCloskey), 57, 62
Oral expression:
  communication in, 231–232
  in conversation, 117, 122–123
  creative play and, 105
  evaluating, 106, 233
  teaching of, 104–105

Oral expression (*Cont.*):
  (*See also* Speaking skills, instruction in;
    Speech)
Oral language (*see* Language; Speech)
Oral reading, 236
Oral reporting, 144
O'Rourke, J., 220
Otto, W. S., 42
Outlining, 170–171

Pantheon Story of Art for Young People
  (Batterberry), 181, 186
Pantomime, 122, 127
Paragraphs, 97
  activities, 97–98
  classifying, 97
Parents:
  conferences with, 59, 64, 119, 134, 135, 182,
    187, 193, 196
  expectations of, 115, 116, 119, 120
  and home involvement, 129, 134
  and teacher cooperation, 182, 187, 191
Parent's Guide to Children's Reading
  (Larrick), 191
Peer groups, 140
Perception, 25, 26
Personke, C., 104
Petty, D. C., 86, 92, 96, 99, 101, 103, 106,
  111, 218
Petty, W. T., 86, 92, 96, 99, 101, 103, 106,
  111, 189, 218, 259
Physical characteristics, 54, 60, 83, 84, 139,
  140, 208–209
Physical development, 54, 60, 83, 84, 208–209
  characteristics of, 83–84
Piaget, J., 85–86, 141, 189, 207
Pilon, A. B., 36, 188
Pinnell, G. S., 24
Placement, 127, 128, 133
Play, creative, 105
Poetry:
  listening to, 30
  memorization of, 36, 37
  writing, 164
Praising students, 78, 119, 124, 136
Prewriting skills, 37, 38
  development of, 37, 38, 41
Professional associations, 264–265
Proofreading, 99, 154
Punctuation, 95–96, 156–157
Puppets, 36, 118, 122, 129
  and dramatization, 118, 122, 127, 129
Pygmalion in the Classroom (Rosenthal and
  Jacobson), 124

Quandt, I., 73
Questioning, 217

R. R. Bowker Company, 172
Rankin, P. T., 141
Rashkis, Z., 225
Rauch, S. J., 261
*Read to Write: Using Children's Literature
    as a Springboard for Teaching Writing*
    (Stewig), 225
Readiness, 27, 58, 77, 78
  for instruction, 192, 194–195
  for spelling, 43, 44, 92
  for writing, 39
Reading:
  ability, 124, 125
  activities, 48, 67–69, 181–182, 186, 190,
      235–236
  assessment of, 49, 117, 126, 174, 182, 187,
      235, 236
  attitudes towards, 116, 120
    reasons for, 69
  beginning, readiness for, 47
  in bibliotherapy, 236
  censorship in, 237
  comprehension in, 69, 71, 170
  in content subjects (areas), 169–170, 205,
      236, 237
  and curriculum, 169
  developing independence in, 169
  and drama, 236
  environment for, 10–11
  fluency in, 9, 10
  goals of, 233
  horizontal and vertical approaches to, 117,
      121, 124–125
  instruction in: grouping plans, 117, 121,
      148, 152, 154, 156, 158, 179, 181, 183,
      187, 191, 193–194
    individual rates of, 169
    individualized approach, 69, 71, 72, 216
    interest, using, 124, 125, 172
    language experience approach, 236
  integrating, 234
  and interest inventories, 169–170
  and interests, 237
  in kindergarten, 47
  in language arts program, 107
  listening and, 28, 70–71
  materials and instructional approaches to,
      47, 48, 267–282
  motivation for, 234, 235, 236
  and notetaking, 171
  oral, 173, 231

Reading (*Cont.*):
  and outlining, 170–171
  periods for, 11–13
  problems in, 45, 49, 173–174, 236
  as psycholinguistic guessing game, 6, 48
  readiness for, 47, 58, 63
  recreational, 48, 125, 126, 133, 171
  and spelling, 45, 93, 222
  and storytelling, 236
  and study skills, 169–171
  and television, 168
  and vocabulary, 237
  and writing, 224–226, 236
*Reading Activities for Today's Elementary
    Schools* (Burns and Roe), 68
Reading Ladders for Human Relations
    (American Council on Education), 111,
    235
The Reading Research Quarterly, 264
The Reading Teacher, 264
Reasoner, C. F., 107
Reasoning, 27
Records, keeping of, 67, 69, 73, 78, 79
Reinforcement, 66
Reporting of progress, 129, 133–134
Rickover, H., 2
Robinson, H. A., 261
Roe, B. D., 68, 70, 133
Rogers, C., 206
Role playing center, 55–56, 61
Romano, C. G., 208–215
Rosenshine, B. W., 248, 249
Rosenthal, R., 124
Roser, N., 7
Roy, W., 244
Rubin, D., 105
Rupley, W. H., 249, 253

Samph, T., 246
Saxe, R. W., 135
Schlager, N., 126
School:
  functions of, 243, 244
    meeting individual needs, 203, 204
    meeting societal needs, 203–205
School Library Journal, 125
Sealy, L., 38
Sealy, N., 38
Self-concept, 73, 180, 183–184, 188
Self-fulfilling prophecy, 119, 124
Self-image, 23, 24
Sentences, 158–159, 223, 225
  teaching sense of, 96, 98
  types of, 97

Sequential Tests of Educational Progress
(STEP), 147
Shuy, R., 229, 252
Silverstein, S., 118, 122
Slobodkina, E., 68, 71
Smith, E. B., 229
Smith, F., 224
Smith, J. A., 86, 217
Smith, L. H., 189
Smith, N. M., 248
Smith, S. J., 172
Snowy Day (Keats), 39
Social characteristics, 23, 24, 54, 60, 61, 140,
179–180, 183, 208, 210–213
Social development, 60, 61
Social studies center, 65
Sounds, recognition of, 86
South Carolina Department of Education, 4,
204, 205, 371
Spache, G. D., 23, 77
Speaking (*see* Speech)
Speaking skills, instruction in, 105–107,
166–169, 229–233
Speech:
assessment of, 37, 106–107, 126, 169,
233
development of, 105–106, 167–169
and dialects, 169, 233
instruction in, 166–167, 231–232
objectives, 104–105
and oral development, 105, 126, 166
personal experiences and, 232
self-evaluation of, 233
Speech Communication Association, 230
Speech defect, 167
Speech problems, 37
Speech skills, 229–233
and body control and movement, 168
and classroom environment, 105
and choral reading, 167, 232
in debating, 231
development of, 122, 129, 167
evaluating, 39, 233
in informal conversation, 231
instruction in, 36, 37, 105–106, 166–167,
231–233
problems of, 106, 168–169, 232–233
and language experience, 231
and nonverbal expressions, 168
questioning strategies in, 231
and social behaviors, 106
tape recording, 105, 167, 232
and voice control, 167–168
Speech therapist, 167

Spelling, 43, 44, 147–150, 218–222
activities, 45, 46, 149, 221
assessment of, 46, 47, 94, 150, 222
attitude toward, 43, 44, 46, 88
and composition, 94
in content areas, 219, 222
in creative writing, 91
and dictionary use, 91, 93, 222
homemade dictionary, 45
errors in, 221, 222
games, 45, 92–93, 198–199, 220, 221
habits to learn, 43, 44, 148, 221
and handwriting, 165
instruction in, 43, 44, 91–92, 147–150,
220–221
contract system, 221–222
evaluating, 47
plans, 91, 92, 149, 221
rules in, 149
instructional programs for, 45, 91–93
basic premises, 43
and language arts, 44
lists of high frequency words, 220
objectives, 90–91
problems in, 45, 46, 93–94, 150, 220, 222
program: goals of, 44, 45, 147–148
weekly plans, 149
readiness for, 43, 44, 92
and reading, 44, 45, 93, 222
rules to be taught, 43, 44, 92, 149
scales, 222
skills, 91, 149
teaching of, 43, 91, 220–222
textbooks, 149
VAKT method, 220–221
words, 45
and writing, 93, 94
Spiegel, D. L., 99
SQ3R, 170
Standardized testing, 121, 127
Standards for Basic Skills Writing Programs
(National Council of Teachers of
English), 223
Stauffer, R. G., 40
Stereotyping, 110
Stewig, J. W., 66, 173, 225, 234, 237
Strang, R. M., 174
Strange, M., 135
Strickland, C., 165
Strickland, R. G., 143
Student interests, 76, 77
Study skills, 169–171
Sutherland, Z., 125
Swassing, V. H., 220
Swick, K. J., 73

Teachers:
attitudes of, 119, 128
behaviors of, and student backgrounds, 246
characteristics of, 241–244, 248, 249, 253–254
personality, 242
physical, 242
types of, 243–244
and curriculum, 252
defined, 253
diagnosis skills of, 249
direct instruction by, 249–252
defined, 251
expectations of, 119
importance of, for achievement, 248
knowledge of, 7–8
and language arts, 245
and literature, 107, 109
demonstrating interest in books, 111
and management skills, 242–243, 249, 252
materials for, 196
philosophy for, 254
as political force, 2
qualities of, 204
and reading, 66
aloud, 181, 185
research implications for, 250–252
and schools, 243
self-evaluation of, 118, 119
styles, 242–243
successful, 249
and team planning, 191, 193, 196–197
and time on task, 246
Teaching:
in blocks, 248
of classroom management, 242–243, 249,252
defined, 252–253
of handwriting, 163–165
and individual needs, 203, 204
individualized, 67, 68, 75
of interrelated skills, 65
and language arts, 250–252
of listening, 141–146
materials, 243–244, 247
models, 15, 16
patterns of, 244, 245, 248, 249, 252
of reading, 65, 234, 235, 248, 249
of skills, 65, 243
of societal disadvantaged, 248–249
of speech, 166–169
of spelling, 43, 91–93, 220–222
team, 205
of writing, 66, 151–155
(*See also* Teachers)

Television and reading, 168
Templeton, S., 221
Templin, E., 41
Terry, C. A., 78, 87, 93, 102, 222, 231
Thinking skills, 85
Thought and language, 3, 5
Tiedt, I. M., 77, 106
Tiedt, S. W., 106
Toepfer, C. F., 207

Understanding, levels of, 33, 34
Unicorn, The (Silverstein), 118, 122
Uninterrupted reading, 181–182, 186
Uninterrupted sustained silent reading (USSR), 12, 48, 171, 235
Usage (*see* Language)

VAKT (Visual Auditory Kinesthetic Tactile) spelling method, 220–221
Vars, G. E., 205
Visual perception and discrimination, 22, 23
Vocabulary:
activities, 95, 98, 99
experience and, 97, 98
kinds of, 98
in young child, 98
(*See also* Language; Reading; Spelling)
Voice control, 167–168
Vukelich, C., 31

Wade, E. W., 249
Wadsworth, B. J., 25, 189
Walker, J. E., 133, 262
Wasylyk, T. M., 165
WEB, The (Wonderfully Exciting Books), 125
Weber, G., 249
Westbrook, L. K., 166
What Are the Basics in English? (National Council of Teachers of English), 3, 198
What Did I Write? (Clay), 47
Where the Wild Things Are (Sendak), 55, 61
Wilhide, J. A., 165, 226
Wilson, R. M., 222
Wilt, M., 142
Winkeljohann, R., 188
Winn, M., 173
Writing, 94–101, 151–163, 223–225
activities, 38, 39, 127–129, 151–156, 192, 194, 197–198, 224
assessment of, 40, 99–101, 161–162, 192, 194, 199, 226–227

Writing (*Cont.*):
conferences on, 223
defined, 223
derived from reading, 182, 187, 190
environment for, 95
evaluating, 39, 40, 127, 161–164, 226
    analytic, 162–163, 227
    holistic, 161–163, 227
    primary trait, 163, 227
experiences with, 224
and grammar, 155–157, 191, 194, 198, 224
how to teach, 226
importance of experience in, 38, 127, 130,
    131, 152–153, 197–198, 223
importance of oral discussion to, 127
instruction in, 37, 38, 152–160, 223–225
of journals, 39, 192, 195, 199
and language experience, 224
of letters, 57, 58, 62, 63
mechanics of, reinforcing, 182, 187, 190
motivation for, 160
of own books, 39, 154
problems in, 39, 40, 98–99, 159–160,
    225–226
    causes of, 99
punctuation and, 95–96
purpose of, 223, 224
readiness for, 39
reading and, 224–226, 236

Writing (*Cont.*):
resource area for, 10, 11
samples of, 192, 194, 226
of sentences, 158–159, 223, 225
skill approach to, 153–154
stages of: developmental, 224
    prewriting, 223, 224
    post-writing, 224
    revision, 224
of stories, 182, 186–187
teaching of, 37, 38, 159–160
time for, 95
(*See also* Handwriting; Spelling)
Writing Aids Through the Grades (Carlson),
    98
Writing center, 38, 55, 60–61
Written expression:
evaluating, 118–119, 127
teaching of, 118, 123–124, 127
(*See also* Writing)

Your Reading (National Council of Teachers
    of English), 235

Zaner-Bloser Evaluation Scales, 165
Zutell, J., 148